Hamilton's Paradox

As new federations take shape and old ones are revived around the world, a difficult challenge is to create incentives for fiscal discipline. A key question is whether a politically motivated central government can credibly commit not to bail out subnational governments in times of crisis if it funds most of their expenditures. The center can commit when subnational governments retain significant tax autonomy, as in the United States. Or if the center dominates taxation, it can tightly regulate borrowing, as in many unitary systems. In a third group of countries, including Brazil and Germany, the center can neither commit to a system of market-based discipline nor gain a monopoly over borrowing. By combining theory, quantitative analysis, and historical and contemporary case studies, this book explains why different countries have had dramatically different experiences with subnational fiscal discipline. Moreover, it provides a new perspective on a tension between the promise and peril of federalism that has characterized the literature since *The Federalist Papers*.

Jonathan A. Rodden is the Ford Career Development Associate Professor of Political Science at MIT. He was recently a visiting scholar at the Center for Basic Research in the Social Sciences at Harvard University. He received his Ph.D. in political science from Yale University and his B.A. from the University of Michigan, and he was a Fulbright Fellow at the University of Leipzig. In collaboration with the World Bank, he recently coedited a book titled *Fiscal Decentralization and the Challenge of Hard Budget Constraints* (2003). His articles have appeared in such journals as *The American Journal of Political Science*, *The British Journal of Political Science*, *Comparative Politics*, *International Organization*, *The Virginia Law Review*, and *World Politics*.

Cambridge Studies in Comparative Politics

General Editor
Margaret Levi   *University of Washington, Seattle*

Assistant General Editor
Stephen Hanson   *University of Washington, Seattle*

Associate Editors
Robert H. Bates   *Harvard University*
Peter Hall   *Harvard University*
Peter Lange   *Duke University*
Helen Milner   *Columbia University*
Frances Rosenbluth   *Yale University*
Susan Stokes   *University of Chicago*
Sidney Tarrow   *Cornell University*

Other Books in the Series

Series list continues following the Index.

Hamilton's Paradox

THE PROMISE AND PERIL OF FISCAL FEDERALISM

JONATHAN A. RODDEN

Massachusetts Institute of Technology

CAMBRIDGE
UNIVERSITY PRESS

CAMBRIDGE UNIVERSITY PRESS
Cambridge, New York, Melbourne, Madrid, Cape Town, Singapore, São Paulo

Cambridge University Press
40 West 20th Street, New York, NY 10011-4211, USA

www.cambridge.org
Information on this title: www.cambridge.org/9780521842693

First published 2006

Printed in the United States of America

A catalog record for this publication is available from the British Library.

Library of Congress Cataloging in Publication Data

Rodden, Jonathan.
Hamilton's paradox : the promise and peril of fiscal federalism / Jonathan A. Rodden.
    p.   cm. – (Cambridge studies in comparative politics)
Includes bibliographical references and index.
ISBN 0-521-84269-7 (hardback) – ISBN 0-521-60366-8 (pbk.)
1. Intergovernmental fiscal relations.   2. Central-local government relations.
3. Revenue sharing.   I. Title.   II. Series.
HJ197.R63   2005
336.1'85 – dc22   2005008112

ISBN-13   978-0-521-84269-3 hardback
ISBN-10   0-521-84269-7 hardback

ISBN-13   978-0-521-60366-9 paperback
ISBN-10   0-521-60366-8 paperback

For Ammie

Contents

Preface

This project started in the late 1990s with the simple observation that however compelling and elegant, leading theories of federalism in economics and political science had little to do with most of what was interesting about developments in federations around the world. Optimistic theories promised that decentralization would yield improved efficiency and governance in a wide variety of countries. Yet disastrous debt accumulation among state and provincial governments in Argentina and Brazil had direct negative implications for macroeconomic and political stability, and the literature seemed to provide no hint of an explanation. Moreover, similar problems have existed on a smaller scale for some time in several countries and are sprouting up along with transitions to democracy and fiscal decentralization in others. Next, I learned that episodes of unsustainable borrowing by states and provinces, followed by rancorous debates about federal bailouts, are as old as federalism itself. I set out to rethink theories of federalism and fiscal decentralization, develop some testable arguments about the causes of fiscal indiscipline in multitiered systems of government, and confront them with data from around the world.

Much of the book was written before I realized that Alexander Hamilton had already done something like this. Upon rereading *The Federalist* and then moving on to explore his other writings, I gained an appreciation not only of Hamilton's imprint on the United States, but also his imprint on theories and analyses of federalism. Hamilton and his collaborators drew upon theories of Greek and French philosophers and lessons from previous experience, painting a rich picture of the promise and peril of federalism in the late eighteenth century. But the picture is difficult to interpret today.

Hamilton's ambiguous intellectual and political legacies create a paradox that frames this book.

In fact, the legacy of Alexander Hamilton is rife with ambiguity and paradox from beginning to end. One of the most vociferous American patriots was born in the West Indies, and though an active campaigner against dueling, his participation in the duel that killed him was supposedly meant as a protest. But his gun was loaded, and it is ambiguous whether he shot at Burr or the discharge of his weapon was an involuntary reflex.

An even more controversial legend of his participation in the duel is that it was a form of suicide brought on by his failure and that of the Federalists to build a powerful central government. While this may be far-fetched, there can be little doubt that Hamilton viewed American federalism at the beginning of the nineteenth century as a complete failure. In fact, Hamilton probably would have viewed anything short of a unitary system as a failure. At the Constitutional Convention, Hamilton is said to have argued that the states should be mere "corporations," at best, and that even in that capacity they would pose a danger to the stability of the general government. Hamilton simply did not believe in the wisdom of dividing sovereignty between central and state governments, and most of his writings and actions served the purpose of building "such a compleat sovereignty in the general Government as will turn all the strong principles and passions" to its side (Miller 1959: 230). As secretary of the treasury, he worked tirelessly to wrest away from the states the power to borrow and tax.

He believed that the Constitution negotiated in Philadelphia was deeply flawed, though much better than the status quo under the Articles of Confederation. According to Joseph Ellis, "Hamilton saw his role in the Federalist Papers as that of a lawyer obliged to mount his most brilliant defense on behalf of a dubious client" (2002: 80). According to John Miller, "[W]hile he was justifying the federalist system he was dreaming of the centralized system that he hoped would emerge from the chrysalis of federalism" (1959: 195). The irony is that the "improvised and disingenuous" (Ellis 2002) legacy of *The Federalist* is an eloquent defense of federalism that has stood the test of time and served as the starting point for generations of theory and analysis that celebrate the virtues of divided sovereignty. It is not difficult to find the influence of *The Federalist* in most theories of federalism and decentralization penned by economists and political scientists ever since. The vast majority of these celebrate the benefits of fiscal and political decentralization.

This book pays special attention to the argument that decentralized federalism can enhance the fiscal discipline of government. Hamilton's true convictions about fiscal federalism have largely been ignored by contemporary students of federalism. Yet this book shows that some of his trepidations about decentralized spending and borrowing in the context of federalism were very well founded.

This book returns to the issue of divided fiscal sovereignty with more than two hundred years of hindsight. In seeking to understand the success or failure of decentralized countries to maintain fiscal discipline, it revisits the tension between Hamilton's frustrated political legacy and his celebrated intellectual legacy. It asks whether the disdain for dual fiscal sovereignty that he demonstrated as secretary of the treasury was justified or he was on firmer ground when making his rather disingenuous remarks in *The Federalist* about the intrinsic value of dual taxation, states' rights, and mutual forbearance.

The book argues that both views contained grains of truth. The limits that federalism places on the sovereignty of the federal government can under some conditions sow the seeds of fiscal disaster. But under other conditions, these limitations bolster a rather strict form of fiscal discipline. In short, all federations are not created equal. This book highlights the diversity of federal structures around the world and connects these to widely divergent fiscal experiences. It explains how some countries get stuck in a dangerous equilibrium: The central government – because of its role in funding most provincial-level expenditures – cannot credibly commit to ignore the fiscal woes of troubled provincial governments; but because of its political composition, it also cannot cut off their access to borrowing. In these situations, semisovereign provincial governments can borrow with implicit federal guarantees and overfish the common pool of national revenue, ultimately undermining the creditworthiness of the entire public sector. Other federations have arrived at stable equilibria, where the provincial governments finance themselves primarily through general-purpose taxation, and it is common knowledge to creditors and voters that provinces are responsible for their own debts.

Most of those who build on the optimistic part of Hamilton's rhetoric in *The Federalist* implicitly assume that countries will obtain the latter type of equilibrium. Yet I will argue that this type of federalism is actually quite rare, and in most countries today it would be very difficult to build. Though in retrospect the U.S. experience with divided fiscal sovereignty since the

Civil War seems to bolster Hamilton's disingenuous legacy, policymakers in most decentralizing countries have much to learn from Hamilton's original skepticism about dual sovereignty. The final chapter will parlay this observation into some potentially controversial policy implications for developing countries and the European Union.

Acknowledgments

This book originated as a Ph.D. dissertation at Yale University. I wish to thank David Cameron, Joseph LaPalombara, Juan Linz, Frances Rosenbluth, and especially Geoffrey Garrett and Susan Rose-Ackerman for their guidance and generosity. I thank my colleagues at MIT, where most of the book was written, and at the Center for Basic Research in the Social Sciences at Harvard University, where the final revisions were completed. For comments on parts of earlier drafts and helpful conversations that helped me improve the manuscript, I thank Jim Alt, Lew Bateman, Richard Bird, Carles Boix, Massimo Bordignon, Martha Derthick, Alberto Diaz-Cayeros, Jeff Frieden, Ed Gomez, Steph Haggard, Bob Inman, Daniel Kryder, Chappell Lawson, Margaret Levi, Per Pettersson-Lidbom, Jørn Rattsø, Dan Rubinfeld, Ken Shepsle, Jim Snyder, Ernesto Stein, Al Stepan, Rolf Strauch, Mariano Tommasi, Dan Treisman, and Pieter van Houten. This book also benefited from the insights of my collaborators at the World Bank, including Shanta Devarajan, Gunnar Eskeland, Stuti Khemani, Jennie Litvack, David Rosenblatt, and Steve Webb. Perhaps my greatest debts are to Barry Weingast, who has provided invaluable comments, advice, and encouragement, and Erik Wibbels, whose value as a critic and coauthor is surpassed only by his value as a friend.

I appreciated the warm hospitality and advice of my hosts and guides in Brazil, including Marta Arretche, José Cheibub, Argelina Figueredo, Fernando Limongi, David Samuels, and Celina Souza. Likewise, I am thankful for the kindness and helpfulness of my German hosts and colleagues, including Uwe Leonardy, Wolfgang Renzsch, Fritz Scharpf, Helmut Seitz, and Jürgen von Hagen. Thanks to Juan Llach for bringing me to Argentina and to Tom Courchene and Ronald Watts in Kingston, Ontario. Furthermore, I thank all of those who gave me opportunities to discuss and improve this project at the American Enterprise Institute, the European Central Bank, the European Commission, the International Monetary Fund, the World Bank, Universidad Austral, the University of São Paulo, Harvard University, the University of Minnesota, and Stanford University.

For financial support, I am grateful to MIT, the Yale Center for International and Area Studies, the National Science Foundation (Grant SES-0241523), the Center for European Studies at Harvard, the German Academic Exchange Service, and the Canadian Federal Government. For excellent research and editorial assistance, I am grateful to Diana Rheault and Susannah Webster. Some of the materials in Chapter 2 appeared in *Comparative Politics*; part of Chapter 4 draws from an article that appeared in *The American Journal of Political Science*; and a slice of Chapter 5 appeared in *World Politics*. I thank the publishers for granting permission to use those materials here.

Above all, I would like to thank my family. My parents, John and Judy Rodden, and my sister, Jenell, have provided a lifetime of unwavering support, love, and encouragement, for which my gratitude and appreciation defy easy expression. Likewise, a simple thank-you to my wife, Ammie, is as inadequate as a book dedication. She has offered the support, patience, good advice, and good humor required to help me finish this book, but also the love and companionship that put it in proper perspective.

1

Introduction and Overview

No one can appreciate the advantages of a federal system more than I. I hold it to be one of the most powerful combinations favoring human prosperity and freedom. I envy the lot of the nations that have been allowed to adopt it.

Alexis de Tocqueville, *Democracy in America*

I should wish you to have as many [states] as you now have palatinates. Create in each of these states as many regional administrations. Perfect the organization of your dietines, granting them wider powers within their respective palatinates.

Jean-Jacques Rousseau, *The Government of Poland*

The probable evil is that the general government will be too dependent on the state legislatures, too much governed by their prejudices, and too obsequious to their humours; that the states, with every power in their hands, will make encroachments on the national authority, till the union is weakened and dissolved.

Alexander Hamilton, *Remarks in the New York Ratifying Convention*, 1788[1]

Alexis de Tocqueville was not alone. Federalism, especially the American variety, is one of the world's most admired and copied political innovations. Starting at least with Montesquieu, political philosophers have pointed out the advantages of decentralized, multilayered government structures and, at least since Rousseau, advocated their adoption in a wide variety of settings around the world. Tocqueville's enthusiasm and Rousseau's practical advice have been taken up with renewed vigor in the late twentieth century, as transitions from centralized authoritarianism to democracy in countries from Eastern Europe to Latin America and Africa have been marked by the decentralization of authority to state and local officials. Other than transitions to democracy, decentralization and the spread of federalism are perhaps the most important trends in governance around the world

---

[1] Frisch (1985: 220–21).

1

over the last fifty years. Even long-standing democracies like Spain and Belgium have chosen to adopt explicitly federal structures, and many others have transferred resources and authority to local governments. Moreover, the gradual evolution toward a European federation is perhaps the most impressive political project of our time.

All of these developments have been accompanied by great optimism about expected improvements in the quality of accountability, efficiency, fiscal discipline, and even economic growth. Yet even a cursory look at the history of federalism should give reason for pause. The U.S. federation has been torn apart by a bloody civil war and a legacy of regional and racial strife, and history's dustbin is filled with failed federations from ancient Greece to modern Yugoslavia and Czechoslovakia to the Caribbean. While civil wars and velvet divorces justifiably get a good deal of attention, federalism can also fail in another way that has, until very recently, escaped the attention of pundits and scholars alike. As this book documents, federalism can lead to spectacular debt accumulation and disastrous failures of macroeconomic policy.

The potential perils of federalism did not escape the attention of its most colorful historian and critic, Alexander Hamilton. His well-known fear, illustrated with copious historical examples from the Lycian and Achaean leagues to the German diet, was of a weak federal government falling prey to foreign conquest or internal dissolution. Much less scholarly attention has been given, however, to his related fears about fiscal federalism. Hamilton was very skeptical about the wisdom of giving the "power of the purse" to state governments. He feared not only that they would use taxing and borrowing powers to weaken the center but, more specifically, that they would spend and borrow excessively, attempting to shift their burdens onto the central government and one another. His fears were well founded: A binge of over-borrowing by a group of states in the 1840s led to macroeconomic instability and ruined U.S. creditworthiness abroad. Remarkably similar events involving the Brazilian states and Argentine provinces have recently led directly to debt crises and hyperinflation in those federations, with staggering social and economic costs. Related problems of federalism and fiscal indiscipline have shown up in a number of other countries, including India, Nigeria, Russia, and South Africa (see Rodden, Eskeland, and Litvack 2003). As this book will show, the problem of federalism and fiscal indiscipline is not limited to new democracies or developing countries. Relatively serious problems with borrowing by state and local governments can be documented in Germany, Italy, Spain, and elsewhere.

Introduction and Overview

Tocqueville's enthusiasm for federalism has been echoed by philosophers, politicians, and economists throughout the nineteenth and twentieth centuries. Indeed, such rhetoric has only gained prominence since the 1970s, as a wave of decentralization spread across developing countries and the process of European integration moved forward. Though operations personnel have always been wary, policy discussions at the International Monetary Fund (IMF) and World Bank in the early 1980s often celebrated the advantages of decentralization and downplayed the dangers. Yet by the end of the 1990s, attention has turned from the theoretical advantages of decentralization and federalism to the realities of the Brazilian and Argentine crises, interprovincial trade wars, and growing recognition of problems with corruption and inefficiency among state and local governments and their public enterprises. Easily the most visible and vexing problem is fiscal indiscipline among subnational governments.

Virtually all cross-national empirical studies of public sector deficits and debt have ignored subnational governments. At first glance, this may not seem problematic; during the period from 1986 to 1996, the average subnational deficit was only around one-half percent of gross domestic product (GDP) for a sample of sixty-three countries. However, in eleven formally federal systems – which include several of the world's largest economies – average subnational deficits exceeded 1 percent of GDP and accounted for nearly 20 percent of total government deficits.[2] In some countries, like Argentina and Brazil, the aggregate subnational deficit routinely surpassed that of the central government and exceeded 2.5 percent of GDP, and subnational debt has reached 15 percent of GDP. Moreover, recent studies have shown that increasing subnational deficits are associated with higher central government expenditures and debt (Fornisari, Webb, and Zou 1998), along with higher rates of inflation (Treisman 2000a).

On the other hand, over the course of the twentieth century many countries – ranging from unitary countries like Norway to federations like the United States and Switzerland – have been able to keep state and local deficits under control or even run surpluses. In fact, federalism and fiscal decentralization are often viewed not as creating opportunities for fiscal imprudence, but rather as important bulwarks of fiscal discipline. This book is an attempt to answer a question of growing importance: What accounts for cross-country and diachronic variation in the fiscal behavior of

[2] Source: IMF, *Government Finance Statistics Yearbook* (various years), *International Financial Statistics* (various years), and author's calculations.

subnational governments and with what implications for the entire public sector? Why do some subnational governments appear to behave as fiscal conservatives, while others run up dangerous, unsustainable deficits ?

This book develops a set of arguments about the varieties of decentralization and federalism that go well beyond earlier studies that focus primarily on the overall level of fiscal decentralization or the mere presence of federalism, and as a result it has strong policy implications. Europe is going through a period of debate and negotiation on its constitutional future not unlike that undertaken in Philadelphia, and participants are keenly aware of the potential for fiscal indiscipline among constituent units in federations. Among others, the constitutional futures of long-standing federations like Argentina, Brazil, Germany, India, and Mexico are currently being debated, along with those of decentralizing countries like Belgium, Italy, and Spain. In each case, the issue of fiscal discipline is taking center stage. Thus, a systematic analysis of the relationship between decentralization, federalism, and fiscal discipline is a timely undertaking.

I. Promise and Peril

At the beginning of the twenty-first century, decentralized federalism is to political economy what Prozac is to mental health. Use is on the rise and everyone is talking about it, but some tout its extraordinary benefits while others insist that it just as often makes things worse. It is increasingly clear that the treatment has vastly different effects on different subjects, but no one knows how, why, or under what conditions it succeeds or fails. Abstract theories of federalism have claimed that fiscal and political decentralization can improve the efficiency and accountability of public sector institutions and even facilitate rapid economic growth. One of the most basic claims, first celebrated by Friedrich von Hayek, is that decentralization can improve the fiscal responsibility of government. On the basis of theoretical claims and some impressive success stories, decentralization has been prescribed around the world. Unfortunately, however, harmful side effects appear to have overwhelmed the expected benefits in a number of countries, and skepticism is growing. Like a controversial drug, neither the promise nor the peril of federalism should be accepted at face value until its effects have been assessed on a wide variety of subjects, each with different histories and preexisting conditions. By examining the problem of fiscal discipline, this book takes up that task.

The promise of federalism is a straightforward proposition that has shown up time and again in political and economic theory from Montesquieu to James Madison to Richard Musgrave: In heterogeneous societies, government policy is most likely to be aligned with the preferences of citizens in the presence of multiple layers of government, each charged with different responsibilities. Higher-level governments can provide federation-wide collective goods like common defense and free trade, while lower-level governments can provide goods like trash collection and religious education that will be consumed locally. If each layer of government stays within its bounds and respects the authority of the other, citizens can hold each layer of government separately accountable for its activities. While a single sovereign might be tempted to abuse its authority, federalism provides a valuable protection by dividing power among multiple, competing sovereigns. Political scientists view such divided sovereignty as a path to stability and peace in societies divided by strong linguistic or ethnic cleavages. Economists extol the virtues of preference revelation, information, and the benefits of intergovernmental competition. Both views boil down to increased responsiveness and accountability; decentralized, multitiered systems of government are likely to give citizens more of what they want from government at lower cost than more centralized alternatives.

The potential perils of federalism have received far less attention. Federalism is more than mere administrative decentralization. It implies that the autonomy of the central government is effectively limited, either by constitutional rules or less formal restraints. In fact, the accountability advantages of decentralization *require* that the central government's authority be substantially limited. Industrial organization theorists have shown that in order to strengthen incentives and promote initiative in a decentralized organization, the center must credibly limit its own information and authority. The flip side, however, is a loss of strategic control by the center. In decentralized federations, politically fragmented central governments may find it difficult to solve coordination problems and provide federation-wide collective goods.

As in the private sector, public institutions only produce desirable outcomes when incentives are properly structured. Decentralization within large, complex industrial organizations, for instance, clearly has the potential to increase productivity by giving division leaders greater flexibility and stronger incentives to innovate. But aggregate efficiency is only enhanced if incentive structures discourage division leaders from manipulating information advantages. Decentralization may be quite costly for the organization as a whole if it cannot safeguard against widespread opportunism. This book tells a similar story about borrowing in federations. Like a decentralized firm, a federation can be seen as a complex nexus of interlocking contracts. If these are not properly structured and actors are resistant to renegotiation, decentralized federalism might undermine efficiency and dilute democratic accountability, perhaps ultimately threatening the stability of the federation. In particular, state and local officials might face incentives to expand their expenditures while externalizing the costs to others, turning public revenue into a "common pool" that is overfished by provincial governments.

II. Federalism and Sovereignty

The next chapter starts by revealing a large gap between the dominant theoretical literature and the current trend toward decentralization around the world. The theory literature often envisions decentralization and federalism as essentially the same thing: a neat division of governmental authority into distinct, hierarchical spheres of sovereignty. From the classics of political philosophy to the modern economics literature, this notion of divided sovereignty plays an important role in the promise of federalism. After reviewing the existing theoretical and empirical work, Chapter 2 contributes more-precise definitions of decentralization and federalism than those employed in these literatures and presents a good deal of data drawn from countries around the world, painting a contrasting picture of murky, overlapping authority in which sovereignty is often unclear and contested. These observations create a fresh starting point for a political economy approach to multitiered government that is well suited to examining the diversity of types of decentralization and federalism, as well as the diversity of outcomes seen around the world.

A key insight of the book is that fiscal decentralization rarely entails distinct sovereignty for subnational entities over their debt. When sovereignty is unclear or disputed, actors use the information available to them and assign probabilities to the likely ultimate locus of authority in the event of a conflict. Sovereignty at a given time in a given policy area in decentralized systems is best understood as a set of *ex ante* beliefs about likely winners of future intergovernmental battles. Chapter 3 presents borrowing in a multitiered system as a dynamic game of incomplete information, where voters, creditors, and subnational governments have limited information about how the central government would react in the event of a future fiscal crisis. Subnational governments must make fiscal decisions, creditors lending decisions and voters electoral decisions, without knowing whether the central government ultimately guarantees subnational debt. If all actors have perfect information that the center is committed to a policy of never assuming subnational debts, it makes sense to view subnational governments as distinct, miniature sovereign borrowers. However, this book demonstrates that this is rarely the case. Most multitiered fiscal systems have evolved in the latter half of the twentieth century with institutional features that undermine the central government's commitment and hence the fiscal sovereignty of subnational entities.

To demonstrate how this game works in action, Chapter 3 examines the interaction of the U.S. states and federal government in the 1840s. The federation was still relatively young and had a recent history of debt assumption and rather ad hoc resource distribution from the center to the states. There were good reasons to question the center's "no-bailout" commitment. Bolstered by the good credit of the federal government, many states had undertaken internal improvements funded by debt. In the face of an unexpected fiscal shock associated with a financial panic, many states refused to introduce new taxes or otherwise adjust. Instead, they demanded bailouts from the central government, joining their (mostly British) creditors in arguing that their debt had implicitly carried a federal guarantee. It is difficult to reconstruct the perceived odds of a federal bailout from historical materials, but it is clear that the debt assumption movement was quite powerful and its failure was certainly not easy to predict. Several states held out bailout hopes to the bitter end and defaulted when the bailout proposal failed in the legislature. Ultimately, they were forced to undertake very painful adjustment measures. But state governments, voters, and creditors learned a valuable lesson: The central government – which was actually prohibited from borrowing on international credit markets during the affair – sent a costly signal of its commitment.

After surviving a few more subsequent tests, the game has been played throughout the twentieth century as if all parties have complete information that the center is committed. That is, the U.S. states approximate fiscal sovereignty. States may occasionally dance around the topic of bailouts – witness the most recent state fiscal crisis – but hopes for bailouts are not sufficiently bright that states would actually refuse to adjust while waiting for debt assumption. When subnational governments are viewed as sovereigns, creditors, voters, and investors face strong incentives to monitor their fiscal activities and threaten to punish unsustainable borrowing, either by raising interest rates, withdrawing votes, or withdrawing capital.

The game has played out differently in recent decades in countries like Brazil and Germany, where several key states have correctly judged the center's commitment as noncredible, refusing to adjust and ultimately receiving bailouts. Clues to the center's lack of credibility were built into the basic intergovernmental agreements that emerged as democracy reemerged in Germany in the 1940s and in Brazil in the 1980s. In both cases, the central government remained highly involved in funding the constituent governments with grants and loans, often with considerable discretion. In Brazil, indebted states knew that they would be able to exert influence in the legislature, and logrolling created a way to bring less indebted states into coalitions to vote for bailouts. Reproducing a pattern that has plagued the federation since the turn of the century, the largest states – especially São Paulo and Minas Gerais – expected that the center could not allow them to default because of negative externalities for the banking system and the country's creditworthiness. In Germany, the constitution provided strong indications that the center would not be able to allow the smallest, most transfer-dependent states to fail. In both cases, the central government has promulgated reforms attempting to reassert no-bailout commitments; but given the lessons learned from the central government's moves in previous plays of the game, state governments clearly continue to make fiscal decisions as if they are playing against a noncommitted central government.

III. Fiscal Institutions

Detailed studies of how this commitment game plays out and evolves in different settings are useful, and several are undertaken in this book. A larger goal, however, is to make some generalizations about the institutional and political characteristics of countries that shape the way the game is played and connect these to distinctive patterns of fiscal behavior. Chapters 3 and 4 argue that the most essential factor shaping fiscal sovereignty is the basic structure of intergovernmental fiscal relations between higher- and lower-level governments. Quite simply, bailout expectations are strongest when subnational governments rely on grants and revenue sharing rather than independent local taxation. Even when the distribution of grants is mostly nondiscretionary, provincial governments can hold out hopes of pressing for increased allocations in future renegotiations. When a highly transfer-dependent government faces default and must close schools and fire stations or fail to deliver health or welfare benefits that are viewed as national entitlements, the eyes of voters and creditors turn quickly to the center for a solution, even if the fiscal crisis was actually precipitated by bad decisions at the local level. If local governments believe that the center's role in financing them will cause the political pain of default to be deflected upward, this not only affects their beliefs about the probability of a bailout, but also reduces their own disutility of default.

Chapter 4 argues that one good way to measure bailout expectations – and hence fiscal sovereignty – is to examine the behavior of credit markets and bond-rating agencies. In the guidelines used by rating agencies to assess subnational governments, transfer dependence is clearly viewed as the best indicator of the central government's implicit guarantee. Bond raters reason that if local governments that are highly dependent upon shared revenues and transfers are allowed to access credit markets, the center understands that it is ultimately responsible and provides an implicit guarantee. Thus, in these cases the credit ratings of the subnationals are tightly clustered around or equal to the sovereign rating, as in Germany. At the other end of the spectrum, rating agencies treat the U.S. states, Canadian provinces, and Swiss cantons – the three federations with the heaviest dependence on independent subnational taxation in the world – as miniature sovereigns; credit ratings (and bond yields) are tightly linked to the independent debt-servicing capacities of the subnational entities. Somewhere in the middle is a country like Australia, where rating agencies clearly pay close attention to the debt-servicing capacities of the individual states; yet taking clues from the intergovernmental transfer system, they explicitly assess a high probability that the Commonwealth government would bail out troubled states in the event of a crisis. This allows transfer-dependent states like Tasmania to pay significantly lower interest rates than they would if they were sovereign borrowers.

Understanding this logic, it is reasonable to expect that central governments with a large role in financing lower-tier governments would tightly regulate their access to credit markets. Indeed, Chapter 4 uses cross-country data to demonstrate a high correlation between transfer dependence and centrally imposed borrowing restrictions. It goes on to show that the combination of transfer dependence and top-down borrowing restrictions is associated with long-term balanced budgets among subnational governments. This is the form of top-down, unitary fiscal discipline that Alexander Hamilton advocated, where the center has a virtual monopoly on both taxation and borrowing and carefully regulates and monitors the expenditures of the subservient lower-level governments. This form of fiscal discipline is in effect in many countries around the world, especially unitary systems in which the local governments have few constitutional protections.

Yet large federations – especially where the provinces were parties to the original constitutional bargain and must sign on to any significant alterations – find it difficult to limit the access of their constituent units to deficit finance. Politically powerful subnational governments with borrowing autonomy and limited tax autonomy can be a dangerous combination. In this context, blurred sovereignty can have troubling macroeconomic consequences. Some countries attain neither the competitive discipline of the modern United States nor the hierarchical discipline of a unitary country like Norway. The center retains much of the power of taxation and the constituent units are highly dependent upon it for finance, yet in various ways the window of local borrowing is left open. As a result, voters and creditors view provincial governments not as sovereigns but as wards of the center, and central governments find it difficult to commit to a policy of saying no to the bailout requests of troubled subnational governments. This undermines competitive discipline and gives state governments incentives to avoid adjustment. At the same time, the political institutions of federalism prevent the central government from exerting hierarchical administrative control over local expenditures. In these countries, federalism poses a dilemma – the central government is too strong fiscally vis-à-vis the states to credibly ignore their fiscal difficulties, yet too weak politically to call them to account.

IV. Political Institutions

Thus, the peril of fiscal federalism is ultimately driven by politics. The first task of the book is to examine fiscal institutions, but the second task – an examination of political institutions – to some extent subsumes the first. The way in which the central government's institutions organize political competition has profound implications for the role of fiscal institutions. First of all, the nature of representation for provincial or local governments shapes the central government's ability to say no when pressed for bailouts by lower-level governments. If the center is merely a loose, logrolling coalition of regional interest groups, it has a hard time resisting bailout requests or firmly regulating the fiscal behavior of local governments. Furthermore, intergovernmental grants and loans from the center to the lower-level governments are likely to be highly politicized. The central government party or coalition will be tempted to use its discretion over the allocation of grants strategically, attempting to shift resources to allies or districts with electoral importance. If provincial and local politicians in the politically favored districts expect extra loans and grants from the central government, their incentives for fiscal discipline are reduced *ex ante*.

This view of political parties is consistent with those of the founders of the American federation, who saw parties as yet another divisive source of factionalism and self-seeking that undermined the national interest. Yet with the benefit of hindsight and a much larger number of data points, Chapter 5 explores a very different argument about political parties. Building on some arguments made in the 1950s by William Riker, vertically integrated national political parties might create links between central and provincial politicians, creating "electoral externalities" that give provincial politicians incentives to be concerned with national collective goods rather than purely local interests. This might help ameliorate the peril of federalism in two ways: (1) by reducing provincial incentives to create negative externalities in the first place, and (2) by creating incentives for provincial politicians to renegotiate faulty intergovernmental contracts.

V. Case Studies

Chapters 4 and 5 evaluate their theoretical arguments by examining yearly cross-country data. Of course, these analyses are by nature rather blunt, but they provide strong indications of the importance of intergovernmental transfer systems and partisan arrangements in shaping fiscal behavior in decentralized systems. The rest of the book comes down from this high level of abstraction and tries to refine the theoretical arguments and examine them more carefully using case studies and the analysis of disaggregated data. One useful feature of the cross-national quantitative analysis is that it helps identify countries that provide useful targets for more in-depth case studies. Leaving behind the countries that approximate subnational fiscal sovereignty and the countries where the center has a firm grip on subnational borrowing, the remaining chapters take a closer look at some countries that have suffered the ill effects of blurred sovereignty – especially Brazil and the Federal Republic of Germany.[3] Although the problem

---

[3] For a wider range of case studies, see Rodden et al. (2003).

has received little attention abroad, state-level debt has become a serious problem in the German federation. While the problem has been exacerbated by the recent economic downturn and the challenges of reunification, Chapter 7 shows that it has been brewing for some time and is in fact rooted in the basic fiscal and political incentives of the modern German system of federalism. Brazil's state-level debt crises in the 1980s and 1990s led directly to its macroeconomic instability and hyperinflation. Chapter 8 examines the political and fiscal causes of these crises, drawing some comparisons to the early American experience.

Both of the case studies help refine and clarify the arguments made in earlier chapters. These two case studies are included not only because they are interesting and important, but because the two systems display variety on the key fiscal and political variables of interest. Drawing on what Przeworski and Teune (1970) refer to as the "most-different-systems" approach to comparative research, Chapters 7 and 8 use time series cross-section data from the states in these federations to test arguments about intergovernmental transfers, the size and structure of jurisdictions, political parties, elections, and business cycles. Germany and Brazil are different systems in almost every imaginable sense: levels of economic development, regional and interpersonal inequality, party discipline, and legislative-executive relations, to name a few. But one thing they share is a strong system of federalism and a pronounced role for the constituent units in federal politics. The case studies show that federalism has played a remarkably similar role in the fiscal troubles of both countries. Yet important systemic differences are discovered as well, and these help illuminate additional nuances and contours to arguments developed in earlier chapters.

VI. Endogenous Institutions

Taken together, Chapters 3 through 8 identify a rather stubborn form of political equilibrium in which the center cannot commit, yet governments with bailout expectations are allowed to borrow, with results that are bad for the country as a whole. Though collectively suboptimal, such systems are difficult to reform because key provincial officials with veto authority have private interests in perpetuating them. These chapters fit within an emerging approach to political economy that relies on politics to explain the persistence of economic inefficiency. When an inefficient but sticky political equilibrium is identified, two further questions emerge naturally: How can a country get out of the bad equilibrium, and how does it emerge in the first place? The first question, taken up in Chapter 9, makes basic features of intergovernmental fiscal contracts endogenous and focuses on moments when renegotiation of these contracts appears to carry substantial collective benefits, seeking to explain the conditions under which political entrepreneurs in a democracy can break through federalism's natural status quo bias. The second question, taken up in Chapter 10, requires a deeper historical approach, one that attempts to explain the longer-term evolution and stability of subnational sovereignty.

In both Germany and Brazil, in response to problems with debt accumulation and bailouts of lower-level governments, the reform of the intergovernmental system has been high on the public policy agenda in recent years. The same can be said about many other countries that have either already fallen prey to the perils of federalism (e.g., Argentina and India) or fear going down that path (e.g., Mexico and the European Union). Chapter 9 examines the challenge facing political entrepreneurs who wish to renegotiate collectively suboptimal intergovernmental contracts that create private benefits for key provincial politicians. Applying the concepts developed in Chapter 5, it argues that reform is most likely to succeed when provincial politicians who have something to lose from the reform can receive offsetting electoral benefits associated with improvements in the provision of national collective goods like macroeconomic stability. In general, this is most likely to happen in countries where voters use the party label of the national executive to reward or punish politicians at both levels of government. When this is the case in general, the provincial politicians who are most likely to sacrifice private benefits are those who belong to the party that controls the federal executive. The chapter concludes by providing evidence drawn from case studies of Germany, Brazil, Canada, and Australia.

Chapter 10 returns to a deeper question about the origins of institutions: Why did some federations, like the United States and Canada, emerge from the twentieth century with credibly limited central governments and fiscally sovereign provinces, while in other federations, like Brazil and Germany, the credibility of the center's no-bailout commitment slipped away along with provincial sovereignty over the course of the century? Rather than providing a complete and convincing answer, this chapter attempts to set the agenda for further research by providing some explanations based on the countries examined in this book.

VII. Policy Implications

Not only does the book contribute to the positive comparative literature on federalism, but the final chapter also explores some implications for current normative policy debates. Above all, it suggests that subnational sovereignty, whereby fiscal discipline is enforced merely through competition for capital and votes, is quite rare – and more fragile than typically thought. This fits with a growing recognition that the larger promise of federalism – improved accountability and better governance – is more elusive than previously thought, especially in countries that decentralize rapidly from a starting point of authoritarianism or extreme centralization. The policy implication is not that trends toward fiscal and political decentralization should be abruptly reversed. Rather, careful attention should be paid to the nature of fiscal and political incentive structures. In some countries, expectations should be altered and second-best alternatives – centrally imposed rules or multilateral intergovernmental cooperation – may be preferable to cycles of provincial debt and bailouts. The final chapter expresses skepticism about the common belief that subnational fiscal discipline should be left to credit markets in newly decentralizing countries.

The concluding chapter also explores the book's implications for current debates about fiscal rules in the European Monetary Union (EMU). Quite in contrast to the German or Brazilian states, the member states of the EMU are clearly sovereign debtors, and market actors have very little reason to expect bailouts from the nascent central government. The European Union (EU) is well positioned to retain distinct spheres of fiscal sovereignty for the EU and the member states. If this is true, it calls into question the bailout logic often used to justify the centrally imposed limitations on member state deficits associated with the Stability and Growth Pact. At the same time, by making central governments accountable for overall public sector deficits, EMU may have had a positive impact by encouraging some central governments to strengthen oversight and accounting procedures for local governments. The book concludes with an eye toward the future, discussing the key problems and prospects for federalism and fiscal decentralization in the twenty-first century.

2

Promise and Peril

INTELLECTUAL HISTORY

This book asks a very specific question: Under what conditions do the actions of state and local governments strengthen or undermine the overall fiscal discipline of government? Yet the question is posed with an eye on older and larger questions about the relationship between decentralization, federalism, and the efficiency and accountability of government. Thus, it is useful to situate current debates about fiscal discipline within a larger current of intellectual history that runs through the classics of political philosophy to modern public economics. Moreover, an important first step in doing theoretical and empirical work on this topic is to cut through the array of definitions and measurements of decentralization and federalism used in diverse literatures and settle on some concepts that will be used throughout the book. In doing so, this chapter also serves to highlight the ways in which the approach taken in this book departs from previous studies.

After introducing in broad terms the classic themes that motivate modern research, this chapter reviews the contributions of welfare economics and public choice theory to the notion that federalism and decentralization can enhance the efficiency and accountability of government. It pays special attention to theories suggesting that decentralization, especially in the context of federalism, can enhance overall fiscal discipline. Next, these abstract arguments are confronted with attempts to define decentralization and federalism with more precision and pin them down with cross-country empirical measures. A key observation made here will be developed further throughout the book: By ignoring too many institutional details, existing theories implicitly assume a type of federalism that is rather infrequently found in practice. More attention to the varieties of decentralization and federalism, along with more realistic assumptions about the motivations

15

of politicians, provide an improved starting point for the theoretical and empirical analyses that follow in later chapters.

I. A Brief Intellectual History of Federalism in Economics and Political Science

If a republic is small, it is destroyed by a foreign force, if it be large, it is ruined by an internal imperfection. . . . Very probable it is therefore that mankind would have been at length obliged to live constantly under the government of a single person, had they not contrived a kind of constitution that has all the internal advantages of a republican, together with the external force of a monarchial, government. This form of government is a convention by which several small states agree to become members of a larger one which they intend to form.

Montesquieu, *Spirit of Laws*

Large populations, vast territories! There you have the first and foremost reason for the misfortunes of mankind. . . . Almost all small states, republics and monarchies alike, prosper, simply because they are small, because all their citizens know each other and keep an eye on each other, and because their rulers can . . . look on as their orders are being executed. Not so the large nations: they stagger under the weight of their own numbers, and their peoples lead a miserable existence. . . . In a word, make it your business to extend and perfect the federal system of government. . . .

Jean-Jacques Rousseau, *The Government of Poland*

By enlarging too much the number of electors, you render the representative too little acquainted with all their local circumstances and lesser interests; as by reducing it too much, you render him unduly attached to these, and too little fit to comprehend and pursue great and national objects. The federal Constitution forms a happy combination in this respect; the great and aggregate interests being referred to the national, the local and particular to the State legislatures.

James Madison, *The Federalist* 10

The federal system was devised to combine the various advantages of large and small size for nations. Alexis de Tocqueville, *Democracy in America*

The promise of federalism was first touted by Montesquieu and was later transformed into a fixture of modern constitutional theory by James Madison and Alexander Hamilton. The same refrain shows up in the writings of modern political theorists and economists. All of these thinkers are attracted to the intuitive idea that was perhaps best expressed by Ralph Waldo Emerson (1835): "The township is the unit of the republic and the school of the people. In the town meeting the great secret of political science was uncovered and the problem solved – how to give every individual his fair weight in government without any disorder from numbers." Quite simply, it seems more likely that citizens can get what they want from government if it encompasses a small, relatively homogeneous area – the township for Emerson and the city-state for Montesquieu – rather than a vast territory. However, the problem with small units of government in the classical view is their vulnerability to attack by larger units. The advantage of large, diverse jurisdictions is the avoidance of internal warfare and the pooling of resources to repel attacks by outsiders. Madison and Hamilton made note of some additional advantages of large size – above all, free trade – and modern public economics has added a few more, including advantages in tax collection, interregional risk sharing, common currencies, and scale economies in the production of public goods.

The promise of federalism is *e pluribus unum*, to make one of many and achieve simultaneously the advantages of small and large governmental units. But each of the philosophers cited above was aware that the creation of such a union entails perils as well. A federation might well be plagued with Emerson's "disorder from numbers" or Montesquieu's "internal imperfection." Tocqueville feared that a large, diverse federation ultimately would be insufficiently powerful to fight effectively against a despotic centralized opponent. Likewise, the "internal imperfection" feared by Alexander Hamilton was an impotent central government. However, the fear of such Virginians as Thomas Jefferson, George Mason, and Patrick Henry in the debates surrounding the adoption of the U.S. Constitution was that the center would accumulate too much power and run roughshod over the rights of the constituent units.

Herein lies the central tension of most scholarship on federalism among political scientists since *The Federalist*. The peril of federalism in virtually all of this literature is twofold: Federations have a natural tendency either to become too centralized – perhaps even despotic – or so decentralized and weak that they devolve into internal war or fall prey to external enemies. Thus, the task of achieving the promise of federalism while minimizing its peril involves a problem of institutional design: how to create a central government that is simultaneously strong and limited. The center must be strong enough to achieve the desired collective goods – free trade, common defense, and the like – but weak enough to preserve a robust sense of local autonomy. This was the central project in William Riker's classic work on federalism and remains the focus of the political scientists who have followed in his footsteps.

Many of the political scientists writing about federalism have been keenly aware of its perils – especially the problem of secession. In fact, much of the recent theoretical work on federalism in political science comes from scholars attempting to understand Russia's rather precarious balance between despotism and dismemberment (Ordeshook 1996; Ordeshook and Shvetsova 1997; Treisman 1999a, 1999b). From Madison to Riker to these recent contributions (see especially De Figueredo and Weingast 2004; Filippov, Ordeshook, and Shvetsova 2003), the key goal of the political science literature has been the search for institutional, cultural, and political circumstances that allow for stable federalism and the avoidance of oppression or war in diverse societies.

In short, political scientists take federalism as a necessity in large, diverse societies and have been preoccupied with avoiding its greatest perils: instability, despotism, and war. Economists, on the other hand, have assumed away problems of politics, incentives, and stability and have focused instead on the rather abstract efficiency and accountability advantages noted above by Montesquieu. Economists have set out to rigorously define the difference between Madison's "great and aggregate interests" and those that are "local and particular," in the process creating a normative framework to establish the optimal level of fiscal and administrative decentralization.

Some of the most basic insights of public finance theory reflect the optimism expressed in Rousseau's quotation above, suggesting that decentralization should have positive, even if unintended, consequences for efficiency, accountability, and governance. Above all, decentralization is thought to align the incentives of political officials with citizen welfare by improving information and increasing competition. The most basic observation was expressed in the quotations above: In any political entity larger than a city-state, local governments will have better information than distant central governments about local conditions and preferences. Second, a vast literature on "competitive federalism" examines the supposition that, under decentralization, governments must compete for citizens and firms, who sort themselves into the jurisdictions that best meet their preferences for bundles of governmental goods and policies.

The welfare economics literature on federalism and decentralization takes its name from Wallace Oates's 1972 book *Fiscal Federalism*, which is still the most important theoretical contribution.[1] This literature generally assumes that political leaders at all levels of governments are benevolent despots who maximize the welfare of their constituents. The most important

---

[1] Oates's work was preceded by Musgrave (1959). For recent updates, see Oates (1994, 1999).

task of the fiscal federalism literature is to solve the assignment problem: "[W]e need to understand which functions and instruments are best centralized and which are best placed in the sphere of decentralized levels of government" (Oates 1999: 1120). This literature prescribes decentralization according to the subsidiarity principle: "the presumption that the provision of public services should be located at the lowest level of government encompassing, in a spatial sense, the relevant benefits and costs" (Oates 1999: 1122). When preferences are spatially heterogeneous, local governments are thought to be better informed about the local costs and benefits of policies and in a better position than more distant central governments to tailor policies to fit local circumstances.

The link between decentralization and improved efficiency has also been made in the public choice literature. Theories of competitive federalism analogize decentralized governments to the private market and celebrate the efficiency gains that may be associated with competition among decentralized providers of public goods. This literature was inspired by the work of Charles Tiebout (1956), which views citizen landowners as "voting with their feet" by sorting themselves into communities that offer their desired tax levels and bundles of goods, thus enhancing preference revelation and forcing government to be more accountable.[2] More recently, Tiebout's competitive logic has been combined with assumptions about self-interested, rent-seeking politicians, and capital and labor mobility are viewed as constraints on rent extraction. Instead of a single Leviathan with monopoly power over the tax base, decentralization creates competition among self-serving politicians and bureaucrats over mobile sources of revenue, which prevents them from lining their pockets with public money, thus reducing the size and wastefulness of government spending[3] and the prevalence of debilitating taxes or regulations.[4] Persson and Tabellini (2000) model tax competition as a way for government to commit not to overtax

---

[2] It is important to note that Tiebout's "pure theory" was specifically geared toward small jurisdictions within one metropolitan area. In spite of a very restrictive set of assumptions spelled out in the original article, the model's implications have been greatly expanded by others to include constituent units in vast federations. Other contributions to this literature include Thomas Dye (1990); Albert Breton (1991, 1996); and Wallace Oates and Robert Schwab (1991).

[3] Brennan and Buchanan (1980); Buchanan (1990, 1995); Tullock (1994).

[4] Weingast (1995); Montinola, Qian, and Weingast (1994); Qian and Weingast (1997); Parikhand Weingast (1997).

capital, and Weingast applies the same logic to regulation, stressing that under federalism, "only those economic restrictions that citizens are willing to pay for will survive" (1993: 292).

To sum up, while political scientists have been concerned with a rather extreme though real set of perils, economists have been concerned with an intellectually intriguing though elusive set of promises. Yet many of the world's federations are plagued neither with centralized dictatorship nor armed insurrection, but simply with bad policies, poor fiscal management, and in some cases recurrent economic crises. Policymakers in Brazil and Argentina, for example, are less concerned with interstate military conflict than with interprovincial trade wars and distributive battles over revenues and debt burdens. These problems stand in stark contrast to the abstract normative world of decentralization in economic theory. The possibility that federalism might lead to costly nonmilitary conflicts between states – for example, rancorous distributive conflicts and trade wars – was recognized by Madison and Hamilton (see *Federalist* 7, especially), but little attention has been given to these issues among modern political scientists and economists.

II. The Promise of Fiscal Discipline

It is better to keep the wolf out of the fold, than to trust to drawing his teeth and claws after he shall have entered.　　　　Thomas Jefferson, *Notes on Virginia*

The conclusion that, in a federation, certain economic powers, which are now generally wielded by the national states, could be exercised neither by the federation nor by the individual states, implies that there would have to be less government all around if federation is to be practicable.

　　　Friedrich von Hayek, "The Economic Conditions of Interstate Federalism"[5]

A common refrain among those who emphasize the promise of federalism – from Montesquieu to modern public choice theorists – is a belief that government has a natural tendency toward excess. Once authority is delegated from citizens to government, it tends to expand and invite abuse, and the danger is all the greater when populations are large and territories vast. The *Oxford English Dictionary* defines "sovereignty" as "supreme dominion, authority, or rule." As a response to the sectarian violence of the sixteenth and seventeenth centuries, Jean Bodin and Thomas Hobbes advocated the

---

[5] Hayek (1939).

elevation of a single domestic sovereign with absolute authority over a distinct territory. Recognizing that such supreme authority invites abuse, later thinkers have sought ways to protect liberty and improve governance by finding ways of dividing and limiting sovereignty without destroying it. Decentralization and especially federalism have always been attractive from this perspective. In this libertarian tradition of thought, the uncontrollable Leviathan might abuse not only its military and police authority, but also its ability to tax, borrow, and spend. Federalism – by creating a limited central government and dividing sovereignty among multiple governments – provides a solution.

If government has a natural tendency to overtax and overborrow, a republican form of government alone might not resolve the problem. In fact, it might make things worse – above all, representatives might try to externalize the costs of governmental expenditures in their jurisdiction onto citizens of others, turning public revenue into a "commons" that is quickly overgrazed (Buchanan 1975; Weingast, Shepsle, and Johnsen 1981). A basic problem is that public budgets funded through general taxation are often oriented heavily toward targeted rather than general benefits. As a consequence of this incongruence between spending and taxation, each policymaker misperceives the costs of spending and demands an "excessive" amount, because she takes into account all of the benefits but only considers the share of taxes that falls on her constituents. This might lead to spending that exceeds the socially optimal amount, and if governments are allowed to fund expenditures with borrowing, it might also lead to a higher than optimal deficit (Velasco 1999, 2000). According to Buchanan and Wagner (1977) and others, a further problem is that voters do not fully understand the relationship between current deficits and future taxes – they simply reward spending and punish taxation. Politicians with electoral motivations, then, face incentives to take advantage of their "fiscally illuded" voters with excessive deficit-financed spending, especially in election years. Once excessive deficits can no longer be maintained and adjustment is necessary, democracies might be poorly suited to make the necessary spending cuts or tax hikes if representatives of interest groups or geographic jurisdictions can delay stabilization as they attempt to shift the burdens of adjustment onto one another. The problem of a democratic Leviathan might only be compounded in large, diverse countries with many legislative jurisdictions (Weingast et al. 1981) or large, fragmented cabinets (Alesina and Drazen 1991).

According to Geoffrey Brennan and James Buchanan (1980), "[F]ederalism is a means of constraining Leviathan constitutionally." First of all, building on the accountability logic of the classic view, the problem might be reduced simply by bringing government "closer to the people" in Montesquieu's sense. In the traditional fiscal federalism literature, a key principle is only to give the central government authority over spending activities that have clear interjurisdictional spillovers, thus keeping the "wolf" out of the fold in the first place and reducing the size of the commons. Above all, the promise of federalism and fiscal discipline has to do with mobility: Competition among regional governments in attracting mobile capital might increase the opportunity cost of public spending and underscore the utility of fiscal restraint. When taxing and spending are decentralized, it will be clear to everyone that highly indebted states will eventually be forced to raise taxes, and even if tax rates are currently low, mobile citizens and firms will weigh future tax increases when making location decisions. Thus, large deficits drain the tax base and erode the popularity of incumbent politicians. If a state's public sector is wasteful, investors and voters can move to jurisdictions where their taxes are used more efficiently. This situation contrasts with a single unitary Leviathan whose expansionary tendencies are relatively unchecked, because capital tends to be much less mobile across national boundaries than it is across states within nations.

Moreover, horizontal fiscal competition creates comparable information about governmental finances and fiscal performance across jurisdictions and provides voters with incentives to gather such information. This is referred to as horizontal "benchmark" or "yardstick" competition (Besley and Case 1995). Decentralization may even allow for vertical benchmark competition if voters contrast local fiscal performance with that of higher levels of government (Breton 1996). Thus, decentralization in a federal context might increase the requisite information and incentives of voters to oversee local spending and borrowing decisions, creating a more direct link between fiscal decisions and the welfare of voters. This accountability mechanism might be particularly strong for owners of land and other fixed assets, for whom poor local fiscal decisions might translate rather quickly into lower asset prices.

In addition to voters and owners of real estate, creditors can play a valuable role in keeping Leviathan at bay. They will face strong incentives to oversee local fiscal decisions, monitor debt levels, and collect and publish data about the potential returns of local infrastructure investment projects.

This information is summarized in credit ratings, which are available to citizens as low-cost information to use in making location and investment decisions.

According to the literature on political business cycles, politicians might benefit from expanding national economies unexpectedly. As a result, they face incentives to overspend and increase the money supply in the short term – especially in the run-up to elections – even if the long-term results are suboptimal. Under these conditions, it is crucial to design institutions that credibly commit policymakers to stable prices and spending restraint. According to Lohmann (1998), Qian and Roland (1998), and others, federalism often serves exactly this purpose by providing checks and balances on central policymakers, thus preventing them from reneging on their macroeconomic commitments. According to Qian and Roland (1998) and Moesen and van Cauwenberge (2000), simply decentralizing some share of public expenditures to provincial or local governments who do not have access to the money supply is enough to harden the overall budget constraint. Subnational governments, in essence, police the inflationary and deficit bias of central officials.

In sum, this book addresses a more specific, positive, and testable elaboration of a larger set of normative arguments stressing that decentralized governance can enhance overall citizen welfare through increased information and competition. The importance that one accords to this particular notion of "welfare" is likely to be wrapped up in one's ideological predisposition. The idea of federalism as a constraint on Leviathan betrays a certain disdain for government and taxation, and indeed this literature – from Thomas Jefferson to Friedrich von Hayek to James Buchanan – has a pronounced conservative ideological thread running through it. Yet one need not share a fear of Leviathan to appreciate and evaluate the logic of the positive arguments. Moreover, the normative implications of unsustainable macroeconomic policies are unpleasant regardless of one's ideological starting point. In the wake of recent macroeconomic disasters in large federations, the distance between theory and experience with fiscal discipline in multitiered systems of government invites a closer look.

III. A Closer Look at Definitions and Data

These arguments have a good deal of intuitive appeal and enjoyed considerable popularity in policy circles in the 1980s. But the difficult experiences with decentralization among developing and transition countries – and even some rich countries – in recent decades invites a rethinking of the basic questions. First of all, surprisingly little explicit attention has been given in this literature to the institutional details of the "decentralized" or "federal" institutions required to bring about the desired efficiency advantages. Reflecting the usage in the theory literature, the words "decentralization" and "federalism" have been used interchangeably in the discussion above. In most cases, decentralization and federalism are viewed as essentially the same thing. Though assumptions about the precise institutional form of decentralization often remain implicit in this literature, most of it assumes a rather far-reaching independence and autonomy for subnational governments (see, e.g., Weingast 1995). These theories require extremely powerful lower-level governments with full autonomy over most policy spheres, in particular over the regulation of the economy. Moreover, from Tiebout to Buchanan or Weingast, the competitive federalism literature assumes that subnational governments have wide-ranging autonomy over setting the tax rate and base, borrowing, and determining budget priorities. As a result, citizens and creditors are able to evaluate the policy choices made by individual governments as they make investment and location decisions. The center is generally conceived as responsible only for providing truly national public goods like defense, a common currency, and the enforcement of a common market. Intergovernmental grants are assumed to follow the dictates of normative fiscal federalism theory: attempts by a benevolent central government to internalize externalities.

Empirical attempts to estimate the effects of decentralization on various outcomes – from government spending to inflation to growth rates – have examined one very simple variable: the share of total government expenditures undertaken by subnational officials. Alternatively, some studies use a dummy variable to capture the presence of "federalism."[6] Surprisingly little thought has gone into defining and measuring decentralization and federalism in ways that facilitate empirical analysis, and communication between economists and political scientists has been so limited that they often use the same words to mean very different things. In any case, neither expenditure decentralization nor a binary, ill-defined notion of federalism captures the kind of decentralized federalism implicitly assumed in the theory literature. Just how far from reality are the assumptions driving the traditional

---

[6] For a review of the empirical literature, see Rodden (2004).

theory literature? To answer this question and build a firmer foundation for more-realistic theoretical and empirical work, it is necessary to define and measure the various dimensions of decentralization and federalism with greater rigor.

Decentralization

Decentralization is often seen as a shift of authority toward local governments and away from central governments, with total government authority over society and economy imagined as fixed. But authority in this context is very difficult to define and even more difficult to measure. For instance, a "decentralization" reform program might increase highly conditional grants to local governments, thus raising their expenditures but lowering their discretion, as has often been the case in Scandinavian countries. Or the central government may cede policy responsibilities to local governments without giving them additional grants or taxing authority, as in many newly "decentralizing" developing countries. Alternatively, the central government may cede authority and money in a certain policy area to local governments, but continue to conduct its own activities while reserving the right to override local decisions when dissatisfied. To further complicate things, political scientists sometimes speak of "political" decentralization that involves the devolution neither of policy autonomy nor funds, but rather a shift in the selection mechanism for local leaders from central appointment to local election. Or in a system that already features local elections, one might speak of decentralization if the slate of candidates is chosen locally rather than by central officials.

Clearly, there is no encompassing definition of government decentralization. Among other things, one might consider local policy discretion, fiscal authority, or political independence, and each of these clearly has several subcategories. Although comparisons across countries and over time are difficult, it is possible to identify some broad trends and patterns for each of these types of decentralization.

Figure 2.1 summarizes several recent attempts to measure decentralization across countries and over time. Using twenty-nine countries for which satisfactory time series data are available from the IMF's *Government Finance Statistics*, Figure 2.1a simply displays average shares of total government expenditure undertaken by state and local governments since 1978, demonstrating a pronounced upward trend. This trend has been particularly

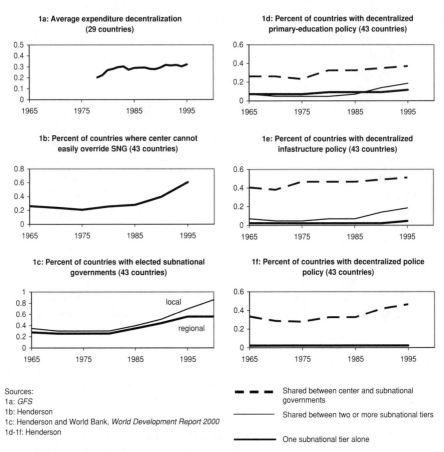

Figure 2.1. Selected time series indicators of decentralization.

strong in Spain and Latin America. Figure 2.1b summarizes data collected by Vernon Henderson on the legal ability of central governments to override the decisions of subnational governments, demonstrating that local governments are gaining increased autonomy, especially since the wave of democratizations in the late 1980s.[7] A similar trend can be seen in the share of countries where central appointment of mayors and governors has given way to popular elections (Figure 2.1c). Figures 2.1d through 2.1f also draw on the Henderson study, which characterized the level of government

---

[7] Data and codebook for Henderson (2000) available at http://econ.pstc.brown.edu/faculty/ henderson/.

responsible for decision making in each of three policy areas: primary education (control of curriculum and hiring/firing of teachers), infrastructure (local highway construction), and local policing. The plots show an unmistakable trend toward increasing influence for local and regional governments in each policy area.

Perhaps the most striking aspect of the latter charts, however, is the prevalence of shared authority. The portion of the sample in which the central government and one or more local governments have joint policy authority is plotted with a dashed line. Very rarely do central governments fully cede autonomy to subnational governments. In the vast majority of cases, decentralization entails a move from complete central dominance to joint involvement of the center and one or more subnational tiers. Even in the cases where the central government is not involved, authority is often shared between two or more subnational tiers (plotted in normal font). Situations in which a single subnational tier is solely involved in policymaking (plotted in bold font) are extremely rare.

This is an important lesson that informs the rest of this book: The process of decentralization unfolding around the world is not a clean delegation of distinct spheres of authority to state and local governments, as envisioned in existing theories. More often than not, "decentralization" means that one or more subnational layers of government is empowered (or even created from scratch) and officials are popularly elected rather than appointed, then asked to share in decision making or simply administration that was formerly the exclusive domain of the center. Very rarely do subnational governments gain new autonomy over the determination and collection of taxes. Virtually every cross-national empirical study to date on the causes or consequences of decentralization uses the indicator from Figure 2.1a: expenditure decentralization. Yet a quick look at these data does not inspire much confidence about their usefulness as a composite measure of decentralized authority. The first column in Table 2.1 displays the average over the 1990s for twenty-nine countries. For instance, Denmark is the third-most decentralized country in the world according in Table 2.1 – even more decentralized than the United States – though the central government tightly regulates virtually every aspect of local government finance. Nigeria appears as number seven, even though the states during this period of military rule were little more than administrative outposts of the central government.

Table 2.1. *Fiscal Decentralization Variables (Averages over 1990s)*

	1 State-Local Exp./Total Exp.	2 Grants/State-Local Revenue	3 Own-Source State-Local Rev./Total Rev.	4 Grants + Revenue Sharing/State-Local Revenue	5 Own-Source State-Local Rev./Total Revenue	6 State-Local Tax Rev./Total Rev. (Rate Autonomy)	7 State-Local Tax Rev./Total Rev. (Rate and Base Autonomy)	8 Borrowing Autonomy
Source	GFS	GFS	GFS	GFS & Country Sources*	GFS & Country Sources*	OECD	OECD	Country Sources*
Argentina	0.44			0.56	0.18			4.0
Australia	0.50	0.40	0.32	0.37	0.33			2.5
Austria	0.34	0.27	0.27	0.58	0.16	0.02	0.01	1.6
Belgium	0.12	0.56	0.06			0.16	0.02	
Bolivia	0.21	0.09	0.18	0.43	0.11			1.5
Botswana	0.03	0.83	0.01	0.84	0.01			1.0
Brazil	0.41	0.34	0.28	0.36	0.27			4.5
Bulgaria	0.19	0.35	0.15	0.92	0.02			1.0
Canada	0.65	0.26	0.51	0.32	0.47	0.32	0.30	2.7
Colombia				0.38				3.0
Denmark	0.54	0.43	0.31	0.43	0.32	0.29	0	1.5
Finland	0.41	0.34	0.33	0.36	0.31	0.20	0	3.0
France	0.19	0.35	0.13	0.39	0.12			3.0
Germany	0.45	0.25	0.34	0.70	0.13	0.04	0.001	2.5
Guatemala	0.10	0.65	0.04	0.67	0.03			2.0
Hungary	0.10					0.02	0	

Iceland	0.23	0.09	0.23	0.42	0.34	0.18	0	2.5
India	0.49	0.43	0.33					
Indonesia	0.13	0.73	0.03					
Ireland	0.29	0.72	0.09	0.74	0.08			1.8
Israel	0.14	0.40	0.08	0.38	0.09			2.4
Italy	0.23	0.66	0.09	0.80	0.05			2.5
Malaysia	0.14	0.19	0.16					
Mexico	0.26	0.11	0.20	0.59	0.09	0.02	0.02	2.6
Netherlands	0.30	0.70	0.09	0.70	0.09	0.02	0	2.3
Nigeria	0.48	0.86	0.09	0.86	0.09			1.0
Norway	0.35	0.40	0.22	0.39	0.22	0.007	0	1.6
Paraguay	0.02		0.01	0.23	0.01			2.0
Peru	0.23	0.73	0.07	0.05	0.23			2.5
Philippines	0.08	0.46	0.05	0.41	0.06			1.0
Poland	0.17	0.31	0.13	0.54	0.09	0.03	0	2.0
Portugal	0.09	0.48	0.05	0.40	0.06	0.02	0.01	2.5
Romania	0.11	0.44	0.07	0.44	0.07			1.0
Spain	0.36	0.60	0.16	0.56	0.17	0.09	0.04	2.5
Sweden	0.37	0.18	0.33	0.20	0.32	0.33	0.01	3.0
Switzerland	0.55	0.25	0.41	0.19	0.45	0.35	0.20	3.0
Thailand	0.06	0.28	0.05					
UK	0.29	0.71	0.09	0.74	0.08	0.04	0	1.5
USA	0.53	0.30	0.42	0.34	0.39	0.32	0.32	3.0

*See appendix

GFS: *Government Finance Statistics Yearbook*. Various years. Washington, D.C.: IMF.

OECD: *Taxing Powers of State and Local Governments*. OECD Tax Policy Studies No. 1. Paris: OECD.

In short, it is difficult to know what to make of expenditure decentralization data without additional data on the regulatory framework for subnational finance. Perhaps the most basic consideration is whether expenditure decentralization is funded by intergovernmental grants, revenue that is shared with the center according to a fixed formula, or the mobilization of own-source revenue through independent taxes, user fees, and borrowing. Until recently, virtually all cross-country studies have ignored these distinctions. The International Monetary Fund does include a line in its subnational revenue accounts called "grants," but for many countries these do not include constitutional revenue-sharing programs. One can use this to calculate overall "transfer dependence" – averages are presented in the second column of Table 2.1. Moreover, one can obtain an alternative measure of fiscal decentralization by calculating own-source revenue as a share of total government revenue (the third column in Table 2.1). While a useful source of variation over time, one should be careful about drawing inferences based on cross-section variation because the coding of grants and subnational own-source revenues seems not to be consistent across countries.

One way to improve upon the IMF measure is to draw on country sources to develop a measure of subnational revenue autonomy that does not code automatic distributions from revenue-sharing schemes as own-source revenue. The fourth column of Table 2.1 presents a measure of grants plus shared revenues as a share of subnational revenue, and the next column includes a measure of own-source revenue as a share of the total.[8] The latter is an alternative to the simple "expenditure decentralization" variable – it attempts to measure the share of total government revenue that is actually raised through revenue efforts of subnational governments.

However, even this variable severely overestimates the extent of subnational revenue autonomy. While subnational governments may collect the revenues labeled as own-source, the central government may nevertheless maintain the power to set the rate and the base, leaving the subnational governments as mere collectors of centrally determined taxes. A recent OECD (1999) study tackles this complex issue, but unfortunately only for a small number of countries. From this study, it is possible to calculate two additional variables: the share of total tax revenues over which subnational governments possess full autonomy to set (1) their own tax rates, and (2) their own rates and base. These variables, also presented in Table 2.1, paint

---

[8] For sources, see Appendix 2.1.

a very different picture of subnational fiscal autonomy. Several countries in which subnational governments account for large shares of total spending (column 1) and taxation (column 5) have very little autonomy over tax rates and base (column 7). In fact, the study makes it clear that the United States, Canada, and Switzerland are in a class by themselves when it comes to autonomous subnational revenue authority.

Additionally, central governments might attempt to restrict the fiscal autonomy of subnational governments not only through conditional grants and regulations governing local taxation, but also by placing formal limitations on subnational borrowing. The ability to independently access credit markets or other sources of deficit finance is an important component of subnational fiscal autonomy. An index created by the Inter-American Development Bank (IDB) considers debt authorization requirements, numerical limits, and restrictions on the use of debt imposed by the central government, along with the ability to borrow through banks and public enterprises owned by subnational governments (in 1995). This variable, which ranges from 1 to 5, is presented in the last column in Table 2.1.[9]

In sum, decentralization is indeed taking place around the world, but theories or empirical studies that envision a clean transfer of authority to highly autonomous local governments can do little to address its causes or effects. In most cases, decentralization implies the introduction of local elections and increased local expenditures, but in the context of increasingly overlapping, intertwined authority with centralized taxation and a good deal of top-down regulation. In any case, the fiscal, political, and administrative framework of decentralization varies dramatically from one country to another. These facts about decentralization – annoyances to be assumed away in most existing theories – are the starting point for the analysis in this book.

Federalism

The subtleties and varieties of decentralization are generally understood but swept under the rug for reasons of analytical or empirical clarity. Federalism, however, is often left ill defined out of confusion or simply conflated with decentralization. Federalism is best understood not as a particular distribution of authority between governments, but rather a

---

[9] The coverage was extended beyond Latin America by the author. See Appendix 2.1 for sources and Appendix 2.2 for a complete description of the formula.

process – structured by a set of institutions – through which authority is distributed and redistributed. "For an economist, nearly all public sectors are more or less federal in the sense of having different levels of government that provide public services, irrespective of the formal constitution" (Oates 1999: 1121). For political scientists, however, federalism is a special kind of decentralization. Federalism can be traced back to the Latin *foedus*, or "covenant." According to the *Oxford English Dictionary*, the original use of this word was for a covenant between God and mankind. The word eventually was used to describe cooperative, contractual agreements between states, usually for the purpose of defense. Covenants and contracts imply mutuality – to serve any purpose, both parties must fulfill some obligation to one another. Federalism implies contractual relations between central and subnational governments.[10] If the central government can get everything it wants from local governments by simple acts of administrative fiat, it makes little sense to see the two as engaged in a contractual, or federal, relationship. If on the other hand, for some subset of the central government's decisions or activities it is necessary to obtain the consent or active cooperation of the subnational units, the two are engaged in a contracting process.

Before filling in the details on the institutions that underlie federal contracts, it is important to understand how and why federal contracts are made in the first place. Both the definition and the operation of federalism are wrapped up in the historical conditions that give rise to the original contract. In his famous book, William Riker (1964) builds on Montesquieu's logic and posits that *all* modern federations originated as bargains aimed at achieving military defense against a common enemy. Perhaps Riker has identified the most important collective good for which states pool sovereignty and aggregate territory, but there are clearly others, like the benefits of free trade and a common currency.

A common pattern from alliance to federation can be identified. Previously independent entities recognize that they face a cooperation problem: They are unable to repel an aggressive neighbor without pooling their troops, or they are unable to capture the gains from cross-border trade. The first step is often a loose alliance or confederation that requires the agreement of all signatories for significant action and can easily be dissolved; but lacking adequate enforcement mechanisms, these are often plagued by

---

[10] For a brief intellectual history of the relationship between contracts and federalism, see King (1982: 96–107). See also Riker (1964); Elazar (1987); and Ostrom (1987).

instability, free riding, and collective action problems. This is the history of the American Articles of Confederation in a nutshell. If the incentives for cooperation are strong enough and political incentives are properly aligned, representatives of the entities might negotiate a new governance structure featuring a central government with stronger enforcement powers and decision rules that require something less than unanimity. Once this contract is made, it takes on a life of its own and continues even after the enemy has been defeated or a common market and currency achieved.

Riker's notion that federations originate as voluntary bargains aimed at achieving collective goods is widely accepted. However, an important critique by Alfred Stepan (1999) identifies another path to federalism. While Riker sees federalism as a bargain that aggregates territory and peoples without military conquest, Stepan points out that sometimes aggregation via conquest comes first, and the federal bargain follows much later (if at all). It is difficult to see the aggregation of Nigeria or the Soviet Union – or even today's Russian federation – as voluntary bargains. Many multinational states are formed instead by the vagaries of conquest, colonialism, and postwar deals. Faced with the challenge of holding multinational states together, especially in a democratic context, the central government learns that a federal bargain is necessary if the country is to stay together. In India, the federal bargain coincided with independence. In Belgium and Spain, central governments agreed to restrict their authority and enter into bargaining relationships with newly empowered regional governments only after conflict-ridden experiences trying to hold together multinational societies with unitary institutions.

In both the "coming-together" and "holding-together" scenarios, the original federal bargain is an agreement about the composition and powers of the central government and the "rules of the game" that will structure future interactions between the central government and the units. These rules were often struck in a context where secession of some states or dissolution of the entire federation was a realistic possibility. Even years later, when secession or dissolution seems less realistic, the aftermath of the original bargain makes federations distinct from unitary systems. The units will not cede authority to the center without safeguards against future exploitation, either by the center itself or by other states. Thus, federal bargains generally include (1) constitutional language protecting the sovereignty and autonomy of the units, in some cases including (2) clauses that vest them with all "residual powers" not explicitly designated to the center. The credibility of such language often hinges on the presence of

(3) a strong, independent constitutional court. More importantly, federal bargains require (4) majorities and often supermajorities of the territorial units for a wide range of policy changes, especially changes to the basic vertical distribution of policy and fiscal authority or the constitution itself. Sometimes, states successfully insist on maintaining (5) control over their own militias.

From Philadelphia in 1776 to the Nice Summit of the European Union in 2000, it is clear that when striking a federal bargain, the most serious concerns about exploitation come from small territories that would be consistently overwhelmed if votes were apportioned according to population. Thus, small states always insist on representation schemes based on territory while large states argue for population-based representation. The compromise usually involves a "one person, one vote" lower chamber and (6) a highly malapportioned upper chamber that overrepresents small states.[11] Comparative data on legislative malapportionment collected by Samuels and Snyder (2001) for seventy-eight countries demonstrate that, on average, federations have much higher levels of upper-chamber malapportionment than unitary systems. As a result of the original federal bargain – which is usually between asymmetrically sized units – federalism is a form of preference aggregation that relies more heavily on bargains among representatives of territorial governments than majority rule among individuals (Cremer and Palfrey 1999; Persson and Tabellini 1996a, 1996b). Figure 2.2 depicts a continuum that reflects the role of territorial governments in the central government's policymaking process. At the far left, decisions are made by majorities of individuals – territorially based districts play no role. Perhaps the best modern examples are town meetings in rural New England or in Switzerland. Or to provide a more realistic national-level example, Israel – with only one nationwide electoral district – is a country in which lower-level governments have no formal role in the central government's decision procedure. Moving along the continuum, we find legislatures with representatives elected from territorial districts – the model for most modern legislatures. Even if these districts do not correspond to the boundaries of territorial governments, one might expect more territorial bargaining than in systems without districts. Further along the continuum are

---

[11] Another reason for malapportionment is that as elite groups expanded the franchise or presided over "pacted" transitions to democracy, the wealthy beneficiaries of the authoritarian or limited-franchise regimes tried to reduce the likelihood of future redistribution by overrepresenting rural allies – who often were able to control the votes of agricultural workers – and underrepresenting urban areas.

	Unitary			Federal		Confederal
Decision-making units	Individuals	Elected district reps that do *not* correspond to territory governments	Elected district reps who correspond to territory governments	Elected district reps who correspond to territory governments	District reps who are appointed by territory governments	District reps who are appointed by territory governments
Apportionment of districts	n.a.	one person, one vote	one person, one vote	mal-apportionment	mal-apportionment	mal-apportionment
Requirement for policy change	simple majority	simple majority	simple majority	simple majority	simple majority	Qualified or supermajority
Example	town meeting	UK Parliament	Italian upper chamber	United States Senate	German Bundesrat	EU Council of Ministers

Figure 2.2. The role of territorial governments in legislatures.

legislatures in which the boundaries of territorial governments correspond with those of electoral districts, but seats are allocated by population, as in the Italian upper chamber.

The next slot in Figure 2.2 is that occupied by the upper chambers of most modern federations, including the United States – as a result of a federal bargain between large and small states, each has a similar number of directly elected representatives, regardless of population. But the next slot on the continuum is even more "federal"; in the original U.S. Senate or the modern German Bundesrat, representatives are directly appointed by the state governments. Finally, at the far right of Figure 2.2 are legislatures in which delegates are directly appointed, small states are overrepresented, and changes from the status quo require supermajorities or, at the extreme, unanimity. For constitutional changes, the German Bundesrat falls into this slot, as does the EU Council of Ministers for most important policy issues.

With each move to the right along this continuum, territorial governments take greater precedence as the relevant units in constructing legislative majorities, and one might say that representation is more "federal." It is much easier to ignore the interests of Rhode Island or Wyoming when trying to construct a majority in the U.S. House of Representatives than when trying to do so in the Senate. In the German Bundesrat, it is necessary not only to obtain the support of a majority (and sometimes two-thirds) of state representatives, but an additional wrinkle is added: It is necessary to please the state-level administrations themselves. For instance, the German states have banded together to veto legislation that they perceived as imposing unfunded mandates, a luxury not available to U.S. governors. At the extreme, in the EU Council of Ministers and the United States under the Articles of Confederation, territorial bargaining with a unanimity decision rule is the *modus operandi* for most major decisions.

The representation of states in central government policymaking is clearly part of the essence of federalism. Preston King argues that the defining characteristic of a federation is "the fact that its central government incorporates regional units in its decision procedure on some constitutionally entrenched basis" (King 1982: 77). King's strict definition would seem to exclude Canada from the federal category. The Canadian provinces are not formally represented as veto players in the decision-making process of the federal government. Yet the Canadian federal and provincial governments are clearly locked into an ongoing process of intergovernmental contracting that takes place primarily outside of central government institutions. The Canadian central government goes so far as to sign formal, contractlike agreements with the provinces in a number of policy areas. Even though the Canadian central government need not obtain the approval of the provincial governments to make policies, it often cannot implement them without cajoling, striking bargains with, and even paying off the provinces from time to time. Federal contracting takes place outside of the legislature in a number of other countries as well. For instance, the Russian and Spanish central governments engage in direct bilateral and multilateral bargaining with regional governments, and a variety of rather formal, policy-specific multilateral bargaining bodies including the states and the central government have evolved in Germany and Australia and to a lesser extent in India.

Formal theories of legislative bargaining help demonstrate that there are clear differences between unitary and federal legislative processes and hence policy outcomes (see, e.g., Crémer and Palfrey 1999; Persson and Tabellini 1996a). First, in the standard Baron-Ferejohn (1987) model, a randomly drawn jurisdiction is allowed to propose a change from the status quo with simple-majority voting rules. It needs to structure its proposed policy so that it is superior to the status quo for one more than half of the jurisdictions and will try to assemble the cheapest winning coalition. This type of bargaining does not favor jurisdictions with a strong preference for the status quo, because they will be left out of winning coalitions. However, because of supermajority or unanimity requirements, intergovernmental bargaining in a federal context often requires the approval of these jurisdictions and resembles some form of Nash bargaining. In this context, these jurisdictions derive bargaining strength from their strong status quo bias and can expect favorable policies. As we shall see, depending on the nature of the rules, federations can exhibit strong status quo bias, and provinces that stand to lose from proposed alterations of the status quo can often extract substantial compensation.

It is also important to realize that the basic contracts that create and maintain federations, no matter how well specified, are fundamentally incomplete. Constitutional contracts are often incomplete for the same reasons that business contracts are incomplete:

(1) the inability to foresee all the possible contingencies
(2) the complexity of specifying rules, even for the numerous contingencies that can be foreseen

(3) the difficulty of objectively observing and verifying contingencies so that the specified procedures may be put into action.

(Dixit 1996: 20)[12]

Just as it is not possible for the parties to a business contract to foresee all future changes in demand, weather, or regulatory policy, it is not possible for the framers of a federal constitutional contract to foresee all future governmental activities and assign them to a jurisdictional level. Nor is it possible for the participants in a constitutional convention to devise a foolproof formula that will resolve all future jurisdictional conflicts. In fact, federal constitutions are notoriously poor guides to the distribution of authority in modern federations. If some positive political benefit is expected to result, central or subnational governments are likely to find ways to enter the policy areas technically reserved for the other level. New policy areas may present themselves years after the constitutional contract has been negotiated, and in many situations both levels of government try to get involved. Even in federal systems where the constitution or founding document goes into great detail to assign specific revenue sources and expenditure responsibilities to each level of government, most policy areas are characterized by the simultaneous involvement of two or more levels of government. Oliver Hart suggests that "the contract is best seen as providing a suitable backdrop or starting point for renegotiations rather than specifying the final outcome" (Hart 1995: 2). A federal constitution is best seen as a backdrop or starting point that lays out some of the basic rules and incentives that structure an ongoing intergovernmental contracting process. Federalism is much more than a set of formal rules; it is an ongoing process (Friedrich 1968: 193). Federal constitutions are important not because they solve the assignment problem, but because they structure the ongoing intergovernmental contracting process.

In sum, federal contracting is largely a product of institutional incentives arising from previous bargains, but sometimes the relevant institutions are not identified in the constitution. Thus, classifying countries as "federal" requires some difficult assessments of constitutional language and protections; the power, autonomy, and purpose of constitutional courts; control over state militias; the representation of the states in the legislature; and the role of the states in the process of constitutional change. It is difficult to make federalism into a binary concept. Some countries, like Germany,

---

[12] On the incompleteness of business contracts, see Oliver Williamson (1985) and Oliver Hart (1995: 1–5).

Table 2.2. *Federal Systems of the World*

Elazar (1995) and Watts (1999)	Watts (1999) only
Argentina	Ethiopia
Australia	Micronesia
Austria	St. Kitts and Nevis
Belgium	
Brazil	
Canada	
Comoros	
Germany	
India	
Malaysia	
Mexico	
Nigeria	
Pakistan	
Russia	
Spain	
Switzerland	
United Arab Emirates	
United States	
Venezuela	
Yugoslavia	

Brazil, and the United States, possess virtually all of these qualities. India, Austria, and Canada, however, are generally considered federations even though their upper legislative chambers are neither strong nor highly malapportioned. India's federal credentials are sometimes challenged because of the prime minister's constitutional authority to dismiss state governments, but this power has been used with diminishing frequency over time.

In spite of these gray areas, attempts at cross-national measurement of federalism treat it as an essentially binary concept. Several empirical studies draw on the classifications of two well-known constitutional scholars, Daniel Elazar (1995) and Ronald Watts (1999), both of whom identify federations by relying more on common sense and experience than rigorous lists of coding criteria. Fortunately, there is not much disagreement among these scholars. Table 2.2 presents their lists of federations – only Ethiopia and two island federations are not common to the two lists.

The Elazar-Watts classifications seem to employ the most expansive possible definition of federalism, placing the United States and Switzerland in the same category as countries like Malaysia and Pakistan. All of the countries listed in Table 2.2 involve some element of central-provincial contracting for some issues, but clearly the classification masks important differences across countries, and some of these countries (e.g., Nigeria as it slips in and out of military authoritarianism) can only be considered federal for some years and not others.

Several things stand out from the lists in Table 2.2. First of all, a large portion of the world's population lives in some sort of federal system, even without considering the semifederal nature of China and the nascent (con)federal system in Europe. Second, many of the countries with the largest territories are federations. Third, countries with a high degree of regionally concentrated ethnic or linguistic diversity tend to have federal structures. In fact, Stepan (1999) points out that all of the world's long-standing multiethnic democracies have adopted federal constitutional structures. The Belgian and Spanish democracies ultimately succumbed to pressures for federalism, and the UK may be beginning to respond to such pressures as well. Recent transitions to democracy in vast countries like Argentina, Brazil, Mexico, and South Africa have been accompanied by reforms that have bolstered federalism. Thus, it appears that Rousseau may have been right: The combination of large populations, vast territories, and a republican form of government is associated with the institutionalization of federal bargaining.

Hopefully, it is now clear that federalism and decentralization are conceptually distinct. Yet it should not be surprising that they are highly correlated. Using the data from Table 2.1, subnational governments in federations spend, on average, over 40 percent of total public sector revenues, while the comparable figure for unitary systems is around 19 percent. Eighty-six percent of the federations feature popularly elected state and local executives, while among unitary systems 34 percent elect regional executives and 53 percent elect local officials. Moreover, decentralization in each of the policy areas displayed in Figure 2.1 is more pronounced in federations.

IV. Sorting Out the Promise and Peril: The Political Economy Approach

This chapter has emphasized key weaknesses and blind spots in the prevailing approaches to federalism in political science and economics, and the gap between theoretical and empirical approaches to the subject. The remaining task is to clarify how this book, along with other recent contributions, proposes to move forward. This book joins a nascent "second generation" of positive political economy research on federalism that starts with the long-held insights from public finance theory and the first generation of public choice theory, but replaces apolitical assumptions about the goals of public officials and vague notions about institutions, drawing on some insights from industrial organization theory and political science in order to lay out the conditions under which the expectations of traditional theories are most likely to be found in practice.[13] This new literature is drawn together by several common threads. First, drawing from the modern political science literature, it thinks of central, provincial, and local decision makers as politicians with career goals rather than benevolent despots or rent-seeking Leviathans. Second, emphasis is placed on bargaining within legislatures or directly between representatives of states and the central government. Third, because decentralized systems do not resemble the division of tax and expenditure authority laid out in fiscal federalism textbooks, the new literature considers a more complex, intertwined form of multilayered government that has much in common with the incomplete contracts described above, giving rise to an emphasis on incentives for opportunism. Finally, drawing on theories of public goods and notions from industrial organization theory, the new literature pays greater attention to Alexander Hamilton's warnings about the dangers of a weak central government.

First of all, fiscal federalism theory has made very strong assumptions of benevolence and foresight of the central government, which is granted a wide-ranging set of fiscal and regulatory tools to counteract the self-interested impulses of the component units. According to Breton (1996), the central government is the *deus ex machina* of fiscal federalism theory; it is called upon to identify, measure, and craft grant programs to internalize all interjurisdictional externalities. Leviathan theorists make equally strong assumptions in the opposite direction. Yet while characterizing local officials as malevolent rent seekers, this theory relies on the same powerful, selfless, omniscient central government to provide national public goods and enforce a common market (see Buchanan 1995).[14] A more realistic set of assumptions can be drawn from the political science literature. Whether they ultimately seek to enhance aggregate efficiency or line their own pockets, politicians must obtain and retain positions of power to do so. The assumption of electoral and other career motivations allows for

---

[13] For literature reviews, see Qian and Weingast (1997); Wibbels (2005); and Rodden (2005).
[14] For a more thorough critique, see Rodden and Rose-Ackerman (1997).

powerful insights into the behavior of politicians. Political institutions create incentive structures, and these can account for important cross-national differences in political and economic outcomes. Under some conditions, self-seeking politicians may face electoral incentives to promote aggregate efficiency; and under other conditions, uncoordinated self-seeking may lead to results that are bad for everyone. Thus, the incentives provided by elections, legislatures, and political parties take center stage in this book.[15]

Second, perhaps the most basic reason for the wide divergence between normative theory and the real-world functioning of federalism is the lack of resemblance between decisions made by a hypothetical benevolent despot and those made in real democracies through some variant of majority rule. A key goal of the emerging positive political economy literature on federalism is to model central government decisions – especially concerning the distribution of intergovernmental grants – as bargains struck among self-interested, reelection-seeking politicians attempting to form legislative coalitions (Dixit and Londregan 1998; Inman and Rubinfeld 1997). Intergovernmental fiscal decisions are made in a context of vote trading and vote buying rather than reflections on collective goods and the internalization of externalities. In the traditional view, the normative case for decentralization in a particular country hinges on the heterogeneity of tastes for public goods and the nature of externalities. From the political economy perspective, Inman and Rubinfeld (1997), Besley and Coate (2003), and Lockwood (2002) present models that focus on legislatures and redistribution, each concluding that the case for decentralization depends critically on the nature of legislative bargaining. As explained above, such bargaining has a special quality in federations, where bargains are struck between representatives of regional governments that are in many cases endowed with equal voting weights regardless of population.

Third, the incompleteness of federal contracts is another key starting point for the new political economy approach. Federalism would resemble the efficient world of fiscal federalism theory if far-sighted actors were able to write complete contracts that solve the assignment problem.[16] When contracts are incomplete, however, there is considerable room for opportunistic behavior by the parties to the contract (Williamson 1985: 47–49). These opportunism problems may be especially severe when the

---

[15] The same approach is taken in Filippov et al. (2003) and Wibbels (2005).

[16] For a more developed "incomplete contracts" approach to the study of federalism, see Tommasi and Saiegh (2000).

contracting parties are politicians in a highly competitive electoral environment. Federal intergovernmental contracts are often characterized by what Oliver Williamson refers to as "bilateral dependency" (1996: 377): The ability of one level of government to get what it wants – in terms of revenue collection, policy, or administration – is affected by decisions made at the other level. In many situations, as we shall see, politicians at one level have no reason to be concerned with whether their counterparts at the other level get what they want. Moreover, politicians are apt to withhold or distort information from officials at other levels of government.

Political scientists and economists alike who celebrate the promise of federalism have been keen to draw on the propaganda of *The Federalist* and view federalism as a form of "dual sovereignty," whereby the federal government and states are sovereign over their own spheres of authority and citizens can hold each separately responsible within their respective spheres (See Buchanan 1995; Ostrom 1987; Riker 1964). An incomplete contracting perspective brings about the realization, however, that these spheres are actually shifting Venn diagrams that overlap and move around in response to court decisions, power struggles, and opportunistic attempts to shift credit and blame. As intimated by Figure 2.1 above, clear divisions of authority tend to give way over time to complex vertical overlap between two and usually three levels of government.[17] Overlapping and blurred sovereignty are central to this book's approach, and it will argue that the dual sovereignty envisioned in the classical view of federalism is only approximated under extremely narrow conditions.

Finally, the emerging political economy perspective brings attention back to the most basic concern of federal design running from *The Federalist* to Riker: the notion that the center must be strong enough to provide public goods but sufficiently weak that it will not "overawe" the provinces. From Rousseau to Tiebout, all of the optimistic normative assessments of decentralization are ultimately about giving politicians stronger incentives to gather information about citizen preferences and transform them into policies at the lowest cost. But in order to achieve these gains, the information and authority of the central government must be credibly limited. This tension has been addressed most clearly in the study of decentralized industrial organizations. Aghion and Tirole (1997) show that in order to strengthen incentives and promote initiative in a decentralized organization, the

---

[17] On Argentina, see Saieghand Tommasi 1999; on Canada, see Courchene 1994; on Germany, see Scharpf 1988; and on the United States, see Grodzins 1966.

center must credibly limit its own information and authority. The flip side of the dilemma, however, is a loss of strategic control by the center.

The same dilemma characterizes decentralization in government. The information and competition advantages summarized above are not likely to materialize if the local governments are mere administrators of plans drawn up by the center. If the central government can arbitrarily overturn local decisions, remove local officials from office, or change the distribution of responsibilities at will, local officials face weak incentives to collect information and mobility has little effect on outcomes. The dual sovereignty ideal outlined in *The Federalist* is impossible if the center's authority knows no limits. Citizens would recognize local governments not as independent entities, but merely as tentacles of the central Leviathan. Such a centrally dominated system would do little to restrain rent seeking. As in the firm, if decentralization is to strengthen incentives, the center must make a credible commitment not to interfere in at least some subset of local affairs.

Thus, the normative theories establishing decentralization's promise seem to assume implicitly not only a wide range of local taxing and spending authority, but also some modicum of political federalism. Yet the new political economy perspective pays equal attention to the flip side of the dilemma pointed out by Aghion and Tirole. If the central government's authority is effectively limited, it may not be able to muster up the coordination necessary to provide federation-wide public goods such as a common market, a common currency, or a common defense. Both the benefits and the dangers of decentralization are amplified when the center is constrained by the bargains and institutional protections associated with federalism.

The remainder of this book builds on this political economy approach, focusing on the smaller, more manageable set of questions about fiscal discipline introduced above. It rethinks the abstract arguments linking decentralized federalism to increased fiscal discipline by adding politics. It theorizes about election-motivated politicians who operate in complex, overlapping spheres of authority where taxing and spending decisions are not tightly linked, intergovernmental transfers are subject to political bargaining, and politicians may face incentives to shift their fiscal burdens onto residents of other jurisdictions. This problem demonstrates the federal dilemma in a nutshell. If the central government controls local borrowing and spending decisions by administrative fiat, many of the information and competition advantages of decentralization may be lost. If it is restrained from doing so, under some conditions it faces a moral hazard problem that threatens the fiscal health of the entire federation.

Appendix 2.1: Years and Sources

Case	Years	Grant Information	Borrowing Autonomy Index	Borrowing Autonomy Sources
Argentina state	1986–1996	IMF, IDB	4	IMF, IDB
Australia local	1986–1996	IMF	2.1	IMF
Australia state	1986–1996	IMF	2.6	IMF
Austria local	1986–1995	Bird 1986	1.35	IMF, Bird 1986
Austria state	1986–1996	Bird 1986	1.85	IMF, Bird 1986
Bolivia	1987–1995	IMF, IDB	1.5	IMF, IDB
Botswana	1990–1994	Segodi 1995	1	Segodi 1995
Brazil local	1986–1993	IMF, IDB, Shah 1994	3	IMF, IDB, Shah 1994
Brazil state	1986–1994	IMF, IDB, Shah 1994	5	IMF, IDB, Shah 1994
Bulgaria	1988–1996	IMF	1	IMF
Canada local	1986–1994	IMF, Courchene 1994	1.4	IMF, Kitchen & McMillan 1986
Canada state	1986–1995	IMF, Courchene 1994	3.25	IMF
Chile	1986–1988	IDB	1	IDB
Colombia	1985–1986	IMF, IDB	3	IDB
Denmark	1986–1993	GFS, Harloff 1988, Bury & Skovsgaard 1988	1.45	IMF
Finland	1986–1995	GFS, Harloff 1988, Nurminen 1989	3	IMF
France	1986–1996	GFS, Guilbert & Guengant 1989	3	IMF
Germany local	1986–1994	IMF	1.7	IMF
Germany state	1986–1995	IMF	2.675	IMF
Guatemala	1990–1994	GFS, IDB	2	IDB
India	1986–1994	IMF	2.5	IMF
Ireland	1986–1994	GFS, Harloff 1988	1.75	IMF
Israel	1986–1994	Hecht 1988	2.4	Hecht 1988
Italy	1986–1989, 1995–1996	GFS, IMF	2.5	IMF
Mexico local	1986–1994	IMF	2	IMF
Mexico state	1986–1994	IMF, IDB	2.8	IMF, IDB

(continued)

Case	Years	Grant Information	Borrowing Autonomy Index	Borrowing Autonomy Sources
Netherlands	1987–1996	GFS, Blaas & Dostal 1989, Harloff 1988	2.3	IMF
Norway	1986–1995	GFS, Harloff 1988, Rattsø 2000	1.6	IMF
Paraguay	1986–1993	IDB	2	IMF, IDB
Peru	1990–1996	IDB	2.5	IMF, IDB
Philippines	1986–1992	GFS, Padilla 1993	1	Padilla 1993
Poland	1994–1996	Cielecka & Gibson 1995	2	Cielecka & Gibson 1995
Portugal	1987–1995	GFS, Harloff 1987	2.5	IMF
Spain local	1986–1994	Newton 1997	2.2	IMF, Newton 1997
Spain state	1986–1995	Newton 1997	2.8	IMF, Newton 1997
Sweden	1986–1996	GFS, Harloff 1988	3	IMF
Switzerland local	1990–1995	IMF	3	IMF
Switzerland state	1990–1996	IMF	3	IMF
UK	1986–1995	GFS, IMF	1.5	IMF
US local	1988–1995	IMF	3	IMF
US state	1988–1996	IMF	3	IMF
Zimbabwe	1986–1991	Helmsing 1991	1	Helmsing 1991

GFS: *Government Finance Statistics Yearbook.* Various years. Washington, DC: IMF.
IMF: Teresa Ter-Minassian, ed. 1997. *Fiscal Federalism in Theory and Practice.* Washington, DC: IMF.
IDB: Inter-American Development Bank. 1997. *Latin America after a Decade of Reforms.* Washington, DC: IDB.

Appendix 2.2: Construction of Borrowing Autonomy Index

This index is constructed based on the method developed by the Inter-American Development Bank (see IDB 1997: 188). It is built according to the following criteria:

  1. Ability to Borrow:
      If the subnational government cannot borrow, 2 points.

2. Authorization:

   This number ranges from 0 to 1. If all borrowing by the subnational government requires central government approval (or state government approval for local governments in federal systems), 1 point. If no subnational borrowing requires approval, 0 points. If the authorization constraint only applies to certain kinds of debt or the approval requirement is not always enforced, a score between 1 and 0 is given according to the level of constraint.

3. Borrowing Constraints:

   If there are numerical constraints on borrowing, such as maximum debt service/revenue ratios, up to .5 point, according to the coverage of the constraints.

4. Limits on the Use of Debt:

   If debt may not be used for current expenditures, .5 point.

   The value of the first part of the index (criteria 1 through 4) is equal to 2 minus the sum of the points from criteria 1 through 4. For example, if subnational governments in a country cannot borrow, the total for this part will be $2 - 2 = 0$.

Additional criteria are:

5. Subnational Government Banks:

   If subnational governments own banks, 1 point. If these banks have substantial importance, an additional .5 point. If subnational governments have special relationships with banks, but do not actually own them (as in the German Länder), .5 point.

6. Public Enterprises:

   If subnational governments own important public enterprises and these have liberal borrowing practices, .5 point.

To obtain the final index for each country, the scores from criteria 5 and 6 are added to the first part of the index. One is added so that the final index varies between 1 and 5.

3

Sovereignty and Commitment

This depends on principles of human nature, that are as infallible as any mathematical calculations. States will contribute or not, according to their circumstances and interests: They will all be inclined to throw off the burthens of government upon their neighbors.

Alexander Hamilton, *Speech in the New York Ratifying Convention*, 1788

The previous chapter argued that in order to bring the theory literature closer to evolving empirical realities around the world, the old notion of decentralization as a clean division of sovereignty among vertically arranged governments must be replaced by an approach that highlights the murkiness and contestability of sovereignty in a world with opportunistic, politically motivated actors. The previous chapter also reviewed some rather attractive and time-honored arguments linking decentralization, federalism, and fiscal discipline, but then examined cross-country data suggesting that modern forms of decentralization and federalism seem inconsistent with their basic assumptions.

In order to pave the way for an explanation of the wide range of experiences related to decentralization, federalism, and fiscal discipline around the world, this chapter takes a political economy approach to the issue of sovereignty over debt in multitiered systems. It presents a dynamic game of incomplete information played between higher and lower-level governments, each of which has incentives to see that the other government undertakes painful adjustment to negative income shocks. A key lesson is that when sovereignty is unclear or disputed, actors use the information available to them and assign probabilities to the likely ultimate locus of authority in the event of a conflict. Sovereignty at a given time in a given policy area in multitiered systems is best understood as an *ex ante* set of beliefs about likely winners of future intergovernmental battles. When applied to battles over debt burdens, this framework provides useful insights into the fiscal incentives faced by subnational governments, and a platform for the cross-national and diachronic comparisons made in later chapters.

According to the conventional definition, central governments are sovereign debtors with "supreme authority" over their debt – no higher government guarantees it or can compel them to repay it. On the other hand, nonsovereign debtors like firms *can* be compelled to repay, or in special cases the sovereign will have incentives to bail them out (e.g., the United States Savings and Loan crisis). When lending to individuals or firms in a developed domestic credit market, lenders have recourse to a variety of legal sanctions imposed and enforced by the sovereign if borrowers do not repay their debts. When lending to sovereign central governments, however, they have no recourse. Their hopes for repayment must be based on either the government's interest in preserving its reputation in order to maintain access to credit markets (Eaton and Gersovitz 1981) or the creditor's ability to mobilize trade or military sanctions against the borrower (Bulow and Rogoff 1989).

For subnational governments, however, this chapter argues that the line between sovereign and nonsovereign debt is blurred. Creditors must make educated guesses about whether the center implicitly guarantees their debt. In countries where the center can commit never to assume subnational debts, lower-level governments can be viewed as miniature sovereign borrowers. However, this chapter begins to explore the many institutional, political, and demographic factors that can sow seeds of doubt about the credibility of the center's commitment not to bail out troubled subnational governments. It introduces an argument that will be refined throughout the book: a separate realm of fiscal sovereignty for subnational governments – something taken for granted in optimistic theories linking decentralization to enhanced fiscal discipline – is quite rare in practice. When the fiscal sovereignty of subnational governments is undermined, the door is open to the kind of strategic burden shifting that Alexander Hamilton believed was unavoidable in decentralized federations.

After introducing the bailout game and discussing its equilibria in abstract terms, this chapter makes it concrete by applying it to the fiscal crisis of the U.S. states in the 1840s. The U.S. case is useful because it highlights some of the factors that undermine commitment, but just as important, it also sheds light on some of the factors that bolster it. The resolution of the debt crisis, while painful for voters in some of the states, was a watershed event in U.S. federalism that clarified for voters and creditors the sovereign status of the states. The lessons from this chapter – above all about the origins of subnational sovereignty and the factors that undermine it – will be refined and tested in later chapters.

I. The Bailout Game

The literature on "soft budget constraints" among firms in socialist economies, which views the central government as falling prey to a dynamic commitment problem, is a good starting point for understanding the relationship between central and local governments.[1] The basic problem in this literature is that the government cannot commit not to extend further credit to a loss-making organization after providing initial financing, which creates bad incentives for managers when choosing projects. In the same way, the central government's inability to commit not to bail out local governments affects their incentives. Consider a simple game played between a central government (CG) and a single subnational government (SNG), both of whom are concerned with the expected electoral consequences of their fiscal policy decisions. A dynamic game of incomplete information is displayed in extensive form in Figure 3.1.[2]

Information is incomplete because subnational governments do not know the central government's "type." That is, they do not know if, in the event of a future fiscal crisis at the final stage of the game, the central government will prefer to allow the subnational government to default (the resolute type) or will prefer a bailout (the irresolute type). The subnational government is faced with an adverse fiscal shock with lasting effects – for example, a recession. In its first move after experiencing a negative shock, the subnational government may choose to adjust immediately and end

---

[1] This literature was inspired by Kornai (1980); most of the formal literature flows from Dewatripont and Maskin (1995). For a literature review, see Kornai, Maskin, and Roland (2003).

[2] The bailout problem has also been modeled as a sequential game driven by the central government's incentives by Wildasin (1997), who focuses on the structure of jurisdictions, and by Inman (2003), who considers a range of factors, including some of those discussed below. The approach in this chapter is distinct, however, in that it focuses on incomplete information. In the spirit of Dewatripont and Maskin (1995), Qian and Roland (1998) use a sequential game to address the impact of devolution on incentives to provide bailouts, but their focus is on the budget constraints of state-owned enterprises rather than local governments themselves, and political considerations play no role. In their model, fiscal decentralization causes competition among local governments, which increases the opportunity costs of bailing out state-owned enterprises that have chosen bad projects.

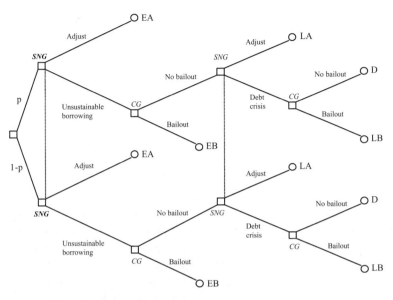

Figure 3.1. Dynamic bailout game.

the game, for which it receives the payoff from "early adjustment" (EA). Alternatively, it can refuse to adjust and deal with the shock by pursuing borrowing that may ultimately be unsustainable, hoping for an eventual bailout from the central government. The center must then decide whether it will quietly resolve the burgeoning problem by providing some additional funding to reduce the subnational government's growing debt burden. If it decides to do so, the game ends with the payoffs for "early bailout" (EB). If it decides not to provide the bailout initially, a second stage ensues where the stakes are higher, a debt crisis has emerged, and default is imminent. Again, the subnational government faces a choice between adjusting and attempting to externalize the costs of adjustment, although this time the bailout will be more expensive and explicit. Once again, the central government must decide whether to provide it.

The expected utilities of the subnational government are driven by the expected electoral values of each outcome. Subnational officials are concerned about the negative electoral consequences of adjustment and would prefer that the costs of adjustment be paid by citizens of other jurisdictions. The subnational government prefers a quiet early bailout, but if it cannot get a bailout at the fist stage, it prefers to get one at the later stage (LB). If no bailout will be provided and the subnational government must pay the costs of adjustment itself, it would prefer a less costly early adjustment to a painful late adjustment (LA). The worst of all worlds is default without federal assistance (D). Thus, the subnational government's payoffs, common knowledge to everyone, are:

$$U_{sng}(EB) = 1 > U_{sng}(LB) > U_{sng}(EA) > U_{sng}(LA) > U_{sng}(D) = 0.$$

The central government's preferences are less clear. All players know that the central government prefers for the subnational government to adjust by itself rather than run a large deficit and demand a bailout. The game is interesting, however, because the subnational government does not know the central government's preferences as the game continues. The subnational government does not know with certainty whether it will be more politically costly for the center to provide or deny a bailout. This is similar to a scenario that has been modeled by students of international conflict as the "deterrence game" (Morrow 1994: 200), in which military challengers must make decisions about whether to wage war or back down without knowing the resolve of defenders. In the same way, subnational governments do not know the resolve, or commitment, of the central government to resist the demand for bailouts.

The most intuitive way to deal with this kind of limited information is to follow Harsanyi (1967–68), capturing the uncertainty in the mind of the subnational government by thinking of the game as beginning with a chance move that determines the central government's type – either resolute or irresolute. The central government is informed of its own type, but the subnational government is not. The central government may try to announce its commitment up front, but the subnational government knows that it may be cheap talk. If the central government is of the resolute type, it always prefers *not* to provide the bailout. The payoffs for a resolute and irresolute central government, respectively, are

$$U_{cgr}(EA) = 1 > U_{cgr}(LA) > U_{cgr}(D) > U_{cgr}(EB) > U_{cgr}(LB) = 0.$$

$$U_{cgi}(EA) = 1 > U_{cgi}(LA) > U_{cgi}(EB) > U_{cgi}(LB) > U_{cgi}(D) = 0.$$

At each of its decision nodes, the subnational government does not know whether it is playing in the upper or lower branch of Figure 3.1, though it updates its beliefs about the center's type after observing the first round. The subnational government starts out believing that the center is resolute with probability p, irresolute with probability $1-p$. When it reaches its second information set, p has been updated to $\overline{p}$.

First, consider the equilibria under perfect information. By backward induction, it is clear that if $p = 1$ (the subnational government believes with certainty that the center is resolute), the game ends quickly because the subnational government plays "adjust" in its first move, foreseeing that the center will play "no bailout" every step of the way, leaving the subnational government in the future with even less attractive options than adjustment. If the center is known to be irresolute ($p = 0$), the subnational government will allow a fiscal crisis to develop by refusing to adjust, knowing that the center cannot tolerate a default. The game ends with an early bailout, since the irresolute center can gain nothing by waiting.

We now have a clear way to think about subnational fiscal sovereignty. At one end of a continuum, if $p = 1$ a subnational government is best understood as a miniature sovereign borrower. At the other end, where $p = 0$, the government is a nonsovereign. A key argument that will gain strength throughout this book, however, is that information about the center's preferences over future bailouts is often incomplete. As we shall see in the case studies that follow, subnational governments are often unsure about the center's resolve. In these cases, the subnational government's decision about whether to adjust is shaped in large part by its evolving assessment of the central government's resolve.

The appropriate solution concept in this dynamic game with incomplete information is a perfect Bayesian equilibrium (PBE). The solution is discussed in detail in the appendix to this chapter, but the key insights are easily summarized. First of all, it is important to note that there is no separating equilibrium in pure strategies. In other words, the subnational government – though it updates its beliefs after the first round – cannot surmise that an irresolute center always plays early bailout and a resolved center always plays no bailout in the first stage. Such a posterior belief for the subnational government is not consistent with the incentives of an irresolute center, which would take advantage of these beliefs by always masquerading as the resolute type in the first period, playing no bailout and inducing its preferred outcome, late adjustment by the subnational government.

This means, quite simply, that if p is sufficiently high initially, the subnational government might mistake an irresolute for a resolved center after observing no bailout in the first round. The subnational government knows it might be making this mistake, but the probability of running into a resolute center is perceived to be sufficiently high that the subnational government prefers the fourth-best late-adjustment payoff to prolonging the crisis and taking its chances by pressing further for bailouts. In this equilibrium, the subnational government has essentially tested the resolve of the center and backed down. It was sufficiently uncertain about the center's resolve that it was willing to avoid adjustment and borrow heavily at first; but after the center has done nothing and default emerges as a realistic possibility, the subnational government chooses to back down. Of course, the game can also end in late adjustment if a resolved center plays no bailout and the subnational government wisely backs down.

Other things equal, lower initial values of p increase the likelihood that subnational governments will avoid adjustment in the first round. The appendix establishes a critical value for p, below which it makes sense for a rational subnational government to push for bailouts in the first round. As these "resolve-testing" equilibria demonstrate, this does not mean that bailouts will ultimately be received, nor does it mean that the subnational government will experience disastrous defaults. Irresolute central governments might use the intergovernmental transfer system to relieve debt burdens of subnational governments well before full-blown fiscal crises develop. Subnational governments might angle to position themselves for such transfers but ultimately give up before the debt-servicing crisis emerges. A dramatic last-minute bailout on the eve of default only happens when an irresolute center attempted to masquerade as resolute and the subnational government called its bluff. A dramatic default without a bailout should only happen when the subnational government misperceives the center's type.

As a guide to empirical research, the model suggests that manifestations of bailout expectations among subnational governments are not limited to dramatic defaults or last-minute bailouts under pressure from creditors, but in many plausible scenarios imply more routine early bailouts (gap-filling intergovernmental transfers) or delayed adjustment. Much of the analysis to follow in this book attempts to identify the factors shaping the utilities of subnational governments and their beliefs about the center's commitment. The simplest empirical implication of this model, then, is that if one can identify institutional, demographic, or other factors that are associated with high values of p, one should expect to find that subnational governments adjust to external shocks and maintain long-term fiscal balance on their own. If institutional and political arrangements suggest sufficiently low values of p, one should expect a greater willingness of subnational governments to avoid or delay adjustment, resulting in larger and more persistent deficits.

It is also useful to consider that the game may be repeated over and over again within countries, meaning that with every negative shock requiring adjustment, subnational officials have a long history of past play on which to base their assessments of p. If the center has a recent history of providing bailouts, it will be very difficult to make a credible no-bailout commitment. Thus, a central government, if concerned with future plays of the game, faces strong incentives to establish a reputation for resolve. When a new political and fiscal system is taking shape, the first rounds of the game are especially important because subnational governments have no past play on which to base their assessments of the center's resolve. Thus, early tests of the center's resolve can be among the most important. In the case studies to follow, past play is extremely important and historical legacies loom large. Yet past play does not necessarily determine current play. Subnational governments also take cues from the political and fiscal institutions that shape the central government's payoffs. Changes in political circumstances and institutions can drive changes in the utilities of subnational governments as well as their perceptions of the center's preferences.

This game provides a framework that will facilitate cross-national as well as cross-province and diachronic comparisons within countries. The key questions about subnational fiscal discipline can now be posed more precisely: What are the conditions under which all subnational units believe sufficiently in the center's resolve that they eschew the later stages of the bailout game? As the history of fiscal federalism evolves in a country, why does the center's resolve crumble – seemingly irretrievably – in some countries, while it strengthens in others? Under what conditions are subnational governments most uncertain about the center's resolve? Why might different subnational units within the same country have different payoffs or different beliefs about the center's resolve? The goal of the chapters that follow is to craft and test systematic arguments about the geographic, institutional, and political factors that can help answer these questions. A useful way to introduce these factors is with a brief analytical narrative that draws on the early American experience.[3]

II. The United States in the Nineteenth Century

The public debt of the Union would be a cause of collision between the separate States or confederacies. The apportionment, in the first instance, and the progressive extinguishment afterwards, would be alike productive of ill-humor and animosity. . . .   Alexander Hamilton, *The Federalist* 7

---

[3] For an alternative spin on these events, see Wibbels (2003).

No conduct was ever more profligate than that of the State of Pennsylvania. History cannot pattern it: and let no deluded being imagine that they will ever repay a single farthing – their people have tasted the dangerous luxury of dishonesty, and they will never be brought back to the homely rule of right.

The Reverend Sydney Smith, in a letter to *The London Morning Chronicle*, November 4, 1843

Though some of his disingenuous writings in *The Federalist* are part of the dual federalism canon, Alexander Hamilton did not believe in separate spheres of sovereignty for the states and the federal government, especially when it came to the power of the purse. "The idea of an uncontrolable sovereignty in each state will defeat the other powers given to Congress, and make our union feeble and precarious."[4] In Hamilton's view, the route to prosperity and good government was through a unitary state with a strong executive. His reasoning is familiar to students of positive political economy: "[I]t is the temper of societies as well as of individuals. . . . to prefer partial to general interest."[5] The strong local accountability so often celebrated by advocates of federalism is for Hamilton merely a mechanism for promoting self-seeking and private goods over the common interest. When speaking of states attempting to "throw their burdens" upon their neighbors, Hamilton was complaining not only about the free-rider problem that characterized requisitions under the Articles of Confederation,[6] but also something like the bailout game above.

In arguing for federal assumption of state debts in the *First Report on the Public Credit* (1790), Hamilton anticipated the modern public choice literature on fiscal competition by pointing out that capital mobility and state politics placed severe constraints upon the ability of states to tax. Rather than celebrating this as a constraint on Leviathan, however, Hamilton feared that states would be able to borrow heavily – bolstered by the good credit of the federal government – but then fall easily into default when faced with negative shocks because of their lacking revenue base, thereby damaging the creditworthiness of other states and the federal government. Next, he feared that due to the influence of the states in the federal policy process, rational decisions about issuing and retiring federal debt would be precluded by squabbles between states based on the strength of debt holders in each state, with indebted states pushing hard for federal bailouts.

---

[4] Letter to James Duane, September 3, 1780, published in Frisch (1985).
[5] *The Continentalist No. II*, July 19, 1781, published in Frisch (1985).
[6] For a public choice perspective on this problem, see Dougherty (1999).

Perhaps his most passionate endeavor as a statesman was to convince Congress to form a national bank and assume all the debts of the states. This was defended as a matter of morality and justice, because the states with the largest debts had borne the brunt of the expenditures in conducting the Revolutionary War. His logic went beyond morality, however. Given his fears about externalities and bailouts, his hope was to establish the federal government as the sole creditor to the states and cut off their independent access to credit markets in the future. Hamilton ultimately succeeded by making the famous deal with Jefferson on the location of the national capital, and the federal government assumed the debts of the states in 1790. Of course, one of the dangers of assumption was that the central government would set a precedent by encouraging states to believe that it was the irresolute type. One of Hamilton's most vocal critics, Albert Gallatin, criticized the debt assumption because it proceeded "without examining whether the debts they then owed arose from the greatness of their exertions during the war, or from their remissness in paying taxes" (quoted in Ratchford 1941). But Hamilton was not concerned about creating a moral hazard problem: His scheme did not make room for future independent borrowing by the states. He perished in his famous duel shortly thereafter, and the states soon resumed their independent borrowing, with troubling results. Many of Hamilton's fears about state borrowing seemed to be well founded after the first half of the nineteenth century. Fifty years after the initial debt assumption, it was held up as precedent during urgent pleas for another much larger assumption. By briefly revisiting these events, it is possible to gain a useful perspective on the bailout game in action.

The Bailout Game in Action

At the beginning of the 1820s, most of the states had only nominal debts or none at all. State budgets were quite small, and they engaged in almost no direct taxation. States were able to get by without significant taxation by relying on proceeds from issuing bank charters, sales of public lands, and various investments. Borrowing, however, became a very attractive way to dramatically increase expenditures on popular banks, canals, and railroads without increasing taxation. With the advent of Jacksonian democracy, the federal government was curtailing its activities and weakening the United States Bank at a time when massive population movements led to increased demand for transportation infrastructure and banking, especially in the new states. Moreover, some of the states – especially Maryland, New York, Ohio, and Pennsylvania – were locked in a battle over preeminence in the race to open up westward trade routes. Borrowing to set up banks and build canals and railroads was extremely popular in these states, as well as southern and western states, and the success of New York's Erie Canal (the tolls exceeded the interest charges before the project was completed) left other states scrambling to initiate similar projects. Illinois, Indiana, and Michigan used federal land grants to start aggressive internal improvement projects. For example, with a population of less than 200,000 and total assessed property value under $43,000, the Michigan legislature approved a $5,000,000 loan (McGrane 1935). Much of the borrowing by the western states was undertaken with the notion that interest payments would be funded by future taxes on recent sales of federal lands (Sylla, Grinath, and Wallis 2004). The southern states especially became involved in chartering numerous banks. Meanwhile, the federal government had rapidly paid off all its debts from the War of 1812 and faced a large, growing surplus, which it decided to simply transfer to the states, along with numerous land grants. These grants served only to encourage additional borrowing, and debt burdens grew steadily. In the years between 1836 and 1839, the growth was explosive, and the states incurred more new debt than in their entire previous history combined. All of the states were encouraged to borrow because of rapidly rising land values, and the belief that even if property taxes were not currently in place, this resource could be tapped in case of emergency (Sylla, Grinath, and Wallis 2004).

These new securities were very popular among Dutch and especially British investors. There was an abundance of funds in the London money market, and the American state securities carried higher interest rates. While other loans to foreign countries disappeared into military campaigns, British investors had very good experiences loaning money to the U.S. federal government, and the American states were viewed as engaged in productive investments in a prosperous land. These securities were backed up by the full faith and credit of the states, and the contracts specified that the principal and interest were payable in London and Amsterdam in local currency.

A negative shock came with the financial panic of 1837 and the onset of a major recession from 1839 to 1843. Reaching the first decision node for subnational governments in the bailout game, many of the states continued to borrow even more aggressively, even though debt servicing became difficult and banks and infrastructure projects were not yet bringing in revenue

(Sylla, Grinath, and Wallis 2004). They continued to borrow until the entire financial structure collapsed with the banking collapse of 1840. Borrowing ceased, work on canals and railroads came to a halt, and meager tax revenues dried up completely. Above all, the land values that propped up borrowing in the first place began to fall. As the crisis deepened, some of the most heavily indebted state governments refused to adjust, resisting any increases in direct taxation to the end, and resorted to a wide variety of tricks that juggled funds between the books of the states and their banks until, one after another, nine states defaulted in 1841 and 1842.[7] All of the defaulting states, excluding Maryland and Pennsylvania, were newer states in the South and West – Arkansas, Florida, Illinois, Indiana, Louisiana, Michigan, and Mississippi. Movements aimed at repudiating debts gained strength in some states, and in Arkansas, Florida, Michigan, and Mississippi, substantial portions of the debt were actually repudiated, to the great consternation of their British and Dutch financiers. Repudiation movements in these states hearkened back to Hamilton and questioned the constitutional powers of the states to contract debts in the first place.

The final stage of the bailout game – the movement for federal assumption of state debts – began in earnest in 1839, well before the state defaults. It is difficult to say with certainty whether foreign creditors truly viewed the states as sovereigns when buying the securities or ultimately expected that the debts of individual states were backed up by the resources and powers of the federation as a whole. The sources cited by McGrane (1935) demonstrate considerable difference of opinion on this point among different British investment houses and financial publications. The difficulty of assessing the sovereignty of the states is demonstrated by the case of Florida, where bonds – marketed in Europe as indistinguishable from other state securities and fully approved by Congress – were issued by a bank chartered by the territorial (pre-statehood) government that was legally under the direct supervision of Congress. Many of the newest, most sparsely populated states certainly did not have sufficient revenues backing their debts, and it is difficult to imagine that investors did not envision some implicit federal support (Sbragia 1996).

Whatever their initial understandings of state sovereignty may have been, British investors ultimately argued forcefully that the debts carried

---

[7] Sylla, Grinath, and Wallis (2004) point out that unlike most other states, Illinois, Indiana, and Ohio did try to increase property taxes in order to service their debts.

an implicit federal guarantee, and placed immense pressure on the U.S. federal government to assume the state debts. The defaults carried externalities for other states, whose bonds were selling below par even though they had punctually made payments. As Hamilton had predicted, negative externalities extended directly to the federal government, which found itself completely cut off in 1842 from European financiers, who claimed they would never lend again to any U.S. entity until the debts of the states were assumed by the federal government. Foreign capitalists had no other recourse than to pressure the central government. Bulow and Rogoff (1989) argue that foreign creditors must be able to impose direct sanctions on sovereign debtors – like military or trade sanctions – in order to force repayment. As relations between the United States and Great Britain grew increasingly hostile, John Quincy Adams believed that war with Britain was imminent if the state debts were not assumed (McGrane 1935: 35). But war with the United States was an expensive proposition, and as most of the bondholders were private citizens, the British government eventually distanced itself from the dispute. Moreover, trade sanctions were not a very useful threat because they would be ineffective if levied against individual states (who could freely export to other states) and too costly if levied against the entire country (see English 1996).

Not surprisingly, support for assumption was strong among politicians and voters in the most heavily indebted states – especially Maryland and Pennsylvania – and among foreign and domestic bondholders, but quite unpopular among many of the older states that had not borrowed significantly (see Table 3.1). Moreover, even some voters in the indebted western states were leery of assumption proposals that would have been funded by land sales that might undermine legislation that they saw as crucial to their own ability to secure lands. After years of debate, a committee headed by William Cost Johnson of Maryland submitted a report to Congress in 1843 advocating assumption. First of all, the committee argued that assumption was justified because a clear precedent had been established, starting with the first assumption, continuing with the War of 1812[8] and then the 1836 assumption of the debt of the District of Columbia, whereby states borrowed and were eventually reimbursed by the central government. Furthermore, the committee argued that without the right to levy tariffs, the

---

[8] During the War of 1812, some states spent and borrowed for their own defense and later submitted receipts to the federal government.

Table 3.1. *U.S. state debts, 1841 (current $)*

State	Total Debt	Total Debt per Capita
Florida	4,000,000	73.43
Louisiana	23,985,000	68.06
Maryland	15,215,000	32.43
Illinois	13,527,000	28.41
Arkansas	2,676,000	27.43
Michigan	5,611,000	26.43
Alabama	15,400,000	26.07
Pennsylvania	36,336,000	21.08
Mississippi	7,000,000	18.63
Indiana	12,751,000	18.59
New York	21,797,000	8.97
Massachusetts	5,424,000	7.35
Ohio	10,924,000	7.19
South Carolina	3,691,000	6.21
Tennessee	3,398,000	4.10
Kentucky	3,085,000	3.96
Maine	1,735,000	3.46
Virginia	4,037,000	3.26
Missouri	842,000	2.19
Georgia	1,310,000	1.89
Connecticut	0	0
Delaware	0	0
Iowa	0	0
New Hampshire	0	0
New Jersey	0	0
North Carolina	0	0
Rhode Island	0	0
Vermont	0	0
Total, all states	192,744,000	11.35

Sources: Debt data: U.S. Tenth Census; Population: ICPSR Study 0003.

states could not be expected to fulfill their obligations by relying on direct taxation, which was not considered a realistic possibility. Furthermore, Johnson made the argument that defaults would halt the construction of important public works with interstate spillovers. Moreover, the committee argued that the states had donated public lands to the federal government in order to retire the federal debt, and now that this had been achieved, the funds should be used to retire the debts of the states.

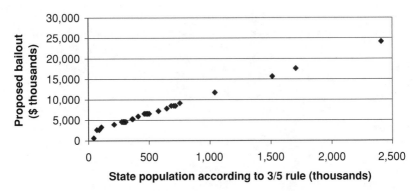

Figure 3.2. State population and Johnson's proposed 1843 bailout. *Sources*: bailout proposal: McGrane (1935); population: ICPSR Study 0003.

Opponents decried the demonstration effect – the possibility that the center would signal a lack of resolve. They argued that fiscal burdens would be shifted from fiscally irresponsible to fiscally prudent states, and states' rights advocates argued that Congress had no power to pay the debts.

The Johnson committee did not propose to distribute the bailout funds in relation to actual state debts. On the contrary, Figure 3.2 makes it quite clear that the committee hoped to buy the votes of nonindebted states with a population-based subsidy – benefiting even the states that had not borrowed at all.[9] However, neither the Whigs nor the Democrats publicly advocated assumption, and Johnson's report was tabled. Even though the committee proposed a simple per capita transfer, one of the best explanations for the defeat of the assumption movement may simply be in the numbers – the majority of states did not have large debts, and outside of Maryland and Pennsylvania, most of the debtor states had small populations. According to McGrane (1935) and Ratchford (1941), the bailout was perceived by voters in nondebtor states as an unfair shifting of debt burdens.[10] Presidential candidates did not wish to lose votes in the older states

---

[9] The committee appears to have used the three-fifths rule (free white population plus three-fifths of the slave population) used for the apportionment of legislative seats when making its bailout proposal. Figure 3.2 looks rather similar if white population or total population is used instead, but the relationship is clearly tighter using the three-fifths calculation.

[10] Johnson's own state of Maryland stood to receive around $6 million even though its debt burden was over $15 million. In spite of its $4 million debt, Florida was to receive only $650,000. On the other hand, debt-free Connecticut and Vermont were each slated to receive around $4.6 million.

or among Western settlers by giving support to a policy that was thought to shift debt burdens and reduce access to federal lands. Moreover, it is important to note that the vast majority of the creditors were foreigners, and the opponents of assumption successfully portrayed the movement as a plot by foreigners and a cabal of wealthy Americans that would harm ordinary voters.

Given the newfound difficulties of the states and the federal government in obtaining loans, it is somewhat surprising that the negative externalities of repudiations and delayed payments alone did not compel Congress to act. Initially, many Americans apparently believed that cutting off dependence on European capitalists was a positive development, and given recent experience, there was strong sentiment against further borrowing. It also became apparent that ultimately the most serious threats of long-term capital flight were empty. Threats of war in Europe and a return to prosperity quickly made the United States an attractive investment once again. It also became clear in 1843 that, though the process would be politically and financially painful, most of the biggest defaulters would find ways to resume interest payments. The states increased tax rates, liquidated banks, sold bank stocks and railroad holdings, and turned projects over to bondholders. In order to please angry and fearful voters and investors, most of the states – even those that did not overborrow – adopted constitutional debt limitations in the 1840s and 1850s.

Borrowing for public works resumed in the 1850s, but none of the defaulting states participated, and although British investors cautiously returned, most of the bondholders were now American citizens. Through the experiences of the 1840s, creditors and voters learned some painful lessons about borrowing and sovereignty. By resisting calls for assumption, the federal government established with costly action rather than parchment a new precedent that the states are truly sovereigns, and even under the most severe conditions, the central government is neither responsible for their debts nor capable of compelling repayment. Realizing this, investors learned to be more discerning in distinguishing the states from one another and began insisting on much more substantial information about the quality of investment projects, the organization of state institutions, and above all the strength of state tax systems. Voters also learned some extremely valuable lessons: Borrowing is not always a substitute for taxation in building infrastructure, and borrowing decisions ultimately do affect citizen welfare – potentially quite dramatically.

Lessons

It is very difficult to discern the beliefs of the governors and state legislators about the federal government's resolve when it issued debt in the 1820s and 1830s. Many historians stress that state officials truly believed that the projects would pay for themselves. It seems evident, however, that p was not sufficiently high to induce early adjustment to the crisis of 1837 for most of the defaulting states. For the troubled states – though it was becoming increasingly clear that they were on a path to imminent default – the expected electoral utility of admitting defeat and instituting painful new taxes was exceeded by the expected utility of avoiding adjustment and lobbying the federal government for a bailout. Moreover, there were a variety of cues embedded in the history and institutions of the new nation to create rational bailout expectations.

On the other hand, with the benefit of hindsight, one can identify countervailing reasons to anticipate the center's resolve. Overall, there was a high degree of uncertainty about the center's type on the eve of the defaults. The episode is of great historical interest because it demonstrates the possibility that playing no bailout at the final stage – even when this is painful for the center – sends a costly signal of the center's resolve that pushes p above the critical value for future plays of the game. The weakening of the fiscal powers of the central government that emerged from Jacksonian democracy, followed by the no-bailout resolution to the 1840s crisis, contributed to a set of perceptions among state governments, voters, and creditors that the federal government preferred disastrous defaults to bailouts. These perceptions ossified in the wake of the Civil War and the negative shocks to state finances experienced in the 1930s. It is going too far to suggest that p has reached 1 for all states – in 2003, there was a short-lived movement for explicit debt reduction transfers in the wake of the most recent state fiscal crisis – but throughout the twenty-first century, there is little evidence that states harbor bailout expectations that lead them to delay or avoid adjustment.

In addition to lessons about the possibility of signaling resolve through costly action, the events leading up to the 1840s crisis teach some useful lessons about the geographic, institutional, and political factors that shape the center's evolving commitment.

Expenditure Assignment and Reasons for Borrowing   First of all, the 1790 assumption and subsequent bailouts and ad hoc resource distributions may have been perceived by some as evidence of the center's lacking resolve.

However, in contrast to the debts of the Revolutionary War and the War of 1812, these debts had been incurred for projects whose potential beneficiaries were primarily residents of the respective states, and this may have ultimately strengthened the credibility of the center's commitment. Johnson's arguments notwithstanding, the debts funded private banks and private transportation companies, often through corrupt local deals, and (with a few exceptions) did not provide anything that could be construed as national collective goods. The rhetoric of "morality" was on the side of Hamilton and the assumption movement in the 1780s, but the moral high ground seems to have been occupied by the anti-assumption movement in the 1840s. In other words, the center's overall resolve is more believable when the states are responsible for providing goods that are purely local in character and over which the center clearly has no jurisdiction or responsibility. The center's resolve is bolstered when government responsibilities are organized according to the dictates of classic fiscal federalism theory discussed in the previous chapter.

Recall from the previous chapter, however, the data on policy decentralization, showing that in most countries around the world in recent decades the center often shares jurisdiction and responsibility with subnational governments, even over basic infrastructure investments. And as we shall see, though the fiscal federalism canon urges the centralization of welfare, health care, and macroeconomic stabilization, in many (especially European) countries with large welfare states, expenditures on politically sensitive national collective goods take place at the local level, funded through intergovernmental grants. When compared with modern cases, the extent to which the U.S. states were free of federal involvement or responsibility in the rush for internal improvements in the 1800s is quite distinctive. As we shall see in some of the case studies later in this book, the center has a much more difficult time establishing its resolve when the local governments are borrowing to assist in the provision of nationwide collective goods or can credibly make that case.

Basic Powers and Obligations of the Center   More generally, it is important to understand the nature of the center's powers, obligations, and responsibilities, both as expressed in the constitution and as understood by citizens, politicians, and creditors. As Hamilton feared, the ambitions and obligations of the U.S. federal government were extremely limited from the very beginning and had even contracted in the early 1800s. The federal government was barely fifty years old and had been formed through a very

65

tenuous delegation of authority from states that already possessed a certain protosovereignty. It was a classic case of "coming together" for the purpose of military defense, and the expressed mandate of the federal government did not go far beyond providing for the "pursuit of happiness." In stark contrast to many of the other countries that will be discussed later in this book, it had no explicit or implicit mandate – in fact, it was expressly forbidden – to redistribute wealth from one state to another or oversee policy outcomes in the states. These limitations clearly bolstered the credibility of the center's commitment to stay out of the states' budget difficulties. The contrast with the German case discussed in Chapter 7 is quite striking.

Perhaps one of the most important limitations of the U.S. central government was in the judiciary. In general, a central government's commitment not to provide bailouts might be undermined by its obligation to protect the property rights of creditors in the event of defaults by lower-level governments. If the courts and the central government's coercive apparatus have accepted the job of enforcing property rights – as is generally the case in democracies – creditors will demand that the center force the lower-level government to repay their debts. If it refuses to comply, the center appears to have shirked in protecting property rights – perhaps the most basic task of government. Wishing to avoid this embarrassment, the center might find it less costly to simply pay the creditors itself. This dilemma is partially circumvented in the United States, however, by the Eleventh Amendment to the Constitution: "The judicial power of the United States shall not be construed to extend to any suit in law or equity, commenced or prosecuted against one of the United States by citizens of another state, or by citizens or subjects of any foreign state." This can be interpreted as preventing the federal courts from reviewing claims of states' creditors and absolves the central government of enforcing claims. There were some potential end runs around the Eleventh Amendment, like bringing a suit through an agent not covered by the amendment – for example, a citizen of the state, a foreign government, or another state (English 1996). In fact, Nicholas Biddle, a prominent defender of the foreign creditors, recommended in a public letter that the investors scheme to attempt all of these, going so far as to suggest that the city governments of Zurich or Lucerne file federal suits. However, Europeans and Americans alike ridiculed the plan as legally suspect and, perhaps more important, impossible to enforce (McGrane 1935: 80).

Differential perceptions of the center's powers and obligations might also help explain some interstate differences in fiscal behavior. Note that the most clearly unsustainable borrowing – aside from Pennsylvania – took place in the new states that lacked a previous history of independence. Perhaps these states – or at least their creditors – had better reason to view their fiscal sovereignty as limited. Some of these states started issuing bonds before they achieved statehood, and it may have appeared that the center could compel them to pay or feel compelled to take over payments in the event of a crisis. Perceptions of incomplete sovereignty might help explain the dismal fiscal performance of the District of Columbia or Puerto Rico in recent decades. This factor also helps explain the only other instance of unresolved debt repudiation by the states in American history to rival the 1840s: the repudiations of the southern states in the wake of bond offerings approved by corrupt "carpetbag" legislators during Reconstruction.

Externalities and the Structure of Jurisdictions

Whatever shades of distinction we may find among ourselves, to foreign nations we are essentially one single people. The stain which falls on the youngest member of the Confederacy spreads over the whole.

Nicholas Biddle, *New York American*, June 5, 1840

The U.S. experience in the 1840s also makes it clear that fiscal externalities – both real and perceived – are an important part of the strategic interaction between local and central governments. The costs for the central government of *not* providing a bailout were increased by the credit downgrades affecting nondefaulting states and the federal government. This was certainly the goal of the investors. However, this externality was insufficient to outweigh the costs of providing the bailout. By the time assumption was brought before Congress (1843), it was clear that most of the states could find ways to resume payments and restore their credit, and it seemed possible that the damage to the U.S. credit reputation would not be permanent.

In assessing the likelihood of bailout expectations and attempts at strategic burden shifting in decentralized countries, it is important to analyze the likely role of externalities. Basic elements of a country's institutional design – like the constitutional obligations of the center – shape the effect of externalities. David Wildasin (1997) draws attention to the size and structure of jurisdictions. An implication of his model is that bailouts are less likely when jurisdictions are small and evenly sized than few and asymmetric. Large jurisdictions – especially those containing capital cities (see Ades and Glaser 1995) – might avoid adjustment because they believe they are "too big to fail." That is, they understand that the center's commitment to them is less credible because their defaults would impose heavy costs on the rest of the federation.

The only large state that defaulted in the 1840s was Pennsylvania. It had by far the largest number of foreign bondholders, and Pennsylvania's defaults clearly had the largest externalities for the nation's credit reputation. According to McGrane (1935: 72), "To the outside world Pennsylvania became a synonym for American discredit." It had been viewed as one of the most financially stable states, and many of its debt holders were ordinary British citizens. An important part of the story of fiscal profligacy in Pennsylvania was its decision to recharter the United States Bank as the United States Bank of Pennsylvania (see McGrane 1935: Chapter 4), after which the balance sheet of the state and that of the bank were virtually indistinguishable. The bank became heavily involved in activities with externalities for the rest of the federation. For instance, the bank was a key player in selling the bonds of other states abroad and held the debts of American cotton growers. For these reasons, the state government may have viewed itself as too large and important to fail. Indeed, according to Ratchford (1941) and McGrane (1935), federal assumption seemed more plausible to investors and policymakers in Pennsylvania than in any other state. Chapter 8 will tell a strikingly similar story about São Paulo, Brazil.

The Identity of Debt Holders   In a related matter, the central government's credibility is also influenced by the identity of bondholders. When deciding whether to provide a bailout, the central government is faced with a choice between serving the interests of the taxpayers/bondholders of the troubled jurisdictions or those of the national taxpayers. If holders of local government debt are also the national median voter, it is more likely that the central government will find it difficult to resist bailout demands (Aghion and Bolton 1990; Inman 2003). However, the domestic bondholders in the 1840s were a small number of wealthy capitalists, and the majority of the bondholders were foreigners. In attempting to explain the failure of the assumption movement, historical studies give a great deal of weight to voter sentiment against foreign capitalists. However, one should not conclude that bailouts are always less likely when debt holders are foreigners. Ronald McKinnon (1997) makes a very plausible argument to the contrary, suggesting that externality-induced bailouts are more likely when the subnational debt is held in international capital markets that may punish the entire country for defaults. Indeed, this was part of the logic that kindled bailout hopes among Pennsylvanians.

The case studies in later chapters will ask a variety of questions about debt holders in order to sort out the political costs of failing to satisfy domestic bondholders and the externality costs of disappointing foreign bondholders. It may also be useful to ask more-specific questions about the political influence and costs of collective action facing foreign bondholders. Central governments will be more likely to assume subnational debts if they fear military or trade sanctions in the event of subnational default. Such government-imposed sanctions are much more likely if bonds are held by foreign individuals and institutions who can successfully force their governments to take on the high costs of implementing such sanctions. This was not the case in Great Britain and the Netherlands, where debts were dispersed among individual investors.

Finally, the experiences of the southern and some northeastern states demonstrated the dangers of allowing subnational governments to own banks. Public sentiment favored repudiation in some southern states in part because the debts were incurred through corrupt deals by state banks favoring small groups of planters. Moreover, the banks helped some states postpone the necessary increases in property taxes. Similar moral hazard problems will be discussed in greater detail in the German and especially the Brazilian case studies below.

Revenue Sources and Autonomy   Perhaps the most powerful explanation for the inability of several U.S. states to service their debts in the 1840s is that they engaged in little or no taxation. There was no link between taxes and benefits at the state level, and voters may have been subject to the purest form of fiscal illusion. Ever since the colonial period, voters were accustomed to forms of public finance that promised benefits without taxation. Tariffs levied on foreigners were viewed as the only truly legitimate form of taxation, and this power belonged to the federal government. State expenditures during the colonial period were funded by debt that was assumed by the central government, and subsequent revenue came from bailouts, special federal transfers, and further borrowing, along with one-shot deals like land sales and bank charters. It is important to note that in 1837 the federal government decided to "return" the federal surplus to the states on a per-capita basis, which created a one-time bonanza that may have created a false sense of security at a critical moment. It may have even kindled hopes among creditors that future federal windfalls would help underwrite state debts.

In the 1800s, the belief was widespread that states could fund massive infrastructure and banking projects without taxation. For example, the state of Pennsylvania repealed *all* state taxes when it rechartered the United States Bank. When it became clear that the investments would not perform as expected and defaults loomed, the states had no ability to raise additional revenues to make interest payments – their tax administration systems were nonexistent or insufficiently developed. Even where the capacity may have been present, state voters were quite hostile to all forms of direct taxation, which had never before seemed justified. Voters and creditors, not to mention governors and legislators, learned painful lessons from the defaults and the subsequent attempts to clean up state finances. In attempting to restore their creditworthiness, many states started to levy direct taxes and build more sophisticated tax administrations for the first time. Above all, many of these states developed extensive, progressive property taxes in the latter half of the nineteenth century (Sokoloff and Zolt 2004). In the wake of the debt crisis, many states altered their constitutions in ways that made future "taxless-finance" schemes impossible (Wallis 2004).

This observation will be expanded in the next chapter and serves as a major theme throughout the book. The revenue autonomy and flexibility of subnational governments have a very important influence on the beliefs of voters, creditors, and subnational politicians about the likelihood of successful burden shifting.

Electoral Motivations and Political Institutions   As argued in Chapter 2, central governments are generally not unitary decision makers, but groups of politically motivated individuals, and the decisions they make about bailouts will likely be shaped by their political incentives and the rules that govern the decision-making process. The factors mentioned thus far only matter insofar as they are translated into policy through legislative and executive institutions. As the game reaches the subnational government's second decision node, it will look around at the debts of other states and update p by assessing the likelihood that it will be able to construct a pro-bailout legislative majority. If a clear majority of the other states experienced the same negative shock and have also embarked on an unsustainable debt path, it will be more likely to believe it is playing against an irresolute center (see also Wibbels 2003, 2005).

Yet it is difficult to establish a clear general hypothesis about the distribution of debt across states and bailout expectations. If externalities are important, one very large and important indebted state may be enough. If subnational entities are highly asymmetric in size, as is often the case in federations, a majority of states with unsustainable debts may not translate into a legislative majority in a legislative chamber that is based on the principle of one person, one vote. On the other hand, a group of states encompassing less than half of the population may be able to control a legislative majority in a highly malapportioned legislative chamber based on territorial representation. Even if bondholders and citizens of states threatening to default constitute a legislative minority, they may be able to secure a vote in favor of bailouts even in the absence of externalities. Legislators who have the most to lose from defaults might be able to mobilize support for bailouts by arranging vote trades. In the 1800s, debt assumption advocates hoped to put together a core coalition of bondholders, bankers, and voters from indebted states, and the proposed bailout package clearly attempted to buy off representatives of other states by including large federal transfers even for states without substantial debts. A tradition of logrolling (vote trading) in the U.S. legislature may have enhanced bailout expectations even though it appears that the median voter had little interest. Chapters 7 and 8 will return to the issue of legislative logrolling over bailouts.

Ultimately, however, to understand the failure of the bailout movement in the United States, it is important to look beyond the regional interests of the individual legislators. When the bailout proposal was considered, all eyes were on the 1844 presidential election. Because the assumption movement was viewed with suspicion in several key states, party leaders and presidential candidates from both parties were unwilling to support it, and congressional gatekeepers saw to it that the bill never came to a vote. The comparative lesson from this experience is that important cross-country and over-time differences in the likelihood of bailouts might be explained by different or changing political incentives and institutional configurations. This observation will be developed further in Chapter 5 and explored in the chapters that follow.

III. Looking Ahead

If one assumes that fiscal decentralization entails a neat division of sovereignty over taxation, borrowing, and spending between higher- and lower-level governments and politics is ignored, the traditional arguments linking decentralization and especially federalism to enhanced fiscal discipline may be compelling. However, this chapter has introduced a framework for thinking about incentives in multitiered systems when fiscal sovereignty is unclear and contested and political incentives take center stage. If subnational governments believe that the center will ultimately prefer bailouts to subnational defaults, they face incentives to delay or avoid fiscal adjustment. Subnational governments pick up cues about the center's likely future behavior, constantly updating their beliefs by assessing institutional and political incentives as well as the center's past behavior.

This chapter also showed how the framework helps make sense of a very interesting historical case that will serve as a baseline for others later in the book. Partially as a result of strident disagreements among the founders of the federal system, the U.S. states entered the nineteenth century with a great deal of uncertainty about the ultimate locus of fiscal sovereignty. The states had been able to borrow based in part on the good credit of the federal government without extensive taxation. However, by the twentieth century, through its institutions and its actions, the central government had established a rather firm commitment not to bail out troubled states, even in the face of default. State policymakers learned that future borrowing would have to be supported by taxation and negative shocks would have to be endured alone.

The detailed discussion of the failed debt assumption movement also served as a vehicle for introducing some of the most important institutional and political factors shaping the incentives of central and subnational governments. These factors will serve as building blocks for the development of more careful, systematic arguments in later chapters. Now that this chapter has established the basic strategic scenario and introduced some building blocks, the task is to refine these into testable hypotheses and conduct some structured comparative analysis. Some of the factors described above – like the basic structure of fiscal and political systems – can be molded into arguments that are amenable to the cross-country quantitative analysis pursued in Chapters 4 and 5. Others – like the identify of bondholders, the nature of legislative coalitions, and the importance of past bailout episodes – are best examined with the case studies that follow.

Appendix 3.1

Proceed by backward induction using beliefs. Begin with the subnational government's final decision whether to provoke a debt crisis. There is a critical updated belief about the resolve of the center, $\overline{p}^*$, that makes the SNG indifferent between late adjustment and provoking a debt crisis. Equate expected utilities:

$$U_{sng}(LA) = U_{sng}(D)\overline{p}^* + U_{sng}(LB)(1 - \overline{p}^*)$$

Solve for $\bar{p}^*$:

$$\bar{p}^* = \frac{U_{sng}(LB) - U_{sng}(LA)}{U_{sng}(LB)}$$

If $\bar{p} > \bar{p}^*$, SNG prefers "late adjustment" to provoking a debt crisis.

If $\bar{p} < \bar{p}^*$, SNG is sufficiently optimistic about the likelihood of a bailout to provoke a debt crisis rather than adjust.

Next consider the central government's first move. The resolute type always plays no bailout. The irresolute type, however, conditions its move on the likely response of the SNG. The SNG adopts a mixed strategy that avoids adjustment with probability z and conducts late adjustment with probability $(1 - z)$. Find the probability, z, of the SNG playing debt crisis that makes an irresolute center indifferent between no bailout and early bailout at its first decision node:

$$U_{cgi}(EB) = U_{cgi}(LB)z + U_{cgi}(LA)(1 - z)$$

Solve for z:

$$z = \frac{U_{cgi}(EB) - U_{cgi}(LA)}{U_{cgi}(LB) - U_{cgi}(LA)}$$

The SNG must have beliefs equal to $\bar{p}^*$ in order to play this mixed strategy. Now consider the CG's mixed strategy that creates these updated beliefs for the SNG. Upon observing no bailout in the first round of the game, the SNG must assess the probability that the center is in fact resolute. There is no pure strategy separating equilibrium. That is, the SNG knows that there is a positive probability, q, that an irresolute center is masquerading by playing no bailout in the first round. Using Bayes's rule:

$$p(R|nobailout) = \bar{p}^* = \frac{p(R)p(nobailout\,|R)}{p(R)p(nobailout\,|R) + p(I)p(nobailout\,|I)}$$

where R and I refer to resolute and irresolute central governments. This can be expressed as:

$$\bar{p}^* = \frac{p}{p + q - pq}$$

Solve for q:

$$q = \frac{p(1 - \bar{p}^*)}{\bar{p}^*(1 - p)}$$

Expressed in terms of SNG's utilities for the outcomes:

$$q = \frac{p[U_{sng}(LA)]}{(1-p)[U_{sng}(LB) - U_{sng}(LA)]}$$

Now it is possible to discuss the first move made by the subnational government. If the game starts with $p > \bar{p}^*$, the SNG will always adjust early. It is already sufficiently convinced of the center's resolve that it would be foolish to avoid adjustment in an effort to attract bailouts. However, when $p < \bar{p}^*$, the SNG is not necessarily deterred. It will compare the expected utility of pressing for a bailout, calculated from the center's mixed strategy, with the expected utility of adjusting. The critical value for p can be obtained by finding the original belief at which the SNG is indifferent between early adjustment and starting down a path of unsustainable borrowing:

$$U_{sng}(EA) = p^*[U_{sng}(D)] + (1-p^*)\{(1-q)[U_{sng}(EB) + q[U_{sng}(LA)]\}$$

Substitute for q and solve for p.

$$p^* = \frac{[U_{sng}(LB) - U_{sng}(LA)][U_{sng}(EA) - 1]}{[U_{sng}(LA)]^2 - U_{sng}(LB)}$$

To sum up, when p is greater than this expression, the SNG will adjust in the first round. This is a Perfect Bayesian Equilibrium. When beginning beliefs in the center's resolve are below this threshold, the subnational government plays unsustainable borrowing in its first move and the Perfect Bayesian Equilibrium involves the mixed strategies described above. In its first move, the resolved government always plays no bailout while the irresolute government plays no bailout with probability q and early bailout with probability $1 - q$. If it observes no bailout, the region chooses debt crisis with probability z, and late adjust with probability $1 - z$. At the final stage, the resolved government always plays no bailout while the irresolute government always plays late bailout.

4

The Power of the Purse

INTERGOVERNMENTAL GRANTS
AND FISCAL DISCIPLINE

The creation of Debt should always be accompanied with the means of
extinguishment.   Alexander Hamilton, *Report on Public Credit*, 1790[1]

This chapter expands on a key observation from Chapter 3 that was first
suggested by Alexander Hamilton: Perceptions of the center's commitment
not to intervene in subnational fiscal crises are shaped in large part by the
intergovernmental fiscal system of taxes, revenue sharing, and transfers. A
key argument in this chapter is that when subnational governments depend
heavily on intergovernmental grants, loans, and revenue-sharing schemes as
opposed to subnational taxes and fees, the central government's *ex ante* commitment to a policy of no bailouts lacks credibility. For a variety of reasons
elaborated below, when a higher-level government has undertaken heavy
obligations to fund the expenditures of lower-tier governments, doubts
creep into the minds of voters, creditors, and local governments about the
center's ability to withstand the political costs of allowing subnational governments to default.

Hamilton alluded to this problem when expressing concerns that the
states presided over insufficient tax base to sustain sovereign borrowing,
making the federal government – with its deeper pockets and good credit
history – an implicit guarantor. He feared that after a negative shock, borrowing by the states under these circumstances was bound to culminate
in a legislative battle over debt renegotiation. For him, the solution to this
moral hazard problem was not to expand the taxes available to state governments in order to firm up their sovereignty, but rather to clamp down on

---

[1] "Report Relative to a Provision for the Support of Public Credit, New York, January 9,
  1790," published in Syrett (1962: 106).

their access to deficit finance by placing all public borrowing firmly under the control of the central government.

This chapter presents evidence that both techniques are effective in reducing subnational and overall deficits. Analysis of a cross-country dataset covering recent decades shows that deficits have been relatively modest among subnational governments where either (1) the higher-level government approximates the Hamiltonian ideal by strictly regulating lower-level borrowing or (2) lower-level governments approximate sovereigns in that they have wide-ranging taxing and borrowing autonomy. Long-term deficits have been largest among subnational sectors that are heavily dependent on intergovernmental transfers yet relatively free from central restrictions on borrowing. This combination is most often found in formal federations.

The first section presents the argument linking dependence on intergovernmental transfers and bailout expectations; then the second section uses cross-national data on credit ratings to demonstrate that transfer dependence affects perceptions of subnational sovereignty. The next section considers how this argument affects fiscal incentives of higher- and lower-level governments and develops some hypotheses linking intergovernmental fiscal structure, borrowing restrictions, federalism, and fiscal behavior. In particular, it considers the incentives of central governments – looking down the game tree and foreseeing that transfer dependence creates a moral-hazard problem – to clamp down on local borrowing *ex ante* and the ways in which federal institutions might prevent them from doing so. The following sections are occupied with cross-national empirical analysis, and the final section pulls together the key arguments and findings.

I. Intergovernmental Finance and Commitment

Of all the institutional factors that shape beliefs about the likelihood of eventual burden shifting, perhaps none is more important than the sources of revenue at the disposal of state and local governments. The mixture of local taxes, fees, user charges, intergovernmental transfers, and borrowing that fund the expenditures of state and local governments help shape the incentives of subnational officials and provide important signals to voters and creditors. In the bailout game, the preferences of the center and lower-level governments are driven by their expected electoral consequences. It is natural to assume that the electoral fortunes of subnational governments are driven primarily by their performance in providing local collective goods ranging from schools to police cruisers to a healthy local business climate. Central government officials are retrospectively evaluated by voters according to their performance in providing nationwide collective goods like national defense, macroeconomic stability, and economic growth. Yet an insight of the previous chapter was that when they are funded by intergovernmental transfers, the center can be held responsible for the provision of purely local goods. Moreover, the center will be held responsible for the provision of goods that are perceived as national entitlements, like health care and welfare, even when the actual expenditures and implementation are in the hands of local governments.

Thus, intergovernmental grants are at the heart of the commitment problem. If subnational governments were financed purely by local taxes, charges, and borrowing, voters and creditors would view the obligations of local governments as autonomous and "sovereign," like those of central governments. That is, p in the bailout game would be close to 0. As a matter of both normative theory and descriptive fact, however, intergovernmental systems always involve the vertical flow of funds between governments. The notion of competitive fiscal discipline described in Chapter 2 implicitly envisions a system that is driven by resident-based taxation where, as in the normative fiscal federalism view, the central government only steps in with grants to internalize specific externalities. In a more realistic world of politics, intergovernmental transfer programs go well beyond the efficient world of fiscal federalism theory – they are well suited for politically motivated redistribution. In all countries, a sizable share of intergovernmental grants are specifically designed and/or ultimately spent to provide goods whose benefits are purely local in scope.

Theoretical and empirical studies in public economics suggest that individuals view grants and own-source local revenues through different lenses. A key proposition of the fiscal illusion literature discussed in Chapter 2 is that when the link between taxes and benefits is distorted or broken, as is the case with intergovernmental grants, voters are less likely to sanction overspending by politicians. Intergovernmental grants create the appearance that local public expenditures are funded by nonresidents.[2] Grant programs often supply concentrated local benefits that are funded by a common (national) pool of resources. Local voters, local politicians, and regional

---

[2] This literature is too large to review here. For an overview of concepts and measurements of fiscal illusion and a literature review, see Oates (1991). For a theoretical application to intergovernmental grants in particular, see Oates (1979).

representatives within the central legislature all receive fiscal or political benefits from grant programs without internalizing their full cost, causing them to demand more expenditures funded by grants than own-source taxation. The vast empirical literature on the so-called flypaper effect shows that increases in intergovernmental grants rarely lead to local-level tax reductions, and increases in transfers stimulate much higher expenditures than do similar increases in locally generated revenues (for an overview, see Hines and Thaler 1995).

Although some aspects of the flypaper effect are still something of a mystery, the common theme in this literature is the notion that intergovernmental grants, as opposed to local taxation, alter perceptions and beliefs about the levels of local expenditure that can be sustained. As a result, decentralization might exacerbate rather than resolve the basic "common-pool" problem of budgeting in representative democracy if it is driven by grants rather than own-source taxation. An empirical literature has established a link between transfer dependence and the growth of government (e.g., Rattsø 2000; Rodden 2003a; Stein 1998; Winer 1980). A central proposition of this chapter is that transfer dependence also alters beliefs about the sustainability of subnational *deficits* by encouraging local politicians – along with their voters and creditors – to believe that the central government will ultimately find it impossible to ignore their fiscal woes. The previous chapter stressed the importance of citizens' and creditors' perceptions of the central government's powers and obligations. Quite simply, when the central government is responsible for providing a large and growing share of local budgets, in the event of a local fiscal crisis, the eyes of voters and creditors will quickly turn to the central rather than the local government for a resolution.

When a highly transfer-dependent local government faces an unexpected adverse fiscal shock, it may not have the flexibility to raise additional revenue, forcing it to cut services, run deficits, or rely on arrears to employees and contractors. If the situation escalates into a fiscal crisis in which the subnational government is unable to pay workers or may default on loans, it can claim – in many cases with some justification – that it is not responsible for the situation. Alexander Hamilton put it well when speaking of the likely "pecuniary delinquency" of states: "It would be impossible to decide whether it had proceeded from disinclination or inability. The pretence of the latter would always be at hand" (*Federalist* 16). If successful in this strategy, eventually pressure from voters and creditors will be directed at the central government, which quite likely *can* resolve the crisis.

It is then difficult for the central government to resist political pressure from bondholders, banks, local parents, or public sector unions. Knowing this, transfer-dependent local governments face weaker incentives for fiscal responsibility. Even if subnational governments can take simple but politically costly steps to avoid an impending fiscal crisis, it may be more rewarding to position themselves for bailouts.

High levels of vertical fiscal imbalance also undermine the type of fiscal discipline expected by advocates of decentralization by dampening horizontal tax competition between jurisdictions. In fact, Brennan and Buchanan (1980) and Winer (1980) view intergovernmental transfers as collusive "cartels" between subnational governments who wish to escape the harsh realities of intergovernmental competition for mobile capital. Without wide-ranging and properly structured local tax autonomy, horizontal competition will not have the expected effects on subnational fiscal decisions. In contrast, when subnational governments have sufficient tax autonomy and intergovernmental competition is strong, it is costly for a regional government to avoid adjustment and demand a bailout in the first stage of the bailout game.[3] Risk-averse taxpayers and owners of mobile assets, fearing that they will eventually pay some of the costs associated with the late-adjustment or no-bailout outcomes, will move (or threaten to move) to other jurisdictions with more sound finances.

The vulnerability of transfer-dependent governments to shocks might be exacerbated by something similar to the so-called Samaritan's Dilemma.[4] Stephen Coate (1995) presents a model in which the government represents altruistic wealthy individuals and makes transfers on their behalf to the poor. In this context, the dilemma arises because "the poor may have an incentive not to buy insurance and to rely on private charity to bail them out in the event of loss. The rich are unable to commit not to help out the unlucky poor even if the government is making the *ex ante* desirable transfer" (Coate 1995: 46). Coate goes on to demonstrate adverse efficiency effects associated with the poor failing to take out insurance in anticipation of private charity. A similar problem might arise in the intergovernmental arena. If the center reveals its redistributive preferences with large transfer programs, the poorest and most transfer-dependent provinces might

---

[3] For a related argument involving subsidies to state-owned enterprises, see Qian and Roland (1998).

[4] The term comes from James Buchanan (1975); for recent analysis of the Samaritan's Dilemma and government transfer policy, see Coate (1995) and Bruce and Waldman (1991).

have few incentives to insure themselves against negative shocks, knowing that the center is unlikely to tolerate excessive suffering and will step in with special emergency transfers. When this is the case, provincial governments have no incentives to save during good times or adjust to negative shocks.

II. Credit Ratings and Bailout Expectations

A difficulty with testing this argument is that bailout expectations are very difficult to measure. Lacking appropriate survey data, it is difficult to measure the beliefs of voters or subnational officials. However, the perceptions of creditors can be ascertained through default premiums and credit ratings. Because dates of issue and maturity vary so widely across bond issues even within one country, it would be extremely difficult to come up with a comparable dataset of bond yields. However, credit ratings assembled by the major international rating agencies are assessments of default risk that allow for comparisons within a national and international peer group.

In the late 1990s, the number of subnational entities around the world formally subjecting themselves to the credit-rating process has dramatically increased. By obtaining credit ratings, subnational governments hope to increase their access to lower-cost international capital and promote investor confidence. Along with the proliferation of credit ratings has come a rising tide of optimism about the likelihood of increased market discipline among subnational governments. However, a brief look at some ratings and a discussion of their logic should stem the tide.

The most important rating agencies are Moody's, Fitch (Fitch, IBCA, Duff, and Phelps), and Standard and Poor's (S&P). Ratings are based on many of the same criteria used to assess sovereign debtors: GDP per capita, the strength and growth of the tax base, debt and interest payments relative to GDP and revenues, recent budget deficits, whether borrowing is undertaken for capital or current expenditures, the diversification of the economy, and several judgmental factors pertaining to the quality of institutions, political leaders, and recent fiscal decisions.[5]

In addition, rating agencies pay careful attention to the system of intergovernmental finance in which the local or regional government is embedded. First of all, agencies take stock of the overall country risk, and the

---

[5] See Fitch IBCA (1998) and Standard and Poor's (2000).

sovereign rating generally acts as a ceiling on subnational foreign currency ratings. This is because local governments may eventually be forced to rely on the central bank to secure the foreign exchange needed for external debt service. However, each of the major rating agencies also assembles separate domestic ratings that exclude the sovereign risks associated with converting and transferring currency outside the country.

One of the most important tasks of credit-rating agencies when assessing a subnational government's default risk is assigning some probability to the likelihood of federal bailouts in the event that local governments are unable to service their debts. This requires a careful analysis of the system of intergovernmental transfers. Agencies clearly take a dim view of highly discretionary and unpredictable transfers, which may expose governments to sudden or arbitrary loss of revenue and cannot be relied on for debt-servicing capacity in the future. On the other hand, stable and predictable transfers are viewed quite favorably, and whether or not governments explicitly pledge transfers as collateral to lenders, it would appear that rating agencies view guaranteed transfers as a reliable income stream for future debt servicing. "In some cases, the terms may come close to guaranteeing regional revenues and debts, and the implications for credit ratings will be favorable" (Fitch IBCA 1998: 2). The most attractive transfer programs from the rating agencies' perspective are general-purpose equalization transfers that guarantee certain baseline revenue levels among all governments. "Certainly, these programs raise the credit profile of the recipients – economically disadvantaged regions. If the equalization system quickly adapts to changing fortunes, this type of system is a positive, even for those that are net contributors, in that they provide a safety net of varying importance during difficult times" (Standard and Poor's 2002: 7).

Rating agencies are quite clear in stating that highly transfer-dependent local governments are viewed essentially as extensions of the central government. In countries like the UK, Norway, or the Netherlands, local governments are able to finance infrastructure projects at subsidized interest rates through a guarantee by the central government or a public bank, but in return the central government allocates the capital and places restrictions on borrowing. In this scenario, there is little reason to bother with local credit ratings, and traditionally such municipal governments have not been rated. Recently, decentralization reform programs have focused on facilitating more-autonomous local borrowing, especially in Western Europe, and investors have displayed a strong appetite for municipal bonds. Hence, rating agencies have started to look carefully even at countries where the center essentially guarantees local borrowing by transfer-dependent entities. A Moody's report comments that if UK local governments apply for ratings – as seems possible as part of the government's decentralization program – centralized funding and regulation of local budgetary decisions lends sufficient comfort to investors that the local governments would probably receive the AAA rating of the central government or something very close (Moody's 2001). Standard and Poor's acknowledges that "a track record that demonstrates general intergovernmental supportiveness may be cited as an extraordinary item incorporated into the entity's stand-alone rating" (2002: 7). In this scenario, where local governments receive 74 percent of revenue from transfers, rating agencies attach relatively little weight to local fiscal and economic outcomes in the presence of a perceived central guarantee.

But very often when central governments allow independent access of subnationals to international credit markets, they do not provide an explicit guarantee. In most cases, they make some form of no-bailout pledge. In such cases, it is the job of the rating agency to assemble as much information as possible to gauge the likelihood of an implicit guarantee and assess the speed with which federal funds would likely be released. Above all, this requires analysis of the intergovernmental transfer system. Table 4.1 allows for some explicit comparisons of the decisions of one rating agency – Standard and Poor's – in four federations. These countries were chosen purely on the basis of the availability of credit ratings and comparable supplementary data, and only the states receiving S&P ratings in the late 1990s are displayed. Standard and Poor's has a long history of rating all but a handful of U.S. states and all of the Canadian provinces. Because the Australian Commonwealth government stopped borrowing on behalf of the states and allowed them to access international credit markets on their own in the late 1980s, S&P has rated all of the Australian states and the Capital Territory. In addition, relatively new ratings have now been assembled for the Spanish Autonomous Communities and German Länder.[6] Table 4.1 presents domestic currency credit ratings, as well as a numerical equivalent

---

[6] Table 4.1 presents data from 1996 for the U.S., Canada, and Australia because of limits on availability of more recent comparable debt data for Australia. It was necessary to present data from 1999 for Spain and Germany because this was the first year for which ratings were assigned to most of the autonomous communities and Länder.

Table 4.1. *Credit rating comparisons*

	Federal Transfers and Revenue Sharing/Total Revenue	Population	GDP per Capita (Local Currency)	Total Debt as Share of Own-Source Revenue	Total Debt as Share of Total Revenue	S&P Rating (Long-Term Domestic Currency)	S&P Rating (13-Point Scale)
United States (1996)							
Sovereign domestic-currency rating: AAA							
Sovereign foreign-currency rating: AAA							
Alabama	0.26	4,291,000	23,138	0.39	0.29	AA	11
Alaska	0.12	605,000	42,602	0.44	0.38	AA	11
Arkansas	0.25	2,505,000	22,673	0.33	0.25	AA	11
California	0.22	31,762,000	30,647	0.47	0.37	A	8
Connecticut	0.19	3,264,000	38,038	1.85	1.50	AA–	10
Delaware	0.18	727,000	39,891	1.44	1.18	AA+	12
Florida	0.20	14,425,000	25,395	0.46	0.37	AA	11
Georgia	0.24	7,334,000	29,932	0.36	0.28	AA+	12
Hawaii	0.19	1,187,000	31,584	0.99	0.80	AA	11
Illinois	0.21	11,934,000	31,502	0.77	0.61	AA–	10
Louisiana	0.29	4,340,000	26,928	0.73	0.52	A–	7
Maine	0.29	1,238,000	23,364	1.04	0.74	AA+	12
Maryland	0.19	5,058,000	28,680	0.75	0.60	AAA	13
Massachusetts	0.21	6,083,000	34,543	1.48	1.16	A+	9
Michigan	0.19	9,734,000	27,238	0.45	0.36	AA	11
Minnesota	0.17	4,648,000	30,452	0.28	0.24	AA+	12
Mississippi	0.29	2,710,000	20,876	0.36	0.25	AA–	10

(continued)

Table 4.1 (*continued*)

	Federal Transfers and Revenue Sharing/Total Revenue	Population	GDP per Capita (Local Currency)	Total Debt as Share of Own-Source Revenue	Total Debt as Share of Total Revenue	S&P Rating (Long-Term Domestic Currency)	S&P Rating (13-Point Scale)
Missouri	0.22	53,69,000	27,293	0.53	0.42	AAA	13
Montana	0.28	877,000	20,609	0.91	0.65	AA−	10
Nevada	0.13	1,600,000	34,103	0.43	0.38	AA	11
New Jersey	0.18	8,008,000	35,682	0.87	0.71	AA+	12
New Mexico	0.21	1,708,000	25,828	0.34	0.26	AA+	12
New York	0.24	18,142,000	34,937	1.02	0.78	A−	7
North Carolina	0.23	7,309,000	27,956	0.25	0.19	AAA	13
North Dakota	0.25	643,000	24,658	0.42	0.32	AA−	10
Ohio	0.19	11,170,000	27,425	0.36	0.29	AA	11
Oklahoma	0.20	3,296,000	22,711	0.46	0.37	AA	11
Oregon	0.21	3,195,000	28,704	0.49	0.39	AA−	10
Pennsylvania	0.21	12,034,000	27,394	0.45	0.35	AA−	10
Rhode Island	0.25	988,000	26,980	1.71	1.29	AA−	10
South Carolina	0.24	3,737,000	24,044	0.56	0.42	AA+	12
Tennessee	0.32	5,307,000	26,767	0.30	0.21	AA+	12
Texas	0.25	19,033,000	29,064	0.38	0.28	AA	11
Utah	0.25	2,022,000	25,481	0.49	0.36	AAA	13
Vermont	0.30	586,000	25,020	1.15	0.80	AA−	10
Virginia	0.17	6,667,000	29,991	0.52	0.44	AAA	13
Washington	0.15	5,519,000	29,313	0.43	0.36	AA	11
West Virginia	0.30	1,820,000	20,451	0.59	0.41	AA−	10
Wisconsin	0.15	5,174,000	27,261	0.44	0.37	AA	11

Mean	0.22	6,052,538.5	28,440	0.66	0.51	AA	10.9
Standard Deviation	0.05	6,235,392	5,084	0.40	0.31		1.4

Canada (1996)

Sovereign foreign-currency rating: AA+
Sovereign domestic-currency rating: AAA

Alberta	0.10	2,759,460	32,632	0.12	0.10	AA	11
British Columbia	0.10	3,834,660	27,025	0.24	0.22	AA+	12
Manitoba	0.27	1,130,790	24,174	1.33	0.96	A+	9
New Brunswick	0.34	752,332	21,404	1.38	0.91	AA−	10
Newfoundland	0.42	564,307	17,841	2.43	1.41	BBB+	6
Nova Scotia	0.40	929,645	20,251	2.74	1.65	A−	7
Ontario	0.14	11,029,000	29,289	1.90	1.63	AA−	10
Quebec	0.19	7,259,020	24,162	1.57	1.27	A+	9
Saskatchewan	0.17	1,016,290	26,016	1.72	1.42	BBB+	6
Mean	0.24	3,252,834	24,755	1.49	1.06	A+	8.9
Standard Deviation	0.12	3,423,502.4	4,338	0.83	0.54		2.0

Australia (1996)

Sovereign foreign-currency rating: AA
Sovereign domestic-currency rating: AAA

Australia Capital Territory	0.46	308,549	32,779	0.26	0.14	AAA	13
New South Wales	0.37	6,241,899	28,339	0.89	0.56	AAA	13
Queensland	0.46	3,369,344	24,104	0.41	0.22	AAA	13
South Australia	0.48	1,476,917	23,946	1.62	0.84	AA	11
Tasmania	0.58	474,233	21,416	2.71	1.15	AA−	10
Victoria	0.39	4,584,649	28,087	1.49	0.90	AA+	12

(continued)

Table 4.1 (*continued*)

	Federal Transfers and Revenue Sharing/Total Revenue	Population	GDP per Capita (Local Currency)	Total Debt as Share of Own-Source Revenue	Total Debt as Share of Total Revenue	S&P Rating (Long-Term Domestic Currency)	S&P Rating (13-Point Scale)
Western Australia	0.45	1,782,700	30,752	1.00	0.55	AA+	12
Mean	**0.46**	**2,605,470**	**27,060**	**1.20**	**0.62**	**AA+**	**12.0**
Standard Deviation	**0.06**	**2,052,624**	**3,767**	**0.77**	**0.34**		**1.1**
Spain (1999)							
Sovereign foreign–currency rating: AA/AA+*							
Sovereign domestic currency rating: AA/AA+*							
Andalucía	0.76	7,340,052	10,999	6.60	0.52	AA−	10
Aragón	0.59	1,189,909	15,864	2.14	0.54	AA−	10
Baleares	0.19	845,630	16,809	0.39	0.26	AA	11
Cataluña	0.63	6,261,999	18,172	2.76	0.76	AA	11
Galicia	0.65	2,731,900	12,177	4.06	0.65	AA−	10
Islas Canarias	0.52	1,716,276	14,305	0.70	0.22	AA	11
Madrid (autonomous community)	0.20	5,205,408	20,149	0.98	0.62	AA	11
Navarra	0.02	543,757	18,856	0.36	0.32	AA+	12
Valencia	0.66	4,120,729	14,172	2.90	0.59	AA−	10
Mean	**0.47**	**3,328,407**	**15,723**	**2.32**	**0.50**	**AA**	**10.7**
Standard Deviation	**0.25**	**2,364,003**	**2,904**	**1.94**	**0.18**		**0.7**

Germany (1999)

Sovereign Domestic Currency Rating: AAA
Sovereign Foreign Currency Rating: AAA

Baden-Württemberg	0.88	10,449,000	53,363	11.27	1.36	AAA	13
Bayern	0.87	12,117,000	54,750	5.43	0.70	AAA	13
Hamburg	0.88	1,702,000	81,293	29.62	3.56	AA	11
Hessen	0.88	6,043,000	57,308	13.77	1.69	AAA	13
Nordrhein-Westfalen	0.89	17,984,000	48,219	18.16	2.03	AA+	12
Rheinland-Pfalz	0.91	4,028,000	42,368	22.88	2.11	AA	11
Sachsen	0.95	4,475,000	31,558	12.86	0.70	AA	11
Sachsen-Anhalt	0.95	2,663,000	30,195	40.05	1.83	AA–	10
Mean	**0.90**	**7,432,625**	**49,882**	**19.26**	**1.75**	**AA+**	**11.75**
Standard Deviation	**0.03**	**5,609,085**	**16,301**	**11.21**	**0.91**		**1.16**

* Upgraded to AA+ on March 31, 1999

Sources:
Credit ratings: Standard and Poor's
All U.S. data: Census Department
All Canada data: Statcan
Australian data: Grants Commission, "Report on State Revenue Sharing Relativities," 2002 Update (Supporting Information);
Courchene (1999); and Australian Bureau of Statistics
Spanish data: *Spain Regional Accounts 2000* (available at http://www.ine.es) and "Spanish Regions: An Analytical
Overview," (published by Fitch, IBCA, Duff & Phelps)

to facilitate some calculations.[7] The numerical scale starts with B+ = 0 and runs through AAA = 13. The table also presents some basic data on transfer dependence, population, and GDP per capita.

Perhaps the most basic indicator for assessing default risk is a jurisdiction's existing debt burden. But an interesting question is whether the risk associated with a jurisdiction's debt burden should be evaluated relative to a state's total revenue – including shared taxes and grants over which it has little control – or only the revenue it raises from its own taxation. Both measures are provided in Table 4.1. Although a simple comparison of debt burdens, transfer dependence, and credit ratings is likely to miss a great deal of subtlety – for instance, important determinates of creditworthiness like economic diversity and unfunded pension liabilities – it can teach some important lessons.

Note that the average level of dependence on federal transfers for the sample of U.S. states and Canadian provinces in 1996 is only around 23 percent, while the average for the Australian states and Spanish Autonomous Communities is roughly twice as high. The German system – to be described in much greater detail below – relies heavily on shared taxes that the Länder do not directly control and thus provides even less revenue autonomy.

If S&P assesses the *ex ante* probability of an irresolute center as 0, provincial debts should be evaluated relative to own-source provincial taxes and similar debt burdens should be associated with similar credit ratings in different countries. Figure 4.1 provides scatter plots and a fitted line for debt burdens and credit ratings in four federations. Within each country, provinces with higher debt burdens can expect lower credit ratings and presumably higher interest rates. Yet this correlation does not imply that credit markets "discipline" provincial governments. A Canadian province or U.S. state with a debt/own-source revenue ratio of 100 percent (the dashed vertical lines) can expect to be rated AA−. However, an Australian state with a similar debt burden can expect either AA+ or AAA. A similarly situated Spanish Autonomous Community can expect an AA rating.

---

[7] Foreign and domestic ratings are identical in the United States, Germany, and Spain at both central and subnational levels. The Canadian and Australian federal governments have consistently faced lower foreign-currency than domestic-currency ratings due to perceived foreign-exchange risk. Curiously, the foreign- and domestic-currency ratings have always been identical for the Canadian provinces until a recent upgrade of Alberta's domestic-currency rating to AAA. Only in Australia are there systematic differences between the foreign and domestic ratings of the federated units.

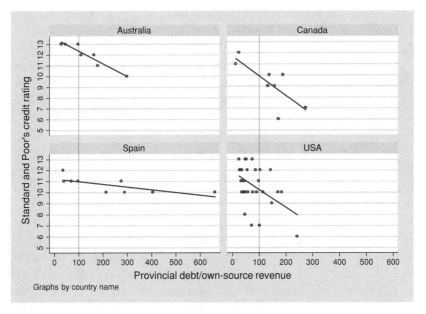

Figure 4.1. Debt burdens and credit ratings in four federations. Sources: See Table 4.1.

The boost to Australian and Spanish subnational entities clearly comes from S&P's assessment of an implicit federal guarantee. When taken as a share of own-source revenue, the Australian states' average debt burden was almost twice that of the U.S. states and only slightly lower than that of the Canadian provinces. Yet all of the Australian states were clustered tightly around the commonwealth government's AAA domestic rating. Until 1990, all borrowing on behalf of the Australian states was undertaken by the commonwealth government and on-lent to the states at the same interest rate. Since then, the states have been allowed to undertake independent borrowing and are progressively redeeming the debt issued by the commonwealth government, with flexible yearly limits placed on new borrowing through negotiations with the central government in the Australian Loan Council (Grewal 2000). Prior to 1990, it was very difficult to view the states as sovereign borrowers; the commonwealth government has implicitly stood behind the states' debts since the 1930s. Reforms in the 1990s have aimed at extracting the commonwealth government from state borrowing while increasing the accountability and independent fiscal responsibility of the states, but "Standard & Poor's believes . . . that the

Commonwealth would probably provide emergency support to the states in a time of financial crisis" (Standard & Poor's 2002: 75). Moreover, the commonwealth government has been successful in influencing state borrowing by threatening to reduce the transfers of governments (Queensland in particular) that did not abide by global borrowing limits set by the Australian Loan Council (Grewal 2000). This creates the perception that Canberra would be able to withhold grants in the future in order to force debt repayment.

By 1996, the Australian states only had a six-year track record of truly independent borrowing, yet two of six states and the capital territory received AAA ratings. Contrast this with the U.S. states, where after more than one hundred years of independent borrowing without a default, only four of thirty-nine states rated by Standard and Poor's received AAA ratings. In spite of a higher debt burden and a nagging problem with off-budget pension liabilities, the average credit rating of the Australian states was higher than that of the U.S. states. The contrast with Canada is even more striking. No province has defaulted since the Great Depression, yet even the consistently low debt burdens of British Columbia and Alberta did not earn AAA ratings,[8] and the average rating was A+ compared with Australia's AA+. In fact, according to Standard and Poor's, the default risk for Newfoundland and Saskatchewan in 1996 was similar to that of Colombia, Croatia, or El Salvador.

The only way to make sense of the Australian ratings – especially that of Tasmania – is if Standard and Poor's assumes no implicit federal support and evaluates the debt burden relative to *own-source* revenue in Canada and the United States, while seeing the transfer system as implying a federal guarantee in Australia and evaluating the debt burden relative to *total* revenue.

Standard and Poor's assumption of an implicit federal guarantee is even clearer in the Spanish case. While the debt burdens of all the autonomous communities seem quite reasonable in international comparison when taken as a share of total revenue, they were extremely high (over 250 percent of own-source revenue) in four of the most transfer-dependent communities. Yet none of the autonomous communities received a rating below AA–. In the most extreme case, in the late 1990s Andalucia raised only 24 percent of its revenue from taxation, its debt was over 600 percent of own-source revenue, yet it received S&P's AA– rating, similar to Pennsylvania.

---

[8] Alberta finally received a AAA rating in 2002.

In the Spanish case, to infer a central government guarantee requires little imagination. With the exception of Navarra and País Vasco, the Spanish Autonomous Communities had extremely limited tax autonomy in the 1990s.[9] The intergovernmental fiscal system ensured that each autonomous community's share of the personal income tax would rise at least in line with Spain's nominal GDP on an annual basis. Furthermore, if any region's growth rate should fall below 90 percent of the average for other regions, compensating transfers were to be made from a "guarantee fund." An additional guarantee mechanism stipulated that per capita revenue for each region may not fall below 90 percent of the national average over a five-year period.[10] The message taken away by rating agencies was clear:

Thus far, the Spanish financial system has been supportive for those regions with a weaker economic base and Fitch has placed much value on the present revenue equalization system and guarantees in place that cushion the economically weaker regions and promote solidarity. The agency would like to see some kind of equalization mechanism kept in place.... (Fitch 2000: 5)

Finally, debt burdens among the German Länder are so high that they require their own graphs with a different scale. Figure 4.2 includes scatter plots with both debt/total revenue and debt/own-source revenue on the horizontal axes. The story is similar to Spain. The rating agencies clearly perceive an implicit federal guarantee in the fiscal constitution and equalization system and have taken comfort in recent bailouts of troubled Länder. The states would not be creditworthy if their debt burdens were assessed relative to their meager own taxes (on average, the ratio is almost 2,000 percent). Debt is even quite high as a share of total Land revenue (175 percent). Yet Fitch is so confident in the federal government's implicit guarantee that it assigns its AAA rating to each of the sixteen Länder – even bankrupt Berlin. Standard & Poor's rates only eight of the Länder, three of which receive AAA ratings, and on average the Länder are more highly rated than the U.S. states and Canadian provinces. Unlike Fitch, Standard & Poor's differentiates between the credit quality of the Länder primarily out of concern over the speed with which bailouts would be administered in the event of a debt-servicing crisis.

---

[9] Even some of the revenues not counted as grants in Table 1 were actually ceded taxes, over which the Autonomous Communities had very little control (see Garcia-Milà et al. 1999). But note that the Spanish system has gone through considerable reform since 2000, giving additional tax powers to the Autonomous Communities.

[10] Recent reforms have done away with this mechanism.

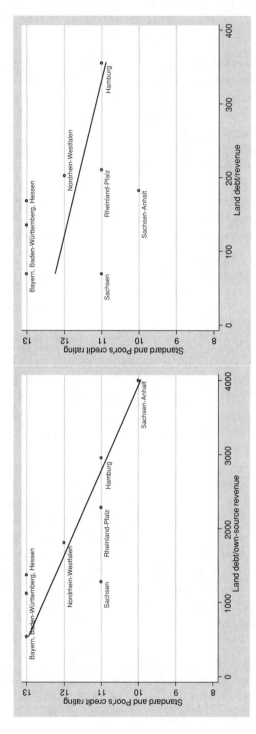

Figure 4.2. Debt burdens and credit ratings in the German Länder. Sources: See Table 4.1.

These credit market perceptions of Australia, Germany, and Spain are in stark contrast to analyses of Canada and the United States: "Fitch's evaluation . . . centers fundamentally on the creditworthiness of the (Canadian) provinces themselves and not on any benefits the provinces derive from federal support" (Fitch 2001a: 2). In fact, an ordered probit analysis of Canadian provincial S&P ratings by Cheung (1996) shows that even controlling for GDP and unemployment, transfer dependence has a negative effect on credit ratings. Compared with the German and Australian central governments, the Canadian and U.S. federal governments have a great deal of discretion over intergovernmental transfers and have a history of balancing their own budgets by slashing transfers to provincial and state governments. Relatively poor, transfer-dependent provinces in Canada and the U.S. may be perceived as more vulnerable to arbitrary cuts in transfers than the disadvantaged federated units in Australia, Germany, and Spain.

It appears that Fitch's statement about the Swiss cantons sums up market perceptions of the U.S. states and Canadian provinces as well: "[They] should be considered more as small sovereign powers than simply local governments" (Fitch 2001b). Hopes for credit market discipline are reasonable when subnational governments are fiscally autonomous and have long histories of independent borrowing. In federations like Australia, Germany, and Spain – where the central government has a history of regulating subnational borrowing and financing a large share of subnational expenditures through predictable rule-based transfers – creditors take comfort in the possibility that the central government would ensure timely interest payments in the event of a subnational debt-servicing crisis. In more transfer-dependent and regulated subnational sectors, credit ratings are tightly clustered around the central government's sovereign rating, and rating agencies give much greater weight to the central government's economic and fiscal performance than those of the provinces. Note the relatively low standard deviations for credit ratings in Australia, Germany, and Spain, despite relatively high standard deviations in debt burdens.

That is not to say that credit ratings are irrelevant in transfer-dependent systems. Fitch's uniform AAA assessment of the German states is rather extreme; S&P ratings are correlated with debt burdens and other fiscal indicators within Australia, Germany, and Spain, and because bailouts might be slow to arrive or even denied, rating agencies defend cross-state ratings variation with careful analysis of each jurisdiction's budgets and economy, even in countries where they acknowledge that bailouts are likely. To the extent that jurisdictions issue bonds, these ratings probably correspond to different borrowing costs across units. This may very well provide governments with some incentives to improve fiscal management.

Yet if voters perceive the same implicit guarantee as creditors, these incentives will only go so far. Facing a debt crisis, a provincial government might be forced to choose between taking politically devastating actions to preserve the credit rating (e.g., firing workers and raising taxes) and threatening to default while requesting federal intervention. If voters believe the bailout is possible and even justified, the latter strategy is extremely attractive, even if borrowing costs might go up in the future as a result.

III. Transfer Dependence and Fiscal Incentives

Though much hinges on the specifics of the transfer system and there is considerable variation across subnational units within countries, the credit-rating data do suggest a clear cross-national relationship between overall transfer dependence and bailout expectations. What are the implications for the fiscal behavior of subnational governments? Examination of more refined arguments, along with more careful parsing of incentives created by specific transfer systems, will be undertaken in later chapters, but the goal of this chapter is to paint with a sufficiently broad brush to facilitate testing with cross-national data. The simplest baseline argument is that if transfer dependence shapes bailout expectations – applying the logic of the bailout game from Chapter 3 – incentives for fiscal discipline should be weaker among more transfer-dependent tiers of government, resulting in higher long-term deficits.

> H1: *Vertical fiscal imbalance is associated with fiscal indiscipline among subnational governments.*

Yet this hypothesis is almost certainly too simple, above all because it ignores the likely response of vulnerable central governments.

Borrowing Restrictions

> H2: *Central governments will place restrictions on subnational borrowing autonomy when vertical fiscal imbalance is high.*

Aware of its vulnerability to manipulation, the central government's first line of defense is to make a credible no-bailout commitment (Inman 2003). If this commitment is undermined by its cofinancing obligations in a system with high vertical fiscal imbalance, it will turn to a second line of defense. Like a vulnerable parent who refuses a child's request for a credit card, the central government may head off the moral hazard problem by formally restricting local governments' spending and access to credit. The bailout game from Chapter 3 no longer characterizes the interaction, because the central government, known to be irresolute, can force subnational governments to adjust by administrative fiat. A wide range of strategies have been used around the world, including outright prohibitions on borrowing, limits on foreign debt, numerical debt ceilings, restrictions on the use of debt, and balanced-budget requirements.[11] In fact, empirical evidence seems to suggest that such restrictions emerge as a direct response to the commitment problem associated with intergovernmental grants – Eichengreen and von Hagen (1996) examine H2 in a sample of currency unions and demonstrate that fiscal restrictions are indeed most often found where levels of vertical fiscal imbalance are high.

H3: Vertical fiscal imbalance is only associated with fiscal indiscipline when subnational governments are allowed to borrow.

Previous studies have not asked whether hierarchical borrowing restrictions are mere parchment barriers or whether they restrict subnational fiscal behavior in practice.[12] If they are effective, one should modify H1 and expect the interactive relationship between transfer dependence, borrowing autonomy, and fiscal performance suggested by H3. If vertical fiscal imbalance is indeed associated with subnational fiscal indiscipline, the relationship should only hold when the bailout game is actually played, when subnational governments have relatively unrestricted access to borrowing. That is, subnational fiscal indiscipline should be most pronounced in cases where vertical fiscal imbalance and borrowing autonomy are both high. This is represented by the upper right-hand corner of Figure 4.3, which depicts vertical fiscal imbalance on the horizontal axis and borrowing autonomy on the vertical axis. At low levels of vertical fiscal imbalance and high levels of borrowing autonomy (the upper left-hand corner), voters and creditors view subnational governments as sovereigns (p is low) and face incentives to keep them on a tight leash. Creditors punish profligacy with higher interest rates, and voters, knowing that the costs ultimately fall on them, punish

[11] For a review, see Ter-Minasian and Craig (1997).
[12] Studies of the U.S. states have addressed voter-imposed local restrictions, but not hierarchical restrictions imposed by central governments.

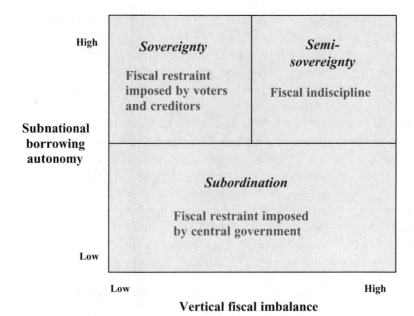

Figure 4.3. Hypothesized relationship between vertical imbalance, borrowing autonomy, and fiscal restraint.

politicians at the polls. Thus, the expected utility of pushing the bailout game to its later stages is low for subnational politicians. When borrowing autonomy is low (both lower quadrants in Figure 4.3), subnational governments resemble wards of the center and deficits are kept under control by the heavy hand of the central government.

But if H3 is correct, it merely raises an additional question: Why should any cases fall into the upper right-hand cell? Why would a vulnerable central government with heavy cofinancing obligations ever allow subnational governments to borrow?

Political Federalism and Territorial Representation

H4: Federalism undermines the central government's ability to restrict subnational borrowing.

Chapter 2 pointed out that federalism is much more than mere fiscal decentralization. It implies that the autonomy of the central government is effectively limited, either by constitutional rules or informal constraints.

Virtually all of the distinguishing characteristics of political federalism imply limits on the central government's ability to regulate the fiscal activities of the states or provinces. Not only is the expenditure autonomy of the provinces generally protected by the constitution, but provincial representation in the upper chamber often gives them veto power over any proposals that would limit their funding or autonomy. Thus, H4 asserts that constituent units in federations have greater independent access to various forms of deficit finance than local governments in unitary systems.

H5: Political federalism undermines subnational fiscal discipline.

H6: The relationship between federalism and subnational fiscal discipline is conditional on vertical fiscal imbalance.

Even without an effect on borrowing autonomy, one might expect the unique institutional protections and territorial representation of federalism to increase the perceived probability that the center is irresolute. This was precisely the fear that motivated Alexander Hamilton to favor banning state-level access to credit markets. As explained in Chapter 2, policymaking in federations includes an element of bargaining among territorial units that often obviates any notion that decisions are made by a national median voter. The complex regional bargaining and logrolling that often characterize the legislative process in federations might allow distressed states to trade votes on unrelated regional projects or lump-sum transfers for bailouts, as Pennyslvania, Maryland, and other states attempted in the 1800s. Bailout expectations might be less rational in unitary systems where territorial bargaining plays a smaller role and government decisions are more likely to reflect the preferences of the national median voter in a more straightforward way. The asymmetry of jurisdiction size in federations might also exacerbate the commitment problem if the failure of a large state might create negative externalities for the rest of the federation – the too-big-to-fail phenomenon (Wildasin 1997). At the same time, a small overrepresented jurisdiction might be "too small to fail" if it is in an especially favorable position to trade votes for bailouts that would be relatively inexpensive for the other constituent units to provide. Based on such considerations, recent studies by political scientists posit a direct link between federal political institutions and fiscal indiscipline (Treisman 2000a; Wibbels 2000).

In short, political federalism might weaken both lines of defense. H4 suggests that it undermines the center's ability to restrict subnational

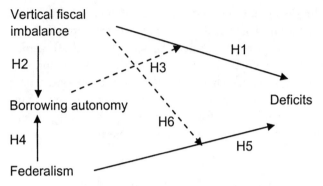

Figure 4.4. Summary of hypotheses.

borrowing. That is, states and provinces in federations will be situated higher in Figure 4.3 than municipalities in unitary systems. But as Alexander Hamilton feared, federalism might have an independent effect on the center's ability to commit in the first place (H5). That is, the presence of federal institutions might be associated with poor subnational fiscal performance no matter where a country falls in Figure 4.3.

Alternatively, H6 suggests an interactive relationship. H1 argues that at low levels of vertical fiscal imbalance, the center can credibly commit to remain uninvolved in the fiscal affairs of subnational governments and voters and creditors hold local politicians responsible for their own fiscal management. If federalism places credible restrictions on the center, this might actually *bolster* its commitment when the constituent units are self-financing, but undermine it when they are dependent on the central government for funds. Returning to Figure 4.3, H6 suggests that federalism should undermine subnational fiscal discipline only on the right-hand side.

Summary of Hypotheses

Figure 4.4 summarizes all of these possibilities, using bold lines to represent direct relationships and dashed lines for interactive relationships. H1 hypothesizes a simple relationship between transfer dependence (vertical fiscal imbalance) and subnational deficits. H5 posits a simple relationship between federalism and subnational deficits. H3 and H6 are the interactive hypotheses: H3 suggests that the effects of vertical fiscal imbalance and borrowing autonomy are conditional on one another, and H6 suggests that the effects of vertical fiscal imbalance and federalism are conditional on one another. Finally, H2 and H4 acknowledge that it may be inappropriate to view borrowing autonomy as exogenous; central government attempts to control subnational fiscal decisions are potentially shaped by vertical fiscal imbalance and federalism.

IV. Data

The rest of this chapter examines these propositions, first using cross-section averages and then using time series cross-section analysis. The dataset is composed of yearly observations for forty-three cases drawn from a cross-section of OECD, developing, and transition countries for the period between 1986 and 1996. Each observation represents an aggregate state or local government sector.[13] Some federal countries provide two separate data points: state and local.[14] Given the arguments above and the important differences between states and local governments in federations, it is necessary to include both states and local governments for the same country separately, introducing appropriate controls and testing for separate effects. The sample contains all state or local government sectors for which complete data could be obtained.[15]

Main Variables

The first task is to come up with a comparable measure of subnational fiscal discipline to use as a dependent variable. Recall that the argument does not predict actual bailouts, but rather a higher tolerance for deficits and debt stemming from rational bailout *expectations*. Subnational debt data are unavailable, but the IMF's *Government Finance Statistics* (*GFS*) collects yearly data on subnational budget balance. Of course short-term budget deficits may reflect intertemporal tax- or expenditure-smoothing or countercyclical budgetary policy. One way to minimize the impact of economic cycles is by using averages over a sufficiently long time period. Another is to include controls for exogenous macroeconomic fluctuations. Both strategies are employed below.

---

[13] For a list of cases and data sources, see Appendix 4.1.

[14] The exceptions are Argentina and India, for which only state-level data were available.

[15] The most important constraint was the availability of data on subnational fiscal performance.

To facilitate cross-national and time series comparison, the deficit/surplus data might be divided either by expenditure, revenue, or GDP. While appropriate for time series analysis within countries, GDP is a less desirable denominator for cross-national comparison because of large cross-national differences in the size of the public sector and the degree of fiscal decentralization. For the analysis of cross-country averages, it makes sense to use deficit as a share of subnational revenue or expenditure. Because revenues are partially determined by the central government (through grants and revenue sharing), the most appropriate cross-national measure of subnational fiscal discipline is the deficit/surplus as a share of expenditures.

To operationalize the most important independent variable, it is necessary to distinguish between intergovernmental grants and own-source subnational revenue. Recall the discussion of data in Chapter 2. While the commonly used data from the IMF might be useful for tracking changes in grants over time, they badly overestimate local revenue autonomy for a number of countries in which subnational governments have very little taxing authority but depend heavily on shared taxes. For this reason, I turn to the more useful (for the task at hand) measure of vertical fiscal imbalance (grants/revenue) that codes shared taxes as grants by consulting a variety of additional sources. The disadvantage of this measure is that it does not vary over time because some of the sources did not include sufficient time series variation. However, as long as the empirical set-up controls for cross-section effects, the *GFS* grants variable may be useful for the analysis of time series variation.

Borrowing autonomy is measured by the legal-institutional index of the Inter-American Development Bank (IDB) introduced in Chapter 2.[16] I have used a slightly modified version of the IDB formula to measure borrowing autonomy for a larger sample of subnational governments.[17]

Among the cases for which the fiscal data are available, a federalism dummy was coded according to the Elazar-Watts classification discussed

[16] IDB (1997: 173–76).
[17] The index is explained in Appendix 2.2. It is similar to the IDB's formula, but instead of calculating a weighted average of state and local governments in federal systems, I calculate separate values for state and local governments and include restrictions placed on municipal governments by state-provincial governments. In addition, I do not count borrowing restraints imposed by state and local governments on themselves. In accordance with the argument, this index seeks to capture the attempts of higher-level governments to restrict local borrowing. In fact, when subnational governments place restrictions upon themselves to appease creditors or voters, this is a powerful indication that their obligations are viewed as sovereign.

in Chapter 2. Part of the argument about federalism above, however, was driven by a specific aspect of federalism – the "incongruent" representation of the states in a strong upper legislative chamber. In order to measure the effect of federal territorial representation, a variable has been created that takes on 0 if the subnational governments are *not* the constituencies for the upper chamber and takes the value of the Samuels/Snyder upper-chamber malapportionment index otherwise (see Chapter 2).[18] This variable is 0 for all of the cases except for ten of the federations.[19] This is, in effect, similar to a "federal" dummy, but it allows for variation in territorial overrepresentation among the federations.

Control Variables

It is possible that central governments in federations make less credible commitments to "say no" to states not because of legislative politics, but simply because states and provinces are larger and more difficult to ignore than municipalities or local governments. To evaluate this claim, I calculate the average number of persons per jurisdiction in each subnational sector.[20] This variable ranges from around fifteen hundred for the French municipalities to over twenty-five million for the Indian states. It is also plausible that political federalism and territorial representation are not important alone, but are mere by-products of large country size. Thus, I include controls for area (square kilometers) and population.[21] It may be more difficult for subnational governments to balance their budgets when they are responsible for a wide range of expenditure activities rather than, for example, mere trash collection. For this reason, I include a control for the overall level of decentralization: subnational expenditures as a share of total public sector expenditures (calculated from the *GFS*).

---

[18] Samuels and Snyder calculate legislative malapportionment using the Loosemore-Hanby index of electoral disproportionality as follows:

$$\text{MAL} = (1/2) \sum |s_i - v_i|$$

where s_i is the percentage of all seats allocated to district i, and v_i is the percentage of the overall population residing in district i.

[19] No data are available for Canada, which has an extremely weak, appointed upper chamber. Each of the other federal upper chambers has significant legislative or veto authority, especially over "federal" issues.

[20] Population data are from the World Bank's *World Development Indicators* (henceforth, *WDI*), and jurisdiction data are taken from the World Bank's *World Development Report 1999/2000*, Table A.1.

[21] Because the data are skewed, natural logs are used for both.

It is also important to control for economic and demographic conditions that may affect subnational fiscal performance. Thus, I include the log of real GDP per capita (PPP, international dollars).[22] Because subnational governments are often responsible for providing primary education and retirement benefits, it is useful to control for the portion of the population that is either too old or too young to work – the so-called dependency ratio. Another common demographic control, population density, is included as well.[23]

Other aspects of a country's institutions might also affect the central government's ability to commit not to provide bailouts. Above all, it might be easier to commit if the center itself faces a hard budget constraint in the form of an independent central bank (Dillinger and Webb 1999). Bailout expectations are more rational if the central government can "resolve" a subnational fiscal crisis by printing more money. Thus, I include Alex Cukierman's (1992) legal-institutional index of central bank autonomy. Additionally, because Persson and Tabellini (1998) find important differences in fiscal behavior between presidential and parliamentary democracies, I include a variable from the World Bank's *Database of Political Institutions* (*DPI*) that takes on 0 for pure presidential systems, 1 for systems with assembly-elected presidents, and 2 for pure parliamentary systems. Furthermore, it may be useful to control for partisan fragmentation in the central government. One might hypothesize that the central government is in a better position to say no to bailout requests if the president presides over a unified legislature in presidential systems or if the Prime Minister in a parliamentary system need not hold together a diverse coalition. Thus, I include the index of political cohesion developed by Roubini and Sachs (1989).[24] Finally, the fiscal woes of subnational governments might also be related to those of higher-level governments. For this reason, I include the central government's deficit/expenditure ratio for all governments and include an additional variable that measures the state's

---

[22] Source: *WDI.*

[23] Ibid.

[24] Taken from the DPI, this variable takes on 0 for presidential systems under unified government and 1 under divided government. For parliamentary systems, it takes on 0 for one-party government, 1 for a two-party coalition, 2 for a coalition with three or more parties, and 3 for minority government. Results similar to those presented below are obtained using a variety of other "government fragmentation" variables from the DPI, including a more complex "veto player" index.

or province's deficit/expenditure ratio for local governments in federal systems.[25]

V. Cross-Section Analysis

Ideally, the propositions above would be tested using time series data disaggregated to the level of individual states and localities. In order to differentiate between countercyclical fiscal management and fiscal laxity, it would also be useful to differentiate between expected and unexpected shocks. In order to discern between various arguments about intergovernmental grants, it would be useful to distinguish between various individual grant programs. While such analysis is possible in single-case studies, data limitations would make cross-national comparison virtually impossible. The goal of this chapter is to make the most of the cross-national data described above. This is best achieved by combining two strategies. This section examines long-term, purely cross-sectional relationships using between-effects OLS regressions on ten-year averages.[26] While the disadvantages are obvious, this approach has some advantages: It allows for the use of more precise measures of vertical fiscal imbalance and territorial representation that cannot vary over time, and it allows for some broad generalizations about the kinds of systems in which subnational deficits are most persistent. Moreover, the cross-section results help provide background for the second empirical strategy: time series cross-section analysis that (by necessity) uses a narrower definition of vertical fiscal imbalance and examines changes over time.

The main goal is to estimate a model of average subnational surplus and ascertain whether vertical fiscal imbalance and federalism have direct or more complex interactive effects. Furthermore, there are good reasons to suspect that the relationship is complicated by an intervening variable: borrowing autonomy. Thus, the empirical model should accommodate H2 and H4 by allowing federalism and vertical fiscal imbalance to affect borrowing autonomy. This calls for a system of equations in which borrowing autonomy is endogenous. Leaving aside H3 and H6 (the interactive hypotheses)

---

[25] This variable is 0 for all states and provinces in federal systems and local governments in unitary systems.

[26] A slightly shorter time-series is available for some of the cases. The results presented below are not affected by the deletion of these cases, nor are they affected by limiting the data period to the years that are common to all cases.

for the moment, the following structural model makes it possible to test H1, H2, H4, and H5 simultaneously:

$$Surplus = a_1 + a_2\text{VFI} + a_3 Borrow\ autonomy + a_4 Federalism \\ + a_i \ldots Controls + v$$ (4.1)

$$Borrow\ autonomy = b_1 + b_2\text{VFI} + b_3 Federalism + b_4 \text{Log} \\ GDP\ per\ Capita + b_5 Log\ population + b_6 System + w,$$ (4.2)

where federalism, GDP per capita, vertical fiscal imbalance, population, system (the presidential/parliamentary variable), and all control variables are treated as exogenous. Using three-stage least squares, the parameters of equations 4.1 and 4.2 are estimated simultaneously.[27]

The results are reported in the first column of Table 4.2. First, note that the borrowing autonomy equation performs quite well. Recall that the Eichengreen/von Hagen hypothesis (H2) assumes that the central government is a rational, unconstrained unitary decision maker, and as such it would choose to tightly regulate subnational borrowing when vertical fiscal imbalance is high. H4 relaxes these assumptions and proposes that federal institutions constrain the central government's range of choices. Strong support is found for both propositions. Countries with higher levels of vertical fiscal imbalance indeed demonstrate lower levels of subnational borrowing autonomy, and states and provinces in federations do have significantly freer access to deficit finance than local or municipal governments. The results also suggest that central governments in wealthier, more populous, and presidential (as opposed to parliamentary) countries allow subnational governments freer access to credit markets.

In the subnational surplus equation, on the other hand, the variables of interest do not approach statistical significance in any specification – even if insignificant control variables are dropped, or if a simpler single-equation OLS model is used. Thus, no support is found for H1 or H5. Though vertical fiscal imbalance helps explain levels of borrowing autonomy, it does not appear to have an independent effect on subnational fiscal performance. Likewise, constituent units in federations do have more borrowing autonomy, but other things being equal, they do not have significantly higher deficit/expenditure ratios than local governments.

---

[27] A variety of other right-hand-side variables have been included in equation 2, but only these approached statistical significance.

Table 4.2. *Simultaneous estimates of average subnational fiscal balance and borrowing autonomy (1986–1996)*

	Model 4.1		Model 4.2		Model 4.3	
Subnational surplus/ expenditure equation						
Vertical fiscal imbalance	−0.062	(0.098)	0.233	(0.052)***		
Borrowing autonomy	−0.037	(0.073)			−0.018	(0.057)
Federal dummy	−0.020	(0.077)	0.020	(0.021)		
(VFI) × (borrowing autonomy)			−0.143	(0.023)***		
(VFI) × (constituent unit in federation)					−0.084	(0.043)**
(VFI) × (local government)					−0.010	(0.110)
Persons per jurisdiction	−0.004	(0.004)	−0.006	(0.003)**	−0.004	(0.003)
Log area	0.005	(0.009)	0.010	(0.006)	0.002	(0.009)
Subnational expenditure/total	−0.190	(0.131)	−0.183	(0.068)***	−0.209	(0.147)
Log GDP per capita	0.017	(0.038)	0.021	(0.014)	0.009	(0.034)
Dependency ratio	−0.010	(0.120)	−0.064	(0.080)	−0.017	(0.125)
Population density	0.00001	(0.0002)	0.0001	(0.0001)	−0.00003	(0.0002)
Central bank independence	0.026	(0.091)	−0.013	(0.046)	0.028	(0.076)
System (president/ parliament)	−0.002	(0.023)	−0.012	(0.010)	0.002	(0.020)
Index of political cohesion	0.003	(0.016)	0.014	(0.011)	0.005	(0.013)
Central govt. surpl./ expenditure	−0.123	(0.205)	−0.203	(0.088)**	−0.124	(0.166)
State-province surplus/expend.	0.724	(0.208)***	0.760	(0.175)***	0.711	(0.206)
Constant	−0.103	(0.320)	−0.262	(0.170)	−0.048	(0.314)
"R^2"	0.68		0.77		0.63	
Borrowing autonomy equation						
Vertical fiscal imbalance	−1.437	(0.490)***	−1.438	(0.490)***	−1.439	(0.490)***
Federal dummy	0.961	(0.224)***	0.962	(0.224)***	0.966	(0.221)
Log GDP per capita	0.411	(0.141)**	0.411	(0.141)**	0.411	(0.141)**
Log population	0.135	(0.078)*	0.134	(0.078)*	0.133	(0.077)*
System (president/ parliament)	−0.206	(0.122)*	−0.206	(0.122)*	−0.207	(0.122)*
Constant	−3.216	(2.042)	−3.199	(2.042)	−3.180	(2.027)
R^2	0.56		0.56		0.56	
Groups	37		37		37	

3-stage least squares, standard errors in parentheses
* significant at 10%;   ** significant at 5%;   *** significant at 1%

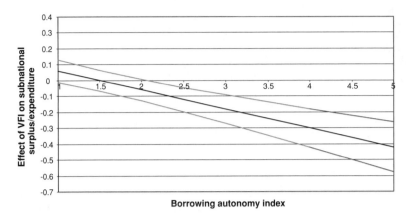

Figure 4.5. Conditional effect of vertical fiscal imbalance on subnational surplus/expenditure.

Model 4.2 estimates the same structural model, but instead of testing for independent effects of borrowing autonomy and vertical fiscal imbalance, it examines H3 by including a multiplicative interaction term. Adding the interaction term raises the R^2 of the surplus equation from .68 to .77, and the variables of interest are individually and jointly highly significant. The best way to interpret the interaction is with reference to Figure 4.5, which plots the conditional effect of vertical fiscal imbalance with a bold line and the 95 percent confidence interval with dotted lines.

The horizontal axis displays the range of the borrowing autonomy index (from 1 to 5) and the vertical axis can be interpreted as conditional coefficients. Figure 4.5 shows that when subnational governments face strict formal limitations on their ability to borrow, vertical fiscal imbalance has a small *positive* (though statistically insignificant) effect on fiscal balance. But as subnational governments gain independent access to credit, vertical fiscal imbalance has an increasingly *negative* and statistically significant impact on budget balance.

Figure 4.6 gives a sense of the model's substantive predictions. It maps directly onto Figure 4.3, displaying the model's predictions when the borrowing autonomy and vertical fiscal imbalance are held at their 20th and 80th percentile values and all other variables are held at their mean values. It shows strong support for H3. Predicted long-run deficits are much higher in the upper right-hand cell (around 14 percent of expenditures), where high levels of borrowing autonomy and vertical fiscal imbalance combine.

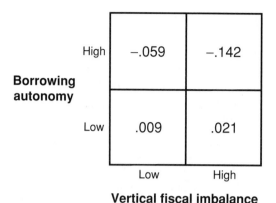

	Low	High
High	−.059	−.142
Low	.009	.021

Borrowing autonomy (left label)

Low   High

Vertical fiscal imbalance

Figure 4.6. Average subnational surplus/expenditure predicted by Model 4.2 at low and high values of vertical fiscal imbalance and borrowing autonomy.

The model predicts balanced budgets when subnational governments face substantial borrowing restrictions (the lower cells), and not surprisingly, it predicts slightly higher deficits on average (around 6 percent of expenditures) when governments are self-financing and have wide-ranging borrowing authority.

Moving on to H6, Model 4.3 holds borrowing autonomy constant and examines separate effects of vertical fiscal imbalance for constituent units in federations and local governments. Consistent with H6, vertical fiscal imbalance only has a significant negative effect on subnational fiscal outcomes among states and provinces. Substantively, once again holding all control variables at their mean values, this model predicts long-term deficits of only around 1 percent of expenditures among *local* governments at both low (20th percentile) and high (80th percentile) values of vertical fiscal imbalance. Among constituent units in federations, the model predicts a 3 percent deficit when vertical fiscal imbalance is at the 20th percentile value and a 7 percent deficit when at its 80th percentile value.[28]

Given the results of Models 4.2 and 4.3, it seems possible that the best model would combine them by using a triple interaction term. Specifically, it is possible that the (VFI) × (Borrowing Autonomy) result in Model 4.2 is driven primarily by federated units. However, a model including separate

---

[28] Very similar results in this regression and all others (not presented, to save space) are obtained using the continuous "territorial representation" measure of federalism based on the Samuels-Snyder index of upper-chamber malapportionment.

effects for federated units and local government (not shown) demonstrates significant, negative coefficients for both that resemble the coefficient for the interaction term in Model 4.2. This suggests that the effect of vertical fiscal imbalance is contingent on borrowing autonomy (and vice versa) among *both* federated units and local governments, but the result should be approached with caution because of the small number of observations within each category.

More generally, one should be skeptical about regression analysis using noncontinuous indexes. As a robustness check, Models 4.1 through 4.3 have been estimated using a simpler dummy version of the borrowing autonomy index (with the median value used as the cut point), and all of the results were quite similar.[29] But it should be noted that with respect to the borrowing autonomy index, ten of the federated units are above the median, and only one (Austria) is below. Of twenty-six local governments in the sample, nine are above and seventeen are below. This underscores the difficulty of distinguishing between the effects of federalism and borrowing autonomy in the cross-section analysis.

To summarize the results, vertical fiscal imbalance and federalism affect long-term fiscal balance, but in a complicated and contingent way.[30] First of all, there is no support for H1 – vertical fiscal imbalance does not have a direct independent effect on subnational fiscal outcomes; but there is strong support for H2: At higher levels of vertical fiscal imbalance, central governments attempt to cut off subnational access to credit markets. Perhaps the most important result is in support of H3: When relatively free to borrow, more transfer-dependent subnational sectors are likely to run larger long-term deficits. As for H5, other things equal, federated units

---

[29] Additionally, none of the main results are affected by including or excluding control variables, including a matrix of region dummies, or dropping individual cases. Similar results have also been obtained using equation-by-equation OLS.

[30] The performance of the control variables can be summarized as follows. "Persons per jurisdiction" has the hypothesized negative sign in each model, but statistical significance is quite sensitive to the precise specification. Land area is unrelated to subnational fiscal performance. As expected, the models show that expenditure decentralization is associated with larger deficits, but statistical significance is sensitive. There is no evidence that wealth affects subnational fiscal performance, and the coefficient for the "dependency" ratio, though negative as expected, does not achieve significance in many specifications. Coefficients for population density, central bank autonomy, executive-legislative relations, and central government political cohesion are not significantly different from 0. Surprisingly, the central government's long-term fiscal performance is not positively correlated with subnational fiscal performance, but the fiscal performance of local governments in federal systems is intertwined with that of the states and provinces.

do not run significantly larger deficits than local governments. But federated units have much greater access to credit than local governments (H4), and the largest subnational deficits in the sample are found among federations with high levels of transfer dependence (H6). The coincidence of wide-ranging borrowing autonomy, high vertical fiscal imbalance, and large deficits is found primarily among constituent units in federal systems, but the contingent relationship between borrowing autonomy and vertical fiscal imbalance appears to hold up among both federated units and local governments.

VI. Time Series Cross-Section Analysis

While cross-section averages are admittedly blunt, these results establish some key correlates of long-run subnational deficits. A natural further step is to examine the effects of intergovernmental transfers on the evolution of fiscal performance over time within countries. Building on the cross-section results presented above, this section focuses on time series rather than cross-section variation and asks whether and under what conditions the growth of transfer dependence over time is associated with increasing subnational deficits. That is, it examines diachronic versions of H1, H3, H5, and H6. The logic is that as subnational officials see steady growth over time in their dependence on intergovernmental transfers, bailout expectations solidify and incentives for fiscal discipline weaken. H1 asserts a simple relationship between growing transfer dependence and growing deficits, while H3 and H6 make this relationship conditional on the presence of borrowing autonomy and federalism. Finally, the logic of H5 suggests that subnational deficits grow more rapidly in federations.

Dynamic analysis is particularly useful from a policy perspective: Countries are decentralizing expenditure authority in many countries around the world; and in most cases, these new subnational expenditures are funded by increased intergovernmental transfers rather than new own-source local taxes and fees. Given the growing concern in the literature about the supposed macroeconomic dangers of decentralization, this section provides an exploration of the fiscal and political conditions under which decentralization might push deficits upward.

In order to make use of time series data, it is necessary to rely on the *GFS* distinction between own-source and grant revenue. Problems of cross-national comparability should be obviated by an empirical approach that focuses exclusively on time series variation. The goal of the empirical set-up is to eliminate cross-section variation and focus exclusively on changes. Debates among econometricians and political science method-ologists about the proper empirical technique for this type of dataset are unresolved. Several modeling strategies have countervailing costs and ben-efits, but fortunately in this instance all yield quite similar results. The results presented below use the GMM estimator derived by Arellano and Bond (1991). This approach relies on the use of first-differences to remove the fixed-effects part of the error term and instrumental variable estimation, where the instruments are the lagged explanatory variables (in differences) and the dependent variable lagged twice. As recommended by Arellano and Bond (1991), one-step robust results are presented and used for inference on coefficients.

The most straightforward model – displayed in Table 4.3 (Model 4.4) – explores changes in the same dependent variable used above: the subna-tional deficit/expenditure ratio. The key dependent variable is the change in grants as a share of subnational revenues. An important control variable is subnational revenue as a share of total (combined state, central, and local) revenue. This set-up allows one to compare the impact of growing revenue decentralization and that of having more of the revenue tilted toward grants. The model also includes two lags of the dependent variable, changes in all of the other control variables that vary over time, levels for those that do not, and a set of dummies for each subnational sector.

In order to examine H1, Model 4.4 includes only grants/revenue, while Model 4.5 examines H3 and H6 by estimating separate effects for systems with high and low levels of borrowing autonomy (above and below the median value), and within these categories, separate effects for local/municipal governments and constituent units in federations. H5 is examined in each model by including the dummy variable that distin-guishes between federated units and local governments. In both models, the coefficient for subnational revenue/total revenue is positive and sig-nificant. Controlling for transfer dependence, as subnational governments receive larger shares of total government revenue, their surpluses increase (deficits decrease) relative to their expenditures. In Model 4.4, although the coefficient for grants/subnational revenue is negative as predicted by H1, it is not significantly different from 0. However, in Model 4.5 the coefficient is negative and highly significant, as predicted by H3, among subnational entities with high levels of borrowing autonomy, regardless of status as federated units or local governments. In the dataset, there are ten state-provincial sectors and nine local sectors with high levels of borrowing

Table 4.3. *Determinates of changes in subnational surplus/expenditure: dynamic panel data analysis*

	Model 4.4		Model 4.5	
Dependent variable				
Δ Subnational surplus/expenditure				
Independent variables				
Δ Subnational surplus/ expenditure$_{t-1}$	−0.008	(0.124)	0.044	(0.114)
Δ Subnational surplus/ expenditure$_{t-2}$	−0.187	(0.077)**	−0.183	(0.065)***
Federal dummy	0.001	(0.005)	−0.004	(0.005)
Borrowing autonomy index	−0.003	(0.003)	0.002	(0.004)
Δ Grants/subnational revenue	−0.058	(0.087)		
(Δ Grants/subnational revenue) × (*High* borr. aut.) × (*federal*)			−0.319	(0.081)***
(Δ Grants/subnational revenue) × (*High* borr. aut.) × (*local*)			−0.536	(0.216)***
(Δ Grants/subnational revenue) × (*Low* borr. aut.) × (*federal*)			0.390	(0.072)***
(Δ Grants/subnational revenue) × (*Low* borr. aut.) × (*local*)			0.049	(0.101)
Δ Subnational revenue/total government revenue	0.451	(0.218)**	0.514	(0.227)***
Δ Population (log)	0.019	(0.017)	0.022	(0.019)
Log area	−0.001	(0.001)	0.001	(0.003)
Δ GDP per capita (log)	0.027	(0.019)	0.019	(0.015)
Δ Dependency ratio	−0.075	(0.095)	−0.023	(0.081)
Δ Population density	−0.001	(0.001)	0.003	(0.003)
System (president/parliament)	0.007	(0.010)	−0.010	(0.010)
Index of political cohesion	0.007	(0.003)**	0.004	(0.003)
Δ Central govt. surplus/expenditure	0.002	(0.040)	0.003	(0.044)
Δ State-prov. surplus/expend. (fed.)	0.190	(0.138)	0.191	(0.125)
Constant	0.011	(0.023)	−0.000	(0.031)
Observations	272		272	
Number of groups	37		37	

Robust standard errors in parentheses
* significant at 10%;   ** significant at 5%;   *** significant at 1%
Calculated using Stata 7.0, "xtabond" procedure, one-step results

autonomy, and the coefficients suggest that a 1 percent increase (decrease) in transfer dependence is associated with .32 percent and .54 percent declines (improvements) in fiscal balance, respectively. The positive coefficient for federated units with low levels of borrowing autonomy is driven exclusively by Austria. For the remaining cases – the subordinate local government sectors with low levels of borrowing autonomy – the coefficient is indistinguishable from 0.

The results presented in Table 4.2 lend support to neither H5 nor H6. There is no evidence that deficits grow more quickly among federated units – in no estimation does the federal dummy approach statistical significance. Furthermore, among subnational entities with substantial borrowing autonomy, growing transfer dependence does not have a larger effect on fiscal outcomes among federated units than among local governments. In fact, the negative coefficient is larger for local governments.

The key result in this section is that when subnational governments are allowed to borrow, increasing transfer dependence is associated with larger subnational deficits.[31] Yet this section should conclude with a strong word of caution about correlation and causation. It is not possible to conclude with any confidence that transfer dependence "causes" deficits by changing the incentives of subnational governments. Some other exogenous unmeasured factor – say, an increase in the demand for local public expenditures like a spike in school-age children or a terrorist threat – might lead to increased grants from higher-level governments but also place new pressures on the finances of local governments. Transfer dependence, especially as it evolves over time within countries, is likely to be endogenous to a

---

[31] Similar results are obtained with and without fixed effects and year dummies, and the results are not affected by the deletion of cases. Similar results are obtained when the dependent variable is measured relative to GDP rather than expenditure and with a variety of other estimation techniques. One reasonable alternative is to use OLS with panel-corrected standard errors and include fixed country effects. Using this technique with either levels or first differences and attempting several different strategies for dealing with serial correlation yield reasonably similar results. A concern in the move from theory to data is that the hypothesized connection between transfer dependence and fiscal outcomes is driven by changing perceptions of the center's resolve – something that is likely to unfold slowly over time. Thus, it is also useful to estimate an error correction model – with first differences on the left-hand side and both lagged levels and first differences on the right-hand side – in an attempt to distinguish long-term from short-term effects of transfer dependence on deficits. For subnational entities with borrowing autonomy, the coefficient was negative and statistically significant for the lagged level, indicating a longer-term relationship.

variety of important unmeasured factors.[32] Thus, this type of analysis cannot rule out other explanations for the observed correlation. Yet it may be informative that the relationship is only apparent among subnational entities that have access to independent borrowing. These suggestive results invite more-refined analysis using individual country studies.

VII. Total Public Sector Deficits

There are reasons to suspect that subnational fiscal indiscipline affects not only the state or local government sector in question, but the entire public sector. In fact, one possible objection to the use of subnational fiscal balance as the dependent variable is the possibility that soft local budget constraints and bailouts might affect the finances of the central government in addition to, or perhaps even instead of, the local governments. For this reason, it is useful to reexamine the key results using *total* (combined central, state, and local) fiscal balance as the dependent variable. Of course, this requires some changes to the dataset and model specifications because states and local governments within federations can no longer be individual data points. Vertical fiscal imbalance and borrowing autonomy in federations must now be based on a weighted (by expenditure share) average of state and local governments. Grants/Revenue now refer to totals for all subnational governments. In addition, the control variables measuring fiscal balance for higher-level governments must be left out.

Table 4.4 presents the results of a model that simply reestimates Model 4.2 from above using average aggregate deficit/expenditure as the dependent variable.[33] Though the coefficient on the interaction variable is slightly smaller than in the subnational deficit model, the result is quite similar and survives all of the robustness checks outlined above. When subnational governments are free to borrow, higher reliance on intergovernmental transfers is associated with larger aggregate deficits, not just for the subnational sector, but for the entire public sector.

---

[32] Another possibility is that subnational deficits "cause" transfer dependence by eventually forcing the center to make bailouts through the transfers system. Granger causality tests suggest that past deficits do not help predict transfer dependence; but in the absence of a good instrument for grants, this possiblity cannot be ruled out.

[33] All of the results in this section are quite similar if the dependent variable is calculated as a share of GDP rather than expenditures.

Table 4.4. *Estimates of total (central + subnational) fiscal balance and borrowing autonomy (1986–1996)*

	Model 4.6	
Total surplus/expenditure		
Vertical fiscal imbalance	0.092	(0.086)
Federal dummy	0.019	(0.038)
(VFI) × (borrowing autonomy)	−0.104	(0.032)***
Persons per jurisdiction	0.041	(0.051)
Log area	0.023	(0.009)**
Subnational expenditure/total	−0.109	(0.107)
Log GDP per capita	0.030	(0.027)
Dependency ratio	−0.306	(0.144)**
Population density	−0.000001	(0.000003)
Central bank independence	0.096	(0.080)
System (president/parliament)	−0.008	(0.015)
Index of political cohesion	0.001	(0.019)
Constant	−0.397	(0.306)
"R^2"	0.72	
Borrowing autonomy equation		
Vertical fiscal imbalance	−1.429	(0.644)**
Federal dummy	0.593	(0.296)**
Log GDP per capita	0.371	(0.189)*
Log population	0.190	(0.105)*
System (president/parliament)	−0.056	(0.154)
Constant	−3.826	(2.741)
R^2	0.47	
Groups	28	

3-stage least squares, standard errors in parentheses
* significant at 10%; ** significant at 5%; *** significant at 1%

Table 4.5 presents two models that extend the panel data analysis to total public sector deficits. Model 4.7 is the simple model, and model 4.8 includes separate effects.

First of all, note that the coefficient for subnational revenue/total revenue is negative and significant in both models, suggesting that, other things equal, revenue decentralization is associated with a rather large decline in overall fiscal balance. While this lends some empirical support to the fear that fiscal decentralization can harm budget balance, once again more-precise institutional details are important. As in Table 4.2, the coefficient for the grants/revenue variable has a negative coefficient in the simple model,

Table 4.5. *Determinates of changes in total (central + subnational) surplus/expenditure: dyanmic panel data analysis*

	Model 4.7		Model 4.8	
Dependent variable:				
Δ Total surplus/expenditure				
Independent variables:				
Federal dummy	−0.030	(0.050)	−0.005	(0.048)
Borrowing autonomy index	0.001	(0.012)	−0.003	(0.011)
Δ Grants/subnational revenue	−0.162	(0.121)		
(Δ Grants/subnational revenue) × (*High* borr. aut.) × (*federal*)			−0.453	(0.205)**
(Δ Grants/subnational revenue) × (*High* borr. aut.) × (*local*)			−0.739	(0.235)***
(Δ Grants/subnational revenue) × (*Low* borr. aut.) × (*federal*)			0.220	(0.164)
(Δ Grants/subnational revenue) × (*Low* borr. aut.) × (*local*)			−0.089	(0.135)
Δ Subnational revenue/total government revenue	−0.521	(0.173)***	−0.451	(0.156)***
Δ Population (log)	−1.089	(0.987)	−0.942	(0.865)
Log area	0.012	(0.006)**	0.012	(0.006) *
Δ GDP per capita (log)	0.018	(0.122)	0.003	(0.126)
Δ Dependency ratio	−1.511	(2.083)	−0.422	(2.283)
Δ Population density	0.0002	(0.0001)	0.0002	(0.0001)
System (president/parliament)	−0.041	(0.021)*	−0.039	(0.019)**
Index of political cohesion	0.009	(0.004)**	0.009	(0.004)**
Constant	−0.107	(0.061)	−0.095	(0.067)
Observations	209		209	
Number of groups	29		29	

Robust standard errors in parentheses
* significant at 10%;   ** significant at 5%;   *** significant at 1%
Calculated using Stata 7.0, "xtabond" procedure, one-step results

but it does not quite reach statistical significance. Model 4.8 shows that as in the subnational deficit models, the negative coefficient is driven by the cases with substantial borrowing autonomy, the coefficients for which are negative, substantively large, and significant. Thus, when subnational governments are free to borrow, growing transfer dependence is associated with growing total deficits, and once again, contrary to H6, the effect is larger in unitary systems.

VIII. Summary of Results

Fiscal decentralization and political federalism may indeed complicate macroeconomic management, but their effects are contingent on other institutional factors. The empirical analysis shows that it is useful to look beyond the rather frustrating and simple binary distinction between federal and unitary systems. Intergovernmental fiscal systems and hierarchical rules are among the important building blocks in a more nuanced approach to the "varieties of federalism."

First of all, the results lend no support to the simple proposition that higher levels of transfer dependence are associated with larger or faster-growing deficits (H1). Rather, it is clear that higher-level governments can assuage the intergovernmental moral-hazard problem by cutting off the access of subnational governments to credit. The cross-section models show that indeed, at higher levels of vertical fiscal imbalance, central governments attempt to restrict subnational borrowing (H2). The cross-section models predict relatively small deficits among subnational governments that either (1) face relatively strict formal borrowing limitations or (2) are relatively fiscally independent, while the largest long-term deficits (subnational and total) are found when subnational governments are simultaneously transfer dependent and free to borrow (H3). Similarly, growing transfer dependence over time is associated with larger deficits only when subnational governments are free to borrow.

The role of federalism is somewhat more complicated. A very simple argument linking federalism and fiscal profligacy is not borne out – other things equal, federated units display neither larger nor faster-growing deficits than local governments in unitary systems (H5). However, they do have significantly higher levels of borrowing autonomy (H4) – so much so, in fact, that it is difficult to differentiate between the effect of borrowing autonomy and that of federalism. Though the degrees of freedom are low, the cross-section analysis does suggest that the conditional relationship between borrowing autonomy and transfer dependence holds up among both federated units and local governments. Moreover, the panel data results show that when free to borrow, growing transfer dependence is associated with increasing deficits, both among federated units and local governments. But H6 posits that the negative effect of transfer dependence will be more pronounced among federated units. Here the results of the long-term averages and dynamic analysis are discordant, but understandably so. The largest *long-term* subnational deficits are found among federated units with relatively high levels of vertical fiscal imbalance, though the marginal effect of increasing transfer dependence is larger among local governments.

IX. Looking Ahead

This chapter points out two distinct paths to long-term fiscal discipline. In the lower half of Figure 4.3, higher-level governments tightly regulate local access to credit, as recommended by Hamilton. An important finding is that these prohibitions seem to achieve their objective: Long-term subnational deficits are negligible in such systems, and fluctuations in grants have no effect on deficits. However, the data also show that this method of fiscal discipline is rarely in place among constituent units in large federations. It is found primarily among local governments in unitary systems, though as we shall see, some troubled large federations like Brazil have recently been pondering the Hamiltonian solution: attempting to implement sweeping new legislation aimed at enhancing central control over subnational spending and borrowing.

A very different path to fiscal discipline is found in the upper left-hand cell of Figure 4.3. Here, the central government limits its cofinancing obligations and allows local governments to borrow, leaving the enforcement of fiscal discipline up to self-interested voters and creditors. Subnational governments are essentially miniature sovereigns in the eyes of voters and creditors. Although Hamilton was advocating a strengthened fiscal role for the *central* government in the quote that introduced this chapter, in the upper left-hand cell of Figure 4.3 the lower-level governments themselves live up to Hamilton 's dictum: The independent creation of debt is accompanied by independent taxation. Long-term deficits are largest in the upper right-hand corner of Figure 4.3, where high vertical fiscal imbalance and wide-ranging subnational borrowing autonomy coexist. This combination – let us call it "semisovereignty" – entails that when subnational governments issue debt, the center presides over the "means of extinguishment." It is found most frequently (but not exclusively) among constituent units in federations.

Thus, formal federations demonstrate most clearly the promise and perils of decentralization. The stakes of decentralization appear to be higher in these systems. The wide-ranging subnational autonomy required for optimistic theories of decentralization is most present in federations, yet the danger of moving to the later stages of the bailout game is most pronounced in these systems as well. For this reason, the remainder of the book focuses primarily on the analysis of formal federations. The next chapter introduces and analyzes partisanship – an important variable omitted from this chapter's analysis. The following chapters use case studies and disaggregated data within countries to shave away some of the blunt edges cut by the analysis of aggregate cross-country data.

5

Disease or Cure?

POLITICAL PARTIES AND FISCAL DISCIPLINE

Party-spirit is an inseparable appendage of human nature. It grows naturally out of the rival passions of Men, and is therefore to be found in all Governments. But there is no political truth better established by experience nor more to be deprecated in itself, than that this most dangerous spirit is apt to rage with greatest violence in governments of the popular kind, and it is at once their most common and their most fatal disease. Alexander Hamilton, *The Defense No. 1*[1]

The one agency that might be expected to harmonize the policies of central and constituent governments is a political party. If the officials of both sets of governments are adherents of the same ideology or followers of the same leader or leaders, then they might be expected to pursue harmonious policies.
William Riker and Ronald Schaps "Disharmony in Federal Government"

The peril of decentralization is that along with increased responsibility for local officials – and the potential for increased local accountability – comes increased local self-seeking that can impose externalities and undermine the provision of national collective goods. The previous two chapters have explored a serious implication for fiscal discipline and macroeconomic stability: Subnational governments might manipulate the central government's cofinancing obligations and make fiscal decisions that shift their burdens onto others. This can create a cooperation problem. All of the provinces would be better off if everyone adjusted to shocks and spent within their means, but if the center cannot make a credible no-bailout commitment, it may be individually rational for some provinces to play burden-shifting strategies, even if the result is collectively suboptimal. If the center is prevented from simply compelling lower-level governments to play the cooperative strategy, as in many federations with strong provincial representation

---

[1] Published in Frisch, ed. (1985: 390).

and institutional protections, provincial governments might overfish the common revenue pool, sowing the seeds of a national debt crisis, hyperinflation, or both.

However, the story presented thus far has been too vague about the political incentives underlying this outcome. First, in cases where subnational fiscal indiscipline and central debt assumption have clear macroeconomic implications, it is not entirely clear why the central government – if its reelection prospects are based in part on the provision of national collective goods – would ever prefer bailouts. This chapter argues that, in fact, if bailouts are expected to have high macroeconomic costs, the political party of the central-level executive has much to lose by providing them. If voters hold national political parties responsible for the provision of national collective goods, legislators belonging to the executive's political party only hurt themselves by pressing for destructive bailouts.

Second, the preference ordering for subnational governments in the bailout game in Chapter 3 was based on the simple assumption that state and local officials can always maximize their expected electoral utility by shifting their fiscal burdens to others, even if this clearly imposes costs on the country as a whole. Yet once again, a national system of political parties can tilt incentives away from bailouts. If voters use national party labels to punish politicians across all levels of government for poor macroeconomic performance, governors or first ministers at the provincial level who share the partisan affiliation of the central executive will face disincentives to seek destructive bailouts.

Alexander Hamilton, like James Madison and many of his contemporaries, viewed political parties as sources of dangerous factionalism standing in the way of the public interest. However, this chapter proposes the opposite argument. Rather than undermining cooperation, political parties encourage politicians to work together in the pursuit of political power. In the context of federalism, parties can provide incentives and tools that help resolve intergovernmental cooperation problems. The arguments presented in this chapter attempt to clarify a theme with a long pedigree in political science. Riker and Schaps (1957) argue that federal-state partisan "disharmony" (control of the states by the federal opposition party) is associated with lower levels of intergovernmental cooperation. More recently, Dillinger and Webb (1999), Garman, Haggard, and Willis (2001), and Filippov, Ordeshook, and Shvetsova (2004) argue that if national party leaders have substantial capacity to discipline co-partisans at other levels of government, it is easier for the central government to implement a coherent, unified policy agenda that transcends jurisdictional divisions. Thus, strong, disciplined political parties that compete in all of the states can be a solution to underlying collective-goods problems in federations. National party leaders with incentives to respond to a nationwide constituency have "encompassing" interests in national collective goods like price stability and fiscal restraint.

To be sure, partisan coalition building and electioneering can also create incentives to use public resources inefficiently. Yet the key argument of this chapter is that under the right conditions an integrated national system of political parties linking the national executive and legislature with subnational governments can alter the incentives of the bailout game in a way that limits its macroeconomic damage. The first section adds detail to the bailout game from Chapter 3 by putting the emphasis firmly on electoral incentives. The second section examines partisanship, electoral incentives, and relations between the national legislature and executive. The third section explains the role of national political parties in creating "electoral externalities" that shape the incentives of subnational officials. The next section tests the resulting hypotheses with a cross-national dataset of federations. The penultimate section helps set up the more refined analysis undertaken in the case studies that follow by addressing alternative measures of the chapter's key concepts, and the final section concludes.

I. Bailouts and Political Incentives

Chapter 3 considered the bailout game played between the central government and only one province, though in practice the center plays the game simultaneously with several provinces. The crux of the bailout game is a moment when some province or group of provinces faces a fiscal disaster that will carry severe consequences for their voters. Chapter 4 argued that when the center is heavily responsible for funding the expenditures in these localities, it cannot escape the political pain associated with firing public employees and cutting local programs. Thus, the center must weigh the electoral value of maintaining a steady flow of local public goods in the affected localities versus the longer-term political advantages of avoiding bailouts. Subnational governments are rewarded or punished for the provision of local collective goods, while in transfer-dependent systems the center is held responsible for both national collective goods and local expenditures. This allows subnational governments to manipulate the center in attempts to obtain a greater share of a fixed pool of transfers – a scenario that will be referred to as "zero-sum" or "redistributive" bailouts. Or worse, because provincial governments do not experience the political pain associated with underprovision of national collective goods like macroeconomic stability, subnational governments might attempt to extract "negative-sum" bailouts that go beyond interprovincial redistribution of fiscal burdens, creating adverse collective consequences like excessive inflation, taxation, or debt at the central level. The key argument of this chapter is that an integrated national political party does not necessarily reduce incentives for subnational governments to seek zero-sum bailouts or enhance the credibility of the center's commitment to avoid them, but it can reduce incentives for subnational governments to seek negative-sum bailouts.

Zero-Sum Bailouts

Bailouts need not have collective consequences. Provinces might extract bailouts that can be funded without raising national taxes, printing money, or undermining macroeconomic stability. The allocation of transfers would merely increase for some provinces at the expense of others. Thus, bailout expectations magnify the usual allocative distortions of distributive politics in democracies. For the moment, let us conceive of the center as merely a president elected from a single nationwide constituency in a federation with three equally sized provinces. Imagine that the president has the support of large majorities in two provinces but little support in the third. If such a president has a clear path to reelection through the two supportive provinces and voters reward the central executive for local expenditures, she will be tempted to favor these provinces in the distribution of expenditure projects. Moreover, in the event of a subnational debt crisis, her no-bailout commitment would be less credible in the politically friendly provinces. She cannot commit *ex ante* to let her supporters suffer breakdowns in local public services in the future if the costs of bailouts can be shifted onto her geographically concentrated political enemies. Alternatively, consider a president elected through a system like the U.S. Electoral College, where each province is a winner-take-all district. If the president expects to win one province by a large margin and lose another by a similar margin while the outcome of the third is unpredictable, her no-bailout commitment is least credible in the "swing" province that will determine the next election. Up to a point, the president can shift resources from the two noncompetitive provinces to the swing province.

Disease or Cure?

Even with very simple assumptions about the political incentives of the center, these examples make it clear that even a minority of provinces might harbor rational bailout expectations. Depending on the precise institutional arrangement and political-geographic scenario, it can be politically rational for the executive to bail out anywhere from 1 to $n-1$ of the provinces at the expense of the other(s). The scenarios multiply when legislative bargaining and fiscal externalities are introduced. In order to promulgate a legislative agenda, the national executive must often forge a legislative majority. In federations, it is usually necessary to obtain a majority in two chambers, at least one of which is malapportioned and composed of representatives of the provinces. Prospective members of a president's legislative coalition might threaten to withhold needed votes on unrelated legislative items in order to extract bailouts. Though the largest states might be able to extract redistributive bailouts because of macroeconomic externalities, small states – if they are overrepresented in the legislature and relatively inexpensive to bail out – might be especially well positioned to extract bailouts through vote trading.

In short, expectations about redistributive bailouts, and hence fiscal behavior, should vary across subnational governments in predictable ways within each country, but hypotheses must be tailored to the specific mix of institutional incentives in each country and time period – a task taken up in the case studies in later chapters.

Negative-Sum Bailouts

The bailout game is interesting because it often implies collective costs for the country as a whole. Whether a large externality-induced bailout of the capital city or a sweeping debt assumption for all provinces, bailouts often cannot be funded by shifting burdens from one province to another. The central government must resort to increased taxes, borrowing, or calling upon the central bank to provide accommodating monetary policy, meaning that the costs of bailouts will eventually be borne in part even by the citizens of the recipient provinces in the form of higher taxes or inflation. The problem may start, as in the United States in the mid nineteenth century, with a minority of provinces attempting to extract purely redistributive bailouts. Their challenge, of course, is to convince the fiscally responsible states to vote for bailouts in the legislature. As in the early American case, a common strategy is to attempt to assemble a broader bailout coalition by crafting a legislative package that would bestow fiscal benefits on a larger group of states. A similar move will be discussed in the Brazilian case below. Such bailout packages, aside from undermining perceptions of the center's resolve for future plays of the game, squeeze the finances of the center.

Thus, a key question has not been fully answered: If the central executive is punished and rewarded in part for the provision of national collective goods, why would it choose to issue collectively suboptimal bailouts? Part of the answer has to do with time horizons: The political costs of subnational defaults might be imminent with an election looming, while the costs of increased federal debt or inflation will accrue more slowly. Yet this answer is incomplete. Eventually, the collective costs of repeated bailouts would be clear to voters – even those in the recipient provinces – and the president or prime minister would be the most likely political victim of anger over increased federal taxes or inflation.

The rest of this chapter argues that accountability for national collective goods, which can only flow through the national executive and its affiliates, can indeed put a ceiling on the collective macroeconomic costs of negative-sum bailouts, but only under the right political conditions. The next two sections explore these conditions, first among legislators and then among subnational executives.

II. Parties and Legislatures

One of the advantages of federalism emphasized by Madison also applies to the division of powers between the executive and legislature: Dividing sovereignty among competing politicians helps protect liberty and prevent abuse of authority. A key disadvantage emphasized by Hamilton, however, is the increased difficulty of holding government accountable for national collective goods. More to the point, if the executive, members of parliament, and senators at two levels of government can all blame one another for increasing debt, borrowing costs, and inflation, it is difficult for voters to use elections to provide politicians with incentives for fiscal restraint. Moreover, individual legislators can claim credit for local collective goods in their jurisdictions without paying the political costs of higher taxes or increased national debt.

A national system of political parties provides a way around these problems. In assessing credit and blame for collective goods, the central chief executive (president or prime minister) provides a natural focal point. Collective responsibility can be attained if voters use a simple rule of thumb: Focus retrospectively on the party label of the federal executive to reward and punish politicians in national legislative as well as subnational elections for the provision of national collective goods. When voters do this, the reelection chances of legislators and subnational politicians are driven in part by the value of the national party label. In this way, co-partisans of the national executive can hurt their own reelection chances by taking actions – like pushing for negative-sum bailouts in the legislature – that reduce the value of the party label by undermining national collective goods.

If bailouts will clearly have collective costs rather than mere redistributive effects, it follows that the no-bailout commitment of the central government is most credible when the national legislature is dominated by the chief executive's co-partisans. The chief executive would not be able to shift blame for tax increases or inflation to legislators belonging to opposition parties. Furthermore, by pushing an agenda that undermines national collective goods, co-partisan legislators would be undermining the value of the party label that sustains them. Yet it is not clear that individual legislators in the majority party – especially in the upper chamber that directly represents the states – would always place the value of the party label above the value of a bailout. The party label is subject to a classic free-rider problem – each legislator hopes to free-ride on the good behavior of the other. If the macroeconomic costs of the bailout are not catastrophic, individual legislators can convince themselves that their province is especially deserving of a bailout while their co-partisans should adjust alone.

Thus, co-partisanship between the legislature and executive is most likely to enhance the central government's credibility when the chief executive and/or party leaders – who have the strongest incentives to avoid destructive bailouts – have additional tools with which to extract compliance from legislators. Examples of such tools include control over nominations, party lists, committee assignments, endorsements, and the allocation of campaign funds. Unfortunately, these are difficult to measure in a comparable way across countries for the cross-national analysis below, but they will be addressed in the case studies in later chapters.

III. Electoral Externalities

A similar logic extends to subnational governments themselves. The assumption employed thus far – that subnational politicians are rewarded purely for providing local public expenditures – is too simple. If voters use the party label of the national executive to retrospectively reward or punish provincial politicians for the provision of national collective goods,

provincial co-partisans of the executive face incentives not to position themselves for bailouts that will clearly have collective macroeconomic consequences. Provincial officials face incentives to cooperate with the center
because their electoral fates are determined in good part by the fates of their
co-partisans at the federal level. In other words, in some countries provincial officials face incentives to internalize fiscal externalities if they face
corresponding electoral externalities. Like national legislators, the reelection chances of subnational politicians are often determined not only by
what they promise and provide in their localities, but also by the value of
their party labels. The self-interested activities of a prominent politician at
one level produce positive or negative externalities that affect the reelection
chances of politicians with the same party label competing at the other level.
In some federal systems, the value of this label may be determined partially
or almost completely by evaluations of the federal incumbent. In other
words, voters may view state elections as something like referenda on the
performance of the governing party or coalition at the central level. In fact,
it may be a rational information-economizing strategy on the part of voters
to do so. Given the complexity of most intergovernmental fiscal systems,
it is difficult for voters to follow the flow of revenue and accountability.
Especially when revenue collection is largely centralized, voters may econ-
omize on information by rewarding and punishing the party of the federal
executive at all levels of government.

In the presence of electoral externalities, the expected electoral utility
of pressing for bailouts declines relative to that of quick adjustment and
balanced budgets for the copartisans of the central executive. This is only
true, however, if bailouts are expected to create collective macroeconomic
costs that damage the party label. In fact, if there are no expected macroeconomic costs, co-partisans of the central executive might view the center's
commitment as *less* credible than provinces controlled by the opposition.
As described above, the central executive might need the support of voters
in stronghold provinces for reelection and thus be unable to commit to
allow fiscal pain in the event of a crisis. Moreover, the center's decisions
affect the value of the party label in the provinces, making this credibility
effect even stronger when the provincial executive is a co-partisan of the
center. If much of the blame for firing teachers and police officers will fall
upon the provincial co-partisan, this does damage to the party label and
bolsters the opposition. Likewise, depending on the specifics of institutions
and political geography in the country, the center's no-bailout commitment to provinces controlled by the opposition is more credible, because

it does not want to provide bailouts if political credit for uninterrupted service provision accrues primarily to the provincial government. Thus, provincial co-partisans of the center are in a better position to manipulate it by avoiding adjustment and extracting redistributive bailouts. A study by Khemani (2003) claims that Indian states controlled by the national ruling party are able to extract extra resources from Delhi according to this logic.

There is no clear universal hypothesis about partisanship, bailout expectations, and fiscal behavior across provinces within countries, however. The relationship depends upon the specific institutional incentives of the country and, above all, upon whether actors believe that bailouts will be redistributive or negative-sum. If all actors believe that unplanned federal assistance will be purely redistributive, incentives for fiscal discipline should be weaker among the central executive's provincial co-partisans because they have greater bailout expectations. Yet if bailouts are expected to carry sufficient macroeconomic costs, the decreased value of the party label outweighs the local electoral benefits of bailouts for co-partisan provinces, leading to the opposite empirical prediction. This hypothesis is consistent with a study by Jones, Sanguinetti, and Tommasi (2000) showing that deficits are significantly lower among the Argentine provinces whose governors are controlled by the party of the president.

This logic also invites a further refinement of the too-big-to-fail hypothesis introduced in Chapter 3. Perhaps a mammoth jurisdiction – a key industrial center whose fiscal behavior carries externalities for the entire country – can hope to avoid adjustment and extract increased redistributive transfers from the periphery. But if the bailouts merely put upward pressure on national taxes, interest rates, or inflation, this strategy quickly becomes self-defeating – particularly if the province's governor shares the party affiliation of the federal executive and hence cannot hope to shift the political blame. Again, if electoral externalities are strong and subnational decisions carry sufficiently clear and immediate implications for national collective goods, provincial officials face incentives to internalize the externalities produced by their decisions.

These hypotheses are best addressed by analyzing disaggregate data within countries, but one clear hypothesis emerges that can be tested with aggregate cross-national data. While redistributive bailouts have no clear effect on aggregate fiscal discipline, negative-sum bailouts do, and the likelihood of this type of bailout should be negatively correlated with the share of provinces controlled by the party of the federal chief executive. If bailouts will have collective costs, electoral externalities and co-partisanship increase the expected electoral utility for provincial governments of the "early-adjust" outcome of the game relative to the other outcomes, all of which put upward pressure on either central or subnational deficits. Thus, a greater number of provinces sharing the party label of the central executive decreases the likelihood of provincial defaults, delayed adjustments, or federal bailouts.

The central government is in a precarious position when the party of the federal executive controls none of the provinces. Provincial governors are positioned to avoid the electoral implications of negative-sum bailouts because the central executive is held responsible for national collective goods. Yet when the center is a major player in funding local services, governors may also be able to shift blame for interrupted services to the center in the case of default. The central government is in a much different position when its co-partisans control the provinces, knowing that if co-partisan governors successfully extract negative-sum bailouts, the reelection chances of incumbents at both levels go down.

This hypothesis has the virtue that it is amenable to cross-national testing, but as with the hypothesis about legislative partisanship, it assumes away the intraparty free-rider problem. Even if all provinces are co-partisans, some governors might argue – and perhaps even believe – that their provinces should receive special consideration due to unique circumstances. Thus, co-partisanship is most likely to limit the damage of the bailout game when party leaders have tools like control of appointments, primaries, provincial party lists, campaign funds, and other ways of shaping the career advancement of provincial politicians. In many countries with strong electoral externalities, provincial chief executives are auditioning for careers in federal-level politics. This may provide especially strong incentives for provincial politicians to avoid triggering bailouts with collective macroeconomic implications. Though systematic cross-national data on these factors might be possible to collect in the future, here they are addressed exclusively in the case studies.

IV. Empirical Analysis

Three variables have been created to correspond to the arguments above for fourteen federations from 1978 to 1996: the shares of seats controlled by the chief executive's party in the lower and upper chamber at the federal level, as well as the share of provinces in which the chief executive shares the partisan affiliation of the central chief executive.[2] In order to examine the largest possible number of federations, this chapter goes beyond the constraints of the *GFS* and uses country sources to supplement the data on intergovernmental transfers and subnational fiscal outcomes presented in the previous chapter.[3] Thus, the group of federations examined here is slightly larger than the group examined there – it includes Malaysia, Venezuela, Pakistan, and Nigeria[4] – though for the sake of consistency the same analysis is also conducted on the smaller group of federations as well. The concepts developed in this chapter need not apply only to federations. Yet the collection of time series partisanship data for that group of countries is virtually impossible – France alone has thousands of local governments. Thus, the remainder of this chapter focuses on fourteen federations primarily because data collection is feasible, but also because Chapter 4 revealed federations to be the most interesting. In contrast to unitary systems, the bailout game is usually not precluded by strict controls over subnational borrowing.

This analysis of federations also allows for a robustness check of some key results from the previous chapter. The dataset used in this chapter contains a smaller number of countries but a larger time series, and all of the fiscal data have been checked against country sources, reducing the possibility of measurement error. The dependent variable indicated in the hypotheses

---

[2] These data were collected as part of a joint project with Erik Wibbels. See Rodden and Wibbels (2002). Coalition governments at the center complicate the collection of these data for Switzerland, Brazil, and Austria. In fact, we are unable to calculate a sensible measure for Switzerland, where the federal executive is a collegial body that represents (by convention) all of the major parties. In Brazil, where the party system is highly fractionalized, national executives must rely on often unstable legislative coalitions. It is plausible that members of such coalitions would be able to expect discipline from their co-partisans at the state level in a manner consistent with the theoretical propositions outlined above. Nevertheless, the variable used in the regressions counts only those states run by the same party as the chief executive. We have also constructed a variable that codes states controlled by junior members of the federal coalition as controlled by the center. This variable is only different for a small number of years in Brazil and Austria and does not affect the results reported below. In the case of *subnational* coalition governments (prevalent in Austria, Germany, and India), we code based on the senior member of the coalition that occupies the office of chief minister, prime minister, president, etc.

[3] Disaggregate country sources were consulted for fiscal data from each of the federations. Happily, for most federations covered by the *GFS*, the *GFS* measure of intergovernmental grants corresponds with the data obtained from country sources. When discrepancies were encountered due to IMF classifications of revenue sharing (see the previous chapter), country sources were used. Because partisan data were only collected at the provincial level, this dataset does not include local and municipal governments.

[4] These countries were not included in the analysis of the previous chapter because some key control variables used in the analysis of cross-section averages were unavailable.

above is the combined central-provincial surplus as a share of combined expenditures. Similar to the previous chapter, a measure of provincial revenue as a share of combined central-provincial revenue captures the effect of fiscal decentralization, and a variable measuring grants as a share of subnational revenue captures the effect of having more of this revenue tilted toward grants. The model also includes the same control variables as the cross-section time series models in the previous chapter and a matrix of country dummies:

$$
\begin{aligned}
Surplus/Expenditure_{it} = {} & \beta_0 + \beta_1 Surplus/Expenditure_{it-1} \\
& + \beta_2 Legislative\ Co\text{-}partisanship + \beta_3 Vertical\ co\text{-}partisanship_{it} \\
& + \beta_4 Decentralization_{it} + \beta_5 Vertical\ Fiscal\ Imbalance_{it} \\
& + \sum \beta_k Controls_{it} + \sum \beta_d Country\ dummies + \varepsilon
\end{aligned}
\quad (5.1)
$$

Because the dataset contains a relatively large number of year observations and a smaller number of countries, OLS with panel-corrected standard errors is on balance preferable to GMM and other techniques. The model presented in Table 5.1 includes a lagged dependent variable, though several alternative estimation techniques yield similar results.

First of all, the results presented in Table 5.1 do not include the executive-legislative co-partisanship variable for the lower chamber because it never approached statistical significance in any estimation. However, the Senate partisanship variable performs very well.[5] This is not surprising, given that bailout demands are likely to focus on the upper chamber, where the interests of the provinces are most directly represented. The coefficient is highly significant regardless of estimation technique. Substantively, moving from five to six out of ten senators sharing the chief executive's party label is associated with an increase in aggregate fiscal balance of around 2 percent of expenditures.[6]

Next, the vertical co-partisanship variable also performs quite well, and the result is consistent with the hypothesis above. Again, the coefficient is highly significant no matter which estimation technique is used. Substantively, moving from five to six out of ten provinces where the

---

[5] Note that the results presented in Table 5.1 only include twelve countries because the Senate variable is inappropriate for Pakistan and Canada. The coefficients and standard errors for all other variables are very similar if this variable is dropped and Pakistan and Canada are included.

[6] A similar result is obtained when senators are coded as co-partisans if they are members of the executive's wider legislative coalition – a distinction that is only relevant in Austria and Brazil.

Table 5.1. *Estimates of combined central-provincial surplus: sample of 12 federations, 1978–1996*

	Model 5.1	
Dependent variable		
Total surplus/expenditure		
Independent variables		
Total surplus/expenditure$_{t-1}$	0.34	$(0.09)^{***}$
Senate co-partisanship	0.19	$(0.05)^{***}$
Vertical co-partisanship	0.08	$(0.03)^{***}$
Grants/provincial revenue	−0.23	$(0.13)^{**}$
Provincial revenue/total	0.94	$(0.17)^{***}$
Log population	0.51	$(0.13)^{***}$
Log GDP per capita	−0.09	(0.07)
Dependency ratio	0.15	(0.16)
Population density	0.0002	(0.0006)
Index of political cohesion	0.01	(0.01)
Constant	−11.49	(2.78)
Observations	177	
Number of groups	12	
R^2	0.76	

Panel-corrected standard errors in parentheses
* significant at 10%; ** significant at 5%; *** significant at 1%
Fixed-effects model, unit effects not reported

executive shares the party label of the federal executive improves overall fiscal balance by close to 1 percent of aggregate expenditure.[7]

---

[7] The results for the other fiscal variables are also quite interesting. In this sample of federations, other things equal, revenue decentralization has a strong positive effect on overall fiscal balance. When vertical fiscal imbalance and partisanship are held constant, the decentralization of expenditure authority to states and provinces within federations appears not to endanger overall fiscal balance. Once again, the danger appears to lie with decentralization that is driven by intergovernmental transfers rather than local revenue mobilization. Increasing transfer dependence is associated with larger aggregate deficits. The focus of this chapter is partisanship and Model 5.1 is intentionally quite simple, but this sample of federations can also be used to bolster the findings of the previous chapter. For instance, the borrowing autonomy index is not included in Model 5.1 because it was unavailable for some cases and does not vary over time. However, using the subsample for which the index is available, an interactive specification reveals that, consistent with the findings in Chapter 4, the negative coefficient for vertical fiscal imbalance is significantly larger at higher levels of borrowing autonomy. Additionally, Rodden and Wibbels (2002) show that the effect of fiscal decentralization is contingent upon transfer dependence. That is, decentralization

A variety of alternative estimations are worthy of discussion. First of all, the results are quite similar if other techniques for dealing with cross-section time series data are used. Second, the results are quite similar if the federations with fewer democratic credentials – Malaysia, Nigeria, Pakistan, and Venezuela – are dropped from the analysis. An additional concern is that the simple vertical co-partisanship rate is a poor measure in countries with frequent occurrence of divided government at the state level during the period under analysis – in particular the United States, Brazil, and Argentina – or countries with frequent occurrence of state-level coalition government – Austria, Germany, and India. Remarkably, the coefficient is still highly significant if this entire group of countries is dropped, though it is much larger (.23).

V. A Closer Look at Measurement

Among federations, aggregate deficits are smaller when the party of the central executive controls a larger share of the upper legislative chamber and is affiliated with a larger share of provinces. While consistent with the arguments above, these rather blunt results invite further analysis using more refined measurements. Above all, it must be stressed that although intimately related, vertical co-partisanship and electoral externalities are distinct concepts. The argument linking vertical co-partisanship and fiscal discipline relies on the notion that the electoral fates of provincial officials are driven in part by voters' evaluations of their national-level co-partisans. Later chapters will delve further into the ways in which partisan and electoral structures shape incentives, but before exchanging blunt cross-national analysis for detailed case studies, it is necessary to get a better sense of how to characterize co-partisanship and electoral externalities across countries and over time.

In order to do this, it is useful to compare federations that are similar in many respects other than the relationship between federal and provincial elections and parties. Figure 5.1 traces co-partisanship over time in three parliamentary federations since the 1940s: Germany, Australia, and Canada.[8]

that is funded by transfers is associated with declining fiscal balance, while decentralization funded by local taxation is associated with improving overall fiscal balance. In addition, Rodden and Wibbels (2002) also include several additional control variables, discuss additional robustness checks, and extend the analysis to inflation.

[8] The index is calculated from data taken from Sharman (1994); Feigert (1989); *Europa World Yearbook*, various years; and http://www.jhu.edu/~aicgsdoc/wahlen.

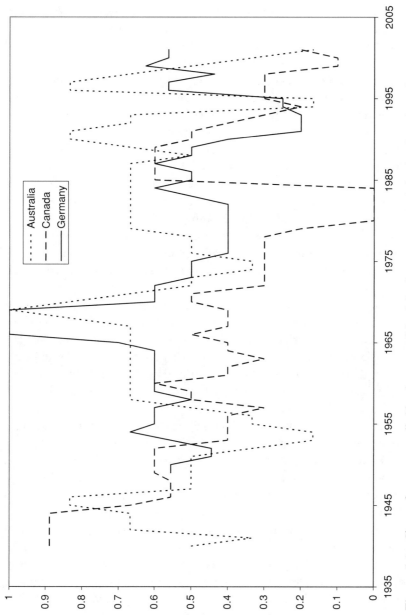

Figure 5.1. Share of states controlled by the party of the federal government in Australia, Canada, and Germany.

If one expects co-partisanship or vertical electoral externalities to affect incentives, one presupposes some amount of horizontal party discipline at both levels. If parties simply do not matter for reelection, party labels will do little to facilitate intergovernmental cooperation. The concepts of vertical co-partisanship and electoral externalities, however, are analytically distinct from the usual notion of party discipline in legislatures; a federal system might have highly disciplined political parties at both levels of government but lack vertical electoral externalities. That is, the electoral fates of individual politicians may be linked by party labels at each level, but they may not be linked across levels. This distinction forms part of the logic for the selection of cases for closer analysis. Australia, Canada, and Germany are comparable cases here because they have parliamentary systems with strong party discipline at both the federal and state levels, and the strength of the party label is an important determinate of any incumbent's electoral success. Australia and Canada are an especially intriguing comparison, given their relatively similar experiences with British colonialism and institutions.

Because of the small number of states in each country, the index of co-partisanship swings widely from year to year. Both Australia and Germany experienced brief periods of what Riker would refer to as partisan harmony in the late 1960s and 1970 and Australia also in the mid-1940s and early 1990s, though the index in both countries falls as low as 20 percent. The Liberals in Canada enjoyed strong control of Ottawa and the provinces in the early 1940s, but since 1960 the governing party rarely has controlled more than half the provinces. Remarkably, the Liberals controlled no provinces while in power in Ottawa in the early 1980s.

On average since World War II, the party in power in Canberra has controlled 57 percent of the states, while the governing party in Bonn has controlled 54 percent, and for Ottawa the figure is 36 percent. Thus, in the long run, rates of co-partisanship are lower in Canada than in Australia or Germany and have fallen somewhat in recent decades in Germany and dramatically in Canada.

This index should not be mistaken, however, for a measure of electoral externalities. Because federal and state elections are generally not held simultaneously in these countries, the federal government might lose votes in state elections because of a "midterm-punishment" phenomenon. Voters often express dissatisfaction with the federal executive in midterm elections by punishing its co-partisans in other branches of government.

This phenomenon would put temporary downward pressure on the co-partisanship rate displayed in Figure 5.1, even though it actually demonstrates the *strength* of vertical partisan externalities.

A measure of vertical electoral externalities consistent with the intuition above would quantify the extent to which the vote shares of provincial-level politicians are shaped by those of their partisan colleagues at the federal level. A simple technique is to estimate a model of provincial vote share for the most successful party in each federation during the postwar period as follows:[9]

$$
\begin{aligned}
State\text{-}level\ vote\ share_{it} &= \beta_0 + \beta_1 Corresponding\ federal\text{-}level\ vote\ share_{it} \\
&\quad \text{X } pre\text{-}1970\ dummy + \beta_2 Corresponding\ federal\text{-}level\ vote\ share_{it} \\
&\quad \text{X } post\text{-}1969\ dummy + \beta_3\ State\text{-}level\ vote\ share_{it-1} \\
&\quad + \sum \beta_d State\ dummies + \varepsilon
\end{aligned}
\tag{5.2}
$$

The dependent variable is the party's share of the vote in province i in election t. The independent variable of interest is the party's aggregate provincial-level vote share in the corresponding federal election.[10] In order to compare provincial and federal voting trends and deal with serial correlation, the party's aggregate vote share in the preceding state election is also included. In order to control for long-term intrastate differences in support and state-specific determinates of fluctuations, a panel of state dummies is included. Moreover, because Figure 5.1 suggests a dip in rates of co-partisanship since 1970, it is useful to divide the period roughly in half and interact the federal vote share with dummy variables for the periods up

---

[9] The AustralianLabor Party (ALP), the Canadian Liberals, and the German "Union parties" (the Christian Social Union in Bavaria and the Christian Democratic Union in the other Länder).

[10] With occasional exceptions in Germany, state-level elections are not conducted on the same dates as federal elections. The simplest pairing technique would be to use the immediately preceding federal election, but this would pair up, for instance, a federal election that was held three years before rather than one held a few days after the state election. Thus "corresponding" federal elections are coded as follows: (1) use the federal election held within a twelve-month period before or after a state election; (2) if a federal election was held during both of these periods, use the preceding election; (3) if no federal election was held during either of these periods, use the most recent federal election held after the preceding state election; (4) if no federal election meets these criteria, drop the case from the dataset. (This only happens when a minority government at the state level falls quickly and a new election is held.)

Table 5.2. *Estimates of state-level vote share for major parties in three federations*

	Model 5.2 Australia (ALP)		Model 5.3 Canada (Liberals)		Model 5.4 Germany (CDU)	
Dependent variable						
State-level vote share						
Independent variables						
Federal vote share X pre 1970	0.48	(0.10)***	0.11	(0.09)	0.65	(0.14)***
Federal vote share X post 1969	0.47	(0.11)***	0.07	(0.09)	0.71	(0.16)***
Lagged state-level vote share	0.42	(0.11)***	0.59	(0.11)***	0.38	(0.09)***
Constant	4.08	(6.44)	5.58	(3.82)	−0.04	(0.06)
R-squared	0.47		0.80		0.83	
Observation	91		125		105	
Number of states	6		10		10	
Years	1964–1992		1947–1993		1954–1994	

Panel-corrected standard errors in parentheses
*** significant at 1%
Estimation: OLS with panel-corrected standard errors, fixed effects
Coefficients for state dummies not shown

to and after 1970. The estimation technique is OLS with panel-corrected standard errors, and the results are presented in Table 5.2.[11]

While the coefficients for the lagged state election variables are rather similar in each of the three federations, the coefficients for the federal election variable point to an important difference between Canada and the other two federations. For the German Christian Democratic Union (CDU) and the Australian Labor Party (ALP), the vote share at the federal level has been a good predictor of vote share at the state level throughout the postwar period, and the federal vote share coefficient is larger than that for the lagged state-level vote share. These highly significant results provide strong evidence of a tight link between federal and state elections.

[11] Australian data were kindly provided by Campbell Sharman. Note that no data are included for Western Australia (WA) until 1955 because the ALP did not compete in WA until that year. The results from Canadian elections prior to and including 1988 were collected from Frank Feigert, *Canada Votes, 1935–1980* (Durham, NC: Duke University Press, 1989). Results for all federal and provincial elections held after 1988 were provided by John Wilson at the University of Waterloo. German data were downloaded from the *Statistisches Bundesamt* (http://www.statistik-bund.de). Because the low number of federal elections held since unification, I report data only from the "old" Länder.

In Canada, on the other hand, the Liberal vote at the federal level does not help predict the Liberal vote at the provincial level.[12]

Thus, over long periods of time the co-partisanship index and the electoral externality coefficients tell relatively similar stories. The worlds of federal and state electoral politics are highly intertwined in Germany and Australia but quite distinct in Canada. Chapter 9, which discusses the reform of intergovernmental systems, will return to these three cases, relate these results to the existing literature in each country, and show that these differences have important implications for the way federalism works in each country. Moreover, Chapter 7 will take a closer look at the role of Germany's strong electoral externalities in limiting the macroeconomic damage of the bailout game.

It is useful to contrast these relatively similar parliamentary countries in order to hold constant such factors as legislative coalition building and possible differences in the roles played by political parties in presidential systems. Further reasons for this case selection will become apparent in later chapters. Yet the arguments established in this chapter should also provide insights into a much broader group of federations. Chapter 8 argues that, on the whole, Brazilian parties created weak incentives for state-level politicians to consider the collectively destructive implications of their fiscal decisions, and Chapter 9 examines the role of partisan externalities in facilitating reform of the intergovernmental system.

VI. Conclusion

This chapter has shown that in federations, overall fiscal deficits are lower at times and in countries where larger shares of both senators and provincial chief executives share the party label of the federal chief executive. In a separate study using the same dataset, Rodden and Wibbels (2002) find a striking negative relationship between vertical co-partisanship and inflation. The causal logic behind these results lies in the electoral incentives that drive the bailout game in Chapter 3. First, co-partisan senators are

---

[12] Similar results can be obtained using a variety of different empirical approaches. For instance, the units of analysis can be state-level incumbents rather than parties, but this rules out even the possibility of significant results in Canada since provincial incumbent parties sometimes do not field candidates in federal elections. The key independent variable can also be coded as a moving average of federal election results. Additionally, similar results can be obtained using changes rather than levels, generalized least squares, and the generalized method of moments.

less likely to push for bailouts that will have collective costs if by doing so they stand to devalue the party label and thereby hurt their own reelection chances. As a result, when the Senate is dominated by the governing party, provincial politicians revise upward their assessments of the central government's resolve and make fiscal decisions accordingly. Second, if their electoral prospects are shaped by voters' assessments of the central executive's ability to provide nationwide collective goods, co-partisan governors and first ministers at the provincial level have incentives to avoid positioning themselves for bailouts that will impose collective costs. As a result, high rates of vertical co-partisanship make large, destructive bailouts incompatible with politicians' incentives and thus limit the macroeconomic damage that can result from the bailout game.

These arguments are consistent with the empirical findings, but considerable refinement is needed. Partisan ties only reduce the utility of pushing for bailouts if the collective costs of the bailouts are clearly understood and are expected to have electoral consequences. Sometimes, the collective costs of bailouts only become apparent over time, and in the short run individual co-partisan senators and governors can hope that bailouts will allow them to tilt resources their way in an ongoing game of geographic redistribution. As long as politicians believe bailouts can be redistributive and collective electoral punishment can be avoided, the utility of bailouts will not be altered for co-partisans of the central executive. Moreover, the center's no-bailout commitment to them will be less credible because the central executive would be unable to escape the electoral costs associated with local defaults. Thus, as long as provincial politicians believe they can get away with redistributive bailouts, incentives for fiscal discipline are weaker among co-partisans of the center. On the other hand, when bailouts are clearly negative-sum, the center's co-partisans face stronger incentives to spend within their means and adjust to shocks.

While these considerations do not affect the logic underpinning the cross-national results, they encourage a careful approach to the case studies that follow. When the redistributive game dominates, co-partisans of the center are expected to extract extra resources from the center by running larger deficits. Yet when the macroeconomic costs of bailouts are well known and begin to translate into electoral costs for the federal chief executive, its co-partisans face stronger incentives to play cooperative strategies. More generally, this chapter makes it clear that hypotheses about cross-province differences in fiscal behavior must be carefully tailored to each institutional setting. In particular, this chapter casts doubt on a simple version of the too-big-to-fail hypothesis. A large externality-producing province may correctly infer that the center's no-bailout commitment is compromised because its default would impose collective costs; but in the presence of electoral externalities, those costs provide a good reason *not* to push for bailouts. When electoral externalities are strong and voters reward and punish the central executive for nationwide collective goods, leaders of a large dominant jurisdiction – if linked in the minds of voters with the central executive – only hurt themselves by pushing for destructive bailouts. Leaders of large jurisdictions are most likely to use their size to their advantage if they feel confident that they will avoid the collective costs. The following chapters argue that this was clearly the case in Brazil in the 1990s but has not been the case in postwar Germany.

Another important factor raised in this chapter but best addressed with case studies is the internal organization of political parties – for example, the tools available to national party leaders to shape incentives of lower-level officials as well as patterns of intraparty career movement. In attempting to prevent its co-partisans from playing burden-shifting strategies, the central executive faces a collective-action dilemma that is best resolved when it controls resources that are valuable to subnational officials. The next chapters turn attention to these more subtle arguments using case studies.

6

An Approach to Comparative Case Studies

Sacrificing subtlety for breadth, the last two chapters made broad arguments about fiscal and political structures and supported them with aggregate cross-national data. This approach is advantageous above all because it provides a context to guide the selection of countries for more-nuanced case studies and the raw material for more-refined arguments. Faced with an overwhelming array of countries, data, and stories but limitations on time and tractability, this chapter explains how the arguments and results above point to a clear strategy for (1) placing existing single-country studies in a comparative framework, and (2) selecting countries to analyze more carefully. At the heart of Chapter 4 was a two-by-two table depicting aggregate transfer dependence on the horizontal axis and subnational borrowing autonomy on the vertical axis. Analysis of credit ratings suggested that in countries on the right, where transfer dependence is higher, the center is more likely to be perceived as an implicit guarantor of subnational debt. Yet as long as such countries also sit near the bottom of the table, where subnational governments are unable to borrow independently, the resulting moral-hazard problem is circumvented. Indeed, the empirical model estimated long-term balanced budgets for these subordinate subnational governments.

Thus, the bailout game is most interesting in the top two quadrants of the table in which subnational governments are relatively free to borrow. Most of the occupants have a long history of federalism. Chapter 4 hypothesized that in the upper-left quadrant – home to such federations as the United States, Switzerland, and Canada, where the subnational units are funded primarily through independent taxation and borrowing takes place without federal oversight – subnational governments are miniature sovereigns, and fiscal discipline is enforced by credit markets and political competition within individual provinces. On the other hand, for countries in the upper-right quadrant – where aggregate transfer dependence and borrowing autonomy are both high – bailout expectations are commonplace among semisovereign governments and the bailout game can have its most troubling macroeconomic costs.

Existing research on the three clearest examples of subnational sovereignty – the U.S. states, Swiss cantons, and Canadian provinces – is consistent with the arguments made above about credit markets, electoral competition, and fiscal discipline. This chapter begins by briefly reviewing and reinterpreting these existing studies in light of this book's theoretical framework. However, as pointed out in Chapter 2, a problem with the prevailing literature in recent decades was a presumption that these cases are typical of decentralized federalism more generally, which led to an overly simplistic lesson that decentralization will enhance competition, accountability, and discipline elsewhere.

Thus, the most promising targets of further research are the countries occupying the upper-right quadrant, which include some of the world's largest and in recent decades most fiscally troubled countries. The key arguments about fiscal structure and political parties await further refinement and testing using disaggregated data. Moreover, some additional arguments generated in Chapter 3 were not amenable to quantitative analysis but are well suited to detailed case studies. The approach in the chapters that follow is to take up these tasks with case studies of recent decades in Germany and Brazil. The main purpose of this brief chapter – taken up in the second section – is to explain the logic and structure of this comparative case study approach.

I. Subnational Sovereignty and Fiscal Discipline

A key implication of Chapter 4 is that when all subnational governments are funded primarily with taxes and the center refrains from overseeing and regulating subnational finance, officials face disincentives to avoid or delay fiscal adjustment. Their perceived likelihood of receiving bailouts is low, and they expect electoral punishment for excessive debt. In the dataset used in this book, the three prime examples of this combination of independent subnational taxation and borrowing are the U.S. states, Swiss cantons, and Canadian provinces. A reexamination of the rich empirical literature on fiscal management among these entities in recent decades provides support for these claims about credit markets, electoral politics, and fiscal discipline.

141

Without any debt limitations imposed by the central government, the U.S. states and Swiss cantons have borrowed essentially as sovereigns and adjusted on their own to negative shocks through most of the twentieth century. The U.S. state sector has actually been in aggregate surplus through most of the past fifty years, and no state has defaulted since the Civil War. Most of the states contribute to so-called rainy-day funds during good times in order to withstand future adverse shocks that may come from recessions, unexpected increases in costs, or sudden cuts in federal grants. The states had to deal with all three of these in the late 1980s and early 1990s. Regional economic downturns, major increases in health care costs, and cuts in federal grants associated with the "new federalism" of the Reagan administration all contributed to serious fiscal challenges in all of the states, and some states ran large deficits.[1] Although some states reacted more quickly than others (Poterba 1994), all of the states were able to adjust without calling upon the central government for help, and most had returned to a relatively strong fiscal position by the middle of the 1990s. In 2002, the states experienced another serious fiscal ordeal as revenue growth fell far short of projections and states encountered rising health care and unfunded mandates in education and homeland security. Though some governors and members of the legislature called for a federal debt relief package, states did not behave as if such relief was forthcoming. Most responded with aggressive adjustment measures on both the expenditure and revenue sides.

A similar story can be told about the Swiss cantons. Aggregate canton budgets have been balanced on average through the second half of the twentieth century. Along with the central government, the cantons also faced a brief period of recession and fiscal stress during the early 1990s that led to sizable deficits and increasing debt burdens. As in the U.S. states, compensating payments from the federal government were never on the table, and the cantons adjusted on their own quite rapidly – mostly by cutting expenditures – returning to aggregate balanced cantonal budgets again by the turn of the century.

The Canadian case is somewhat more controversial. One province has defaulted in this century. After experiencing depression and drought and electing a prairie populist, antibanking government, Alberta defaulted on one-third of its bonded debt in 1936. Alberta stayed in default until 1945, when the federal government bailed out the province. The federal

---

[1] According to a study conducted by Edward Gramlich (1991), the most important factor in the state and local fiscal crisis was the rapid growth in health care costs.

government had also effectively bailed out Saskatchewan in the 1930s (Buck 1949). The bailout of Alberta was explicitly aimed at restoring Canada's creditworthiness in international markets, which had been adversely affected by the problems in Alberta (Boothe 1995). Thus, it would appear that markets did not view Alberta as a true sovereign. This impression may have been furthered by the activities of the federal government and courts that combated prairie populism by overruling or striking down much of the legislation of the government of Alberta.

Furthermore, in spite of the credit ratings presented in Chapter 4, some Canadian scholars question the sovereign-borrower status of the provinces even today. Since 1957, the Canadian fiscal system includes a federal-provincial fiscal stabilization agreement guaranteeing that any province whose revenues from certain specified sources fall below the previous year's revenues would receive a compensating stabilization payment (Perry 1997).[2] One might argue that by explicitly putting a floor under provincial revenues, the central government is essentially issuing a "letter of comfort" to creditors, assuring them that provinces will be able to service their debts.

However, much has changed in the Canadian federal system since the events of the Depression and World War II. Above all, dependence on transfers decreased and provinces gained control of the income tax. As demonstrated in Chapter 5, the Canadian party system has become increasingly decentralized and fragmented since World War II. Both politically and fiscally, the Canadian provinces are among the most independent subnational units in the world today. The Canadian provinces have weathered serious fiscal storms without any discussion of bailouts, and no defaults or ad hoc debt reduction bailouts have been provided since the Alberta affair. Kneebone and McKenzie (1999) describe painful adjustments by the Canadian provinces to growing debt burdens in the 1980s and again at the turn of the century.

In fact, in Canada as well as in the United States and Switzerland, a plausible argument can be made that the constituent units face harder budget constraints than the federal government. In each of the adjustment scenarios described above, the constituent units reacted to lasting negative shocks more quickly than did their respective federal governments. Even though each of these federations has notoriously independent central banks, the central government still might hold out hope that the central bank will

---

[2] This provision was not actually used until 1987 and has been used by several provinces during the recession of the 1990s.

eventually be forced to monetize its deficits. Sargent (1986) provides such an interpretation of the Reagan deficits, and Kneebone (1994) suggests that this was explicitly the strategy of the Canadian federal government in the 1980s.

Over years of repeat play of the bailout game, a clear separation from the money supply, a strong tax–benefit link, and a relatively disengaged and explicitly limited central government provided strong signals to creditors and especially voters that the bailout probability is very low. An influential study of bond yields across the U.S. states demonstrates that, other things equal, more highly indebted states pay higher interest rates on similar bonds, with interest rate penalties imposed gradually at low levels of debt but eventually rising in a steep, nonlinear way at higher levels (Bayoumi et al. 1995). Empirical research also suggests that the local electorate plays an important role in monitoring and disciplining the fiscal decisions of the constituent units. Peltzman (1992) asserts that voters in the U.S. states are fiscal conservatives in that incumbent governors who preside over expansions in state expenditures lose votes. A study by Lowry, Alt, and Ferree (1998) shows that the incumbent governor's party is punished in legislative elections for failure to maintain fiscal balance. Descriptive accounts assert that Canadian voters punish provincial administrations that preside over large increases in budget deficits and debt burdens (Bird and Tassonyi 2003; Kneebone and McKenzie 1999).

Voters constrain the expenditure decisions of their representatives in the U.S. states and Swiss cantons even more directly through popular initiatives and referenda. Over the years, voters have gained increasingly direct control over the ability of their representatives to run deficits and incur debt. Several cross-section studies of the states and cantons show that the extent to which citizens have access to direct oversight has a strong effect on fiscal outcomes. For example, in twenty-three of the American states citizens can initiate and approve laws by popular vote, while in the other twenty-seven states laws can be proposed only by elected representatives. John Matsusaka (1995) shows that spending is significantly lower in states with initiatives than in pure representative states. Furthermore, Kiewiet and Szakaly (1996) show that public debt is significantly lower in states where citizens have the possibility of voting on the issuance of guaranteed debt in a referendum.

Initiatives and referenda play a particularly important role in constraining the fiscal behavior of the Swiss cantons (Spahn 1997; Wagschal 1996). Increases in cantonal spending and borrowing require obligatory referenda in most cantons. Like those of the U.S. states, the constitutions of the cantons vary in the extent to which they allow for elements of direct democracy,[3] and these variations are highly correlated with fiscal outcomes. Werner Pommerehne (1978, 1990) shows that government expenditure is significantly lower in the cantons that make use of direct-democracy mechanisms. Feld and Matsusaka (2003) show that mandatory referenda on new spending reduce the size of cantonal budgets by 17 percent for the median canton.

Perhaps the best example of voters attempting to rein in public spending in the U.S. states and Swiss cantons is the imposition of constitutional limitations on borrowing and indebtedness. In contrast to most of the other countries examined in this book, such restrictions in the U.S. states and Swiss cantons were not imposed by the central government in response to an intergovernmental moral-hazard problem, but rather by local citizens who wished to constrain the fiscal decisions of their representatives. In most cases, these constitutional amendments and statutory restrictions were pushed into effect through popular movements that arose directly out of painful fiscal crises. In the United States, these restrictions originated in direct response to the crisis of the 1800s discussed in Chapter 3. According to Ratchford (1941: 121),

Many taxpayers were rudely disillusioned by the developments of the 1830's and 1840's. They saw how the abuse of state credit increased tax burdens at the most inopportune time and led to overexpansion, waste, extravagance, and fraud. It was not surprising that they should demand safeguards to prevent the repetition of such events. Previous to 1840 no state constitution limited the debt which the legislature might incur, but within a period of fifteen years thereafter the constitutions of nineteen states were amended to include such limitations.

Rhode Island led the way in 1842 by adopting an amendment forbidding the legislature, without the consent of the people, to incur debts amounting to more than $50,000. Later, New Jersey adopted a similar amendment, which was subsequently copied by most of the other states (Heins 1963: 8). These restrictions were introduced not only to placate voters, but creditors as well. Only after introducing constitutional safeguards were defaulting states allowed to borrow again in international markets. Moreover, a study

---

[3] Pommerehne and Weck-Hannemann (1996) identify four dimensions of direct democracy in the Swiss cantons: (1) whether the tax rate must be approved by the voters in an obligatory or optional referendum, (2) if deficits must be approved by voters, (3) if the budget draft must be approved by voters, and (4) if there is direct democracy on budgetary decision making. In Jura and Bern, for example, each of these mechanisms is present, while none are present in Valais and Neuchâtel. Most of the cantons fall somewhere in the middle.

by Poterba and Rueben (1999) demonstrates that in modern times, other things equal, states with stricter and more easily enforceable expenditure limitations and antideficit provisions pay lower default premiums on their bonds.

Additional stipulations have been added over the years, and voters have now imposed balanced-budget requirements and borrowing restrictions on their representatives in all of the states except Vermont. A good deal of scholarly attention has been given to the question of whether these restrictions are associated with lower debt.[4] Most of these studies find evidence that such restrictions do affect state budgeting decisions, but there is considerable debate about nagging problems of endogeneity and enforcement. States with more fiscally conservative voters or more competitive elections might be more inclined to enforce existing restrictions or impose them in the first place. The various rules and restrictions themselves contain rather weak enforcement mechanisms or none at all. For the most part, "electoral accountability (or the threat of it) is the mechanism of enforcement" (Alt and Lowry 1994: 823). Constitutional or statutory fiscal restrictions are best understood as benchmarks or focal points that can be used by opposition politicians to embarrass incumbents when they are broken or circumvented. After all, such restrictions originate in the wake of painful fiscal crises as ways of signaling debt reduction commitment to voters and creditors by inviting voters to assess in future elections the government's ability to meet specific targets.

In response to a growing debt burden in the 1990s, several Canadian provinces, starting with Alberta and now extending across the federation, have recently introduced balanced-budget rules for the first time. However, even the strongest among these are quite weak when compared with those of the U.S. states (see Bird and Tassonyi 2002; Millar 1997). Most focus on the budget rather than actual expenditures; several make provisions for "contingencies" and "unforeseen circumstances"; most do not specify enforcement mechanisms;[5] and above all, they do not formally bind future governments. However, as in the United States, these provisions emerged as signaling devices to assure voters and creditors that the government is serious about debt reduction and their effects on fiscal

---

[4] See Alt and Lowry (1994); Bohn and Inman (1996); Endersby and Towle (1997); Inman (1997); Kiewiet and Szakaly (1996); Poterba (1996); Poterba and Rueben (1999).

[5] An interesting exception is Manitoba, where salaries of cabinet members are to be reduced if balanced-budget commitments are not kept.

outcomes are left in the hands of voters, who may choose to punish violators or not.

II. The Political Economy of Semisovereignty: The Logic of the Case Studies

In sum, existing literature suggests that a combination of federalism, independent taxation, and borrowing autonomy is associated with minimal bailout expectations, independent adjustment, and long-term fiscal discipline enforced by creditors and voters. This is consistent with the view of federalism celebrated by fiscal conservatives at least since Hayek, and it lies behind much of the optimistic policy literature reviewed in Chapter 2. Yet these examples of subnational sovereignty are quite unique. Such farreaching tax autonomy is rare among federations and rarer still among unitary systems. In recent decades, in most of the world's federations the central government retains a much larger role in funding provincial expenditures while leaving the provinces with relatively independent access to various forms of credit, ranging from bonds to state-owned banks and enterprises.

There is a great deal of diversity among these countries – in the structure of fiscal federalism, partisan incentives, and in fiscal outcomes. Moreover, several of these countries have undergone significant changes over time. Brazil and Argentina have experienced macroeconomic disasters resulting directly from dysfunctional fiscal federalism. In both countries, subnational officials appear to have had few incentives to exercise fiscal restraint (Dillinger and Webb 1999), though radical reforms have been undertaken under the Cardoso administration in Brazil. The problem of subnational deficits has been limited to only a few jurisdictions in Germany and Spain, though concerns are growing as these countries struggle to maintain Maastricht deficit criteria. The severity of the crisis in state-level public finance in India is only now becoming a top public policy issue (McCarten 2003). Serious problems have also developed in Nigeria (World Bank 2002) and South Africa (Ahmad 2002). State-level deficits in Mexico were controlled in the past by the heavy hand of the PRI, which dominated the governments of all states in the 1980s and early 1990s. However, in the post-PRI setting the moral-hazard problem is now a reality, and the Mexican government is working to develop new ways of controlling the borrowing of the states.

The next steps in developing a more nuanced understanding of the potential macroeconomic pathologies of federalism are to identify (1) some of the systemic factors that explain cross-country differences among these examples of semisovereign subnational governments, and (2) sources of cross-province variation within federations. Chapter 3 provided several avenues of inquiry for the first step: historical experiences, the assignment of expenditure and borrowing responsibilities, the basic powers and obligations of the center, the structure of jurisdictions, the role of externalities, and the identity of debt holders. These factors are best analyzed with case studies. Furthermore, it is clear that the two key incentive structures analyzed in this book – fiscal and political – display subtle variations across countries and across provinces that are not easily captured with cross-national quantitative indicators.

For instance, while the overall mix of transfers and taxes is important, credit ratings agencies pay a good deal of attention to the precise obligations and incentives created by each country's tax transfer system, which create different incentives for different provinces in the same system. Furthermore, Chapter 5 presented a cross-national result suggesting that higher rates of co-partisanship are associated with lower deficits in federations. But this requires considerable fleshing out through more refined analysis within countries. Provinces with chief executives sharing the party label of the federal chief executive should have stronger bailout expectations, and hence weaker incentives for fiscal discipline, if they believe they can extract purely redistributive bailouts that will not harm overall macroeconomic stability. But if bailouts are likely to cause macroeconomic harm and the electoral fates of subnational governments are tightly linked with those of their federal-level colleagues, party ties create disincentives for provincial officials to push the bailout game to its later stages.

Some system-level explanations – like historical experience with bailouts and perceptions of the center's obligations – are best addressed with descriptive case studies. Others – like the influence of transfers, co-partisanship, and jurisdiction structure – are best addressed with disaggregated provincial-level data analysis. As we shall see, the perils of fiscal federalism are sometimes concentrated in certain jurisdictions. As demonstrated by the U.S. case, sometimes the most instructive type of variation is over time within countries, as the structure of the bailout game evolves through experience and learning.

Time, data, and tractability impose constraints such that careful case selection is essential. When attempting to isolate the effect of one variable, a common approach to case selection in comparative politics is to choose countries that are quite similar in many respects – Canada and Australia, Brazil and Argentina, or the Scandinavian countries for example – in order to control for such potentially confounding factors as language, colonial experience, executive-legislative relations, or level of economic development.

This approach may indeed have benefits for certain types of inquiry. For example, it was useful in Chapter 5 to make sensible cross-national comparisons of electoral externalities, and the parliamentary comparison of Canada, Australia, and Germany will be employed again in Chapter 9 when assessing the prospects for reform. The disadvantage of this approach, of course, is that one is left wondering whether the results hold up in developing countries, presidential systems, non-British colonies, and so on. When disaggregated within-country data are available and similar within-country relationships can be established in very different types of systems, this should instill greater confidence in the general applicability of the relationship. This approach to comparative inquiry, referred to by Przewoski and Teune (1970) as the "most-different-systems" approach, requires variation over time or across units below the system level (individuals, provinces, or local governments). If one finds, for instance, that grants and co-partisanship have similar effects on provincial-level fiscal outcomes in very different types of countries – crossing the presidential/parliamentary divide, using different types of electoral rules, and at different levels of economic development, for example – one can be more confident in the strength of the relationship than if one found a similar result in two relatively similar systems.

It is difficult to imagine two more different federal systems than Germany and Brazil. Germany has been a wealthy, stable democracy for several decades, while during the same period Brazil has battled persistent poverty and vacillated between authoritarianism and democracy. At least until unification, the Federal Republic of Germany has been a relatively homogeneous country with relatively mild interregional income disparities, while Brazil is a vast federation encompassing a panoply of social groups, topography, and ways of life and demonstrates some of the world's most pronounced interpersonal and interregional income inequality. Moreover, the two federations have completely different political institutions. Brazil is a presidential, division-of-powers system with difficult executive-legislative relations and a famously fragmented party system. Germany is a parliamentary system with highly disciplined political parties. Describing high levels of party switching and apparent indiscipline, a generation of Brazil specialists has characterized the Brazilian party system as chaotic and irrelevant (e.g., Mainwaring 1992). At the other end of the spectrum, parties are at

149

the heart of the German political process, and German specialists have long referred to it as a "party state" (Schmidt 1992). The interregional distribution of fiscal resources by the Brazilian central government is thought to be highly political and driven by a pork barrel logic in Brazil (Ames 1995, 2001), while grants in Germany are generally characterized as rule-based and nondiscretionary (Spahn and Föttinger 1997).

Yet both have key features of federalism, including a constitution that protects the rights of states and powerful, malapportioned upper chambers that represent the interests of politically important state-level executives. In both countries, complex interstate bargains are required for reform. Both countries have also experienced recent travails with subnational debt and central government bailouts. By taking a closer look at the unfolding of state-level debt crises in such different contexts as nineteenth-century United States and modern Germany and Brazil, greater confidence might be built about some of the system-level arguments introduced in earlier chapters. Each case study will start with a brief description of the most important facets of the country's system of fiscal and political federalism, followed by an analytical discussion of recent debt accumulation and bailouts that draws on arguments developed throughout the book.

The main advantage of the most-different-systems approach lies in the observation of cross-state and time series variation in factors like jurisdiction size, political representation, transfer dependence, and co-partisanship. The third section of each case study provides a cross-section time series analysis of state-level expenditures and deficits. If similar state-level relationships are found in such diverse federations, the findings should inspire confidence, while divergent relationships will demand system-level explanations.

An additional advantage of these cases is that they provide difficult challenges for the key hypotheses developed above. Brazil is claimed by many observers to be a country in which parties are irrelevant, so it is a good test case for the proposition that parties shape state-level fiscal behavior. Likewise, it is often said that intergovernmental transfers only create incentives for fiscal indiscipline if they are highly discretionary (e.g., IDB 1997), so Germany's rule-based transfer system is a good context for examining the relationship between transfers and fiscal discipline.

As a result of recent bailout episodes and ongoing problems with the finances of state governments described in Chapters 7 and 8, the costs associated with the existing German and Brazilian systems of fiscal federalism are becoming clear not only to policy specialists but increasingly to average citizens. In both countries, reform of the intergovernmental system has been a hot topic in recent years, but federalism creates strong impediments to reform. Perhaps the most important peril of federalism highlighted in both case studies is a bias toward the preservation of the status quo, even when it is clearly deficient. Both the Brazilian and German constitutions are examples of what Chapter 2 described as incomplete federal contracts, and the case studies point out that existing intergovernmental contracts have been producing collectively undesirable outcomes, especially in Brazil. Yet the renegotiation of basic contracts in federations often requires the consent of politicians who stand to lose some benefits produced by the status quo contract.

Chapter 5 suggested that political parties might provide a way out of this trap. If the electoral fates of state-level officials are strongly shaped by those of their central government co-partisans, they may have incentives to give up some private benefits and sign onto a reform program that is perceived to be a collective good for the federation as a whole. Chapter 9 examines more carefully the problem of renegotiating intergovernmental fiscal contracts in federations, paying special attention to the role of political parties. It discusses the role of political parties in shaping reform efforts in Brazil and Germany and broadens the analysis to the three relatively similar cases from Chapter 5.

Finally, after characterizing the nature of incentives and obtaining some empirical results from recent decades, it is useful to make current incentives and expectations endogenous. Why have creditors and voters developed bailout expectations in some provinces? Has this always been the case? Or is it possible to identify historical moments when the basic game of fiscal federalism shifted *away* from a set of institutions and incentives consistent with competitive discipline? From its nineteenth-century unification to the twilight of the Weimar Republic, Germany's system of fiscal federalism was radically different than today's. In fact, the federal states in the old system had a relatively long history as truly sovereign borrowers up to World War I. The system evolved during the Weimar period and was radically transformed in the 1930s, after which the states were completely co-opted into an authoritarian system that destroyed their sovereignty. The Brazilian states also had a period of autonomous international borrowing in the late nineteenth century, but any perceptions of state sovereignty came to an end with a massive bailout of São Paulo in the 1930s. Though the states were never irrelevant during periods of authoritarianism, their status as sovereign borrowers was undermined. In many respects, the recent bailouts replay a Brazilian script that is almost a century old.

Chapter 10 builds from these historical experiences and broadens the analysis to include several additional federations, attempting to make endogenous some of the key institutional variations pointed out in previous chapters. Above all, it asks why subnational governments in some federations – like the United States, Canada, and Switzerland – solidified their status as miniature sovereigns in the first half of the twentieth century while others – like Argentina, Brazil, Germany, and Mexico – emerged as semisovereigns.

7

Fiscal Federalism and Bailouts in Postwar Germany

> The fundamental principle on which it [the German Confederation] rests, that the empire is a community of sovereigns, that the diet is a representation of sovereigns, and that the laws are addressed to sovereigns, renders the empire a nerveless body, incapable of regulating its own members, insecure against external dangers, and agitated with unceasing fermentations in its own bowels.
>
> Alexander Hamilton and James Madison, *The Federalist* 19

> A closely knit institutional web limits the exercise of unilateral political initiatives by any one actor and encourages incremental policy change. In a word, it makes the West German state semisovereign.
>
> Peter Katzenstein, *Politics and Policy in West Germany*

When making the case for a single, centralized sovereign to replace the system under the Articles of Confederation, Alexander Hamilton cited the loose eighteenth-century German confederation as an example of provincial sovereignty gone awry. He advocated a centralized system of finance and decision making that would relegate subnational governments primarily to the administration of policies conceived and funded by the center. Two hundred years later, the German federation is much closer to Hamilton's vision of centralized legislation and taxation than a "community of sovereigns." Yet the German postwar constitution is nevertheless extremely federal in every respect outlined in Chapter 2. Above all, the Länder are very important players in the federal policy process, and the constitution provides them with a number of robust institutional safeguards. Though in possession of very limited tax autonomy, the Länder have been able to retain wide-ranging autonomy over their expenditure and borrowing decisions. Thus, the modern German federation is an example of what previous chapters have deemed fiscal semisovereignty.

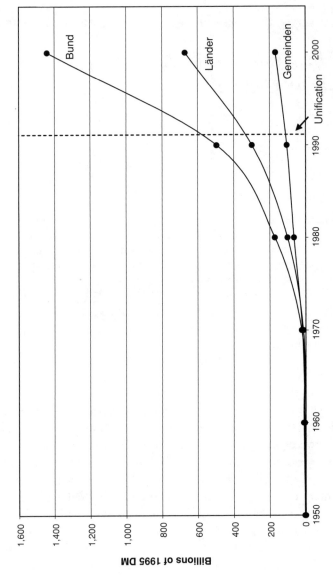

Figure 7.1. Real accumulated debt in Germany by government level. Source: *Statistisches Bundesamt* 2002 and author's calculations.

This chapter explains how incentive problems embedded in the German system of federalism have led to a growing debt problem among the Länder and placed heavy burdens upon the federal government. Germany has run afoul of the criteria of the Maastricht Stability and Growth Pact and has undermined the pact's credibility by flouting it.

Figure 7.1 displays the debts of the German Bund (federal government), Länder, and Gemeinden (local governments) since 1950 in inflation-adjusted 1995 Deutschmarks. In the immediate postwar period, borrowing by the Länder outpaced that of the Bund. Public debt was quite modest and rather evenly distributed between the three levels until the explosion of public debt in the 1970s and 1980s, most of which took place at the Bund and Land levels. The Länder are the largest subnational debtors in Europe, and the central government has been powerless to restrict their borrowing.

Table 7.1 displays the accumulated debts of each Land in 2000. Bremen and Saarland have accumulated massive deficits since the 1970s, and in spite of debt reduction transfers from the central government starting in 1994, they still have among the highest per capita debt burdens. Moreover, after only a decade of existence, the five new eastern Länder attained debt

Table 7.1. *Per capita debts of Länder (DM as of Dec. 31, 2000)*

Baden-Württemberg	5,497
Bayern	2,884
Hessen	6,967
Niedersachsen	8,424
Nordrhein-Westfalen	8,333
Rheinland-Pfalz	8,907
Saarland	11,210
Schleswig-Holstein	10,893
City States	
Berlin	19,338
Bremen	25,193
Hamburg	19,035
New Eastern Länder	
Brandenburg	9,625
Mecklenburg-Vorpommern	8,214
Sachsen	4,432
Sachsen-Anhalt	10,079
Thüringen	8,723
Average	**10,485**

Source: Statistisches Bundesamt 2002.

burdens similar to those of the "old" Länder, Saxony (Sachsen) being the only exception. The problem is not only the growing debt burden of the Länder, but also the pressure placed on the finances of the federal government. Figure 7.1 gives some indication of the extent to which the Länder have used their power in the Bundesrat to force the Bund to bear the burdens of unification and the bailouts of Saarland and Bremen.

By examining the recent problem of fiscal discipline among the Länder, this chapter builds on the arguments developed in previous chapters and tailors them to a specific institutional context. One goal of the chapter is to examine more closely some of the general arguments about what happens when subnational governments have limited tax autonomy but unlimited borrowing autonomy in the context of robust federalism. But a more important goal is to make use of the rich cross-sectional and time series variation displayed in Table 7.1 and Figure 7.2. In fact, at least up to the early 1990s, unsustainable borrowing has been limited to a handful of states, and bailouts have only been received by two of the smallest states. The chapter will build on some of the insights developed earlier to explain as much of the time series and cross-section variation in fiscal outcomes as possible.

Above all, the chapter explains how the system of fiscal federalism, as established by the constitution and interpreted by the courts, creates a strong relationship between a state's position in the equalization system and the credibility of the center's no-bailout commitment. States with a large and growing dependence on federal transfers have the most rational bailout expectations, and the empirical analysis shows that they incur the largest deficits.

The chapter also allows for a closer examination of the role of political parties. The electoral fates of incumbents at the Land level are driven in good part by voters' assessments of the performance of the federal government, and top Land officials are often very clearly attempting to position themselves for federal posts. Moreover, federal party leaders control a variety of resources that are valuable to Land politicians. Thus, Germany's highly integrated political parties put a ceiling on the incentives of Land officials to position themselves for bailouts. Consistent with the arguments in Chapter 5, this helps explain why Germany's bailout problem pales in comparison with Brazil's (described in the chapter that follows) and why Germany's largest states – unlike the largest states in Brazil – have exhibited fiscal discipline in spite of the center's weak no-bailout commitment. Yet it also appears that states sharing the federal government's partisan affiliation – especially small states that can hope for redistributive bailouts that will not undermine national macroeconomic stability – spend more and run slightly larger deficits than states controlled by the opposition.

The first section describes and analyzes the incentives built into the German system of fiscal and political federalism in greater detail. The second section describes the way the bailout game was played in Saarland and Bremen. The third section parlays concepts from earlier chapters into testable hypotheses about Land-level fiscal outcomes, and the fourth section provides empirical analysis for the years 1975 to 1995. The final section concludes.

I. The German Federal System

Fiscal Federalism

The German system of federalism is deeply at odds with the notion of dual federalism that was feared by Hamilton and admired by so many other students of American federalism. Yet it is also at odds with Hamilton's preferred centralized sovereignty. Rather than carving out two distinct realms of sovereignty at the federal and state levels or placing it firmly at the center, the German state intertwines each level into a dense network that Peter Katzenstein deems a "semisovereign state." Although some tasks, like national defense, are clearly allocated to the Bund alone, legislation and implementation in Germany is in most policy areas a complex, cooperative process between the highly interdependent Bund and Länder. The German Länder have few exclusive areas of legislative competence, and federal law generally overrides state law.

The Länder are nevertheless important players in the German policy process. This is not because they possess an autonomous role in legislation within a constitutionally protected set of responsibilities, but rather because they are key players in the formulation of policy at the federal level and in its implementation at the Land level. Unlike the states in most other federal systems, the governments of the Länder are directly represented in the upper chamber. Recall from Chapter 2 that this places Germany at the extreme end of a continuum running from population- to territory-based modes of political representation. Every law that affects the interests of the states must be approved by the Bundesrat, which gives the states a very important role as veto players in the federal policymaking process. Additionally, in contrast to most other federations, the German central government has a very limited bureaucratic apparatus under its own control;

it relies on the Länder and local governments to implement most federal policy. Given this structural interdependence of Bund and Länder, it is very difficult for either level of government to achieve its goals without bargaining, cajoling, or cooperating with the other level.

Multilateral bargaining between the interdependent Bund and Länder is also the modus operandi in the collection and distribution of revenue. All of the most important taxes accrue to the federal and state governments jointly. Most decisions about tax base and rates are made by the federal government (subject to the approval of the Bundesrat). While some taxes are collected by the Bund, most are administered by the revenue authorities of the Länder, which act as agents of the federation. The fiscal equalization system goes to great lengths to redistribute revenue from the wealthy to the poor Länder, and the parameters of this system are renegotiated periodically between the Länder and the central government.

Expenditures The states are responsible for public spending in a wide variety of areas, such as culture, education, law and order, health, environmental protection, and regional economic policy. Despite the constitution's attempt to divide authority between the governmental units, however, it is difficult to identify a policy area in which only one level of government is involved. Because the Länder and local governments are responsible for implementing the vast majority of policies determined at the federal level, neither the constitution nor outlays by level of government reflect very accurately the actual distribution of authority or spending. Even in policy areas that had previously been the exclusive competence of the Länder, the activities and finances of the Bund and Länder have gradually become intertwined. The most important step away from dual federalism was the 1969 renegotiation of the Basic Law, which established the so-called joint tasks. The Länder agreed to give up their exclusive authority in several policy fields in exchange for complex forms of multilevel cooperation in policymaking and funding. While the discretion of the Länder in spending is limited in most areas by uniform federal law, they enjoy relatively wide autonomy over the budget in practice. In many fields, they can vary the amount of support they give to programs required by federal law, and they remain free to supplement services prescribed by federal statute. The Länder are the largest public sector employers in Germany. In this capacity, they also enjoy a good deal of discretion, again within federally imposed legal constraints.

Revenue   The constitution specifies in great detail the assignment of revenue to the Bund and Länder, and major revisions in federal financial arrangements can only be made by amending the constitution, which requires a two-thirds majority in both the Bundestag and the Bundesrat. The flow of revenue laid out in the German constitution is far removed from the principles laid out in most fiscal federalism textbooks. Instead of assigning specific taxes to the layers of government and matching them with specific expenditure responsibilities, the provisions of the German constitution stipulates that all of the most important revenue sources are shared. Taxes assigned directly to specific layers of government are extremely limited. The income tax, corporation tax, and VAT, which yield almost three-quarters of total tax revenue, are each jointly appropriated.[1] Legislation regarding tax base and rates for each of these is the domain of the federal government, although these taxes are administered by the revenue authorities of the Länder. In the administration of the shared taxes, the state authorities act as agents of the federation and are subject to uniform federal administrative guidelines.

The vertical distribution of the shared taxes between Bund and Länder is very stable over time because the actual percentage shares are laid out in the constitution and can only be changed by amendment. In order to ensure that the Länder receive sufficient funds to fulfill their federally mandated responsibilities in the face of changing fiscal circumstances, the vertical distribution of the VAT is frequently renegotiated between the Bund and the Länder and approved by the Bundesrat.

By far the most important sources of funding for the Länder are the shared taxes. First of all, the primary system of tax sharing distributes the proceeds of the major shared taxes to the states as follows: Income tax revenue is apportioned to the states according to the derivation principle; corporate tax revenue is divided according to a formula based on plant location; and a portion of the VAT is distributed to the states on a per capita basis. Next, the secondary system of revenue equalization proceeds in three stages. The first two states are horizontal, while the third involves vertical transfers from the Bund.

In the first stage, around 75 percent of the VAT is distributed by population, and up to 25 percent of the VAT is redistributed to the Länder with the lowest revenue after the primary tax-sharing receipts are calculated. After this stage, the "financial endowment" of each state is calculated and

---

[1] For additional details, see Spahn and Föttinger (1997: 229) and Seitz (1998).

compared with its financial needs. Then at the second stage of equalization, revenue is redistributed from states whose endowments exceed their needs to those for whom the opposite is true. The concept of need is based on the per capita tax income for the entire country.[2] After this stage, the "weak" states reach 95 percent of the average national tax capacity.

In the third stage of the equalization system, the federal government steps in to lift the recipient states up to at least 99.5 percent of average fiscal capacity. It does this with federal supplementary grants (*Bundesergänzungszuweisungen*). At this stage, the Bund also bestows additional supplementary grants on some states to compensate them for "special burdens." Special supplementary grants are also received by smaller Länder to compensate them for higher administrative costs and recently by some of the old (preunification) Länder to compensate them for the higher fiscal burden they must bear because of reunification. Massive supplementary transfers are also currently being made to the East German Länder. As will be discussed in greater detail below, the federal supplementary grants are also now being used to provide bailouts to Bremen and Saarland because of their debt-servicing obligations. Finally, the Bund also funds specific activities and capital investments for joint tasks, as laid out in the 1969 renegotiation of the Basic Law.

Borrowing   The central government has no power to place numeric restrictions on the borrowing activities of the Länder. Nor must the borrowing decisions of the Länder be approved or reviewed by the Bund. Like the federal government, however, the Länder have their own constitutional and statutory provisions that restrict them from borrowing more than the outlays for investment purposes projected in the budget. These so-called golden rule provisions at the Land level, however, have a number of well-known loopholes. First of all, "investment purposes" is an extremely slippery concept, and it is not difficult to recast a variety of expenditures as investment outlays. Second, financing arrangements associated with the contracting out of local public infrastructure projects provides an additional way around the golden rule provisions. Private investors are given guarantees and asked to prefinance and build infrastructure projects. Upon completion of the work, the government redeems the building costs over

[2] The benchmark for determining differentials in tax capacities is, roughly, the average tax revenue per capita multiplied by the population for each state. However, the procedure is complicated by a weighting that favors the city-states.

a certain period (Spahn and Föttinger 1997: 237). Third, since 1969 the constitutions of the Länder have allowed them to break the golden rule in cases of "disturbances of general economic equilibrium." In addition to the problem of loopholes, Bremen and Saarland have chosen simply to ignore these constitutional provisions.[3]

It is important to note that while most of the federal government's debt is in the form of bonds, the Länder rely primarily on direct bank loans to finance their deficits. The Länder indirectly control a network of commercial banks – the *Landesbanken* – that make loans to the municipalities and Länder. The officials of the Landesbanken generally have strong political connections with Land politicians, who frequently accept lucrative stints on their Landesbank's supervisory board. Some suggest that the Landesbanken are used to channel cheap credit to politically favored businesses.[4] Borrowing on international bond markets has been limited until recently. The Länder occasionally issue local currency bonds, which are typically managed by the state's Landesbank. Bonds have been a less significant part of Land-level borrowing, however, because of the attractiveness of the *Schuldschein* market. *Schuldscheindarlehen* are credits that are documented by negotiable promissory notes called *Schuldscheine*. They are not quoted on any exchange but can be transferred to third parties by way of a written assignment. In most cases, these are negotiated with the state's Landesbank.[5]

The German equalization system provides little reason for creditors to distinguish between the creditworthiness of the states. In the mid-1990s, some of the Länder have started to make use of a wider range of instruments as their overall debt requirements grow and as barriers between domestic and offshore markets come down. Some Länder have recently structured new forms of debt securities to attract international investors, which has led some of the Länder to apply for credit ratings. As described in Chapter 4, Fitch IBCA is so certain of the central government's implicit support of

---

[3] According to the data collected by the central government on the finances of the Länder and the author's calculations, deficits have surpassed capital expenditures quite regularly over the last twenty years in Bremen and Saarland and only sporadically in Hamburg and Niedersachsen. On paper *ex post*, the other Länder have abided by the "golden rule." However, it seems clear that these numbers should be taken with a grain of salt if the division between capital and current accounts is as fluid as most observers suggest.

[4] "German Banking: Can Dachshunds be Whippets?" *The Economist*, January 4, 1997, p. 70.

[5] For a more detailed discussion of this system, especially the evolving role of the Landesbanken, see Rodden (2003).

the Länder that it gives all of the Länder AAA ratings, and even the more circumspect Standard & Poor's drastically overrates their creditworthiness based on an assumption of implicit federal support.

Political Federalism

The unique German system of administrative and fiscal federalism is accompanied by a highly integrated yet unmistakably federal political system. The most central characteristic of German political federalism was measured and discussed in Chapter 5: the highly intertwined nature of federal and state partisan politics. Like state elections in Australia, Land elections in Germany are widely seen as the equivalent of federal by-elections; they often appear to be referenda on the competence of the chancellor and his government (Fabritius 1978; Lohmann, Brady, and Rivers 1997). Throughout the postwar period, the German political parties have become increasingly vertically integrated (Chandler 1987; Lehmbruch 1989). This is not surprising, because the Bundesrat possesses the power either to veto, delay, or rewrite most federal legislation, and Land elections determine the makeup of the Bundesrat. As a result, the media, voters, and Land politicians themselves have come to interpret Land elections as something like nonsimultaneous midterm federal elections (Abromeit 1982).

Another reason for the tight relationship between federal and state elections is the complex interdependence of the fiscal and administrative systems. It is difficult for citizens to obtain and interpret information about the competence and performance of their representatives at the Land level. Since they have no autonomous control over local tax rates, most policy decisions are made through cooperative intergovernmental processes, and most of their expenditures are for the implementation of federal programs, Land-level officials can always credibly claim that the blame for local policy failures or revenue shortfalls lies elsewhere, even though this is not always true. Voters simply have no way of accurately sorting out credit and blame for outcomes. Thus, it might make sense for information-economizing voters simply to assess the performance of the governing coalition in Bonn and reward or punish those parties at each level of government.

As in Australia, the Bund and Land parties coordinate their funding and campaign activities, Land-level leaders play an important part in the nomination process for federal party leaders, and career paths frequently move back and forth between federal and state politics. In fact, every modern chancellor started his career with years of service in the party's Land-level organization and served as a Land-level minister-president.

By no means do the tight links between state and federal elections imply that the states are homogeneous, however, or that Land-level officials are mere prisoners of the actions taken by their partisan colleagues in Berlin. A good number of Land chancellors have gained sufficient independent popularity to withstand short-term vote losses stemming from voters' displeasure with their central co-partisans. Some parties have developed such regional dominance that, though their vote totals may fluctuate with evolving assessments of the federal government, they are unlikely to lose their grip on power. This has been true of the Christian Social Union (CSU) in Bavaria, the Christian Democratic Union (CDU) in Baden-Württemberg, and, until recently, the Social Democratic Party (SPD) in Bremen.

II. The Bailout Game in Action: Bremen and Saarland

The system described above has produced a growing problem of federalism and public debt. Before elaborating and testing some hypotheses about the institutional, macroeconomic, and political sources of the problem, it is necessary to describe in greater detail the recent history of borrowing, intergovernmental gamesmanship, and court decisions involving Bremen and Saarland.[6] Although Saarland has always been a receiving Land in the equalization process, Bremen was a contributor prior to the 1970s. Both Länder have faced major economic downturns and had to deal with vexing unemployment problems in recent decades. Thus, it is not surprising that these Länder have faced significant pressure on their public finances. Given their small size and lack of economic diversity, they were poorly situated to bear the costs of adjustment alone.

In fact, they have not been forced to bear the costs of adjustment alone; prior to unification, they were the largest beneficiaries of the equalization process. In recent years, Saarland and Bremen have been ranked number one and two among all the Länder in fiscal capacity per capita (as measured by the federal government) after equalization. In spite of this and in spite of constantly increasing dependence on equalization payments and supplementary transfers, both Länder continued to increase spending, run large deficits, and rely heavily on debt to fund current expenditures throughout

---

[6] For a more detailed account of the bailout episode, see Seitz (1998)

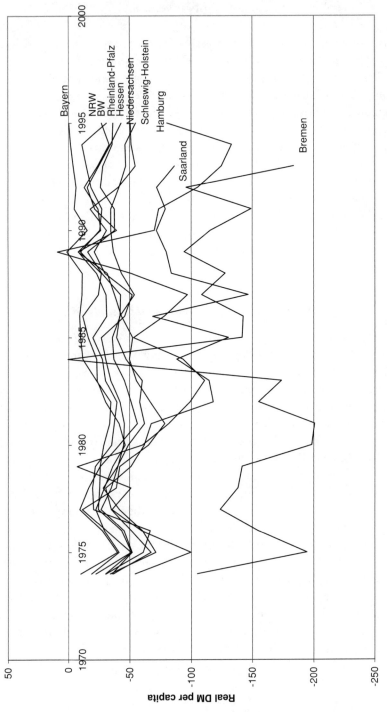

Figure 7.2. Real surplus per capita by Land, 1974-1995. Source: *Statistisches Bundesamt Deutschland* and author's calculations.

164

the 1980s and '90s. Figure 7.2 displays the real per capita budget surplus (deficit) of each Land from 1975 to 1995.

Given their high level of fiscal dependence on other Länder and the Bund, the strategy of the governments of Bremen and Saarland was to tell voters that they were not responsible for growing deficits and debt burdens, arguing that the rest of the federation was not fulfilling its constitutional obligation to ensure adequate funding. Despite alarming debt levels, the governments of Saarland and Bremen had no trouble securing credit from their Landesbanken.

Saarland's Constitution contains a golden rule provision that public debt must not exceed investment spending. The government of Saarland simply ignored this provision despite the highest court in the state's declaration that the budget contradicted the state's constitution. Rather than suffering public embarrassment, the government of Saarland used the "unconstitutional" nature of its deficits as further proof that the rest of the federation was not fulfilling its obligations. In the mid-1980s, it became clear that the accumulated debt levels in Bremen and Saarland were unsustainable, and both Länder declared that they faced fiscal emergencies, calling on the federation and the other Länder to provide special funds to pay down some of their debt. Bremen eventually requested that the Bund explicitly take over its obligations. The 1980s saw a variety of complaints by the Länder to the Constitutional Court over the details of the fiscal constitution, and Saarland and Bremen took their case for bailouts to the courts.

A 1986 decision found that the federal supplementary transfers can be used to assist fiscally troubled Länder. Returning to the game-theoretic presentation in Chapter 3, this enhanced the beliefs of officials in Bremen and Saarland that the central government would eventually be irresolute, weakening even further their incentives to bear the costs of adjustment alone. Through the rest of the 1980s, they made no effort to adjust. Rather, they continued to articulate bailout demands in complaints to the Constitutional Court, and in May 1992 the court declared that the solidarity obligation contained in the Basic Law required that the Bund, as part of the renegotiation of the equalization system in 1993, begin using the supplementary transfers to provide Bremen and Saarland with bailouts amounting to 17 billion DM.[7]

Bremen and Saarland started receiving the special funds in 1994, Bremen an extra 1.8 billion DM per year and Saarland an extra 1.6 billion DM.

---

[7] "Bund fordert Länder zur Mitfinanzierung auf," *Handelsblatt*, March 3, 1998.

Bremen and Saarland were under no obligation to make repayments, though the state governments agreed to limitations on expenditure growth and promised to use the extra funds only for the reduction of public debt and only to use savings on interest for further debt reduction or additional infrastructure investment. The bailouts were sufficient to balance current budgets temporarily. Nevertheless, the Bund still has no carrots or sticks with which to reward or punish changes in spending or progress in reducing debt, and the progress of both Länder in reducing debt has fallen far short of expectations. Empirical analysis by Seitz (1998) shows that primary expenditure growth in Bremen and Saarland continued to outpace some of the other states after the bailout agreements. In fact, both Länder have since argued that the bailouts were insufficient, and they explain their inability to reduce debt by pointing out that they have experienced unexpected revenue shortfalls.[8]

III. Explaining Differences across the Länder

The most crucial facts thus far can be easily summarized. The German Länder have considerable discretion over budgetary and borrowing decisions but very little authority to raise revenue through taxes and fees. As a result, creditors and perhaps even voters do not always see Land officials as sovereign over their own finances, but as parts of a complex intertwined system. Furthermore, the equalization system codifies very strong commitments by the central government to the states and by the states to one another, which have been interpreted by creditors as implicit debt guarantees. Recent court decisions and bailouts in Bremen and Saarland have confirmed this interpretation.

This sounds like a recipe for widespread fiscal indiscipline. Yet the postwar experience with decentralized fiscal management in Germany has not been a disaster. In fact, Figure 7.2 shows that many of the states have recovered from difficulties in the mid-1970s and early 1980s and avoided large sustained deficits. This section develops arguments based on earlier chapters, and the next section attempts to exploit variation over time and across states to explain sources of fiscal indiscipline.

---

[8] "Streit um Hilfen für das Saarland und Bremen," *Frankfurter Allgemeine Zeitung*, February 25, 1998.

Intergovernmental Grants

H1: In the long term, transfer dependence is associated with larger deficits.

Given the centrality of the supplementary transfers in the bailout game, these are an obvious place to start searching for explanations of state fiscal behavior. From the beginning, these gap-filling transfers provided an obvious mechanism through which state officials might hope to receive future debt relief transfers, and indeed, the courts confirmed this in the late 1980s. Bailout expectations are more rational in the states that receive the largest and most rapidly growing transfers. Creditors and voters are aware that local debt burdens are unlikely to result in defaults, school closures, or the firing of public employees, and fiscal decision makers can hope that growing debt burdens will be covered by more-generous transfers in future years. These come from a common pool of revenue raised by the federal government, and redistributive transfers from wealthy to poor states were viewed not only as legitimate, but as part of the cornerstone of German federalism.

Thus, it was reasonable for decision makers in the recipient states to believe that extra support would be forthcoming if debt burdens ultimately became unsustainable – or perhaps even earlier. For the most transfer-dependent states, when faced with tight revenues and growing expenditure burdens in the 1970s and 1980s – the first decision node in the bailout game from Chapter 3 – there was little incentive to undertake painful adjustment measures. If local politicians choose to avoid or postpone fiscal adjustment and maintain current expenditure levels by increasing borrowing – hoping for increased redistributive transfers from the wealthier states in the future – there are few reasons for local voters or creditors to punish them. They can claim with considerable credibility that their fiscal burdens are ultimately not their responsibility. Thus far, only two states have reached the final stage of the bailout game, where default is imminent and a high-stakes bailout drama is a leading newspaper headline.[9] Yet H1 hypothesizes that other transfer-dependent states also faced weak incentives for fiscal discipline.

At the other end of the spectrum, the states that pay into the equalization system and receive no supplementary transfers – only some modest specific-purpose transfers for joint tasks – cannot credibly make such claims to their voters and creditors when faced with similar downturns. If they overspend

---

[9] At the time of this writing, Berlin appears to be heading in the same direction.

and run into debt-servicing difficulties, there is no reason to believe the federation will step in with extra support. The system is designed to fill only the gaps of the states that have fallen behind and become regular recipients of supplementary transfers.

Note that H1 refers to long-term dynamics; temporary fluctuations in transfers should not have this effect. A single-year bump above the trend might, if anything, lead to a larger surplus. For this reason, the estimation technique employed below distinguishes between short-term fluctuations and long-term developments.

Figure 7.3 illuminates trends and interstate differences in real inter-governmental grants per capita. It shows that transfers are relatively low and growth is minimal in the three wealthiest states – Bayern, Hessen, and Nordrhein-Westfalen (Bavaria, Hesse, and North Rhine-Westphalia) – and demonstrates a gentle upward trend in the other states, with a more pronounced increase in Bremen and Saarland. Additionally, Figure 7.3 shows a general downturn in the old Länder associated with unification after 1991.

Jurisdiction Size and Representation

H2: Average deficits are highest in the smallest (most overrepresented) states.

The intergovernmental common resource problem can also be shaped by the size and structure of jurisdictions. As described in previous chapters, some jurisdictions might be large enough that their fiscal activities and credit reputations create sufficient externalities that the rest of the federation cannot allow them to default. Knowing this *ex ante*, these jurisdictions might strategically adopt loose fiscal policies. Yet there are reasons to expect a countervailing logic in Germany. Above all, political parties create electoral externalities that encourage state-level leaders to be concerned with federation-wide collective goods. If the government of a large state like Nordrhein-Westfalen would trigger massive federal bailouts by strategically overspending, it would probably have noticeable macroeconomic effects, bring embarrassment to the party, and undermine the career advancement of state-level politicians. In contrast, the smallest states that produce the fewest externalities are relatively inexpensive to bail out and can hope to achieve bailouts that are viewed as relatively unexceptional receipts in an ongoing game of redistributive pork barrel politics.

Figure 7.3. Real grants per capita by Land, 1974–1995. Source: *Statistisches Bundesamt Deutschland* and author's calculations.

Additionally, small states might have more-rational bailout expectations because their overrepresentation in the Bundesrat enhances their bargaining power (Seitz 1998). When trying to construct the least expensive winning Bundesrat coalition, the government may be tempted to favor the "cheapest" states – those with the most votes per capita. In principle, it is possible to distinguish between the effects of size – measured with population or GDP – and representation – measured as logged legislative seats per capita. However, with such a small number of cross-section observations this is difficult. An additional wrinkle in the analysis is that representation is highly correlated with the level of intergovernmental grants: Other things equal, overrepresented states are more successful in attracting inter governmental transfers.[10] Transfer dependence and bargaining power might independently create bailout expectations, but it may also be the case that the influence of bargaining power on fiscal outcomes works through expectations (and receipts) of transfers. The empirical analysis below will attempt to deal with these possibilities.[11]

Co-partisanship

H3: Deficits are higher when the Land and Bund are controlled by the same party.

Chapter 5 argued that the effects of co-partisanship on incentives for fiscal discipline depend a good deal on the country context. On the one hand, in a country with strong electoral externalities like Germany, sharing the federal government's party label reduces the expected benefit of receiving a bailout if the bailout is expected to impose macroeconomic costs on the federation as a whole. Yet the notion that subnational fiscal indiscipline and debt relief transfers could have important collective macroeconomic costs has not been part of public discussion until perhaps the late 1990s. At first, the discussion of debt relief transfers portrayed them as minor tinkering with the existing system of redistribution. Chapter 5 argued that as long as

---

[10] This relationship between representation and transfers is quite common. See Rodden (2002) on the European Union's Council of Ministers; Lee (2000) on the U.S. Senate; Ansolabehere et al. (2003) on the U.S. states; and Gibson, Calvo, and Falleti (2004) on Argentina and Brazil.

[11] Note that other mechanisms might also underlie a relationship between size and fiscal management. Above all, small jurisdictions are often less economically diversified and hence more vulnerable to shocks (note the volatility for the small states in Figure 7.2), and they may not enjoy scale economies in the production of some public goods.

co-partisan leaders at the state level believe that debt relief transfers will be viewed as mere interstate redistribution that favors their constituents, their bailout expectations are more rational than those of states controlled by the federal opposition party. Expecting that they are in a better position to receive additional supplementary transfers, co-partisan states would spend more and run larger deficits than states controlled by the party in opposition at the federal level. Once again, we are confronted with a variable that might have a direct effect on expenditures and deficits or one whose influence may work through grants. Both possibilities are explored below.

A dummy variable was constructed that takes on 1 for years in which senior coalition partners were the same at the federal and state levels and 0 otherwise. A more complex variable was also created as follows: When the federal and Land governments have no parties in common, the case receives 0 points. When the junior coalition partners are the same but the senior partners differ, the case receives 1 point.[12] When the senior coalition partners at both levels are the same, but each has a different junior coalition partner, the case receives 2 points. When either (1) the coalitions are identical or (2) the Land party governs alone while its federal counterpart is the senior coalition partner in Bonn, the case receives 3 points. Again, election years in which changes take place are weighted averages of the two scores.

Control Variables

Business Cycle   Most empirical studies of government budgeting start with a benchmark assumption based on Barro (1979) and Lucas and Stokey (1983) that governments will attempt to smooth tax rates over time. However, this model is not useful among subnational governments that possess limited authority to tax. Studies of subnational governments have examined the expenditure side, finding evidence for intertemporal smoothing of specific kinds of capital expenditures (Holtz-Eakin and Rosen 1993; Rattsø 1999, 2000), but evidence for nondurable current or total expenditures is lacking (Holtz-Eakin, Rosen, and Tilly 1994; Rattsø 2004). Bayoumi and Eichengreen (1994) examine the hypothesis that state and local governments in the United States and elsewhere conduct Keynesian

---

[12] This was quite rare. The only scenario in which this is the case, in fact, is when the FDP is in coalition with the CDU at one level and the SPD at the other.

countercyclical stabilization policies. Finally, Seitz (2000) presents a theoretical model of subnational fiscal decision making that is tailored to the German Länder. While the tax-smoothing model takes government expenditures as exogenous and posits that a benevolent government smoothes tax rates over time in order to minimize the deadweight loss imposed on consumers by progressive tax rates, the Seitz model assumes that revenues are fixed and derives an optimal policy rule for expenditures. In this model, Keynesian fiscal stabilization is ruled out – expenditures and revenues are modestly procyclical but budget deficits are countercyclical. To account for these possibilities, the model includes real Land-level GDP per capita and unemployment levels. Bayoumi and Eichengreen (1994) use aggregate data on the entire Land sector to conclude that the Land fiscal policy is in fact countercyclical. By using disaggregated GDP and unemployment data and a fully specified model, it is possible to make a much firmer conclusion.

Electoral Budget Cycle   The literature on electoral cycles is too large to review here (See Alesina and Roubini 1997), but the basic propositions are well known. Starting with Nordhaus (1975) and Tufte (1978), political economists have suggested that opportunistic incumbent politicians have incentives to use the tools of fiscal and monetary policy to heat up the economy prior to elections, and several scholars have attempted to assemble empirical evidence of macroeconomic fluctuations prior to elections. Most recently, a second generation of political business cycle models argues that large macroeconomic fluctuations before elections are not sustainable and instead seeks out evidence of electoral cycles on monetary and fiscal policy instruments (Cukierman and Meltzer 1986; Rogoff 1990; Rogoff and Sibert 1988).

This latter view of electoral cycles is most appropriate for fiscal policy at the Land level in Germany. Land governments certainly cannot manipulate macroeconomic conditions during the run-up to Land elections, nor do they control monetary policy instruments, but they do have control over spending and borrowing decisions. And even though they do not set tax rates, they are responsible for tax collection. Incumbent Land governments may face incentives to increase spending on highly visible public goods or particularistic projects for important constituents or reduce their tax collection efforts during election campaigns (Wagschal 1996).

The campaign period is defined as the six-month period preceding any Land election. If the election is held in July or later (the full six-month campaign period falls in the same calendar year as the election), the Land year is coded as 1 for the electoral budget cycle variable. If the election is held during the months of March through June, the year of the election receives a .5, along with the previous year. If the election is held during January or February, the deficit effect would show up primarily in the previous year, so the election year receives a 0, while the previous year receives a 1.[13]

Partisan Budget Cycle   The literature on partisan economic cycles is also voluminous. Since Douglas Hibbs (1987), political economists have argued that parties of the left and right represent the interests of different constituencies and, when in office, promulgate policies that favor them. In particular, Hibbs assumes that left-wing parties are more concerned with the problem of unemployment and right-wing parties are more concerned with inflation. This implies that partisan differences should show up in systematic, permanent differences in the unemployment/inflation combination chosen by different political parties. The Länder certainly do not have the power to choose these combinations, but a more recent literature on fiscal policy may have direct application in the Länder. First of all, the fiscal management of left-wing governments might be marked by greater sensitivity to unemployment. Specifically, because the Länder have little autonomy to set tax rates but considerable borrowing and spending autonomy, left-wing governments with a commitment to combat unemployment may have no other option during downturns than to increase expenditures financed by borrowing. In other words, the short-term counter-cyclicality of deficits with respect to unemployment might be strengthened by left partisanship.

Partisanship might affect not only short-term management of the business cycle, but also long-term expenditure and borrowing patterns. In a study of the U.S. states, Alt and Lowry (1994) argue that Democrats simply prefer higher expenditure levels than Republicans and that states controlled by Democrats spend (and tax) more per capita than those controlled by Republicans. Survey data presented by Manfred Schmidt (1992: 58) show that SPD supporters in Germany prefer higher expenditure levels than CDU supporters. Given the lack of revenue autonomy, the only way for left-wing governments in the Länder to live up to expectations is to rely on deficit spending (Wagschal 1996). In this way, state-level politicians might

---

[13] Another strategy is to weight each year by the number of election campaign months that fall within it. This yields very similar results to those presented below.

use fiscal policy to demonstrate their ideological credentials to voters. Even if the transfer system potentially reduces the costs of lax revenue collection or overspending, CDU politicians might attempt to differentiate themselves from their competitors by demonstrating a commitment to small government and balanced budgets. Gaining a reputation as a fiscal conservative might also be a good career strategy for an upwardly mobile CDU Land finance minister or chancellor.

There are several potential ways to measure partisanship. The simplest way to estimate separate effects of unemployment on deficits for left and right governments is to create a dummy variable that takes the value 1 for years in which the SPD governs alone or is the senior coalition partner and the value 0 for years when the CDU or CSU governs alone or is the senior coalition partner. To examine the longer-term argument, I have created a continuous variable that takes into consideration the possibility that, for instance, demands for expenditures might be lower in an SPD/Free Democratic Party (FDP) coalition than when the SPD governs alone. Of course, party ideology is difficult to scale, but a useful technique has been developed by Huber and Inglehart (1995), who use surveys of expert political scientists, political sociologists, and survey researchers who are asked to place parties on a ten-point scale from left to right. Huber and Inglehart report the following mean positions for German parties: Greens 2.91, SPD 3.83, FDP 5.64, CDU 6.42, and CSU 7.3.[14] For coalitions, I simply take averages of the scores for the coalition members. For election years, I use weighted averages of the scores of the pre- and postelection coalitions, weighted by the number of months in the tenure of each. Averages over the entire period are displayed in Table 7.2. The most left-leaning state is Bremen, with an average score of 3.86, while the most conservative state is Bayern (Bavaria).

Political Fragmentation   Several theories suggest that fragmented or polarized coalitions run larger deficits and accrue higher levels of public debt. Roubini and Sachs (1989) and Alesina and Drazen (1991) argue that when persistent deficits become problematic, parties in government are likely to disagree about who should bear the costs of adjustment. In the case of unified, single-party government, it should be relatively easy

---

[14] Alter (2002) conducts several quality checks and reports that the survey respondents are very consistent with one another and their responses are very consistent with other studies.

to externalize these costs onto some group that is not part of the governing party's constituency. When two or more parties must agree, however, either because of coalition government or of divided government between branches, distributional conflicts over the costs of adjustment may prevent or delay the necessary adjustments to taxes or spending. Again, the empirical method used here does not differentiate between expected and unexpected shocks in order to explicitly examine adjustment, but the logic should lead to larger deficits in states with more veto players.

Although the measurement of such a variable is rather complicated when comparing countries, it is relatively straightforward in the Land context. Following Tsebelis (1995), I assume that each coalition member is a potential veto player, so one point is assigned for each coalition member. A single-party government receives one point and a two-party coalition receives two points (there are no three-party coalitions during this period). Again, when necessary, election years are coded by using weighted averages. Perhaps a better alternative measurement goes beyond the number of veto players and considers their ideological spread. A coalition with large ideological distance separating its members might find it harder to allocate costs of adjustment. This variable takes on the value 0 for one-party governments, and the distance between the Huber-Inglehart scores for two-party coalitions. The largest ideological spread is, of course, a grand coalition of the CDU and SPD (2.59); the smallest is between the CDU and FDP (.78). Table 7.2 (p. 178) shows that the average ideological spread in Bayern and Schleswig-Holstein was 0. Bayern has been controlled by the CSU alone during the entire period, and Schleswig-Holstein moved directly from the CDU alone to the SPD alone in 1988. Hessen has been the most fragmented state, with three different types of coalitions during the period under analysis.

Electoral Competitiveness

Alesina and Tabellini (1990) and Persson and Tabellini (2000) explore the possibility that debt is used strategically by politicians who expect to lose elections and seek to tie the hands of their successors by forcing them to take on debt payments that crowd out other forms of expenditure. This leads to the hypothesis that deficits are larger in extremely competitive political systems where incumbents frequently have low reelection expectations. I use an index of political competition calculated as 1 minus a Herfindahl

175

"political concentration index": $1 - \Sigma \alpha_i^2$ where α_i is the proportion of time in office (as senior coalition partner) for party i. The competition index moves from 0 to 1 as competition increases. This index is useful for cross-sectional analysis, but it does not vary over time. For time series cross-section analysis, it is difficult to come up with a proxy of "incumbent's perceived reelection probability." The most reasonable proxy is the incumbent senior coalition partner's vote share in the most recent election.

IV. Empirical Analysis

Empirical Approach

The dataset consists of observations for each of the old German Länder for each year between 1974 and 1995.[15] A very short time series and vastly different budgeting circumstances preclude the new Länder and Berlin. Additionally, the years 1994 and 1995 are dropped for Bremen and Saarland because massive bailouts received in those years caused grants to balloon and budgets were "artificially" balanced by federal intervention.

Several potential econometric strategies present themselves. Some of the hypotheses presented above are primarily about cross-Land differences, while others require analysis of changes over time within Länder – some short-term and some long-term. To address these concerns, the empirical analysis proceeds in three stages. The first group of time series cross-section models uses the error correction setup to differentiate between short – and long-term effects of key variables. In these models, the dependent variable is first-differenced and Land dummies are included to control for unobserved cross-section effects.[16] The disadvantage of including fixed effects is that it suppresses the effects of variables that differ across states but are quite stable over time, such as Bundesrat representation and ideology. Thus, in order

---

[15] Data on government composition, election timing, and vote shares were taken from the American Institute for Contemporary German Studies (http://www.jhu.edu/~aicgsdoc/wahlen). Fiscal, unemployment, and population data were downloaded from the *Statistisches Bundesamt* (http://www.statistik-bund.de). GDP data were kindly provided by the statistical office of Baden-Württemberg. These data were also used to calculate Land-level deflators used to adjust all fiscal data for inflation.

[16] In order to control for the impact of events like the oil crisis in the early 1970s and unification in the early 1990s, models have also been estimated including a matrix of year dummies, though this does not affect the results.

to allow for some cross-sectional effects, a random-effects model is also estimated. Finally, though the degrees of freedom are low, it is instructive to estimate a simple between-effects model on cross-section averages to illuminate the extent to which the results are driven by persistent cross-state differences.

For the time series cross-section models, there are several reasons to favor an error correction setup in which the endogenous variable is a first difference and the regressors that vary over time are entered both as first differences and lagged levels. First of all, this setup allows one to distinguish between short-term and long-term effects. The coefficient on the lagged level of real grants per capita measures the long-term, lasting effect on fiscal outcomes, while the coefficient for the first difference measures short-term, transitory effects. Similarly, the coefficients for the lagged levels of GDP and unemployment estimate the long-term effects of economic change, while the coefficient for the change variable allows one to examine short-term responses to the business cycle. An additional reason for first-differencing the dependent variable is to minimize the bias created by possible nonstationarity in fiscal variables like expenditures and revenues.

Perhaps the most serious econometric challenge is the possible endogeneity of grants. Past deficits might cause increased grants, or – even though the models control for GDP and unemployment – grants and deficits might be jointly caused by some unobserved factors like the decline of an industry or a demographic shift. Moreover, as discussed above, grant levels may be "caused" by some of the other exogenous variables like representation, co-partisanship, or the macroeconomic controls. Ideally, the empirical setup would instrument for grants. It is very difficult to find a good instrument, however, because variables that are correlated with grants – above all, Bundesrat representation – will also be correlated with the error term of the fiscal performance equation.[17] Another possibility is to use past values of grants as instruments or to use the Arrelano-Bond GMM technique used in Chapter 4, in which the lag structure is used to instrument

---

[17] It is interesting to note that no matter what lag structure is used, grants are not predicted by unemployment or GDP. They do not move with the election cycle, and partisanship variables do not perform well. Grants are apparently targeted neither to co-partisan states nor swing states. The only variable that performs well in predicting grant levels is Bundesrat seats per capita.

Table 7.2. *Estimates of Land-level fiscal outcomes (fixed effects)*

	Dependent Variable		
	Δ Real Surplus per Capita	Δ Real Expenditure per Capita	Δ Real Revenue per Capita
Dependent variable$_{t-1}$	−0.80***	−0.70***	−0.44***
	(0.11)	(0.10)	(0.10)
Δ Grants	0.70**	0.03	0.70***
	(0.33)	(0.28)	(0.15)
Grants$_{t-1}$	−0.19	0.98***	0.46***
	(0.17)	(0.18)	(0.15)
Co-partisanship	−73.92**	53.42*	−13.79
	(35.99)	(28.84)	(23.60)
Δ GDP per capita	0.01	0.06*	0.07***
	(0.04)	(0.03)	(0.02)
GDP per capita$_{t-1}$	−0.02**	0.04***	0.01
	(0.01)	(0.01)	(0.01)
Δ Unemployment	−7.42	−1.1	3.12
	(52.80)	(44.77)	(32.13)
Unemployment$_{t-1}$	6.61	18.95 .	20.02
	(20.27)	(19.29)	(12.44)
Election year	−74.26*	48.56	−21.44
	(38.06)	(31.98)	(24.61)
Ideology	50.37**	−22.16	13.78
	(24.50)	(20.02)	(13.88)
Political fragmentation	40.3	−40.16*	−8.26
	(27.94)	(23.35)	(14.12)
Govt. party vote share	−362.1	−416.51	−730.24**
	(603.71)	(499.32)	(322.90)
Constant	466.96	4,137.41***	3,132.23***
	(707.72)	(790.61)	(731.67)
Number of observations	206	206	206
Number of states	10	10	10
R^2	0.63	0.58	0.72

*significant at 10%; ** significant at 5%; *** significant at 1%
Panel-corrected standard errors in parentheses
Surplus, grants, expenditures, revenues, and GDP are in real per capita terms. Coefficients for Land dummies not reported

for all of the time-variant exogenous variables.[18] All of these approaches yield similar results to the simpler models presented below.

[18] The Arellano-Bond technique is less appropriate here because of the small number of cross-section observations.

The error correction version of the model looks like this:

$$\Delta\,Surplus(t) = \beta_0 + \beta_1 Surplus(t-1)$$
$$+ \beta_2 \Delta\,Grants(t) + \beta_3 Grants(t-1) + \beta_4 Bundesrat\,seats\,per\,capita(t)$$
$$+ \beta_5 Copartisanship(t) + \beta_6 \Delta\,GDP(t) + \beta_7 GDP(t-1)$$
$$+ \beta_8 \Delta\,Unemployment + \beta_9 Unemploymentt(t-1)$$
$$+ \beta_{10} Election\,year(t) + \beta_{11} Ideology(t) + \beta_{12} Veto\,players(t)$$
$$+ \beta_{13} Most\,recent\,vote\,share(t) + Land\,and\,year\,dummies + \varepsilon \qquad (7.1)$$

The results of this model are presented in Table 7.2. In addition to the surplus model, Table 7.2 also reports the results of identical models that use real expenditures per capita and real revenues per capita as dependent variables. For some of the hypotheses, it is helpful to examine whether variables that affect fiscal balance are working through the expenditure side, the revenue side, or both. Similar results have been obtained using other estimation techniques, and experiments with dropping states from the analysis reveal that the results are not driven by outliers (e.g., Bremen or Saarland).

The results presented in Table 7.3 must be approached with more caution, but they provide valuable information. These models drop the Land dummies in order to allow cross-state variation to affect the results. Unsurprisingly, the results are more sensitive to the inclusion and exclusion of states. Note that the regressions in Table 7.2 do not include the time-invariant Bundesrat representation variable because of the inclusion of fixed effects, but this variable is included in the random-effects models.

Finally, Table 7.4 presents the results of the most blunt models: OLS regressions on cross-section averages. All of the variables are the same except the political competition index, which replaces the vote share of the governing party as the indicator of electoral competitiveness. Of course, one should be skeptical of a regression with ten observations, but several variables do approach statistical significance in the full model.

Results

Grants The results tell an interesting story about intergovernmental grants in Germany. First of all, short-term increases in grants have a large positive effect on fiscal balance (the first column in Table 7.2). Not surprisingly, other things equal, short-term increases in grants have large positive effects on revenues (the third column), but no discernible effect on expenditures in the short term (the second column).

Table 7.3. *Estimates of Land-level fiscal outcomes (random effects)*

	Dependent Variable		
	Δ Real Surplus per Capita	Δ Real Expenditure per Capita	Δ Real Revenue per Capita
Dependent variable$_{t-1}$	−0.62***	−0.19***	−0.04
	(0.12)	(0.05)	(0.04)
Δ Grants	0.54	0.11	0.76***
	(0.36)	(0.34)	(0.16)
Grants$_{t-1}$	−0.24**	0.54***	0.09
	(0.12)	(0.17)	(0.09)
Log Bundesrat seats per capita	−115.36*	69.95 *	11.95
	(41.80)	(40.09)	(16.89)
Co-partisanship	−127.25***	117.13***	13.34
	(39.82)	(34.85)	(27.15)
Δ GDP per capita	0.01	0.08**	0.08***
	(0.04)	(0.03)	(0.03)
GDP per capita$_{t-1}$	−0.003	0.03***	0.01
	(0.003)	(0.01)	(0.01)
Δ Unemployment	−67.09	63.13	25.45
	(54.20)	(52.32)	(36.27)
Unemployment$_{t-1}$	−19.66**	29.5**	6.66
	(8.59)	(12.30)	(8.06)
Election year	−79.48 *	49.18	−21.9
	(43.22)	(40.90)	(27.90)
Ideology	69.93***	−40.56**	−5.76
	(20.43)	(17.89)	(11.59)
Political fragmentation	38.8	−20.6	−10.56
	(26.65)	(24.35)	(16.09)
Govt. party vote share	−708.44	935.85 *	88.7
	(499.82)	(511.54)	(285.28)
Constant	−1,766.62***	283.00	−101.93
	(652.95)	(585.67)	(311.72)
Number of observations	206	206	206
Number of states	10	10	10
R^2	0.56	0.36	0.62

* significant at 10%; ** significant at 5%; *** significant at 1%
Panel-corrected standard errors in parentheses
Surplus, grants, expenditures, revenues, and GDP are in real per capita terms

Table 7.4. *Estimates of average Land fiscal outcomes (cross-section averages)*

	Dependent Variable		
	Average Real Surplus per Capita	Average Real Expenditure per Capita	Average Real Revenue per Capita
Grants	−0.41**	3.00**	2.59**
	(0.10)	(0.33)	(0.30)
Log Bundesrat seats per capita	−151.00*	−85.24	−236.24
	(41.78)	(138.83)	(124.71)
Co-partisanship	−450.99*	153.04	−297.94
	(158.11)	(525.42)	(471.95)
GDP per capita	0.0002	0.21***	0.21***
	(0.002)	(0.010)	(0.010)
Unemployment	−63.89**	301.83**	237.94**
	(15.36)	(51.05)	(45.86)
Ideology	73.28**	134.45	207.73 *
	(16.72)	(55.55)	(49.90)
Political competition index	351.4**	−123.94	227.46
	(78.55)	(261.04)	(234.48)
Constant	−2,150.97*	−8,021.93*	−10,172.90**
	(645.14)	(2143.85)	(1925.71)
Number of states	10	10	10
R-squared	0.99	0.99	0.99

Standard errors in parentheses
* significant at 10%; ** significant at 5%; *** significant at 1%
Surplus, grants, expenditures, revenues, and GDP are in real per capita terms
Estimation: OLS (between effects)

However, upon examination of the coefficients for lagged grant levels, there appears to be support for H1. The negative coefficient for lagged grants in the fixed effects model is −.19 and does not quite obtain statistical significance, while it is −.24 and highly significant in the random-effects model. Upon closer examination, the coefficient is also significant (and substantively larger) if the 1970s are dropped from the fixed-effects model. Recall from above that the possibility of using supplementary transfers for debt relief was not formally discussed until the 1980s. Moreover, more-complex models like the Arrelano-Bond GMM approach that use further lags of grants as instruments lead to highly significant negative coefficients for this variable, as do models that allow grants to be endogenous to variables like co-partisanship and Bundesrat representation. Furthermore, due to concerns with reverse causation, I have also replaced the grants per capita

181

variable with a (highly correlated) variable capturing the state's relative position in the equalization system before the final stage, which is purely automatic and exogenous to a state's past fiscal behavior. This variable has the expected sign and is highly significant in every estimation.

What does this mean? The coefficients suggest that controlling for developments in GDP and unemployment, a long-term increase of 100 DM per capita in intergovernmental grants is associated with a decrease of between 19 and 24 DM per capita in fiscal balance. The revenue and expenditure equations are also interesting. The coefficients in Table 7.2, which are driven primarily by time series variation, suggest a large long-term "flypaper effect." In the long run, virtually every pfennig of a grant increase is spent (the coefficient on expenditures is .98).[19] Quite simply, it appears that as states become more dependent on transfers, they are more inclined to increase expenditures and fund part of these increases with borrowing. In the very long run (Table 7.4), we see that more transfer-dependent states spend more per capita and run larger deficits.

Though these results are robust to different specifications, including models that allow for endogenous grants, a word of caution about causation is in order. In the absence of a good instrument, one cannot rule out the possibility that increases in grants, expenditures, and deficits are jointly caused by some unobserved phenomena. One can only say that there is an interesting correlation – but one that is difficult to explain without drawing on the notion of bailout expectations.

Jurisdiction Size   Because the models in Table 7.2 control for fixed effects, the Bundesrat seats per capita variable is only included in the random-effects and between-effects models. In spite of the high correlation with grants, this variable has a significant negative coefficient in the deficit model in Table 7.3 and even in the between-effects estimation in Table 7.4. Not only do they receive more grants, but states with more Bundesrat seats per capita have higher expenditures and larger deficits per capita. Unfortunately, it is not possible to distinguish between the effects of jurisdiction size and representation. Replacing the representation variable with Land population or real GDP tells a rather similar story. In any case, consistent with the arguments made above about the role of the party system in mitigating

---

[19] These results are consistent with a separate paper that explicitly examines adjustment. Rodden (2003b) shows that the more transfer-dependent the state, the less likely it is to adjust expenditures when faced with a negative revenue shock.

the too-big-to-fail problem, the largest German states are the least deficit-prone.

Copartisanship   While partisan incentives might create disincentives for large, wealthy states to use their size to extract bailouts, the analysis supports the hypothesis linking co-partisanship and enhanced bailout expectations. Other things equal, each of the models suggests that Land governments controlled by the party heading the federal government spend more and run slightly larger deficits than states controlled by the opposition. A similar result is obtained with the more complex measure of co-partisanship described above. A variety of interactive specifications were also estimated (not reported). Above all, they revealed that this relationship between co-partisanship and fiscal outcomes is driven primarily by the relatively small states, where – if the logic spelled out above is correct – the potential political costs of seeking redistributive bailouts are lowest.[20] No relationship was discovered between intergovernmental party ties and either grants or overall revenue. That is, it does not appear that co-partisans of the federal government are systematically favored in the game of distributive politics. Yet, other things equal, at least among relatively small states, co-partisans spend more and run larger deficits. The most reasonable explanation seems to be that co-partisans in these states believe that the federal government's no-bailout commitment is less credible.

Control Variables   It is possible to reject rather firmly the notion that the Länder conduct countercyclical fiscal policy. In fact, the evidence suggests pronounced procylicality. The "GDP change" line in Table 7.2 shows that revenues and expenditures move with the business cycle – revenues more so than expenditures – but fluctuations in GDP have no discernible effect on deficits.[21] The coefficients for revenue and expenditures are virtually identical to those in a recent study by Seitz (2000) that uses a different estimation technique.[22] The "change in unemployment" coefficients are indistinguishable from 0, and the same is true when this variable is interacted

---

[20] Further analysis with interactions revealed that the relationship was relatively similar whether the SPD or CDU was in power at the center.

[21] The coefficients for lagged GDP demonstrate that in the long run as states get wealthier, they spend and borrow more.

[22] The only difference is that Seitz finds evidence in favor of modestly countercyclical deficits.

with a partisanship dummy.[23] Together with Seitz (2000) and contrary to the aggregate results of Bayoumi and Eichengreen (1994), these results confirm that there is nothing like Keynesian countercyclical fiscal management going on at the Land level.

However, the analysis shows strong support for the electoral budget cycle hypothesis. The statistical significance of the coefficients for the election year variable in Tables 7.2 and 7.3 are suppressed by the inclusion of year dummies. These coefficients are significant at .01 when the year dummies are dropped. The results suggest that state deficits expands by 75 DM per capita during election years.

While there is no evidence that left and right partisanship affect the government's response to the business cycle, the ideological score of the governing coalition is correlated with fiscal outcomes. Specifically, right-wing governments spend less and borrow less than left-wing governments. The relationship is strongest in the random- and between-effects estimations, suggesting that it is driven primarily by long-term cross-Land variation. There are several potential explanations for this. First, CSU/CDU Land officials might have personal beliefs in smaller government and lower debt. Second, they may represent the preferences of their constituents. Or third, they may wish to impress their federal co-partisans.

No support is found for the common wisdom that the presence of coalition government or the ideological spread between coalition partners is associated with budget deficits. Finally, the vote share of the senior coalition partner in the most recent election – an admittedly imperfect proxy for reelection expectations – does not perform well in time series cross-section models, and the political competition index is quite sensitive in the simple cross-section models.

Summary of Findings It is clear that both within and across states, increasing reliance on intergovernmental transfers is associated with larger expenditures and higher deficits. The highest per capita expenditures and largest deficits are also found in the smallest, most overrepresented states. Though claims of causation must be muted in the absence of a good instrument, these results likely reflect that bailout expectations are more rational in relatively small and transfer-dependent Länder. Furthermore, among smaller Länder who might be bailed out without triggering a

---

[23] Only in the very long term are higher unemployment rates correlated with higher revenues and spending (see Table 7.4).

macroeconomic crisis, co-partisans spend more and run larger deficits than states controlled by the opposition. Finally, deficits expand during election years and are systematically larger in Länder controlled by the left.

V. Conclusion

As discussed in Chapter 2, the American political science literature – from the *Federalist Papers* to William Riker to Barry Weingast – has developed a normative view of federations as either too decentralized (e.g., Hamilton's description of the German empire) or too centralized (e.g., the Third Reich), seeking out some institutional sources of "balance." Yet the problem in postwar Germany is perhaps not that the center is simply too strong or too weak, but that it is simultaneously both. The center has deep pockets, it dominates revenue legislation, and its powers and obligations invite expectations of very similar public services in every corner of an increasingly diverse federation. Yet its ability to legislate and administer policy is severely constrained by the role of the Länder as veto players in the Bundesrat and their dominance of bureaucratic administration. Though the center's fiscal obligations undermine its no-bailout commitment, its constitutional and political limitations prevent it from imposing discipline from above.

The equalization system provides limited insurance against revenue shocks – it does not allow state revenues to fall far below the national average. But it does not provide insurance to fully compensate for income or unemployment shocks, and by no means does it ensure the Länder that expenditures can maintain a constant growth trajectory. In other words, Länder are not relieved of the obligation to undertake politically painful adjustments. However, a steadily increasing flow of discretionary supplementary grants seems to have created this impression for recipients. This chapter has argued that these grants – coupled with the constitutional obligation to maintain equivalent living conditions – provide politicians with rational beliefs that current deficits can be shifted onto residents of other jurisdictions in the future through increased transfers. Even if unsure whether these bailouts will be provided and precisely what form they will take, politicians in the most transfer-dependent states have few reasons to fear the wrath of voters and creditors if their debt-servicing burden increases.

The transfer system is not the only important incentive structure; the chapter also points to a role for partisan politics and elections. States controlled by left-wing parties run larger deficits, and expenditures and deficits are more pronounced in election years. Moreover, expenditures and deficits are higher in smaller states controlled by the federal government's co-partisans. The most attractive explanation is that these states are best able to position themselves for redistributive bailouts without being blamed for undermining national collective goods. Germany has not been plagued by the too-big-to-fail problem that looms large in the next chapter on Brazil. The political embarrassment associated with demanding a bailout is reduced in the smallest states, which can more credibly claim that their fiscal distress – often precipitated by an obvious exogenous shock – is not self-imposed. By contrast, it is likely that the political career of a chancellor or finance minister from a large state running unsustainable deficits and garnering massive federal bailouts would be compromised.

The overall macroeconomic costs of bailouts in Germany are open to debate. Relative to Germany's GDP, the actual bailout packages of Bremen and Saarland were not terribly costly. Yet the possibility of a demonstration effect and rising bailout expectations for all states is cause for concern. The courts have made it clear that the Basic Law implies a federal guarantee of Land debt. The states on the receiving side of the fiscal equalization program have strong bailout expectations. Yet as the dust settles from the Bremen and Saarland bailouts, it is also now clear that bailouts will be neither quick nor politically painless. These administrations had to play the bailout game to the final stage and endure public scrutiny and ultimately embarrassment. While bailout expectations have increased, so have the political costs of seeking them. The costs of fiscal indiscipline and the debt burdens of the Länder have become increasingly salient in the media, and voters are increasingly likely to perceive bailout requests from the Länder as threats to macroeconomic stability.

The distinction made in Chapter 5 between redistributive and negative-sum bailouts is useful. To the extent that state politicians in Germany have positioned themselves for bailouts, it was with the understanding that these would be perceived as redistributive – politicians from relatively poor, sub-sidized states using debt burdens to justify an even larger allocation. Yet the strong, integrated party system provides disincentives for Land politicians to stubbornly refuse adjustment and attract bailouts if voters will perceive these as carrying collective macroeconomic costs. Though the German transfer system and its interpretation by the courts undoubtedly create an intriguing and potentially disastrous moral-hazard problem, the political costs of undermining national macroeconomic stability – made possible by the party system – place limits on its severity.

Nevertheless, debt levels are increasing rapidly once again in Bremen and Saarland along with Berlin and most of the new Länder. It remains to be seen whether the political embarrassment and federal intervention associated with bailouts will dissuade them from extracting bailouts. The inability of the federal government to control state debt played a large role in Germany's inability to abide by the Stability and Growth Pact. In the current political discourse, fiscal irresponsibility among the Länder is portrayed as one of several key threats to Germany's macroeconomic success and international competitiveness. Many observers – especially from the wealthy states – agree that basic reform of the intergovernmental fiscal system is long overdue. But successful reform requires the consent of actors – in this case, the governments of the relatively poor Länder – who have something to lose. The difficult process of renegotiating the German fiscal constitution has been one of the thorniest issues on the German public policy agenda in recent years. Thus, the discussion of Germany is not yet complete. Chapter 9, which addresses the political economy of reform in federations, will return to the German case and address the problems and prospects for renegotiating the German fiscal contract.

8

The Crisis of Fiscal Federalism in Brazil

No Alexander Hamilton has arisen . . . to compel all parties to put aside their petty
jealousies and sacrifice their private interests to the welfare of the (Brazilian) Union.
Haggard's Monthly Report, June 1907[1]

The problem of unconstrained borrowing by states in the presence of a
perceived federal guarantee was a mere annoyance in postwar Germany
when compared with Brazil in the 1990s. While unsustainable borrowing
and bailouts were limited to the smallest states in Germany, this case study
discusses a pattern of fiscal indiscipline and bailouts that extended to a
majority of Brazilian states. Moreover, the crisis of fiscal federalism in Brazil
had direct implications for macroeconomic stability.

Brazil is the most decentralized country in the developing world. It has
a long history of federalism and decentralization and has become considerably more decentralized over the last two decades. On average during the
1990s, the states and municipalities were responsible for over one-third of
all revenue collections, close to half of all public consumption, and almost
40 percent of the public sector's net debt stock. Political and fiscal decentralization were key components of Brazil's transition to democracy in the
1980s. An examination of Brazil's experiences since then demonstrates the
severity of the challenges for macroeconomic management posed by fiscal
decentralization in the context of inequality, political fragmentation, and
robust federalism. Above all, Brazil has been forced to deal with one of the
most serious and persistent subnational debt problems in the world.

Brazil has experienced three major state-level debt crises between the late
1980s and 2000. In each of the crisis episodes, the states – already facing

---

[1] Cited in Wirth (1977: 219).

precarious fiscal situations with high levels of spending on personnel and interest payments – were pushed into debt-servicing crises by exogenous shocks. In each case, their first reaction was to demand bailouts from the central government, and in each case the federal government responded by taking measures to assume state debts.

The task of this case study is to examine the political and economic underpinnings of fiscal indiscipline among the Brazilian states in the 1980s and '90s. In spite of the considerable differences between Germany and Brazil, this chapter unearths some striking similarities in the perils of borrowing by semisovereign states. Above all, the basic fiscal contract clearly creates perceptions among governors, voters, and creditors that the states are not ultimately responsible for their own obligations. In spite of its proclamations, the central government could not credibly commit to refrain from bailing out the troubled states during times of crisis. This commitment was undermined above all by the fact that the states have been able to influence relevant central government decisions regarding subnational finance because of their strong representation in the legislature. But unlike Germany, Brazil had a party system in the 1980s and '90s that provided neither legislators nor governors with reasons to be concerned with national macroeconomic stability.

As in the previous chapter, this study uses cross-state and time series data to get a more precise understanding of the problem. Although the data quality is not ideal and the finding is less robust, it does appear that, as in Germany, increasing transfer dependence is associated with increasing expenditures and deficits. Additionally, the states with the most votes per capita in the legislature not only receive larger transfers, but also spend more and run larger deficits. There is also fleeting evidence that governors sharing the political affiliation of the federal executive run larger deficits. Moreover, the Brazilian states also demonstrate a pronounced electoral deficit cycle.

Yet the analysis also emphasizes interesting differences between the two countries. Only the smallest and most transfer-dependent states had rational bailout expectations in Germany; and when they occurred, bailouts were mandated by the high court rather than negotiated through a political bargain. In contrast, the Brazilian system has a long-established precedent that subnational debt renegotiation is, like discretionary transfers, a prize in an ongoing game of distributive politics played out in the legislature. This provided all states with reasonable bailout expectations. Moreover, in stark contrast to the German case, the largest and wealthiest

189

states in Brazil were the largest debtors and received some of the largest bailouts.

The first section describes and analyzes the incentive structures created by the Brazilian intergovernmental system. The second section analyzes the crisis episodes in greater detail. The following section proposes and tests several potential explanations for cross-state variation in fiscal behavior across the Brazilian states, and the final section concludes by returning once again to the Brazil–Germany comparison.

I. The Brazilian System of Federalism

The structure of Brazil's system of federalism was laid out in the 1988 constitution: It includes the Union, twenty-six states plus the Federal District (Brasilia), and a constantly growing number of municipalities. Unlike Germany, Brazil is a presidential democracy. The lower chamber of Congress (Chamber of Deputies) consists of 513 members elected via a system of open-list proportional representation using the states as constituencies. The Senate is comprised of three senators from each state, elected for eight-year terms with no limits. While the overrepresentation of small states in the upper legislative chamber is a central feature of most federal democracies, this asymmetry is especially severe in Brazil and applies to *both* chambers (See Samuels and Snyder 2001; Stepan 1999).

Brazil's system of federalism is similar to Germany's in that the activities of the federal and state levels are highly intertwined, with a center that is heavily involved in funding and regulating the states. And as in Germany, the states have had wide-ranging access to borrowing – especially from state-owned banks – and federal attempts at oversight have been stymied by strong representation of the states in federal political institutions. A key difference highlighted in this chapter, however, is the fact that Brazil's presidential system and electoral rules have created a much weaker party system than Germany's.

Fiscal Federalism

Expenditure Surely no federal constitution is a perfect guide to the distribution of spending and governmental authority between levels of government, but Brazil's 1988 constitution is even less helpful than most. The National Constituent Assembly leading to the constitution ceded large amounts of revenue through devolved tax authority and guaranteed transfers and ensured a high degree of fiscal and budgetary autonomy for the states. However, it did very little to specify expenditure responsibilities. The constitution does carefully outline some exclusive areas of *federal* competence. These include most of the responsibilities that are generally allocated to the central government in normative fiscal federalism theory: defense, common currency, interstate commerce, and national highways. The constitution also explicitly lays out some spending activities for the municipalities, but it does not itemize any exclusive responsibilities for the states. Rather, it lists a variety of concurrent, or joint, responsibilities of the federal and state governments. This list includes a variety of major spending areas, including health, education, environmental protection, agriculture, housing, welfare, and police. In these concurrent policy areas, the constitution stipulates that the federal government is to set standards and the state governments are to deliver services. The constitution also stipulates that the states are free to legislate in all non-enumerated policy areas.

In practice, most policy areas are jointly occupied by two and sometimes three levels of government. Decentralization since 1988 has been a disorderly process in which the federal government, facing fiscal pressures because of the devolution of revenues, gradually discontinues programs. In the areas of education, health, urban transportation, recreation, culture, child and old-age care, and social assistance, all three levels act in an uncoordinated fashion, which sometimes leads to "confusion and chaos in service delivery" (Shah 1991: 5). The constitution does little to place specific restrictions on the spending activities of the states. The states prioritize their spending according to their own agendas and even try to induce the central government to provide funds for their preferred programs through negotiated transfers in the areas of shared responsibility. Throughout the 1980s and '90s, the constitution has significantly restricted state autonomy, however, in the area of public sector personnel management. According to the 1988 constitution, states cannot dismiss redundant civil servants, nor are they allowed to reduce salaries in nominal terms. During the 1990s, retiring state employees had the right to a pension equal to their exit salary plus any subsequent increases granted to their previous position. These constitutional provisions have seriously restricted states' ability to control personnel costs; and given the importance of these costs in state revenue, it has been very difficult for the states to make adjustments when fiscal conditions require spending cuts.

Revenue   One of the most distinctive characteristics of Brazil's federal system, when compared to its South American neighbors, is the relatively important role of some states in raising their own revenue. Throughout the twentieth century, Brazilian states have funded a relatively large share of their spending through taxation – first through the export tax and then, since the 1930s, through a turnover tax. This was replaced in the 1960s with a value-added tax, now known as the ICMS. Additionally, they have access to motor vehicle, estate and gift taxes, and the federal government allows the states to levy supplementary rates up to 5 percent on the federal bases for personal and corporate incomes. The federal government assumes exclusive responsibility for the taxes on personal income (IRPF), corporate income (IRPJ), payroll, wealth, foreign trade, banking, finance and insurance, rural properties, hydroelectricity, and mineral products. The federal government also administers a type of value-added tax: the IPI. The federal government's revenue from income taxes, rural properties, and IPI must all be shared with the state and local governments.[2]

The ICMS accounts for 23 percent of the total tax burden and for 84 percent of tax collection by the states (Mora and Varsano 2001: 5). The collection of the ICMS is based on origin rather than destination, which makes it difficult for poor states (where consumption generally outpaces production) to raise revenue and allows states to export their tax burdens onto others (see World Bank 2002a). Moreover, though technically illegal, states compete vigorously for mobile investors with lower tax rates and exemptions for producers, leading some critics to complain that a "fiscal war" between the states shrinks the tax base of the states, burdens interstate commerce, complicates tax administration, and exacerbates interstate income disparities.[3] As is the case with spending authority, overlap in the distribution of taxing authority contradicts the basic principles of fiscal federalism and leads to confusion and inefficiency. In particular, the bases for the federal government's IPI, the states' ICMS, and some local government taxes overlap, and administration is extremely complicated.

Although the Brazilian states do have access to an important broad-based tax and some of the wealthier states fund a large portion of their spending

---

[2] One key problem with the Brazilian tax system is that because of its obligation to share such large portions of these taxes, the federal government seeks to overexpand several inefficient, cascading taxes that are not subject to sharing (Mora and Varsano 2000).

[3] The so-called Kandir Law of 1996 substantially altered the ICMS by exonerating exports and investment goods and allowing taxpayers to compensate their liabilities with taxes previously paid on all their inputs.

activities through locally raised revenue, intergovernmental transfers are an extremely important facet of the Brazilian federal system. Although overall levels of vertical fiscal imbalance are low for the state sector as a whole when compared to other Latin American federations, dependence on transfers varies dramatically from one state to another.

The far right-hand column of Table 8.1 displays average levels of transfer dependence over the 1990s for all of the states. During this period, on average São Paulo depended upon the federal government for only 7 percent of its revenue, while for Acre the figure was 75 percent. Revenue is transferred to the states and municipalities by (1) constitutionally mandated tax revenue–sharing arrangements, and (2) nonconstitutional, specific-purpose transfers.

Revenue-sharing arrangements are specified in great detail in the Brazilian Constitution. The Constitution provides strict criteria for the allocation of revenue to the states and municipalities, but does little to stipulate the final use of the funds, other than the requirement that states and municipalities must spend at least 25 percent of all tax revenues on education. The most important fund for the states is the State Participation Fund (FPE). The FPE is funded with 21.5 percent of the net revenues of the three main federal taxes: the personal (IRPF) and corporate (IRPJ) income taxes and the VAT (IPI). The distribution of funds among the states follows a participation coefficient for each state that is based mainly on regional redistributive criteria. The coefficients range between 9.4 percent for the state of Bahia to 1 percent for São Paulo (Ter-Minassian 1997: 449). The fund sets aside 85 percent of the total for poorer regions: the North, Northeast, and Center West.

It is important to note, however, that this fund has not been successful in combating interstate inequalities in private income or public spending. Figure 8.1 illustrates these inequalities by plotting average real GDP per capita on the horizontal axis and average real expenditures per capita on the vertical axis. The wealthiest states have per capita incomes that are five times those of the poorest cluster of states, and there are corresponding interstate differences in public expenditures. These relationships have been quite stable over the last decade.[4] Figure 8.1 displays what are among the largest regional income inequalities of any country

---

[4] The interstate Gini coefficient for real GDP per capita (calculated by the author) has been steady at around .30 from 1986 to 1998, while the coefficient for real expenditures per capita has declined from .36 to .30 over the same period.

Table 8.1. *Key fiscal and demographic data, Brazilian states, 1990–2000 averages*

	Population	Poverty Index	Real GDP per Capita (1995 R$)	Real State Expenditure per Capita (1995 R$)	State Deficit as Share of Revenue	Transfers as Share of State Revenue
Acre	468,867	30.66	2,066.34	890.76	−0.098	0.753
Alagoas	2,636,603	51.40	1,680.58	277.73	0.030	0.463
Amapá	355,923	37.19	3,206.24	1,229.55	−0.017	0.706
Amazonas	2,337,339	32.83	4,849.87	565.16	0.009	0.249
Bahia	12,480,193	51.12	2,252.30	332.57	−0.018	0.273
Ceará	6,731,876	54.11	1,832.65	307.42	0.022	0.311
Distrito Federal	1,774,824	12.98	7,836.46	1,714.53	−0.007	0.551
Espírito Santo	2,773,477	28.24	4,234.46	645.81	−0.088	0.198
Goiás	4,405,601	24.45	2,740.13	456.99	−0.139	0.139
Maranhão	5,187,500	64.20	1,024.06	207.57	0.056	0.557
Mato Grosso	2,227,149	25.83	2,994.60	600.56	−0.125	0.239
Mato Grosso do Sul	1,905,740	23.48	3,542.96	573.29	−0.131	0.188
Minas Gerais	16,517,107	27.64	3,824.05	504.97	−0.043	0.158
Pará	5,425,679	38.34	2,367.17	276.29	0.004	0.385
Paraná	8,867,247	21.59	4,417.68	450.72	−0.011	0.147
Paraíba	3,300,224	47.48	1,589.76	288.81	−0.086	0.536
Pernambuco	7,375,282	46.84	2,373.88	311.16	0.002	0.280
Piauí	2,673,439	60.59	1,137.13	271.97	−0.038	0.555
Rio de Janeiro	13,305,537	14.40	5,580.57	642.50	−0.070	0.125
Rio Grande do Norte	2,545,940	44.32	1,924.42	365.71	−0.086	0.482
Rio Grande do Sul	9,560,723	18.65	5,604.92	675.65	−0.032	0.118
Rondônia	1,243,090	22.90	2,469.33	530.27	−0.140	0.452
Roraima	246,824	10.65	2,212.90	1,334.00	−0.070	0.703
Santa Catarina	4,824,261	15.27	4,951.90	552.24	−0.070	0.151
Sergipe	1,603,101	46.24	2,395.81	506.83	−0.013	0.437
São Paulo	33,704,209	9.89	6,850.41	893.38	−0.080	0.069
Tocantins	1,023,999	51.57	1,192.50	588.80	−0.135	0.630

Sources: IBGE, various years; Ministerio da Fazenda, various years; and author's calculations

in the world, and revenue sharing has had little effect (Shankar and Shah 2001). By way of comparison, the income of the wealthiest German state is not quite twice the income of the poorest, and there is no correlation between GDP per capita and expenditures per capita among the German states.

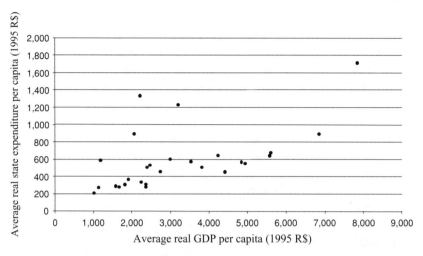

Figure 8.1. GDP per capita and state expenditure per capita, Brazilian states, 1990–2000. Sources: Ministério da Fazenda, various years; IBGE, various years; and author's calculations.

In addition to general-purpose revenue-sharing arrangements, the federal government makes grants to the states and municipalities for a variety of specific purposes. First of all, grant programs have been instituted to comply with laws other than the constitution. States and local governments also undertake investment projects on behalf of the federal government, which funds them through the General Revenue Fund as well as the Social Investment Fund. In addition, a variety of transfers are made to state and local governments through specific central government agencies.

A large portion of the funds transferred to the states outside of the revenue-sharing arrangement have traditionally been made through "voluntary" or "negotiated" transfers. These are not regulated by law and are based solely on negotiations between the federal and state (or municipal) governments individually. These provide support for a variety of activities including regional development, agriculture, education, health, and housing. In most cases, funds are transferred to the state and local governments to undertake spending in areas that are constitutionally assigned to the federal government. The president and his administration enjoy wide-ranging discretion in the distribution of these grants. Ames (2001) demonstrates that these grants have been used by each Brazilian president to favor the states of his political allies. More specifically, although the transfers have become less discretionary in recent years, Arretche and Rodden (2003) show that voluntary transfers during the Cardoso administration have favored the states of members of the president's legislative coalition in the Chamber of Deputies. These transfers often accrue disproportionately to the most politically powerful and often the wealthiest states. These transfers often work at cross-purposes with the redistributive goals of the tax-sharing mechanism and help explain the relationship displayed in Figure 8.1.

Borrowing   In the 1990s, the Brazilian states have borrowed from a variety of sources, including the domestic private sector, the external private sector, federal financial institutions, and a variety of informal mechanisms. First of all, the states borrowed from private domestic banks, primarily for short-term cash management purposes and for medium-term financing. An important form of short-term borrowing has been the revenue anticipation loan (ARO), which has been used as a means of managing cash flow. States have also floated bonds on the domestic capital market. Prior to a recent wave of privatizations, twenty of the states owned at least one public bank, all of which facilitated state borrowing by underwriting state bond issues. Like public enterprises, these banks also carried off-budget liabilities. Their lending activities were highly politicized: The directors were short-lived political appointees, bank personnel were hired for political purposes, and loans were directed to political allies (Werlang and Fraga Neto 1992). Many of the banks were insolvent by the mid-1990s. The state of São Paulo borrowed directly from its commercial bank, BANESPA. States also borrowed from international private sector institutions, most often in the form of medium-term contractual debt. Some states and their enterprises have successfully floated Eurobonds in the 1990s (Dillinger 1997: 3).

Second, states borrowed from federal financial institutions. Since the 1960s, long-term financing has been provided to the states by the Federal Housing and Savings Bank (CEF) and the Federal Economic and Social Development Bank (BNDES). In addition, the federal government mobilized savings through its deposit-taking commercial banks – above all the Banco do Brasil – which were lent to the states (Dillinger 1997: 3). As discussed in greater detail below, the federal treasury and the Central Bank have also become important creditors to the states as a result of recent bailout agreements. The evolving distribution of subnational debt is displayed in Table 8.2.

Finally, states borrowed through a variety of informal mechanisms. Short-term state deficits were frequently financed with arrears on payments to suppliers and state employees. In addition, states sometimes used time

Table 8.2. *Subnational net debt (percentage of GDP)*

	1987	1988	1989	1990	1991	1992	1993	1994	1995	1996	1997	1998
Total net debt*	6.82	5.57	6.15	8.87	7.50	9.50	9.30	9.50	10.40	11.90	13.00	14.30
Domestic debt	5.23	4.18	5.18	7.67	6.40	8.40	8.30	9.20	10.10	11.50	12.50	13.70
Bonded domestic net debt	1.81	1.53	2.49	2.46	2.30	3.10	3.60	4.60	5.40	6.40	4.30	2.40
Banks	3.41	2.65	2.69	4.45	3.20	4.30	3.90	3.30	3.60	4.10	2.60	1.80
Federal government renegotiations								1.10	1.10	1.10	5.50	9.50
Other	0.01	0.00	0.00	0.76	0.90	1.00	0.80	0.20	0.00	-0.10	0.10	0.00
External debt	1.60	1.40	0.97	1.20	1.20	1.10	1.00	0.30	0.30	0.40	0.50	0.70

* Excludes public enterprises
Source: Bevilaqua (2000)

lags in the judicial process to facilitate a unique form of borrowing: Take cost-cutting measures, like land expropriation, that are likely to be over-turned by the courts; but until a judgment is reached, states can avoid payment. Even when an unfavorable judgment is issued, the states can some-times finance payment through special bonds called *precatorios* (Dillinger 1997: 3).

The federal government has taken a variety of measures to control state borrowing in the 1990s, and at first glance it would appear to have had access to an impressive array of hierarchical control mechanisms through the constitution, additional federal legislation, and the Central Bank.[5] Most of these mechanisms have been undermined, however, by loopholes or bad incentives that discourage adequate enforcement. This section describes the regime in place during the 1990s, while more recent (post-1997) reforms are discussed in the next chapter. First of all, the constitution stipulates that the Senate has the authority to regulate all state borrowing. The Senate placed numerical restrictions on new borrowing on the basis of two factors: debt service coverage and growth of the total stock of debt. These reso-lutions were merely guidelines, however, and the Senate was free to grant exceptions, which it did frequently (Dillinger and Webb 1999). Given that the Senate is dominated by the interests of the states, it was a very poor overseer of state borrowing.

In addition to the Senate, constitutional provisions and federal regula-tions also restricted domestic borrowing in theory. Federal laws stipulate that revenue anticipation loans (AROs) must be repaid within thirty days after the end of the budget year in which they are contracted. The issuance of domestic bonds is controlled by the constitution, which since 1993 pro-hibited new state bond issues. The states were nevertheless allowed to issue *precatorios* to finance court judgments and roll over the principal and capital-ized interest on their existing bonds. State external borrowing was exempt from these federal regulations, although most international lenders (includ-ing the World Bank) require a federal guarantee, which may be granted or denied by the Federal Ministry of Finance. State borrowing from donor agencies was controlled by a multiministerial council (COFIEX). An office in the Federal Ministry of Finance also monitored the finances of the sub-national entities and made recommendations to the Senate and the Central Bank.

---

[5] For a comprehensive review of central government attempts to regulate subnational bor-rowing going back to the 1970s, see Bevilaqua (2000).

The Central Bank was also involved in the oversight of state borrowing in its capacity as overseer of borrowing in the domestic banking sector. Under several Central Bank resolutions, private banks were prohibited from increasing their holdings of state debt other than bonds, but "the complexity of these regulations and their subsequent adjustments" (Dillinger and Webb 1999: 12) has undermined their effectiveness. Central Bank regulations also prohibit states from borrowing from their own commercial banks. This regulation has been evaded with great success, sometimes subtly and sometimes blatantly. The most common trick is to allow a contractor on a state project to borrow from a state bank and then default, by prior agreement, leaving the bank with a bad loan that is then assumed by the state government (Dillinger 1997).

The system described above made hierarchical control of state borrowing in the 1990s difficult for two interlocking reasons. First, the constitution seriously restricts the ability of the central government to influence the fiscal decisions of the states; and second, the central government failed to take advantage of the authority it does have because it is itself at times little more than a loose coalition of regional interests. First of all, the hierarchical control mechanisms available in the constitution only restricted the spending activities of the states in counterproductive ways. Above all, the states have until very recently been able to interpret the constitution as preventing them from changing levels of public employment in response to fiscal emergencies. Conditions attached to specific-purpose transfers have traditionally done very little to encourage fiscal discipline. On the contrary, these grants have been ad hoc windfalls negotiated according to a political logic. Owing largely to the politics of federalism discussed below, the Brazilian federal government in the 1980s and '90s had weak or inadequate tools with which to curb the borrowing activities of the states. Perhaps the most serious stumbling block has been the central government's inability – until the Cardoso administration – to regulate the state-owned commercial banks.

Precisely because the central government is so heavily involved in financing, lending to, and attempting to regulate the states, it creates expectations among voters and creditors alike that state debt is implicitly backed up by the central government. This expectation not only weakens voters' incentives and undermines the electoral oversight mechanism, but it destroys the discipline of the credit market as well. Even though the Brazilian states have undertaken significant borrowing from private banks, their spending and borrowing activities have not been disciplined by the need to attract investment capital on the private market. While international investors require an explicit federal guarantee, domestic lenders appear to have assumed an implicit guarantee. This assumption proved to be correct time and again in the 1980s and 1990s.

Fifteen states and two municipalities have issued bonds, while all of the states borrowed in the 1990s through revenue anticipation loans (AROs). As in Germany, bonds have traditionally been underwritten by the states' commercial banks and sold to private banks and investors. Although they bore five-year maturities, the bonds were generally rolled over at maturity (Dillinger 1997: 6). As state finances became precarious in the late 1980s, the credit market began to put pressure on the states: Interest rates demanded by private banks rose, and maturities shortened. Eventually, private investors refused to hold state debt at any price. This credit market pressure was quickly transformed into political pressure on the federal government, which ultimately was forced to take on the debt of the states when they defaulted. In 1989, the federal government agreed with the states to transform the outstanding stock of federally guaranteed external debt into a long-term debt to the federal treasury. This move confirmed the implicit assumption of ultimate federal responsibility for state debts, which was subsequently reaffirmed several times.

In sum, voters and creditors in the Brazilian states receive very few cues to suggest that state governments should be held responsible for their own fiscal health. Voters in the 1980s and '90s had a perception – one that contained a grain of truth – that state-level deficits and debt were not the fault of governors or other state-level officials. This perception was reinforced by the media and even members of Congress (Souza 1996: 340). This may have its roots in the role of the states prior to the democratic constitution, when they borrowed large amounts on behalf of the central government. Thus, starting in the late 1980s, democratically elected governors in the states could claim quite reasonably that their inherited burdens were actually federal burdens (recall Hamilton's arguments for debt assumption after the Revolutionary War). Moreover, the constitution gave the states very little control over personnel decisions, even though payroll accounted for well over 60 percent of expenditures in most states. Furthermore, the overlap of expenditure responsibilities between all three levels of government makes electoral accountability for service provision extremely difficult. On the revenue side, the ICMS does not provide incentives for large, encompassing coalitions of voters to lobby for preferred levels of taxes and public services or overall efficiency in the state public sector; rather, it encourages small, sector-specific groups of constituents with high stakes to lobby for special favors.[6]

In some of the poorest states, most revenue comes from general-purpose transfers. In the case of the transfer-dependent states, the fact that most local expenditures are being funded by other jurisdictions may discourage careful oversight. According to Afonso and de Mello, "[R]igidities in revenue sharing arrangements contributed to delaying subnational fiscal adjustment, since federal government efforts to increase revenues have also led to an increase in total subnational revenues via revenue sharing" (2000: 4). Even in the large, relatively wealthy and fiscally "autonomous" states, voters might not face incentives to punish officials for rising expenditures and deficits and unsustainable debt levels. Although not favored in the distribution of constitutional transfers, these politically powerful states have been particularly adept at attracting voluntary transfers. Voters in these states have come to reward their governors primarily for their ability to attract spending projects that are in effect subsidized by the rest of the federation.

Political Federalism

The most important reason for the central government's inability to gain control over state borrowing in the 1980s and '90s was the responsiveness of both the Chamber of Deputies and the Senate to the interests of state governments. Given the low level of party discipline and the frequency with which legislators change parties in both chambers, most representatives cannot advance their careers by concentrating on national or even statewide issues, but rather on seeking porkbarrel public works projects and other benefits for selected municipalities within their state (Ames 1995) – a common observation in presidential systems with weak party discipline. In order to build a winning coalition on any policy issue, it is necessary for the president to make a complicated set of regional payoffs. Brazil's open-list proportional-representation electoral system perpetuates extreme political individualism and guarantees that parties play a limited role in mobilizing electoral and legislative coalitions at either level of government.[7] Between

---

[6] For a more general discussion of this problem, see Rodden and Rose-Ackerman (1997).

[7] Voters can vote directly for an individual candidate or for a party's entire label. From the candidate's perspective, this creates a strong incentive to make individual appeals to voters through patronage and pork. The party's total list vote equals the sum of the party's

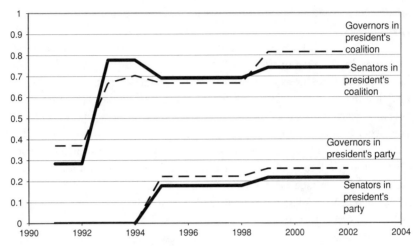

Figure 8.2. Shares of senators and governors in president's party and legislative coalition. Source: Arretche and Rodden (2004).

two and four candidates run for governor in each state, and these candidates attempt to attract as many politicians as possible to their camp, regardless of party. Each of these coalitions makes agreements about divisions of cabinet spoils and electoral lists for state and federal deputy elections (Samuels 2000). Thus, even gubernatorial candidates face few incentives to make statewide appeals to large groups of voters. "In each state, these processes involve personalistic negotiations, and downplay partisan or policy differences" (Samuels 2000: 243).

Term limits have also provided elected officials with short time horizons in the early 1990s. Without reelection incentives, most politicians were striving to build support networks that would allow them to move to a different level of government – city councilmen aspired to be state deputies, state deputies to be federal deputies, federal deputies to be state governors, and governors to be senators. Executive jobs are preferred to legislative positions because they provide power over budgets and patronage (Dillinger and Webb 1999).

Figure 8.2 displays shares of governors and senators belonging to the president's party, showing that throughout the 1990s only a small minority

candidates' votes plus its party label votes. The candidates with the most individual votes get the highest priority in distributing the party's seats, so each candidate prefers a vote for himself or herself over a party label vote (Samuels 1999: 495).

shared the president's party affiliation. However, a new body of literature (e.g., Figueiredo and Limongi 2000) suggests that the traditional wisdom about Brazilian party fractionalization ignores the importance of partisan legislative coalitions painstakingly built by each president, allowing them to obtain relatively stable legislative majorities in both legislative chambers. Figure 8.2 also displays shares of senators (and governors) belonging to the president's broader legislative coalition. It shows that in recent years Senate coalitions have included well over half of the senators, in part because Cardoso needed to secure supermajorities for constitutional changes.

The key question raised by Chapter 5 is whether members of these legislative coalitions, even if not co-partisans, would be inclined to place a national collective-goods agenda over bailout demands from their own states in order to protect the popularity of the president with whom they are allied. This seems doubtful because presidents clearly must continue to pay for the legislative support of coalition members, and bailouts are an attractive form of payment. Federal largesse seems to be the glue that holds Brazilian legislative coalitions together (Arretche and Rodden 2004). Moreover, evidence presented below suggests that the 1993 bailout favored the president's legislative allies.

Through the 1990s, the Senate had the formal authority to restrict borrowing in a number of ways, and it has been the primary overseer of recent debt renegotiations. It is difficult to expect the Senate to hold the line against the states, however, when the senators' interests are so close to those of state governors. On average, three-quarters of the senators are former or future governors (Dillinger and Webb 1999). Mainwaring and Samuels (2003) provide a wealth of examples – from the José Sarney to Fernando Enrique Cardoso administrations – of situations in which presidents attempted through various means to restrain state spending or debts but ran into opposition from influential governors. In each case, the governors had important allies in the Senate or Chamber of Deputies whose votes the president needed, and each time the president was forced to water down or abandon the proposal.

Another question raised by Chapter 5 is whether co-partisan governors, or at least governors belonging to a party in the president's coalition, would think twice about positioning themselves for bailouts out of fear that the resulting macroeconomic damage would hurt the president and thereby undermine their own political careers. Of course, the dataset is very small compared with Australia, Canada, and Germany – where it was possible to test for electoral externalities since the 1940s – but over the four elections since the return to democracy, it is difficult to find systematic evidence that gubernatorial-election outcomes are tightly linked to evaluations of the national executive.[8] Yet in many respects, the relationship between state and federal elections is still evolving, and the possibility should not be dismissed. As will be discussed in greater detail in the next chapter, Cardoso assembled a reform coalition that based its legitimacy on a national collective-goods agenda. Their successful fight against inflation may have indeed created a brief period in which Cardoso's legislative and especially gubernatorial allies were able to ride his coattails. In the 2002 elections, the Workers' Party (PT) made gains in gubernatorial elections that are difficult to explain without the success of their candidate in the presidential election.

Yet in comparison with Australia and Germany, it is safe to say that electoral externalities are rather weak in Brazil, and although unavoidably influenced by the presidential elections that are held simultaneously, gubernatorial elections do not have the flavor of referenda on the performance of the president. In fact, Samuels (2000) argues that candidates for the national legislature coalesce around gubernatorial candidates rather than presidential candidates and organize their campaigns around state-based rather than national issues and candidates (Samuels 2000).

II. State-Level Fiscal Crises and Bailouts

The Brazilian states have been through three debt crises in the last decade. This section briefly discusses the first two crises and then provides a more

---

[8] In Chapter 5, parties' vote shares in state elections were regressed on lagged state election vote shares and corresponding federal vote shares in the state in a model including fixed effects. It is difficult to extend this approach to Brazil because the parties that have had success in gubernatorial elections frequently either did not compete in the state in the previous year or fielded no federal-level candidate. This approach, when applied to the PMDB and PSDB, yields no relationship between federal and state vote shares, though this is not surprising given the small number of observations. It is interesting to note that this approach does yield a significant relationship between federal and state vote shares for the PT, which has maintained a small but stable showing in state elections. Perhaps a better approach, given the importance of coalitions, is to assign one party as the "incumbent" in each gubernatorial election based on the nature of its ties with the previous regime. David Samuels kindly provided information about such affiliations. The vote shares of these incumbents were regressed on the vote share of the party (or its affiliate) in the last gubernatorial election and the vote share of the presidential candidate with whom the incumbent was affiliated in the concurrent presidential election. Once again, there was no evidence of a relationship between state and federal vote shares.

in-depth analytic chronology of the most recent crisis.[9] In the mid-1960s, the debt of all subnational governments accounted for nearly 1 percent of GDP, while by 1998 it reached over 14 percent (see Table 8.2, above). The following historical account demonstrates that the rapid growth in state-level debt came about through a series of crises, each of which was precipitated by events somewhat beyond the control of the states. Each incident ultimately accelerated and transformed into a systemic crisis, how-ever, because of the moral-hazard problems described above. In each case, when faced with growing, unsustainable debt levels, the states refused to bear the costs of adjustment and demanded that the federal government assume their debts in some way. In each case, the credibility of the states' demands for bailouts was enhanced by their professed (and in many cases real) inability to respond adequately to the crisis alone. Moreover, in each case the credibility of the federal government's commitment not to assume subnational debt was undermined by its history of bailouts and the strong representation of the states in Congress and the executive.

Background

The first crisis arose during the international debt crisis of the 1980s. This crisis originated in loans made by the private sector. State bonds and rev-enue anticipation loans (AROs) were held by private banks. Unable to roll over external debt and faced with foreign-exchange constraints, states were unable to service their foreign debt. Throughout the 1980s, the federal government honored the states' federally guaranteed obligations to their respective creditors. In 1989, after lengthy negotiations the federal gov-ernment agreed to transform the accumulated state arrears and remaining principal into a single debt to the federal treasury.

The second crisis involved debt owed by the states to the federal financial intermediaries – principally the Federal Housing and Savings Bank (CEF). In 1993, this debt was also transferred to the federal treasury. In both of these deals, the refinanced debt was rescheduled for twenty years at interest rates based on those specified in the original contracts, with a grace period for payment of principal. The federal government had a difficult time securing

---

[9] The historical information presented in this section has been adapted from interviews, newspaper accounts, and the following secondary sources: Bevilaqua (2000); Dillinger(1997); Dillinger and Webb (1999); Oliviera (1998); Rigolon and Giambiagi (1998); and World Bank (2001).

the agreement of the states to the second deal, and in order to close on the arrangement, the federal government conceded an escape clause: If the ratio of state debt service obligations to revenue rose above a threshold fixed by the Senate, the excess could be deferred. The states would be allowed to capitalize deferred debt service into the stock of debt, which would only have to be repaid when debt service fell below the threshold.

This capitulation by the federal government to the interests of the states created a new set of perverse incentives. The agreements drastically reduced states' immediate debt service obligations in cash terms, but prompted considerable expansion in the stock of state debt. With the new debt service ceiling, states were able to capitalize existing debt service into the stock of debt, which would then expand at a rate that would accelerate whenever real interest rates increased. For the most indebted states, the debt service ceilings drastically reduced the expected future cost of current borrowing and interest capitalization. Moreover, the new incentive structure made it possible for fiscal decision makers to reduce debt service burdens, continue to borrow, and leave the fiscal consequences to future administrations. The agreements reinforced the perception that state debt was in the end backed up by the federal government.

The Most Recent Crisis

These new perverse incentives, combined with those inherent in the Brazilian intergovernmental system, precipitated another debt crisis in the mid-1990s. Debt burdens continued to grow during the 1990s, not primarily because of new borrowing, but because of the capitalization of interest on existing debt. Despite the previous crises and bailouts – or perhaps because of them – the states continued to increase spending, especially during and immediately after election campaigns. Figure 8.3 presents the average total expenditure per capita in the Brazilian states over the entire period, displaying severe spikes for the election years of 1986, 1990, 1994, and 1998 and rapid growth from 1993 – the year of the federal bailout – to 1998.

This expenditure growth was sustainable as long as inflation remained high. With high inflation rates, states could reduce payroll costs in real terms by simply holding nominal salaries constant. With the success of the Plano Real in the mid-1990s, however, dramatically falling inflation rates reduced the states' ability to avoid real salary and pension increases via inflation. Recall that the states' hands have been tied to an extent by the constitution, and they could claim that they were unable to fire workers or

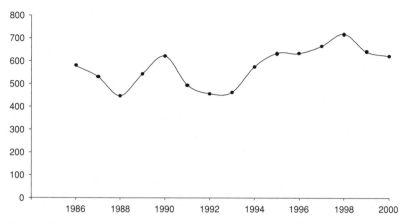

Figure 8.3. Average real expenditures per capita (R$ 1995), Brazilian states. Source: Ministério da Fazenda, various years; and author's calculations.

reduce wages. As a result, real state salary outlays skyrocketed. The states also faced exogenous challenges because of interest rates; much of their debt was vulnerable to short-term interest rate fluctuations. The tight monetary policy of the Plano Real resulted in continued high interest rates. Faced with growing personnel costs and overwhelming debt service obligations, the states' response was to default. The states defaulted in a variety of ways: (1) the further capitalization of interest on bonds, (2) the collapse of state banks, and (3) defaults on revenue anticipation loans and arrears (Dillinger 1997).

The most severe problem was with state bonds, particularly in four of the states: São Paulo, Rio de Janeiro, Minas Gerais, and Rio Grande do Sul. As described earlier, the states began to have difficulty marketing bonds in the late 1980s. Unable to liquidate the bond debt, the states sought relief from the federal government. It was clear that if the federal government refused to act, the states would be forced to default. The federal government was concerned that such defaults would undermine the stability of the entire domestic capital market. Thus, it responded by offering them the so-called *troca* arrangement, under which the federal government authorized the states to exchange their bonds for federal bonds. Under the terms of the agreement, state bonds would be held in the portfolio of the Central Bank, which would float a corresponding amount of Central Bank bonds, transferring them to the states. The Senate was authorized to determine the proportion of the bonds that would have to be liquidated at maturity.

Not surprisingly, the most indebted states were able to achieve their desired outcome in the Senate in the initial years – 100 percent rollovers. In addition, the Senate allowed the states to capitalize the accumulated interest due on the bonds into the outstanding stock of bond debt at each rollover. Thus, the Senate allowed the states to technically avoid defaults, even while they avoided any cash obligations to service their bonds. Interest charges on the exchanged bonds were based on the rate for federal bonds, which remained high. As the interest was capitalized, the total stock of state debt grew at an explosive rate.

Some states also defaulted on debt to their state-owned banks. By far the largest problem was São Paulo and its debt to BANESPA. Throughout the 1980s, the government of São Paulo was able to skirt central regulations and run up massive debts to BANESPA. It did this with loans contracted directly by BANESPA from foreign banks, with short-term revenue anticipation bonds that were transformed into long-term debt, and with loans to state-owned enterprises. São Paulo began to default on this debt during the early 1990s, and by 1994 it had ceased servicing the debt altogether. By the end of 1996, the state's debt to BANESPA had reached US$ 21 billion and was the bank's principal "asset" (Dillinger 1997: 8). By the middle of the 1990s, BANESPA had to meet its cash obligations by borrowing from the Central Bank. Several other state banks suffered heavy operating losses and stayed in business by borrowing from the Central Bank during this period as well.

Because of the importance of BANESPA and São Paulo to the national economy, they were viewed by the central government as too big to fail. The Ministry of Finance feared that the failure of BANESPA would prompt a liquidity crisis and a run on deposits, which would undermine confidence in the banking system as a whole. In 1995, the Central Bank assumed control of BANESPA and the state-owned bank of Rio de Janeiro with the goal of privatizing them, but it ultimately infused them with cash and returned them a year later, unreformed. According to Abrucio and Costa (1998), this was a direct response to pressure from the governor of São Paulo and its congressional delegation. By briefly assuming control of these two state banks and continuing to give liquidity support to them and other state-owned banks, the Central Bank not only permitted them to remain in operation and continue to capitalize the unpaid interest owed by borrowers, but also bolstered the perception that the banks' liabilities carry an implicit federal guarantee.

States also defaulted on short-term cash management debt in the 1990s. As the state fiscal crisis deepened, states lacked the funds to liquidate their short-term debt and appealed to their creditors to roll it over. The states also began to run up arrears to suppliers and personnel. The state administrations blamed the central government as they failed to make payments to contractors and employees, and the political pressure on the central government increased. In November 1995, the federal government responded by establishing the Program for State Restructuring and Fiscal Adjustment. This program provided two lines of credit to the states: one to pay off arrears to employees and contractors, and the other to refinance their revenue anticipation loans. Under the terms of the loans, the states agreed in theory to a series of reform measures dealing with personnel management, state enterprises, tax administration, debt reduction, and overall expenditure control (Bevilaqua 2000; Dillenger 1997). The federal government, however, had very little power to enforce these conditions, and funds were disbursed before any of the conditions could actually be imposed (Dillinger 1997: 7).

The actions of the federal government with respect to each of these forms of de facto state default effectively federalized the state debt. Bonds that had previously been held by private banks are now held by the Central Bank. While the debt to BANESPA had previously been the concern of its shareholders and depositors, it was implicitly assumed by the Central Bank. While the revenue anticipation loans and arrears had been owed to private banks and individuals, the restructured debt is now owed to the federal treasury.

Intergovermental Debt Negotiations

The central government and the states now face a monumental economic and political challenge as they attempt to work out long-term arrangements for the reduction of this debt. As has long been the case in India and more recently in Argentina, state debt is now primarily a matter between the states and the central government, rather than the states and their private sector creditors. As of September 2001, 84 percent of state debt was held by the national treasury. Thus, the reduction of state debt and the improvement of state fiscal health is now a matter of political bargaining between the representatives of the central government – Congress and the executive – and the governors. In the late 1990s, the structure of the Brazilian federal system introduced several roadblocks to successful reform. Executive agencies like the Ministry of Finance – the only actors with any claim to a national constituency – are reluctant to grant explicit

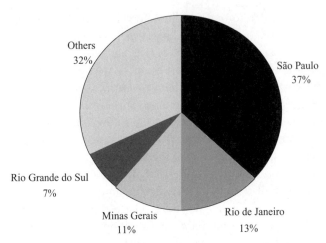

Figure 8.4. Distribution of subnational debt, September 2001. Source: Banco Central do Brasil 2001 and author's calculations.

debt reductions, fearing the exacerbation of the moral-hazard dilemma. The major debtor states – Rio de Janeiro, Rio Grande do Sul, Minas Gerais, and São Paulo (see Figure 8.4) – have had few incentives to make concessions in negotiations.

As a result of the deals described above, their debt service burdens are quite low, and the governors have no incentive to sign any agreement that would increase those burdens, particularly while they are still in office. The major debtor states are the most fiscally autonomous states – they are financed primarily through VAT revenue, over which the federal government has little control. Thus, federal threats to withhold intergovernmental transfers, while important, can only go so far.

The most important roadblock to satisfactory debt renegotiation and reform has been the Senate. Governors have pushed hard collectively for the principle that all state debt negotiations should take place in the Senate. Each state has three Senate seats, which means that the major debtor states control only twelve of the eighty-one seats. Instead of coalescing against the minority debtor states, however, the senators from the other states took advantage of the situation and demanded proportionate benefits for their own states in exchange for their votes to protect the interests of the largest debtors. This is an example of the Senate's norm of "universalism," whereby all of the senators agree not to stand in the way of one another's spending projects and debt relief.[10] Given the weakness of party discipline in Brazil, the president was unable to use national partisan ties to convince representatives to favor a national agenda over their regional interests. All of the senators faced incentives to prolong the debt repayment process (Gomez 2000), and deadlines for agreements came and went while the stock of debt continued to grow from 1995 to 1997.

Eventually, Cardoso succeeded in his plan to pursue separate deals with individual states. In December 1997, the federal government signed its first agreement with a major debtor state: São Paulo. Under this arrangement, the federal government agreed to assume all of São Paulo's bond debt and debt to BANESPA. A large chunk (around 80 percent of the total) was refinanced as a loan to the state government with thirty years to maturity and a real interest rate of 6 percent – well below the prevailing domestic rate. Another chunk (12.5 percent) was to be amortized through the transfer of stock in state enterprises. The remainder was forgiven by the federal government. The agreement also created a debt service ceiling covering not only the newly refinanced debt, but also the debt refinanced under the two previous reschedulings. For São Paulo, this amounted to virtually no increase in actual cash debt service, and it allowed the majority of debt service to be deferred indefinitely.

After São Paulo, Minas Gerais, and Rio Grande do Sul signed similar agreements. In the course of the legislative debate, Congress chose to offer the refinancing terms to all the remaining states in Brazil. Although these agreements will lower the interest rates paid by the states, the federal government will continue to be the states' creditor and continue to pay the overnight rate as the marginal cost of borrowing funds. Moreover, the states will not be prevented from continuing to capitalize interest on debt owed to the federal government, and state debt will continue to grow. As a result, the aggregate interest costs for the public sector will not decline. The costs have merely been shifted explicitly to the federal treasury.

Furthermore, obtaining favorable debt workouts continues to be a high priority for most senators, and demands for further delays in repayment are likely to only grow stronger. In a well-publicized incident in 1999, the governor of Minas Gerais – former president Itamar Franco – bitterly criticized the agreed fiscal targets and debt repayment schedule, threatening to cease all debt payments to the federal government. In fact, the governors

---

[10] On federalism and the norm of universalism in the legislature, see Inman and Rubinfeld (1997). On the Brazilian Senate, see Mainwaring and Samuels (2001).

and senators often appear to stand on reasonably firm ground when making their case. For instance, some governors have argued that as a result of recent reform of the ICMS, they face revenue constraints in addition to high real interest rates and social security expenditures, which make the debt repayment agreements excessively burdensome. In fact, however, ICMS revenue growth has been quite strong in recent years. It has become perhaps even more difficult than ever for potential creditors, investors, or voters – even scholars and journalists – to distinguish between self-imposed and exogenous fiscal problems among the states.

Who Benefited from Bailouts?

In the German case, only two states received formal bailouts, and these were somewhat depoliticized by the fact that they were mandated by the courts. But in Brazil, the bailouts of the 1990s were distributed to virtually every state, and the bargaining was extremely political. Afonso Bevilaqua (2000) has calculated the amount of debt renegotiated and forgiven in the bailouts of 1993 and 1997. Only two states did not have part of their debt renegotiated in 1993, and five states did not in 1997. Since the 1989 debt assumption, debt renegotiation has been a regular episode in the game of distributive politics. It is not a coincidence that each debt renegotiation took place in the heat of a presidential-gubernatorial election campaign. Thus, before moving on to examine state fiscal behavior, it is useful to establish some stylized facts about politics and the distribution of the bailouts.

A series of OLS regressions, presented in Table 8.3, examine the bailouts received by each state per capita in 1993 and 1997.[11] Given the central role for the Senate in the oversight and renegotiation of state debts and the potential importance of small states in bargaining due to malapportionment, it is useful to include the number of senators (three) per million inhabitants. Of course, this variable also reflects any other effects on bailouts that might be related to the size of the state. Any small state bias owing to legislative bargaining might be overwhelmed by the president's interest in pandering to the largest states with the most votes in presidential elections. One might expect this factor to be especially important in the 1997 bailout, when Cardoso was running for reelection. Furthermore, the large states might

---

[11] For 1993, this is the amount of debt renegotiated, and for 1997 it is the sum of the amount renegotiated and the amount forgiven. Both are expressed in per capita terms, 1998 prices. Natural logs are used in the regressions. The data source is Bevilaqua (2000).

212

Table 8.3. *Determinants of bailouts*

	Dependent Variable: Logged per Capita Bailout		
	1993	1997	1997
Log senate seats/million pop.	−2.94***	−0.19	
	(1.17)	(0.95)	
Log senators in president's coalition	1.24**	−0.23	
	(0.53)	(0.44)	
Interaction	1.10**	−0.26	
	(0.52)	(0.48)	
Governor in president's coalition	0.97	2.01***	2.10**
	(0.69)	(0.79)	(0.75)
Log GDP per capita	−0.88	1.42**	1.45**
	(0.55)	(0.72)	(0.67)
Log population			0.65*
			(0.33)
Constant	8.53*	−8.37	−18.74***
	(4.94)	(6.25)	(5.41)
Observations	27	27	27.00
R-squared	0.40	0.56	0.55

Standard errors in parentheses
* significant at 10%; ** significant at 5%; *** significant at 1%

be able to extract bailouts because of the negative externalities associated with letting them default.

If the president attempts to broker deals using his partisan legislative coalition, one might also expect to see that more-generous bailouts flow to the states with stronger representation in the coalition. This is measured with the number of a state's Senate delegation that is in the president's coalition. Seats per capita and coalition representation might also have an interactive effect. If the president favors small-states when building his legislative coalition in the first place, one might expect that small state bias is only enjoyed by states that are part of the president's legislative coalition. Aside from direct legislative bargaining, it seems plausible that presidents will work to broker deals that benefit governors who belong to their coalition. This is captured with a dummy variable. Finally, the regressions control for income per capita.[12]

[12] A variety of other control variables did not achieve statistical significance, including the percentage of population above and below the working age, income inequality, partisanship,

Only the representation variables are significant in the 1993 bailout regression. The model performs much better with the inclusion of the interaction term, which suggests that the effects of overrepresentation and coalition membership are conditional on one another. The conditional coefficients reveal that the effect of coalition membership on bailouts is positive and significant over most of the sample range but grows larger among the smaller states. As for the effect of overrepresentation, the conditional coefficient is negative but not significant when only one or no senator is in the president's coalition, but it is positive and significant when two or three senators are part of the president's coalition. In short, small-state bias holds only for states that are firmly in the president's coalition. The partisanship of the governor and income per capita had no effect on the distribution of the 1993 bailout.

The story is different for the 1997 bailout. The second column estimates an identical model for 1997, but the Senate representation variables do not approach significance. The third column presents a simpler model that drops these variables and replaces them with the state's population. In short, the 1997 bailout clearly benefited larger, wealthier states and those controlled by Cardoso's allies.[13]

These results are quite consistent with the discussion above. Recall that the 1993 bailout was negotiated between the president and the Senate, and the results bear the mark of a bargain struck between the president and his partisan Senate coalition. However, in 1997 Cardoso insisted on bypassing the Senate and dealing directly with governors, starting with the large states controlled by his allies and then moving on to other states.

III. Explaining Variation across States

Now that some facts have been established about federal bailouts, it is useful to examine the fiscal behavior of the states under the 1986 constitution. It is possible to tailor the hypotheses from the previous chapter and revisit them with Brazilian panel data. Expenditure growth was stronger

legislative fractionalization, and variables that capture the state's representation in the president's coalition in the Chamber of Deputies.

[13] A difference between the 1993 and 1997 bailouts is that the former was meant to alleviate debts to federal financial intermediaries, and the latter was primarily targeted at bond debt. No reliable measure of debts to the federal institutions is available, but a control for total bond debt as of 1996 was included in the 1997 bailout regression. The parameter estimate was positive but (surprisingly) not significant, and it did not affect the other results.

and deficits larger in the smallest, most transfer-dependent German states and, surprisingly, among the central government's co-partisans.

In the German case, there were strong indications that dependence on intergovernmental transfers was a reasonable proxy for bailout expectations. Ultimately, these expectations were borne out and bailouts were distributed in the form of special debt reduction transfers. In Brazil, however, neither constitutional nor discretionary transfers have been used for post hoc gap filling or debt forgiveness. Rather, bailouts have taken the form of federal debt assumption, forgiveness, and renegotiation at very favorable terms. Yet it is at least plausible that transfer dependence will have an effect on fiscal behavior. First, more transfer-dependent states have less flexibility in fiscal management. Second, consistent with the flypaper effect discussed in earlier chapters, it is possible that increased transfers spur new expenditure commitments, new public employees, and so on, which are difficult to cut during downturns. Finally, as argued in Chapter 4, it is possible that transfer dependence simply signals to creditors and voters a less credible federal no-bailout commitment than can be made to relatively tax-dependent states.

Yet as in the previous chapter, it is difficult to view grants as exogenous. Indeed, Arretche and Rodden (2004) have conducted an econometric study of transfers in Brazil, finding that like the bailouts examined above, the distribution of grants is highly political. Above all, small states with legislative bargaining advantages are favored, as are members of the president's legislative coalition and states that provided more votes for the president in the last election. Recall that in Germany there are no party-political effects on transfers, only a small state bias. The Brazilian pattern provides an advantage that is discussed further below: Some of these partisan variables may be plausible instruments for grants.

As in Chapter 7, there are reasons to suspect that jurisdiction size and overrepresentation might affect fiscal outcomes, but there are contradictory possibilities. Small states might spend and borrow more if they believe they will be favored in future intergovernmental bargaining. Because overrepresentation is pronounced in both legislative chambers and both are important, the best measure is a two-chamber average of seats per million population. But as made clear in the discussion above, any small-state bias might be overwhelmed by the too-big-to-fail problem; the largest states understood that the rest of the federation would suffer immensely by allowing them to default. And unlike the case in Germany, the party system did not provide disincentives for large states to demand negative-sum bailouts. Moreover, because much of the borrowing in the 1990s was brokered by or directly from state banks, the states with larger banks may have simply been able to borrow more.

Next, the regressions examine co-partisanship. The fractionalization of the Brazilian party system ensures that co-partisan governors are a rarity. Itamar Franco did not belong to a party, and Fernando Collor de Mello had no co-partisan governors. On average, over two administrations, only one-fourth of the governors were Cardoso's co-partisans. But it is also useful to examine the effects of membership in the president's larger coalition. The regressions below include a dummy variable that equals 1 for each observation in which the state's governor is a member of the president's legislative coalition, 0 otherwise.[14]

In order to make comparisons across cases, the econometric models presented in this section are quite similar to those presented in Chapter 7. As before, the dependent variables are surpluses, expenditures, and revenues, expressed in real per capita terms. The control variables include real GDP per capita (unemployment data are unavailable), an index that codes the governor's party on a left–right dimension, a dummy variable for election years, and a Herfindahl index of partisan fractionalization in the state legislature. Once again, error correction models are estimated, and models have been estimated with and without year dummies in the time series cross-section models. Table 8.4 presents the results of a model that, because it estimates first differences and includes fixed effects, is driven primarily by time series variation within states. Table 8.5 presents a random-effects model and includes the representation variable. This model also includes an additional dummy variable for the new states that did not exist prior to the new constitution and therefore did not have to service preexisting debt burdens. These regressions also include a set of regional dummies.[15] The between-effects models presented in Table 8.6 include the "new state" and regional dummies as well, but drop the ideology variable because it never attains statistical significance. Because of the high correlation between grants per capita and seats per capita, regressions are also presented without the grants variable.

Before discussing the results, some caveats are in order. Above all, the data quality is significantly lower than in the German case. There are serious questions about accounting in the states during the period of hyperinflation.

---

[14] Other variables that measure the strength of a state's representation in the president's legislative coalition have also been included, but these had no significant effect on fiscal behavior and are not reported below.

[15] The regions are North, Northeast, Center East, Southeast, and South.

Table 8.4. *Determinates of state-level fiscal outcomes (fixed effects)*

	Dependent Variable		
	Δ Real Surplus per Capita	Δ Real Expenditure per Capita	Δ Real Revenue per Capita
Dependent variable$_{t-1}$	−0.97***	−0.75***	−0.85***
	(0.13)	(0.11)	(0.14)
Δ Grants	−0.02	0.37***	0.37***
	(0.03)	(0.09)	(0.09)
Grants$_{t-1}$	−0.07*	0.38***	0.38***
	(0.04)	(0.12)	(0.12)
Governor in president's coalition	7.88	37.95	53.13*
	(15.66)	(24.34)	(28.17)
Δ GDP per capita	−0.03**	0.07**	0.04
	(0.01)	(0.03)	(0.04)
GDP per capita$_{t-1}$	−0.01	0.04	0.04
	(0.01)	(0.03)	(0.03)
Ideology	14.19	14.47	34.61
	(13.00)	(16.99)	(21.28)
Pres./gov. election year	−16.52	170.18***	134.41***
	(14.62)	(12.15)	(21.63)
State legislative fractionalization	−98.70	−14.06	−69.98
	(99.01)	(143.77)	(142.02)
Constant	612.79***	−18.59	471.19***
	(106.72)	(126.88)	(176.85)
Observations	362	362	362
Number of states	27	27	27
R^2	0.58	0.57	0.56

* significant at 10%; ** significant at 5%; *** significant at 1%
Panel-corrected standard errors in parentheses.
Surplus, grants, expenditures, revenues, and GDP are in real 1995 currency per capita
Coefficients for state dummies not reported

Moreover, as described above, the states had access to off-budget accounts and faced contingent liabilities, which suggests that a cautious approach should be taken in the interpretation of yearly surplus data. In addition, year-to-year variations in the surplus can be quite dramatic, especially in the late 1990s, as states sold off banks and public enterprises.

Perhaps some of these factors, along with the relatively short time series (1986–2000), account for the relatively unstable results. While the signs of the coefficients are quite stable in various estimations, the magnitude

Table 8.5. *Determinates of state-level fiscal outcomes (random effects)*

	Dependent Variable		
	Δ Real Surplus per Capita	Δ Real Expenditure per Capita	Δ Real Revenue per Capita
Dependent variable$_{t-1}$	−0.56***	−0.66***	−0.77***
	(0.11)	(0.10)	(0.13)
Δ Grants	−0.01	0.36***	0.39***
	(0.04)	(0.08)	(0.08)
Grants$_{t-1}$	−0.09**	0.33***	0.38***
	(0.05)	(0.09)	(0.10)
Log seats per million population	−44.11*	92.06***	85.08***
(two-chamber average)	(24.23)	(31.13)	(29.72)
Governor in president's coalition	−16.53	29.31	36.81
	(17.31)	(20.95)	(24.11)
Δ GDP per capita	−0.03**	0.09***	0.07**
	(0.02)	(0.03)	(0.03)
GDP per capita$_{t-1}$	−0.01*	0.07*	0.08*
	(0.01)	(0.01)	(0.02)
Ideology	−2.98	10.96	23.09
	(13.55)	(14.50)	(17.74)
Pres./gov. election year	−32.06*	130.45*	103.86*
	(12.72)	(19.14)	(28.75)
State legislative fractionalization	−221.36*	−43.40	−18.27
	(82.08)	(112.51)	(110.66)
New state	178.129*	88.862*	134.802*
	(40.19)	(44.19)	(42.26)
Constant	281.567*	−93.375	−129.745
	(86.21)	(85.44)	(83.40)
Observations	362	362	362
Number of states	27	27	27
R^2	0.40	0.54	0.53

* significant at 10%; * significant at 5%; * significant at 1%
Panel-corrected standard errors in parentheses.
Surplus, grants, expenditures, revenues, and GDP are in real 1995 currency per capita
Coefficients for region dummies not reported

of some of the coefficients and their standard errors are sensitive to the estimation technique and the exclusion of individual states.

First, consider the effect of intergovernmental transfers. For all the differences in the two systems, the long-term negative effect of transfer dependence on the surplus is rather similar to that found in the German case.

Table 8.6. *Determinates of average state-level fiscal outcomes (cross-section averages)*

	Dependent Variable					
	Real Surplus per Capita		Real Expenditure per Capita		Real Revenue per Capita	
Grants	-0.38***		0.90***		0.95***	
	(0.13)		(0.16)		(0.14)	
Log seats per million population (two-chamber average)	-33.01	-142.46***	-28.44	232.49***	-73.15	202.58***
	(46.62)	(34.59)	(57.52)	(59.95)	(52.13)	(60.55)
Governor in president's coalition	-198.94**	-146.19*	122.79	-2.98	99.68	-33.22
	(69.80)	(81.61)	(86.12)	(141.43)	(78.05)	(142.85)
GDP per capita	-60.32	-137.34**	264.24***	447.85***	248.40***	442.42***
	(50.67)	(52.65)	(62.52)	(91.24)	(56.66)	(92.16)
State legislative fractionalization	-624.92*	-616.49	-203.95	-224.05	-18.46	-39.70
	(348.29)	(421.01)	(429.71)	(729.63)	(389.45)	(736.98)
New state	367.11***	260.65***	220.66**	474.46***	215.68***	483.87***
	(62.80)	(62.38)	(77.49)	(108.10)	(70.23)	(109.19)
Constant	1158.399***	1843.47***	-1726.28***	-3222.3***	-1700***	-3286.8***
	(354.80)	(378.03)	(437.74)	(655.13)	(396.73)	(661.73)
States	27	27	27	27	27	27
R^2	0.83	0.74	0.97	0.92	0.98	0.91

Standard errors in parentheses

* significant at 10%; ** significant at 5%; *** significant at 1%

Surplus, grants, expenditures, revenues, and GDP are in real 1995 currency per capita

Estimation: OLS (between effects)

Coefficients for region dummies not reported

However, the Brazilian result is more tenuous. The coefficient for lagged grants per capita is negative in each surplus model. The coefficient is only marginally significant in the fixed-effects model, and in fact the statistical significance disappears rather easily when influential cases are dropped. In the random-effects model, the negative coefficient – similar in magnitude – is significant at the 5 percent level, but again it dips below standard significance levels when some of the influential cases are dropped from the analysis. The same can be said about the negative coefficient for grants in the between-effects surplus model in Table 8.6.

As in Chapter 7, there are concerns about the endogeneity of intergovernmental grants. While the search for an instrument was fruitless in Chapter 7, here some political variables from Arretche and Rodden (2004) are useful. In particular, the strength of a state in the president's coalition in the legislature is highly correlated with grants but not with state fiscal outcomes. When the surplus regressions are estimated using this instrument, the coefficients for grants per capita are always negative and substantially larger than those reported in the tables, but again the statistical significance was sensitive.[16]

Moving on to jurisdiction size and overrepresentation, the results are again fairly similar to the German analysis. Other things equal, states with more legislative seats per capita have higher expenditures and larger deficits per capita in the random-effects models in Table 8.5. The same is true when grants per capita are dropped from the between-effects models in Table 8.6. Using the coefficient from the first column of Table 8.5, the substantive effect of a move from Minas Gerais, which has a two-chamber average of 1.6 seats per million inhabitants, to Rondônia, which has 4.13 seats per million, is a R$ 92 increase in expenditures and a R$ 44 increase in the deficit.

Finally, a governor sharing the partisan affiliation of the president's governing coalition had no effect on the expenditures or deficits in the time

---

[16] Because of the fuzziness of the boundary between current and capital accounts and the goal of consistency with Chapter 7, the overall surplus has been used in this analysis. However, these results are more robust when the *current* surplus (net of capital accounts) is used instead. Another class of models (not reported to save space) attempted to examine the effect of intergovernmental grants on responses to unobserved common shocks. Models that interact lagged transfer dependence and the lagged dependent variable showed that expenditures and deficits were "stickier" in more transfer-dependent states. In other words, if an unobserved common shock leads to higher per capita expenditures, the increase is more permanent in more transfer-dependent states.

series cross-section models.[17] However, the parameter estimates in Table 8.6 focus solely on cross-section effects and suggest that states with longer periods of control by the president's coalition parties run larger deficits. But again, this result is somewhat sensitive to dropping influential cases. In any event, there is little support for the notion that the president's co-partisans exhibit fiscal restraint.

The control variables are also quite interesting. As in Germany, state fiscal policy is procyclical: Expenditures and revenues move with the business cycle. The electoral budget cycle is also quite pronounced: Revenues, expenditures, and deficits are all larger during election years. According to Table 8.4, expenditures increase by $R 170 per capita during election years.[18] Although the legislative fractionalization variable is rather sensitive and not always significant, the random- and between-effects estimations suggest that a fractionalized state legislature is associated with larger deficits. Finally, the new states spend more per capita than the others, but they also have much higher revenues and higher surpluses.

Because deficit data may be somewhat unreliable for the reasons mentioned above, it is useful to examine debt data as well. Time series debt data were unavailable, but Table 8.7 presents the results of simple cross-section regressions on total debts of the states as of 2000. Of course, this is not an ideal way of assessing long-term state fiscal behavior because of the bailout episodes that included significant debt forgiveness, but it does give a sense of which states had the largest debt burdens when the dust settled from the chaos of hyperinflation, fiscal crisis, and bailouts. Table 8.7 does not include the co-partisanship, ideology, or legislative fractionalization variables, which never attained significance in any estimation. The results also cast doubt on the connection between debt and transfer dependence. This regression is different from the others in that it attempts to distinguish between the effects of the economic externalities created by a state – captured by total real GDP – and the effects of overrepresentation. The GDP variable is correlated with the representation variable at −.84 and GDP per capita at .61. When included in the cross-section surplus regression of Table 8.6 (dropping GDP per capita), the parameter estimate for GDP was marginally significant and suggested that, controlling for

---

[17] Replacing the coalition membership variable with the direct co-partisanship variable does not yield any significant results.

[18] Although the coefficient in the surplus equation is not significant in Table 8.4, it is −.45 and highly significant if the year dummies are dropped.

Table 8.7. *Determinates of total state debt, 2000*

	Dependent Variable: debt per capita, 2000
Grants	0.36
	(0.63)
Log seats per million population (two-chamber average)	808.84**
	(393.26)
Log GDP	483.13***
	(153.53)
New state	−1,011.93*
	(578.77)
Constant	−1,0815.14**
	(3,820.63)
States	27
R²	0.42

Standard errors in parentheses
* significant at 10%; ** significant at 5%; *** significant at 1%
Estimation: OLS

representation, larger states ran larger deficits. In the simple debt regression in Table 8.7, this comes through more clearly. Controlling for GDP, states with more legislative votes per capita have larger debts. But controlling for representation, by far the largest debtors per capita in 2000 were the giants of the Brazilian economy – particularly Rio de Janeiro, Rio Grande do Sul, and São Paulo – even though these states also received the largest per capita bailouts in 1997.

IV. Conclusions: Germany and Brazil

The Brazilian empirical results can be summarized as follows. Though the causal link between transfers and fiscal incentives is less clear than in Germany, it appears that in the long run increasing transfer dependence is associated with increasing expenditures and larger deficits in Brazil. However, these results are not terribly robust, and a single-year snapshot of debt in 2000 yields no significant relationship between transfer dependence and debt.

Next, other things equal, overrepresented states receive larger transfers, spend more, run larger deficits, and accrue more debt. This is consistent with the hypothesis that such states have enhanced bailout expectations owing to their favorable position in legislative bargaining. Though a similar correlation was found in the German case, the link between representation and bailout expectations seems more plausible in Brazil than in Germany. In Brazil, it is common knowledge that the distribution of grants, loans, and ultimately bailouts is a matter of political bargaining, especially between the president and the two chambers of the legislature, where small, overrepresented states are attractive coalition partners. In Germany, bailouts were channeled exclusively through the preexisting system of grants, which are relatively depoliticized to begin with, and the entire federal role in debt reduction for Saarland and Bremen was shaped by court decisions more than interstate bargaining. Moreover, party discipline in the Bundesrat reduces the likelihood of the kind of pure interregional bargaining over bailouts seen in the Brazilian Senate. Pure interstate bargaining is much less pronounced in the German legislative process because of its strong, disciplined parliamentary parties. In Brazil, with its combination of presidentialism and open-list PR, the president must put together complex interstate coalitions in order to implement his legislative agenda.

In the German case study, it was not possible to distinguish between the impact of overrepresentation and other correlates of state size because of the small number of states and the tight multicollinearity between small size, overrepresentation, and deficits. In Brazil, however, controlling for per capita legislative representation, the states that account for larger shares of Brazil's GDP run larger deficits and accrue more debt. These states also benefited most heavily from the 1997 bailout. In contrast with the German situation, these results are consistent with the too-big-to-fail hypothesis.

The best explanation for this stark difference between Germany and Brazil is the party system. Vertical partisan externalities are strong in Germany but weak in Brazil. The electoral success of state-level politicians in Germany is intimately tied up in voters' assessments of the macroeconomic performance associated with their party label, which places limits on the incentives of state governments to extract bailouts. If anything, in Brazil the coattails usually run in the opposite direction. Thus, there were no electoral incentives to discourage large and relatively wealthy states like São Paulo or Minas Gerais from avoiding adjustment and aggressively extracting bailouts, even though this behavior had increasingly visible collective macroeconomic consequences. Similar behavior in Nordrhein-Westfalen or Bayern would have been politically suicidal.

More generally, the lack of concern for national collective goods among legislators and governors in Brazil helps explain the contrast with the more limited bailout problem in Germany. In addition, the German transfer system and its interpretation by the courts enhance bailout expectations, primarily among the poorest and smallest states. Finally, it was helpful that the German system partially insulated bailout decisions from the realm of legislative bargaining and distributive politics by placing them in the hands of the judiciary, while in Brazil bailouts have always been in the domain of legislative bargaining and distributive politics.

Though the Brazilian problem has been more widespread and costly to date, both instances of fiscal indiscipline have a similar underlying structure. The case studies have added flesh to the bones of arguments developed in earlier chapters. In both cases, the central government played a major role in revenue sharing, grants, and loans to subnational governments in the context of interconnected, overlapping spheres of authority, which undermined the credibility of its no-bailout commitment. The German Länder and Brazilian states have significant spending responsibilities, and the political fortunes of their leaders are strongly shaped by their ability to maintain and increase expenditures that are funded from a common pool of national tax revenue. When faced with negative shocks that require adjustment, state-level politicians have weak incentives to endure the political pain of cutting personnel or welfare expenditures. In both cases, voters and creditors have come to believe that when local expenditures are threatened, the central government can and should be forced to step in with extra assistance. *Ex ante*, this weakens state governments' incentives for fiscal discipline. In Germany, incentive problems are built into a highly rule-based system of redistributive transfers. In Brazil, the central government had a long history of discretionary political involvement in state finances, not only in the form of grants, but also loans made by financial intermediaries and flows of resources to state commercial banks.

Yet in spite of these clear incentive problems, the constitutional protections afforded the states – above all, the nature of their representation in the federal policy process – has allowed them to jealously guard their freedom to borrow without federal interference. In both cases, the center has found it extremely difficult to close the most troubling avenue of deficit finance: state-owned banks.

By the end of the 1990s, it was increasingly clear to economists and policy analysts in both countries that the basic structure of fiscal federalism was in need of reform. This perception has become widespread among the Brazilian general public as well in the wake of debt crises and hyperinflation, perhaps less so in Germany, where the potential collective costs of bailouts are less transparent. Yet in recent decades, both countries have been plagued by the status quo bias of federalism. Though reforms like enforceable limitations on state debt and the privatization of state banks might have collective benefits, in each country they require the agreement of state governments that have something to lose.

Now that the case studies have provided a closer look at some of the persistent pathologies of fiscal federalism, the next step is to identify the conditions under which reform is possible. This chapter has purposefully ignored some sweeping changes in the Brazilian system of federalism implemented in the late 1990s as part of Cardoso's broader neoliberal reform agenda. The incentive structure described above has changed in important respects, and perhaps the most glaring pathology – virtually unregulated borrowing from state banks – has been rectified. Thus, an important part of the Brazilian story remains to be told in the next chapter.

9

The Challenge of Reform in Federations

When the concurrence of a large number is required by the Constitution to the doing of any national act, we are apt to rest satisfied that all is safe, because nothing improper will be likely to be done; but we forget how much good may be prevented, and how much ill may be produced, by the power of hindering the doing of what may be necessary, and of keeping affairs in the same unfavorable posture in which they may happen to stand at particular periods.

Alexander Hamilton, *The Federalist* 22

A basic problem of federalism is now painfully clear. After a good deal of bargaining, state representatives sign a constitutional contract, as in postwar Germany or postauthoritarian Brazil, setting the rules of the game for future interactions. A critical component of the bargain is that these rules are difficult to change. At the original contracting stage, states (especially small ones) insist on strong institutional protections out of concern for future expropriation and opportunism on the part of the other states or the federal government. In addition to constitutional protections backed up by courts, these contracts usually directly include the states as veto players over key legislative issues and require supermajorities or even unanimity for the renegotiation of the basic contract.

But as we have seen, the original contracts were not negotiated by benevolent planners behind veils of ignorance. They are political bargains that often deviate dramatically from the optimal distribution of authority laid out in fiscal federalism textbooks. Moreover, the contracts are incomplete: Important issues were left unresolved, and the assignment of responsibilities between governments must be continuously renegotiated through an ongoing intergovernmental bargaining process. But political incentives prevent the federal government and states from negotiating intergovernmental contracts that will provide them with collective goods.

226

It may eventually become clear to all the parties that the division of authority or finances laid out by the original contract imposes significant costs on the federation as a whole. However, the existing arrangement generates private benefits for either the federal government or all or some subset of the states. Even though an alternative contract might promise long-term gains for the federation as a whole, some states will veto it in order to protect their private benefits or attempt to negotiate a second-best contract that fully compensates them for the loss of these benefits. In the kind of unitary system favored by Alexander Hamilton, such inefficient arrangements might be easier to dislodge by putting together a legislative coalition of jurisdictions that stand to gain from the reform. Thus, while federations are often formed in the pursuit of collective goods, they may fall prey to a "joint-decision trap" (Scharpf 1988) that creates status quo bias and undermines the sustained provision of collective goods.

Concretely, we have seen that a common failure of federal bargains is the creation of fiscal structures that allow states to externalize their fiscal burdens onto others through cycles of borrowing and bailouts. The protections for states built into the original contract make it difficult to close the loopholes that undermine overall fiscal discipline. In Germany, this problem puts the country at risk of triggering fines for "excessive deficits" associated with the Stability and Growth Pact. In Brazil, the cost has been massive debt and macroeconomic instability. Although not addressed in detail in this book, faulty federal contracts also frequently make it difficult to prevent another of Hamilton's fears: destructive local protectionism and interprovincial trade wars.

In short, federal contracts are often inefficient but sticky. This is but a specific example of a general problem. Unfortunately, institutions do not always evolve so as to enhance overall social welfare. Rather, they reflect the power and interests of the actors who create them, and even after these actors are long gone, institutions create beneficiaries with incentives to obstruct reform. Nevertheless, institutions do evolve and sometimes even change radically, and an important project spanning the social sciences and history is to understand what drives institutional change.

This chapter contributes to that project in a modest way by explaining the conditions under which intergovernmental contracts – when they come to be widely viewed as collectively suboptimal – are most likely to be reformed within the context of democracy. While the next chapter ventures to ask what drives deeper, long-term trends in federalism and fiscal sovereignty and examines the role of brute force and authoritarianism, here we stay within the realm of stable democracy assumed throughout the book and examine the possibility raised by Douglass North that "incremental change comes from the perceptions of the entrepreneurs in political and economic organizations that they could do better by altering the existing institutional framework at some margin" (North 1990: 8).

Given the costs that can be associated with collectively inefficient intergovernmental contracts, this chapter will provide many examples of political entrepreneurs who believe that pushing for reform has a potentially handsome political payoff. But what shapes the likelihood that such entrepreneurs can break out of federalism's joint decision trap? That is, how can they secure the cooperation of legislators or subnational officials who are elected from regions that stand to lose private benefits associated with the existing intergovernmental contract? For instance, how can Brazilian and German state governments be convinced to give up their state banks? More generally, why would governors agree to reforms that would limit their access to deficit finance and off-budget accounts? If a member of a federal upper chamber represents a province that benefits disproportionately from the current transfer system, why would she vote for a reform that might reduce expenditures in her province?

Chapter 5 introduced the notion of electoral externalities. In some countries, like Brazil and Canada, the electoral incentives of officials whose electorate is confined to one province seem to be shaped primarily by voters' evaluations of what is promised and provided within the province, and provincial elections are rather distinct from national elections. Yet in other countries, like Germany and Australia, provincial elections are more intertwined with federal elections in that voters use national party labels to reward and punish the incumbent national executive. Because of these electoral externalities, provincial politicians can, under the right conditions, face incentives to consider the costs of the externalities produced by their policies.

The key argument of this chapter is that electoral externalities can help political entrepreneurs renegotiate intergovernmental contracts that are widely perceived to be inefficient. If reform requires provincial politicians to give up something of electoral value, reformers must create a situation in which provincial politicians believe they will receive offsetting electoral benefits associated with perceived improvements in collective welfare. This task is easiest in countries where electoral externalities are strong and at times when the center and the provinces in question are controlled by the same party.

The first section clarifies the argument linking electoral externalities and the likelihood of reform, and the remainder of the chapter explores the relationship empirically with case studies. First, section two draws on the "most-similar cases" research design by comparing Australia and Canada – two countries that are remarkably similar in many respects except for electoral externalities. The Australian states were willing to make concessions in negotiations over intergovernmental reform because of party ties with a popular federal-level political entrepreneur. In the Canadian federation, on the other hand, intergovernmental reform has been frustrated time and again because provincial leaders have no partisan incentives to be concerned with federation-wide collective goods.

Next, we return to the "most-different cases" approach by completing the comparison of Germany and Brazil. In Germany, basic intergovernmental agreements have been successfully renegotiated on several occasions – and in each case, partisan ties between the center and states played a crucial role. In Brazil, the lack of electoral externalities has been an impediment to successful reform in the past. Indeed, Brazil's famously fragmented party system would appear to make this an overdetermined case. Yet the recent experience of Brazil demonstrates the importance of electoral externalities even in a country with a hostile institutional environment. President Cardoso, a political entrepreneur whose electoral success was based on an agenda of reform aimed at macroeconomic stability, was able to form a multiparty coalition whose members – including state governors – came to believe that their own electoral prospects were wrapped up in the perceived success of the president's reform efforts. As a result, Cardoso was able to extract concessions from legislators and governors in a major renegotiation of the intergovernmental contract.

I. Breaking out of the Joint-Decision Trap: The Role of Electoral Externalities

The problem of this chapter is simple: An existing intergovernmental contract is collectively deficient in a way that seems obvious to the vast majority of people, yet reform is difficult to orchestrate because representatives of provinces – sometimes comprising a minority of the population – have incentives to veto it. In some cases, the arena for such intergovernmental conflict is the upper legislative chamber. In others, the battles take place in interministerial groups, first-ministers' conferences, or even special constitutional conventions. Alternatively, the central government must negotiate directly with provincial governments in order to achieve reform. In any of these scenarios, a basic problem is that recalcitrant provincial representatives expect to continue receiving electoral benefits from the existing arrangements in the future. Their electoral fates are shaped by their ability to provide benefits to their constituents, and it is difficult to convince them to give up this sure flow of benefits in exchange for reforms with long-term collective benefits that do not translate easily into votes in provincial elections.

The problem may be "symmetric" if all provincial chief executives are equally unwilling to give up their access to some discretion – for instance, over access to credit markets. All German Land minister presidents, for example, would likely join forces in opposing federal restrictions on borrowing by state governments. In most cases, however, the problem is asymmetric, in that reform requires that some provinces sacrifice more than others. A proposal to privatize state banks or public enterprises is most painful for leaders of states with large banks or enterprises that rely on them for patronage and soft credit. Proposals to update intergovernmental transfer systems and abolish outmoded criteria for distributing grants inevitably create winners and losers. Perhaps the most vexing problem is when a supermajority or unanimity is required and the assent of potential losers cannot be avoided.

Let us focus on reforms that are expected to offer sufficient collective benefits that political entrepreneurs in the federal executive find it worthwhile to make them prominent features of their electoral strategies. The most obvious way to achieve reform is through Coasian bargains. If the reform creates considerable collective surplus, the federal executive should be able to make payoffs to the potential losers. In the symmetric case, governors might be persuaded to give up some discretion over borrowing in exchange for more-generous transfers. Or in asymmetric cases, governors who agree to privatize large state banks might be lured with grants or debt forgiveness. Yet such bargains can only go so far. If they place great value on the status quo, the would-be losers can whittle the reform surplus to the point that it is scarcely recognizable as a collective improvement or to the point where it is no longer incentive compatible for the representatives of the "winner" states. Moreover, Coasian bargains are notoriously difficult in the presence of a time inconsistency problem. Collectively, beneficial reforms often require the "losers" to give up future streams of rents, and the central executive cannot credibly commit to a schedule of payoffs that will continue in the future.

The Challenge of Reform in Federations

The key problem is that provincial representatives face electoral incentives only to provide patronage, pork, and public goods that are enjoyed within the province, receiving no political benefit for playing a role in the enhancement of national collective goods. Yet Chapter 5 argued that electoral externalities provide a way around this problem. If many voters use the party affiliation of the federal chief executive to punish and reward politicians in senatorial and gubernatorial elections – as in Germany and Australia – electoral credit for improved collective goods is likely to accrue not only to the national executive, but to co-partisan senators and governors as well. Co-partisans must weigh their share of the potential political payoff for supporting national collective goods against the political value of the rents they must give up. If co-partisan provincial leaders scuttle a high-profile reform initiative in a country with strong electoral externalities, the damage to the party label could be serious. Moreover, in countries where provincial leaders angle for national-level careers for which central party bosses are gatekeepers, such behavior has additional costs. On the other hand, for provincial officials belonging to the federal opposition party, successful reform would create negative externalities, providing them with incentives to obstruct reform, perhaps even if their province stands to be a relative winner, in order to avoid aiding their competitors.

Anticipating all of this, the central executive will be more likely to propose high-profile reform in the first place – and stake its electoral prospects on success – when the crucial provinces are represented by co-partisans. Reforms with symmetric costs are more likely if the requisite supermajority can be achieved among co-partisans. When the costs are concentrated in some provinces whose assent is required, success is much more likely if the losers are co-partisans. Not only might the electoral benefits of reform offset the loss of private benefits for the losers, but a supermajority of co-partisans can help the executive structure a deal that softens the blow to the losers by taking something from the other provinces. Moreover, a co-partisan center is in a better position to commit to a schedule of compensation that unfolds over time.

This logic leads to some simple propositions. In countries where electoral externalities are weak or at moments when they are strong but negative for crucial provinces, significant intergovernmental reform aimed at long-term collective improvements will be difficult to achieve. Provincial leaders who stand to lose future streams of electoral benefits will either withhold assent or bargain for copious compensation. Intergovernmental reform is most likely and can be achieved at lower cost in countries with strong electoral externalities and at moments when the crucial provincial-level veto players are co-partisans of the center.

II. Case Studies

In order to assess these propositions, we return to some of the case studies introduced in previous chapters. We have learned that electoral externalities have been strong throughout the postwar period in Australia and Germany, though these countries frequently face moments when the federal governing party controls only a minority of states. Canada may have demonstrated strong electoral externalities in the earlier part of the century, but since World War II the worlds of provincial and federal party politics have been increasingly distinct. And like provincial premiers in Canada, Brazilian governors do not often ride the coattails of co-partisan chief executives.

Each of these federations features intertwined fiscal and policymaking processes that require the frequent renegotiation of complex intergovernmental contracts. As elaborated in the case studies below, vested interests among state-level politicians almost always make them difficult to renegotiate, and these systems can slip rather easily into socially inefficient but stubborn political equilibria. Above all, in each country the joint-decision trap has complicated attempts to remove barriers to interstate trade and renegotiate arcane intergovernmental fiscal contracts. In Canada, even the basic constitutional contract has been deemed unacceptable by elites for decades, yet reform is notoriously elusive.

The logic spelled out above suggests that the case studies examine scenarios when the federal executive has something to gain by initiating reform that will be painful for some of the provincial representatives whose approval is necessary. The expectation is that reform is most likely at moments when the key provincial governments are controlled by co-partisans of the central executive whose electoral fates are driven largely by the value of the national party label. Over a long period of time, this entails that intergovernmental reform is most difficult and costly in Brazil and Canada, where provincial officials have no electoral incentives to be concerned with national collective goods. In Germany and Australia, the expectation is that the executive will find it easier to elicit the support of the provinces that have something to lose from reform, but only at moments when these provinces are co-partisans.

Because substantial reform of the intergovernmental system in each of these federations generally requires a supermajority, this entails that substantial reform is most likely when a supermajority of provincial chief executives are controlled by the party of the central chief executive. Thus, Figure 9.1, which combines Figures 5.1 and 8.2 by plotting the share of co-partisan provinces in each country over time, is a good guide to the case studies, which demonstrate that intergovernmental reform has been concentrated at moments when co-partisanship peaks.

It is not possible to give a satisfying historical account of intergovernmental relations in four countries in one chapter. Rather, the illustrative case studies focus on scenarios that resemble the discussion above: Reform is viewed as a collective good that can enhance overall efficiency and bring electoral benefits to the central government, but it requires the agreement of state governments who are loath to give up the relative benefits of the status quo intergovernmental contract.

The comparison of Canada and Australia brings the benefits of the most-similar-cases approach to comparative inquiry. While these federations are quite similar in many ways, Chapter 5 demonstrated that at least since World War II the link between federal and subnational political competition has evolved quite differently in the two countries. The links between federal and state-level politics in Germany has much in common with Australia, and the case studies tell rather similar stories. Yet it is useful to continue the German and Brazilian stories and draw on the comparison of most-different cases. While demonstrating the costliness of reform in the absence of a German-style party system, the Brazilian case shows that even in a presidential system with weak and sometimes chaotic parties, a popular chief executive with a widely accepted reform agenda might be able to craft electoral externalities and generate incentives for subnational governments to give up private benefits.

Canada

This book is not the first to point out the separation between provincial and federal party politics in Canada. Throughout the postwar period, provincial and federal party organizations have grown into almost completely distinct entities.[1] They do little to coordinate their electoral strategies, raise their own funds, and select their own candidates and leaders, and party career

---

[1] See, e.g., Bakvis (1994) and Chandler (1987).

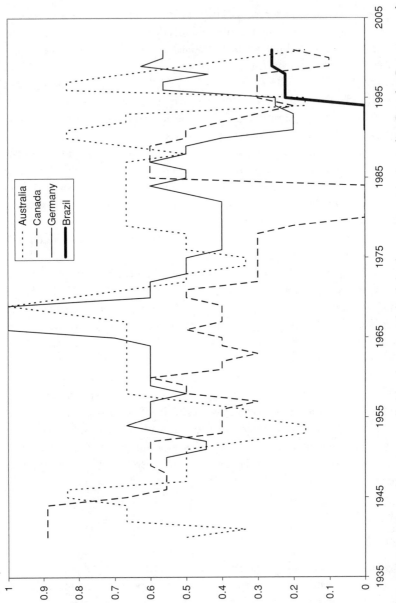

Figure 9.1. Share of states controlled by the party of the federal government in Australia, Canada, Germany, and Brazil.

patterns rarely move between the federal and provincial levels.[2] In fact, one of the most trusted campaign strategies at the provincial level in Canada is to harshly criticize the government in Ottawa, even if governed by a party with the same name. Without electoral links to federal parties, provincial officials face incentives only to push for a regional private-goods agenda. Although scholars and pundits, even Ottawa and most of the provincial governments claim to agree that a new set of multilateral contracts is necessary, intergovernmental compromise is extremely difficult to achieve because provincial officials have no incentives to give up valuable regional benefits.

The basic contracts underlying the Canadian system of fiscal federalism have remained unchanged for several decades – many of them since World War II – even though the challenges facing the system have changed considerably, and there is general consensus that "the existing arrangements are unsustainable" (Simeon 1994: 135). First of all, most observers agree that the outdated "five-province standard" behind the Canadian equalization scheme needs to be restructured. Second, direct provincial access to revenue from natural resources introduces a number of inefficiencies to the system. Third, observers note that major federal–provincial transfer programs – in particular, Established Programs Financing and the Canada Assistance Plan – contradicted basic principles of fiscal federalism from their inception in the 1970s, and a variety of unforeseen circumstances have further undermined their usefulness over time.[3] In short, Canadian fiscal federalism is a nexus of interlocking intergovernmental contracts that have outlived the political and economic conditions under which they were negotiated. Reform proposals are plentiful, and all agree that real progress requires the cooperation of Ottawa and all the provinces.

Yet the political incentives for this kind of multilateral cooperation are lacking. Intergovernmental cooperation in which regional benefits are sacrificed for national gains will not yield electoral rewards. Nor can Ottawa negotiate deals in which relative beneficiaries from reform bargain away some of their benefits to secure the agreement of the relative losers. In the absence of electoral externalities, public debates about reforming Canadian fiscal federalism are dominated by "balance sheet federalism," in which each provincial government explains to its voters why each federal proposal is

---

[2] The NDP's more integrated structure is the exception. There are also differences across provinces within the (traditionally) dominant parties. For instance, the federal and provincial branches of the Liberals and Progressive Conservatives are much more integrated in the Maritime Provinces than elsewhere. See Dyck (1991).

[3] See Courchene (1984); Boadway and Flatters (1994).

skewed against their interests. Over time, the tenor of these debates encourages the spread of a pronounced form of regional envy.

Canadian politicians and pundits are also fond of pointing out that goods, services, capital, and individuals flow more freely across the borders of the member states of the European Union than the borders of the Canadian provinces. The Canadian internal market is surely the most fragmented of all the developed federations (Courchene 1996). In a variety of ways, provincial officials respond to politically powerful groups of local workers or producers and introduce regulations and other policies that discriminate against workers or producers from other provinces, thereby fragmenting the internal market and creating barriers to mobility.[4] These barriers prevent Canadians from realizing the full potential gains from interprovincial trade. A recent study by the Canadian Chamber of Commerce estimates the cost of Canada's internal trade barriers to be $7 billion per year, or 1 percent of GDP.[5]

Intergovernmental negotiations in 1982 and 1994 have addressed the challenge of strengthening the internal market, but in each case key actors were ultimately unwilling to give up the private political benefits associated with the protection of local workers and producers. First of all, the Constitution Act, 1982 and the accompanying Canadian Charter of Rights and Freedoms attempted for the first time to incorporate a binding provision relating to individual mobility. Yet after several rounds of negotiation, in order to obtain provincial support for the charter, the federal government also agreed to enshrine several impediments to the internal economic union.[6] In 1994, the Agreement on Internal Trade was signed by all provincial governments, but the agreement has achieved little.[7] In order to secure provincial agreement, it was necessary to include a loophole stipulating that the agreement does not apply to any measure that is part of a "regional economic development" program, which makes the agreement virtually useless (Courchene 1996: 212).

---

[4] Several detailed examples are provided in Filip Palda, ed. (1994). Examples include beer sales, financial markets, agriculture, commercial transportation, and preferential hiring practices. For an account of a full-scale trade war between Québec and Ontario, see *Globe and Mail*, September 28, 1993: B1–B2.

[5] Dierdre McMurdy, "The Walls that Divide," *Maclean's* 109 (September 23, 1996): 39.

[6] The charter enshrines the rights of provinces to discriminate against residents of other provinces with respect to land ownership and employment, and the Constitution Act protects the right of energy-producing provinces to enact indirect energy taxes. See Courchene (1996: 193).

[7] See the assessment in *OECD Economic Surveys: Canada* (1998).

In addition to fiscal contracts and free-trade agreements, the reform of the most basic underlying intergovernmental contract – the Constitution – requires the agreement of Ottawa and all the provinces. Canada's lack of partisan links between provincial and federal elected officials is an important part of the explanation for its constitutional impasse. On an issue like Senate reform, for example, on which each of the regions has a distinct set of interests, no province faces incentives to compromise or make side payments for the good of the federation as a whole. The constitutional negotiations (or those over free trade or fiscal federalism) would probably play out much differently if a vertically integrated party with a strong base in each of the provinces were to come to power in Ottawa by promising far-reaching constitutional reform. The current fragility of Canada's constitutional contract is not a necessary artifact of the rift between its two main cultural-linguistic groups. The Maritimes, Ontario, and above all the western provinces have also emerged as important veto players with distinctive demands. The simultaneous satisfaction of these demands is impossible, and compromise will be difficult without electoral externalities.

In fact, the last wholesale renegotiation of Canadian intergovernmental contracts took place in the period between 1935 and 1940, when reform was presented to the public by the federal government and the respected independent Rowell-Sirois Commission as a necessity in response to the Depression and the onset of World War II. One of the key reforms was the centralization of unemployment insurance, which was originally opposed by provinces that expected to be net payers: Quebec, Ontario, and Alberta (Beramendi 2004; Struthers 1983). The disintegration of the Canadian party system had not yet taken place, and an intergovernmental reform agenda was an important part of the platform on which Mackenzie King and the Liberals assumed power in Ottawa in 1935. When the Liberals also came to power in Ottawa and Québec in the late 1930s, all the provinces but one were controlled by a vertically integrated party with a reform mandate – a feat that has never been repeated (see Figure 9.1). Once this happened, the crucial provinces dropped their opposition, and electoral externalities clearly facilitated the reforms.

Yet since the era of Mackenzie King, the links between federal and provincial parties have frayed, along with the likelihood of sweeping intergovernmental reform. Even when public sentiment has favored reform, Ottawa finds it very difficult to convince provinces to give up the rents associated with existing intergovernmental contracts without offsetting electoral benefits of reform. The center is increasingly unwilling to buy reforms by paying provinces off with grants and other forms of pork for which provincial officials will get all the credit. Moreover, because most of the reforms will create winners and losers, the federal government finds it very difficult to facilitate side payments between provinces that stand to lose as part of multilateral reform deals. The federal government's only hope for reforming the intergovernmental contract is through expensive bilateral deals with individual provinces, which causes Canadian intergovernmental relations to bear a striking resemblance to relations between independent countries.

Australia

In marked contrast to Canada, the state and federal parties in Australia cooperate closely in funding and conducting election campaigns at each level, state elites play important roles in the endorsement of candidates running for federal office, and party careers frequently move back and forth between levels of government. State elections are frequently "treated almost as federal by-elections," which "are taken as judgments upon the Prime Minister and the leader of the Federal Opposition as much as upon the state party leaders" (Rydon 1988: 168–69).

Some of the same intergovernmental contracting problems – most notably, barriers to free trade and competition – have plagued the Australian federation. Unlike Canada, however, electoral externalities have helped facilitate reform. The most dramatic episode took place between 1990 and 1996. At the end of the 1980s, the federal and state governments alike faced a growing public perception of economic crisis – above all, nationally organized business groups and the media complained of anti-competitive practices, monopoly provision of key goods and services by state-owned enterprises, and an overregulated economy with many unnecessary impediments to interstate trade and competition. The Hawke government responded by making microeconomic and public sector reform the center of its political agenda and stressing potential national income gains. Although some of this agenda could be implemented by the Commonwealth government alone – for example, a floating exchange rate, tariff reduction, and deregulation – much of the agenda required the active participation of the states. In fact, some of the most important reforms required that the states give up their access to regulatory and other policy tools that allowed them to provide constituents with electorally valuable private benefits.

The timing of the most sweeping intergovernmental reforms in the postwar period is quite consistent with the arguments above. Returning to Figure 9.1, note that during the period of negotiation the federal government and five of the six states were controlled by the Labor Party. The states were willing to give up key rents because of the offsetting gains in political credit for the successful implementation of reform. New South Wales was the only state controlled by the opposition Liberal Party, and its premier, Nick Greiner, who had come to power with a platform favoring microeconomic and public sector reform, had nothing to gain by being the lone holdout.

The states had to give up important rents in order to improve the internal economic union and reform public sector enterprises. One of the key complaints addressed in the Australian intergovernmental negotiations resonates with the discussion of Canada above: The states were able to regulate the sale of goods and services and the registration of occupations in ways that served their own regional interests but fragmented the internal economic union. In October 1990, the Australian heads of government agreed to an ambitious program of mutual recognition of regulations and standards relating to the sale of goods and the registration of occupations. In 1991, the states also negotiated agreements on a uniform approach to food standards and the joint regulation of nonbank financial institutions. After the successful implementation of the Mutual Recognition Agreement, Australia's internal union now rivals Germany's as the most integrated of all federal systems.

The intergovernmental agreement on a national competition policy was perhaps the most sweeping and significant of the microeconomic reforms of the early 1990s in Australia. One of the most important factors suppressing competition and a free interstate market was the role of the states in setting up and protecting public sector monopolies in key utilities, transportation infrastructure, and several other areas. The efficiency losses associated with these monopolies for the federation as a whole were well known. Nevertheless, the states had been extremely reluctant to give up any authority over these public enterprises, especially because the monopoly rents from these enterprises made up the largest single component of own-source state revenue (Craig 1997). The final Competition Principles Agreement, signed by the Council of Australian Governments in 1995, compensates the states for some of this lost revenue in return for the implementation of reforms and thus represents a major renegotiation of the fiscal contract as well. It is remarkable that the states were willing to give up the rents, both political and economic, associated with the monopolies. The agreement undoubtedly entailed not only fiscal but political costs for the states, who faced pressure from local interest groups like taxi drivers whose monopoly has been opened up to competition, but they were confident that the offsetting credit for reform, combined with new benefits offered by the central government, would outweigh these costs. The agreement covers all of the public monopolies and state enterprises in gas, electricity, water, rail, urban transit, ports, agricultural marketing boards, and several other areas. According to the OECD, the agreement has produced quick results.[8] The negotiations also led to repeals and alterations of a wide range of redundant or poorly coordinated regulatory policies at the federal and state levels.

Germany

Like state elections in Australia, Land elections in Germany are widely seen as the equivalent of federal by-elections; they often amount to referenda on the competence of the chancellor and his government (Fabritius 1978; Lohmann, Brady, and Rivers 1997). As in Australia, the Bund and Land parties coordinate their funding and campaign activities, Land-level leaders play an important part in the nomination process for federal party leaders, and career paths frequently move back and forth between federal and state politics. The evolution from state-based to highly integrated parties over the postwar period was shaped largely by the incentive structure of the upper chamber of Parliament. The Bundesrat may set the joint decision trap in the first place (by directly including the states as veto players in federal policy), but as it has evolved over time, it also has come to provide the means to break out of it. Opposition parties learned to use the obstructive capacity of the Bundesrat to frustrate the governing coalition, effectively turning Land elections into federal legislative elections and ultimately creating strong electoral externalities (Abromeit 1982; Lehmbruch 1989). A brief look at ongoing intergovernmental fiscal negotiations in Germany will show that intergovernmental contracts are indeed difficult to renegotiate – especially during periods of divided government – but as in Australia, electoral externalities occasionally open windows of opportunity.

The German fiscal constitution contains very specific provisions relating to the division of taxing and spending powers between the Bund and

---

[8] *OECD Economic Surveys: Australia* (1997).

Länder. Such a specific constitutional contract can only produce acceptable outcomes for a limited period of time, and ultimately it must be renegotiated to accommodate changing circumstances. Periodic renegotiation is especially important given that the states are responsible for implementing most federal legislation, and the Basic Law stipulates that "living conditions" should be "equivalent" throughout the federation. The constitution, especially as it pertains to equalization and other transfers from wealthy to poor Länder, is difficult to renegotiate. Contributors, for instance, are not easily convinced that their burden should be increased, while recipients have come to see transfers as constitutionally guaranteed entitlements. Indeed, the basic fault line in most attempts to renegotiate fiscal contracts in Germany is that between the wealthy and poor Länder.[9]

Yet the Bund and Länder have managed to renegotiate basic fiscal contracts on several occasions. The first of these was in 1955. Although the Bundestag and Bundesrat were both controlled by the Union parties, important conflicts arose between the government in Bonn (especially the CSU finance minister) and the CDU-led governments of Nordrhein-Westfalen and Rheinland-Pfalz. The CDU and CSU went to great lengths to hold extensive talks and prevent the public perception of fragmentation in the coalition, however, and they were eventually able to work out a compromise within the party that brought about the concessions necessary to conclude the reform (Renzsch 1991: 161).

By the middle of the 1960s, the intergovernmental fiscal contract had once again become outdated. The basic assignment of fiscal and regulatory tasks was widely perceived by the media, the public, and politicians to be in need of major reform. Furthermore, the Bund and Länder both carried out uncoordinated industrial subsidy programs as part of their sectoral and regional development programs. The Länder competed against one another for limited mobile investment capital, often outbidding each other with subsidy programs (Scharpf, Reissert, and Schnabel 1976: 77–78).

In general, "it was widely felt that the action space and the action perspectives of the Länder governments were too narrowly circumscribed to deal effectively with some of the problems that had become major political issues in the 'reformist' political climate of the mid-1960s" (Scharpf 1988: 244). As with the reform of the Australian intergovernmental system in the 1990s, the reform proposals circulated in Germany in the 1960s required

[9] After unification, the dynamics have become even more complicated, with the interests of the old poor Länder sometimes conflicting with those of the new poor Länder in the east.

that the Länder tie their hands and give up a considerable amount of policy and revenue autonomy in favor of a more multilateral, cooperative process. Some of the Länder – most notably, Bayern – were reluctant to give up any autonomy over their budgets.[10] Reform was difficult not only because it would reduce symmetric rents for the states, but because it had clear distributive implications. As in 1955, the most important conflict was between the wealthy and the poor Länder. In particular, the sweeping reforms proposed by the federal government were opposed by the executives of the wealthy Länder, who expected to be relative losers. Because the proposal required a two-thirds majority in the Bundesrat, the veto threats of the wealthy Länder were potentially fatal.

The reform proposal ultimately was accepted by a supermajority of the Länder because electoral externalities helped overcome the distributive conflicts between the Länder. In the mid-1960s, the SPD took advantage of the popularity of the intergovernmental reform issue and made it the centerpiece of its electoral platform. Both major parties were ultimately able to legitimize the formation of a grand coalition because they promised to use it as an opportunity to achieve the two-thirds majority necessary in both houses to renegotiate the Constitution. After a long period in opposition, the SPD was particularly eager to prove to the public that it was capable of delivering on the reform program; and some of the wealthy SPD Länder,[11] even though they had serious reservations about the proposal, were ultimately willing to compromise in order to allow their party to claim credit for successful reform. Had they held out in opposition to the proposal that had been negotiated and heralded by their SPD colleagues in the Bundestag, they might have undermined their party's credibility and their own political futures. Partisan links also facilitated Bayern's eventual vote for reform: Heavy lobbying efforts by Franz-Josef Strauß, federal finance minister and CSU head, helped sway the state government (Renzsch 1991: 259).

For the period since the Grand Coalition, Figure 9.1 provides a fairly good guide to further contract renegotiation. From 1969 to 1982, a coalition between the Social Democrats and Liberals controlled the Bundestag, but the Union parties had a majority in the Bundesrat. During this period, negative electoral externalities prevented any renegotiation of the intergovernmental fiscal contract, even though it had once again become outdated.

---

[10] This paragraph and the next draw heavily on Renzsch (1991: 246–60) and Renzsch (1995: 179–82).

[11] In particular, Bremen, Hamburg, Hessen, and Nordrhein-Westfalen.

242

In the mid-1980s, however, a CDU-Liberal coalition came to power at the federal level, giving the Union parties temporary control of both chambers. Alterations of the fiscal contract took place during this period directly between the federal government and the Länder under the control of the CDU or CSU (Renzsch 1995: 176–79). A conference committee to resolve conflicts between the Bund and Länder was called for 16 percent of the legislation passed by the Bundestag during the period of divided government between 1969 and 1982, but for only 2.5 percent of the legislation passed between 1983 and 1991.[12] When both houses are controlled by the same party, the federal government and its partisan colleagues in the Länder face strong electoral incentives to avoid calling the conference committee or allowing for open intergovernmental conflict, lest they present to the public the impression that the party is fragmented or incompetent. It is useful for the chancellor to develop collaborative working relationships with his party colleagues in the Länder. Moreover, many Land-level politicians are unwilling to gain a reputation for excessive regional self-seeking because they have aspirations in federal party politics. In fact, making costly concessions in intergovernmental negotiations is a way for Land-level leaders to signal to federal party leaders the credibility of their commitment to the overall success of the party.

Very recently, Germany's underlying fiscal contract has been coming under fire once again in the wake of reunification. The 1995 agreement to incorporate the new Länder into the fiscal constitution is widely criticized, especially by the wealthy Länder. In the wake of bailouts of Bremen and Saarland and the growing subnational debt described in Chapter 7, demands for a complete overhaul of the system are growing. The evolving arrangement of partisan and fiscal interests, however, will make reform extremely difficult. The main problem is that asymmetries have grown, and the character of the problem is not so much the reduction of symmetrical rents for all provinces, but the possibility that reform would have highly asymmetric beneficiaries. Any effective reform to improve incentives would require the agreement of some of the poor Länder, which will be very difficult to achieve. The SPD-led central government has few incentives to introduce serious reform because its support is drawn disproportionately from the poor Länder, while the Länder that have the most to gain from reform are controlled by the opposition Union parties. As a result, the

---

[12] Unpublished data collected by the Bundesrat, Geschäftsstelle des Vermittlungsausschusses (1997).

wealthy Länder are relying increasingly on the courts as the arena for their complaints.

After several complaints to the Constitutional Court by the wealthy Länder and a court decision mandating revisions to the equalization system, in June 2001 the Bund and Länder agreed to a new equalization law that will take effect in 2005. The basic structure of the old three-stage system remains unchanged, but the wealthy states agreed to the new system because it allows them to keep a larger share of the taxes they collect. But the agreement will not reduce the receipts of the relatively poor Länder. As Gerhard Schröder put it, "[T]here are no winners and no losers."[13] This apparent win-win scenario was possible because the central government agreed to make up the difference by committing billions of additional Euros to the system. In other words, the central government will be replacing some of the horizontal redistribution between the Länder with direct, vertical redistribution from the Bund to the Länder, and transfer dependence among the poorest Länder will only grow. Given partisan divisions that overlay rather than cross-cut distributive divisions, the central government was only able to achieve reform by making large payoffs to assuage the relative losers.

In sum, the German federal government can use electoral incentives to extract votes for reform at lower cost when the crucial states are co-partisans. Much of the action is in the Bundesrat, and reform is easiest to achieve when it is controlled by the federal majority party. The only reform that has taken place outside of these brief windows of opportunity was forced by the high court, and the federal government was forced to buy off recalcitrant states at high cost.

Brazil

In the three parliamentary federations discussed above, political entre-preneurs at the center occasionally found opportunities to boost their popularity by spearheading attempts to renegotiate unpopular intergov-ernmental contracts. In the postwar period, it is difficult to find examples of major multilateral renegotiations featuring costly provincial sacrifice without also finding evidence of a strong electoral incentive for reform among co-partisan provincial politicians. Yet more research on a wider array of cases is needed. Perhaps the countries discussed above are spe-cial because they have fused executives and legislatures and strong party

---

[13] Reported by Deutsche Presse-Agentur, June 23, 2001.

discipline at both levels. The process of renegotiating intergovernmental contracts might look very different in presidential countries characterized by the relatively weak parties that emerge when the executive is not dependent upon the confidence of the legislature. In Brazil, party discipline is weakened not only by presidentialism at both levels, but also by the system of open-list proportional representation. Brazil's lack of electoral externalities invites comparison to Canada. It is safe to say that, in general, the route to election and reelection to state-level posts in Brazil – perhaps even national legislative seats and the presidency – has little to do with being a member of a party that is popular for its nationwide achievements. In general, membership in the president's political party does not preclude governors from vigorously criticizing and spurning the federal government.

The simplest application of the argument laid out above is to point out that the Brazilian president cannot extract concessions from governors or senators in the pursuit of intergovernmental reform without a good deal of compensation. This is undoubtedly the case. As pointed out in Chapter 8, there is considerable evidence that Brazilian presidents must pay for legislative support – even from co-partisans and coalition members – with pork barrel projects, loans, debt forgiveness, and the like. The landmark intergovernmental reforms of the Cardoso administration were no exception. Yet a closer look at Cardoso's reform strategy suggests that electoral externalities can help facilitate reform even in a country like Brazil.

It is too early to judge the success of the intergovernmental reforms of the 1990s, but the Cardoso administration did succeed in extracting critical concessions from the states. First and foremost, they persuaded key states to privatize or otherwise reform their commercial banks. The importance of this reform cannot be stressed enough, because state banks were the key avenue of overborrowing in the 1990s. Second, they presided over the passage of the Law of Fiscal Responsibility – a legislative package that, if enforced, would dramatically alter the basic incentive structure of Brazilian fiscal federalism. The first was a matter of bilateral negotiation between states, and the second was pushed through Congress by the president's legislative coalition.

Cardoso built up enormous political capital by bringing inflation under control early in his term. He was able to claim credit for a clear, extremely valuable nationwide collective good. In the process, he built a legislative coalition that supported the measures and, as a result, gained some of the political credit for reform. Legislators and governors who were part of the president's inflation-fighting coalition were able to gain politically by claiming credit for macroeconomic stability. In other words, Cardoso crafted a multiparty coalition that engendered top-down coattails for a brief moment. He then used it to extract concessions from key allies.

First, as a condition for debt relief, each state agreed to a package of adjustment targets. Law 9496 of 1997 spelled out these targets, including scheduled declines in debt/revenue ratios, increases in primary balance, limits on personnel spending, growth in own-source revenues, ceilings on investments, and lists of state enterprises to be privatized. Particular attention has been given to resolving the problem of rigidity in state personnel expenditures. Above all, states and municipalities are limited to a ceiling of 60 percent of tax revenue for payroll expenditures. In addition, the new legislation establishes a set of measures aimed at increasing the ability of all levels of government to control such expenditures, including prohibitions on wage increases and new hires. Above all, after several long struggles, most of the state banks – including the most troubled banks discussed above – have finally been privatized.

These reforms started with bilateral negotiations between the administration and the states controlled by its allies. The president fought hard to keep these issues out of the Senate, which so often resolved such issues through logrolling. In this way, the president mobilized the temporary popularity of reform and used it to bring public pressure on the state governments when attempting to extract concessions. The costs of reform were not distributed symmetrically among states. In particular, the largest debtor states were also those most accustomed to abusing state banks: Minas Gerais, São Paulo, and Rio de Janeiro. Each of these states emerged from the 1994 election with PSDB governors whose political success was tightly linked with the success of Cardoso's reform agenda. These governors did extract compensation in return for bank privatization and other reforms – above all, debt forgiveness and renegotiation – but the potential electoral costs associated with undermining Cardoso's stabilization agenda clearly played an important role.

In the period between 1997 and 2000, the legislature also signed an array of new regulations designed to limit future borrowing of the states. Senate Resolution 78 (September 1998) resolved to put further restrictions on borrowing from state banks, imposed new borrowing ceilings, restricted new bond issues, and forbade the issuance of promissory notes to contractors (World Bank 2001). It also proscribed borrowing by jurisdictions that had not demonstrated a positive primary balance in the previous twelve months. Moreover, the National Monetary Council, through resolution

2653, authorized the central bank to control lending by domestic banks to subnational governments.[14]

Above all, the Fiscal Responsibility Law (Supplementary Law 101, approved in May of 2000) and the Penal Law for Fiscal Crimes (approved in October 2000) may be the most important changes to the Brazilian intergovernmental system since the 1988 Constitution.[15] This legislation obliges the president to set yearly debt limits for all levels of the public sector and stipulates that violating subnational governments will be prohibited from all internal and external credit operations and placed on a list of violators, with penalties for any financial institutions that attempt to lend to violators. The states and municipalities are required to submit multiyear plans and reports on the use of resources from privatization, social security funds, and contingent liabilities. The law also includes a golden rule provision stipulating that credit operations may not exceed capital expenditures. Additionally, it clarifies the legal authority of the federal government to withhold constitutional transfers from states that fail to repay debts to the federal treasury. Governments will be required to publish explicit justifications for revenue targets and detailed information about revenue sources and tax breaks, to make bimonthly comparisons of expected and actual revenues, and to adjust within thirty days to revenue shortfalls.

It is too early to speculate about whether these laws will be successful and whether the judiciary will have the independence and capacity to enforce them. What is clear is that the Cardoso administration set out to transform one of the world's most decentralized federations into a tightly managed, hierarchical regime not unlike that found in many unitary systems. Given the traditional influence of governors and state-based interest groups in the legislature, these reforms are quite striking. The president was able to guide this legislation through by convincing the public that state and municipal fiscal profligacy was an important part of the reason for inflation and macroeconomic instability. Using the language of Chapter 5, it had finally become clear to voters that fiscal indiscipline among state governments was not a matter of extracting short-term redistributive bailouts funded by

---

[14] Outstanding loans to the public sector (including public enterprises) are capped at 45 percent of any private bank's equity. If enforced, this will make borrowing by the states extremely difficult. The national savings bank – an important remaining source of long-term credit for the states – is already close to this limit (World Bank 2001).

[15] It is only possible here to give a broad outline of what is an extremely detailed, far-reaching legislative package. For details on the Fiscal Responsibility Law, see Nascimento and Debus (2001).

others, but involved long-term collective costs. This altered the incentives of the president's political allies, especially in the large, crucial states, creating new political incentives to submit to a national collective-goods agenda. He built a multiparty reform coalition that acted with unprecedented cohesiveness in the legislature; and after achieving success and building up positive electoral externalities for the coalition, he started to extract impressive concessions.

It should be pointed out, though, that the electoral credit associated with being part of the president's reform coalition was not on its own sufficient to secure their cooperation. The coalition members also received grants, loans, and favorable treatment in the distribution of bailouts.[16] While state-level deficits and personnel expenditures have fallen during the Cardoso administration, grants and overall expenditures have risen, and the central government's debt burden – in large part because of bailouts of states – has increased substantially.

In sum, it appears that the logic of electoral externalities helps explain how it was possible for governors and legislators to make such striking capitulations during the Cardoso presidency, even in a country where state elections have not traditionally been viewed as referenda on the chief executive's party. Some of the key concessions were extracted from individuals who stood to make electoral gains from successful reform. Yet while party links provided a useful focal point in creating a reform coalition, electoral externalities were insufficiently strong to erase the need to make side payments to its members.

III. Conclusion

Taken together, these case studies show how electoral externalities can help facilitate reform and reduce its costs. When existing intergovernmental contracts are sufficiently unpopular, the national-level executive will have much to gain by proposing a new contract and securing the agreement of the necessary provincial representatives. This can be done at lowest cost when the relevant provincial representatives are co-partisans who stand to enjoy some of the electoral benefits of successful reform. In each of the federations discussed in this chapter, moments of far-reaching reform requiring provinces to make difficult sacrifices came at moments when the critical provinces were co-partisans of the center.

---

[16] In addition to Chapter 8, see Arretche and Rodden (2004).

But this chapter must end with an important caveat: The argument and the case studies do not imply that the new contracts are optimal in terms of long-term welfare, even if side payments and pork are kept to a minimum. The chapter's message is positive rather than normative. It examined moments when there was widespread agreement that existing contracts were inadequate and accepted the proposed solutions at face value. In some cases, the results clearly enhanced aggregate efficiency, as with the privatization of Brazilian state banks or the reduction of trade barriers in Australia. Yet looking back with the benefit of hindsight, some of the reforms have been judged unfavorably, and by no means does this chapter suggest that federations with strong electoral externalities are more efficient in some aggregate sense than federations like Canada.

For instance, the German reforms of 1969 are now widely criticized for having made the German policy process more complex, less decisive, and less democratic, because decisions previously in the hands of individual states were moved to interministerial bodies (see, e.g., Scharpf et al. 1976). In fact, one of the perceived "problems" with the German federal system at the time was the fact that states were competing with one another over mobile capital. If one is drawn to the promise of federalism reviewed in Chapter 2 – specifically Hayek's notion that robust decentralization bolsters efficiency by enhancing information and competition – some of the reform deals described above were steps in the wrong direction in that they either centralized authority or muddied the division of responsibilities. These possibilities will be entertained more seriously in the next chapter.

10

The Origins of Subnational Sovereignty

This book has made much of a distinction between fiscal sovereignty and semisovereignty among constituent units in federations. By the middle of the twentieth century in the United States, Canada, and Switzerland, voters and creditors had come to see the states, provinces, and cantons as sovereign debtors. On the other hand, detailed case studies of Germany and Brazil in the 1980s and '90s analyzed what can go wrong in federations where subnational entities are semisovereign: They are allowed to borrow freely even though fiscal and political institutions send strong signals to voters and creditors that the central government can ultimately be held responsible for their debts. Yet a more basic set of questions remains unanswered: Why do the institutions that bolster subnational fiscal sovereignty – above all, a limited center and wide-ranging subnational tax authority – so often slip away? In the long run, why do some federations maintain distinct spheres of fiscal sovereignty among the constituent units while others do not?

All modern countries are artificial constructs put together by a combination of brute force and bargaining after a long period in which the only sovereignty – political or fiscal – extended to small communities. At the beginning of the twentieth century, state and provincial governments resembled fiscal sovereigns in Argentina, Australia, Brazil, Canada, Germany, Mexico, Switzerland, and the United States, among other federations, and the same can be said about local governments in many unitary systems. In the federations especially, the fiscal authority of the central government was extremely limited in 1900. In many cases, the center had little direct tax authority and had to depend on contributions from the provinces. By the end of the century, however, autonomous subnational taxation had virtually disappeared in Argentina, Germany, and Mexico and was attenuated significantly in Australia and Brazil, while it has remained robust in Switzerland and the United States. Taxation in Canada went through a period of centralization during World War II, but the provinces quickly regained tax autonomy thereafter.

What accounts for these different trajectories? Rather than attempting to provide a satisfying answer to this question based on deductive reasoning, this chapter proceeds inductively from the case studies in two steps. First, it revisits German and Brazilian history to help explain the roots of the semisovereign equilibria described in earlier chapters. Like Chapter 3's discussion of the U.S. 1840s debt crisis and Chapter 9's discussion of reform, the first section pays special attention to "critical junctures" – moments when institutions are in flux and crucial choices appear to create long-lasting legacies (Lipset and Rokkan 1967). Furthering some observations from Chapter 9, it demonstrates how political entrepreneurs carve out opportunities – especially during crises related to debt, the Great Depression, and World War II – to assemble coalitions that centralize revenue through a combination of bargaining and brute force.

When these centralizing moments pass, however, states and provinces inevitably reassert themselves – especially during transitions from authoritarianism to democracy. Along with democratic legitimacy through elections, state governments often regain the right to borrow independently. Yet once the genie has been let out of the bottle – that is, the center has assumed state debts and come to dominate taxation – it is difficult to put it back. The first section concludes with evidence that semisovereign provinces emerge in a similar way in other federations as well.

Yet it would be preferable to move beyond contingent stories and toward a more satisfying explanation of long-term cross-country differences. After all, some countries experience debt crises, wars, and depressions without succumbing to centralization. Perhaps there are deeper antecedent conditions that shape whether or not a country resists centralization when faced with a crisis that engenders demands for centralization and opens a window for centralizing entrepreneurs. The rather speculative second section of this chapter takes up that task. Its goal is to stimulate further research by drawing out hypotheses that emerge from the case studies. Some promising avenues for further research on "endogenous fiscal sovereignty" include long-lasting regional cleavages, the organization of political parties, and patterns of interregional and interpersonal income inequality.

I. Why Does Sovereignty Slip Away?

At first glance, one might be tempted to conclude – incorrectly – that the Canadian provinces, Swiss cantons, and U.S. states are distinct from their Brazilian, German, Argentine, or Mexican counterparts because they have such long histories of independence, some even predating the federation itself. Yet the power to tax was almost exclusively in the hands of the German Länder and the Prussian provinces all the way up to World War I. In the three large Latin American federations, central governments with the power to tax came about only through decades of battles and bargains between regional sovereigns. In addition to the battles described in the Brazilian case below, fiscal sovereignty in what is today Argentina was exclusively in the hands of the provinces until a modern central state, dominated by Buenos Aires, was crafted under Bartolomé Mitre in the 1860s. In Mexico, wide-ranging tax powers were not ceded by the states to the central government until the 1940s.

Thus, at some point in history subnational entities in each of these countries were well positioned to emerge with the type of market discipline that has characterized the United States and Canada. They funded themselves, and central governments were in no position to back up their debts. In fact, evidence is presented below that the German and Brazilian states *were* sovereign borrowers around the turn of the century. In order to move toward a theory of endogenous subnational sovereignty, it is useful to explain what happened in these two countries between 1900 and the period covered in the case studies above, explaining when and how the possibility of subnational sovereignty slipped away.

Germany

In *The Federalist* 18–20, Madison and Hamilton provided a critical tour of confederations from Greek and Roman antiquity to the eighteenth century in order to illustrate "the tendency of federal bodies rather to anarchy among the members than to tyranny in the head" (Federalist 18: 112). They reserved their most vocal criticism for the German confederation, which they characterized as "a history of wars between the emperor and the princes and states . . . of the licentiousness of the strong, and the oppression of the weak . . . of requisitions of man and money disregarded . . . of general imbecility, confusion, and misery" (*Federalist* 19: 115). Even after unification in the nineteenth century and the end of military conflict within the empire, the decentralization of public finance in the German Reich was a great source of tension and instability. As in the eighteenth-century United States, the governments of Prussia and the other Länder were fearful of allowing the central government to gain autonomy and power at their expense and prevented the Reich from levying direct taxes. After unification in 1871, the Reich was highly dependent on the Länder for funds and since 1879 was even forced to redistribute tariff receipts above a certain amount to the Länder (von Kruedener 1987). Lacking tax autonomy and facing growing expenditure obligations associated with military commitments, the Reich resorted to international borrowing. The Reich and Länder both borrowed heavily; in fact, they competed with one another for funds on international credit markets, driving up the interest rate premiums for all German bonds (Hefeker 2001) – exactly the decentralized borrowing scenario feared by Hamilton. Lacking a reliable tax base, the central government ultimately had to finance World War I almost completely with debt.

Without a doubt, the German states were sovereign debtors in the nineteenth century. German states and cities have borrowed independently since medieval times, and there was no unified "German" debt until the Imperial Reich floated loans in the late 1870s. The various German states, along with the individual provinces of Prussia, issued bonds that were quoted regularly starting in 1815. Homer and Sylla (1996) have assembled interest rates for the German governments throughout the 1800s, which demonstrated a good deal of diversity in the rates paid by the various entities. For instance, in 1820 the province of Silesia paid 3.83 percent for bonds with a four-year maturity, while Prussia paid 5.72 percent. After unification, the rates were more tightly clustered. By 1875, the range was from Prussia, which paid 4.09 percent, to Bayern, which paid 4.26 percent. It seems quite likely that these yields were related to market assessments of creditworthiness.

Similar to the U.S. states, the German states emerged from the nineteenth century with a realistic chance of developing market discipline. However, this began to unravel after World War I. In much the same spirit of Hamilton arguing for a stronger central government in response to the failure of requisitions in the Revolutionary War, advocates of centralization fought for a much stronger central government with broader tax autonomy in the Weimar Constitution. However, the Länder and Gemeinden continued to play an important role in the interwar period, and the central government was unable to control their expenditures and debts, which grew substantially throughout the period. When funds on international markets dried up, the German subnational governments borrowed heavily from their own banks. As in many other federations, the Depression created a serious fiscal crisis for subnational governments. Ultimately, the spectacular default and bankruptcy of several Länder – most dramatically, Prussia – was pushed along by and played into the hands of centralizers and was used by the Nazis in their efforts to discredit and take over the Land and communal governments (James 1986). Through legislation and emergency decree, in the late 1920s the central government began stripping the states and municipalities of their power, forcing them to reduce taxes and dramatically cutting their transfers. The Nazi takeover in 1933 was the culmination of a lengthy battle pitting the central government against the states and communes, and put an end to the era of dual sovereignty in German federalism.

After the upheaval of the Nazi dictatorship and a destructive war, the states became the key players in the negotiation of a new constitution. They reclaimed a central role in spending and borrowing and reverted to their connection with the Landesbanken. Their autonomy over borrowing and spending is protected by their place as key veto players in the federal policy process. Yet they regained virtually none of their old tax autonomy. In the negotiations leading to the new federal contract, most of the representatives, save those from Bayern, were opposed to even the slightest legal independence for the Länder in the realm of taxation, citing the disastrous limitations on the tax authority of the central government from 1871 to World War I, the chaos of the Weimar period, and the perceived needs of a "modern" economy (Kilper and Lhotta 1996; Merkl 1963). In fact, even the limited tax authority ultimately granted the Länder has been attributed to intervention by the allied forces (Renzsch 1991: 54).

In sum, the fiscal sovereignty of the Länder was attacked under Weimar and obliterated under the Nazis, and the subnational tax autonomy required for its restoration was not seriously considered when democracy and federalism returned. Time and again, even in the postwar period discussed in the preceding chapter, centralizing reformers have used past crises and perceived inefficiencies as justifications for reforms that chipped away at the fiscal sovereignty of the states. Policy elites and the public – at least outside Bayern and a couple other wealthy states – seem to have adopted Hamilton's original negative assessment of subnational fiscal sovereignty, and the notion seems to have lost any claim to widespread legitimacy in Germany.

Brazil

More recently, Brazil's states also emerged from a period of dictatorship under circumstances that made subnational sovereignty difficult. Yet Brazil's military dictatorship was not nearly as centralized, and the states have never fully lost control over taxation. Nevertheless, a firm no-bailout expectation among state officials, voters, and creditors would have been extremely difficult to build in the late 1980s given the role of the states in borrowing during the previous regime. Looking back even further into Brazilian history, some basic facts about the structure of Brazilian federalism seem to have stood in the way of market discipline as far back as the beginning of the twentieth century.

The perception in the 1990s that the federal government guaranteed all state borrowing has a long historical lineage. Yet so does the political inability of the central government to control the fiscal activities of the states. As with the United States when it developed a new federal constitution in the late eighteenth century, one of the first policies to be considered under the new Brazilian constitution of 1988 was a federal assumption of state debts. In the United States, the borrowing took place in order to achieve what came to be seen as a national collective good – the defeat of the British – and federal assumption was presented as a moral necessity in order to start the new federal fiscal system on a fair footing. A similar logic accompanied the new Brazilian constitution in the late 1980s. State governments had borrowed on foreign markets at the behest of the previous military regime. The center had formally guaranteed the debt, and there was a strong moral and political logic in favor of federal assumption of state debts when attempting to lay the framework for a new, just federal contract.

In both situations, federal assumption challenged the status of the states as sovereign borrowers and created bad incentives. However, in the United States over fifty years elapsed before the debt crisis and assumption movement, during which time the central government had been relatively disengaged from involvement in the borrowing and spending activities of the states. In Brazil, by contrast, the next debt crisis after the 1989 assumption emerged in a matter of only three years and involved debts owed to the central government's intermediaries. Federal grants, loans, and even bailouts have been part of a game of regional distributive politics well before the promulgation of the new constitution. The central government never even came close to developing the necessary distance from state government finance to credibly disavow their obligations as those of separate, sovereign borrowers. It has been particularly loath to allow states to default on foreign debt because its own creditworthiness would undoubtedly suffer.

Not unlike Germany after World War II, the most recent manifestation of democratic federalism in Brazil followed a period of authoritarian centralization that seriously undermined the sovereignty of the states, making it very difficult to suddenly change expectations. In Brazil, the military eroded the states' tax powers, but in contrast to the complete subjugation of the Länder in the 1940s, the Brazilian states maintained some flexibility over spending during military rule. In fact, the military tried to use the states and their governors to help legitimize their rule (Medeiros 1986; Souza 1997). Ames (1987) provides an account of regional pork barrel politics involving governors during military rule. Support for the regime was particularly strong in the poor, rural northeastern states; and due to the structure of the legislature, the military regime created new states where its support was strongest and combined states where its support was weakest. It used grants and loans to funnel resources to political allies. The military regime also was involved in directly financing the state commercial banks, which in turn funneled resources to regime supporters (Souza 1997). Well before regional elites came together in the Constituent National Assembly to bargain over a new constitution, governors viewed state debt as a way to extract resources from a center with deep pockets. Souza (1997) argues that already in the gubernatorial elections of 1982, with the regime's blessing the governors relied heavily on the state commercial banks to funnel resources to their supporters.

To gain further understanding of why the Brazilian states have not developed anything approaching fiscal sovereignty in the late twentieth century, it is useful to go back even further – to the First Republic of the late 1800s and early 1900s. This period was characterized by strong regional elites in control of state politics and a central government that was principally an arena for the consummation of bargains among regional elites. From the beginning, it was the kind of federation that would have earned the wrath of Alexander Hamilton. The state governments tried to avoid direct taxes, preferring to finance expenditures by taxing trade with foreigners and one another and funding railroads and other internal improvements through foreign borrowing. Bitter interstate trade wars raged throughout the early part of the twentieth century. Central government politics was a complex bargaining relationship in which the well-organized coffee producers of Minas Gerais and especially São Paulo, who were responsible for providing most of the federal budget, attempted to extract favorable interest rate and coffee price stabilization policies from the central government. They did this by controlling the presidential nomination process, buying votes quite literally through bribery in the legislature (see Love 1980), and buying the support of other states with intergovernmental transfers.

Investors were attracted to Brazil's potential, especially its dominance in coffee production. Many of the states borrowed in international credit markets with little federal supervision. The loans were used for railroads, internal improvements, and the promotion of immigration. By far the largest foreign loans, however, were for São Paulo's coffee valorization program. With funding through a mixture of federal loans and federally guaranteed state loans, coffee was stockpiled during times of high production and released on the world markets when production was low (Love 1980). Between 1888 and 1930, São Paulo contracted twenty-five large foreign loans (Levine 1978).

At the turn of the century, some form of market discipline might still have been a possibility. In the late 1800s, international creditors did apparently differentiate between the obligations of the states and the federal government. The large, wealthy states of the south had greater access to credit markets than the relatively poor northern states and paid lower interest rates. For instance, Levine (1978) points out that most of Pernambuco's foreign loans carried interest rates of 7 percent, compared with 4 to 5 percent for the southern states at the turn of the century. According to Wirth (1977), a high level of concern about international credit ratings affected the fiscal decisions of the government of Minas Gerais, and Love (1980) makes the same observation about São Paulo.

However, any nascent perception of state sovereignty quickly disappeared. According to Levine (1978), many of the states lived close to default throughout the Old Republic. When president Manuel Ferraz de Campos Sales went to London in 1898 to refinance Brazil's foreign debt, he reported a threat from the directors of the House of Rothschild that any default could "gravely affect national sovereignty itself, provoking claims that would perhaps end in foreign intervention" (Campos Sales 1908).[1] This was a credible threat – indeed, the British, Germans, and Italians blockaded Venezuela four years later in order to collect debts. When the state of Espirito Santo defaulted on a loan in 1901, the Brazilian central government assumed the debt in response to diplomatic pressure from the French government. Next,

---

[1] Quoted in Love (1980: 208).

the government was pressured into bailing out a bankrupt railroad project funded by German investors in Minas Gerais.

The most dramatic events, however, took place in the 1930s. In 1929, the price of coffee had plummeted, and the failed coffee valorization program left São Paulo with massive debts. Other states were on the verge of default as well. When Getúlio Vargas came to power through an armed rebellion in 1930, his first move was to borrow a strategy from Alexander Hamilton. He attempted to assert once and for all the federal government's sovereignty by assuming the debts of the states. Unlike Hamilton, he may have succeeded. The states – above all, São Paulo – traded debt relief for reduced sovereignty. Under the Estado Novo instituted in 1937, Vargas completed his Hamiltonian project by closing the state legislatures, replacing elected governors with appointed "intervenors," drastically reducing the taxing powers of the states, and asserting federal supremacy over interstate trade. He also instituted a draconian restriction on borrowing: States that failed to maintain balanced budgets were to be transformed into territories. Though the states regained power over their own affairs with the transition back to democracy in 1946 and quickly resumed their role as key players in a complex game of regional bargaining over the federal budget, the Vargas bailout in 1930 was a serious long-term blow to the concept of state fiscal sovereignty. The centralization and suspension of democracy in 1964 was merely a reprise.

It is interesting to note the similarity of the debt-bailout-reform pattern of the First Republic and the most recent crises. A mixture of asymmetric economic development and regional distributive politics looms large in both eras. In both cases, states conducted unsustainable borrowing with a federal guarantee. Tenuous state finances were pushed over the edge by economic downturns, and states pressed the central government for bailouts. In both cases, the largest and wealthiest states – most notably, São Paulo – borrowed the most and received the largest bailouts. Aggressive borrowing with a federal guarantee seems to be a strategy in the game of distributive politics for São Paulo. Since the days of the coffee economy, leaders of São Paulo have known that their economy is too big to fail, which allows them to use debt strategically.

Lessons

The weakness of the central government's no-bailout commitment inherent in the Brazilian fiscal system can be traced to the politics of federal bargains.

As in Germany, strong regional political elites with independent sources of legitimacy and authority antedated the process of building a modern central state with authority to tax and print money. In fact, even the key centralizing figures – Bismarck and Vargas – did not rely exclusively on force. They had to craft delicate interstate coalitions, as have their successors. Once in place, this kind of federal history is difficult to suppress. Neither Nazi dictatorship in Germany nor military rule in Brazil ended the legacies of states as spenders and veto players. In both places, a return to democracy seemed to require a return to federalism, and elites associated with the states negotiated new constitutions that protected their interests. These political bargains provided states with impressive revenues from shared taxes, grants, and loans, and even gave states access to bond markets and borrowing from their own federally guaranteed banks.

But it is difficult to escape the lasting impact of these centralization and debt assumption episodes on market perceptions and expectations. The Brazilian states were borrowing in international markets from the turn of the century to the 1930s, and the federal government's role in guaranteeing the debt was rather unclear. However, uncertainties were resolved and the nature of the game was clarified when Vargas assumed the debts of the states, which have been implicitly or explicitly backed up by the federal government ever since.

In Argentina as well, the construction of a modern central state began with a federal assumption of provincial debts in 1862. Like Hamilton and Vargas, Mitre viewed the assumption of provincial debts as an important way to build the central government's independent sovereignty. Predictable perils of semisovereign borrowing soon followed in the 1880s, when provincial banks were issuing paper money, often at the behest of speculator interests, and borrowing gold abroad (Rock 1985: 157–58). This contributed to a macroeconomic crisis in 1890, when the central government once again assumed unsustainable provincial debts. As with the Vargas centralization of Brazil in the 1930s, the provinces gave up considerable tax autonomy to the federal government in exchange for bailouts. The autonomy of the provinces in the realm of taxation then eroded further throughout the twentieth century, with its fits and starts of semidemocracy and military authoritarianism, as the federal government and provinces reached bargains that led to the famously complex intergovernmental "labyrinth" that is still in place today (Iaryczower, Saiegh, and Tommasi 2001).

In each of these examples, the historical roots of semisovereignty seem to lie in a centralization process characterized by Careaga and Weingast

(2000) as a fiscal "pact with the devil." Whether in response to a military threat, a fiscal crisis, perceptions of chaotic interprovincial competition, or pure hunger for power, Hamiltonian centralizers convince provincial elites to give up their tax autonomy in exchange for a system of guaranteed federal transfers (Diaz-Cayeros 2004). They do this with a combination of carrots, like positions in the federal government or increasing transfers, and sticks like the threat of military attack, federal intervention, and double taxation. According to Careaga and Weingast (2000), such a pact did not come about in Mexico until the 1940s. Debt assumptions are often a prominent carrot in these pacts. Provincial officials are happy to unload debt burdens, and centralizers understand Hamilton's logic: "If all the public creditors receive their dues from one source, distributed by an equal hand, their interest will be the same. And, having the same interests, they will unite in the support of the fiscal arrangements of the Government" (quoted in Miller 1959: 235).

As a result, the legacy of these centralization projects is a central government with dominance in the realm of taxation and an implicit responsibility for state debts. Yet the latter is not a problem in the short term because centralizers often seem to obliterate the autonomy of the states and obviate the need to bargain with them. Hitler completely subordinated the Länder. Vargas appointed federal "intervenors" in the 1930s, and later military regimes appointed governors. Various authoritarian Argentine and Nigerian governments appointed governors and intervened at will in the provinces and states throughout the twentieth century. A dominant party meddled in state politics throughout much of the latter twentieth century in Mexico. The same is true of the Congress Party in India, especially under Indira Gandhi.

But once it takes root, federalism – as defined in Chapter 2 – is incredibly resilient. First of all, beyond the façade of hierarchy, military regimes often rely on provincial governments to help extract revenue, provide services, and augment their legitimacy. Even for military governments, political survival might require intergovernmental bargaining. Even in dominant-party federations like India under the Congress Party or Mexico under the PRI, intense interregional bargaining often takes place within the party. Second, transitions to democracy or challenges to dominant parties often start with protests and organization in the provinces, which hold the first democratic elections and then earn a seat at the bargaining table when a new constitution is negotiated. In any case, advocates of democratization in countries with traditions of federalism often see a return to federalism as a necessary part of the return to democracy. Finally, when authoritarian regimes negotiate the way back to democracy, they may see federalism as a convenient way to enhance the power of conservative rural groups at the expense of urban workers and limit future redistribution.[2] In all of these scenarios, the return to democracy involves the return or even the amplification of interstate bargaining.

When a more robust type of federalism returns after periods of centralized dictatorship or one-party dominance, the "pact with the devil" is difficult to undo. Once autonomous taxation is exchanged for a mixture of revenue sharing, grants, and loans, a return to wide-ranging provincial tax autonomy is quite rare. However, provinces quickly regain autonomy over expenditures and reassert control over provincial banks and public enterprises – sometimes even gaining access to international capital markets. Thus, the dangerous semisovereign equilibrium can arise rather naturally when federal bargains are revived as countries emerge from periods of authoritarian centralization. The period when the new federal bargain is reached is often marked by very high expectations about poverty reduction, improved government services, and reductions in interregional inequality. The result is often a politically fragmented but fiscally dominant central government with a commitment problem.

II. Toward a Comparative Theory of Dual Fiscal Sovereignty

This discussion of the origins of semisovereign borrowing also provides a new perspective on the three clearest cases of dual sovereignty. With the exception of Canada during World War II, the constituent units in these federations have not made centralizing pacts. The Canadian provinces, Swiss cantons, and U.S. states have maintained control over their own taxes, budgets, and debts throughout much of the twentieth century in spite of wars, fiscal crises, and depression. This brings us back to a more precise version of the dominant yet still unanswered question of the political science literature on federalism: Why do some federations centralize while others do not? Though a convincing explanation for the different fates of federations cannot be supplied here, a few possibilities stand out. First of all, in spite of bloody international and civil wars, at no point did these federations succumb to authoritarian centralization or long stretches of

---

[2] Saiegh and Tommasi (1999) suggest that this explains the electoral and financial reforms promulgated in 1972 by the Argentine military regime, which feared a Peronist victory in the 1973 election.

one-party rule. As described above, some of the key moments of tax centralization in Argentina, Brazil, and Germany have come during periods of authoritarian rule. However, significant centralization has also taken place in democracies, as in Weimar Germany or Canada and Australia during World War II.

A second possibility is that at key moments the pact with the devil may have been too difficult to make because of simmering conflicts over slavery, language, race, or national identity. Switzerland and the United States had civil wars during the nineteenth century, and Québec has flirted with secession as recently as the 1990s. The decentralized nature of American federalism has been shaped in large part by its divide over slavery. Canadian and Swiss federal histories have been shaped by divides between ethnic and linguistic communities. A reasonable proposition, then, is that long-term tax decentralization stabilizes when a country has regionally based, mutually suspicious groups that stand in the way of centralizing pacts or undermine the efforts of centralizing entrepreneurs. This type of argument fits comfortably within an older political science literature asserting that robust, decentralized federalism is most likely to persist in countries with federal "societies" or "political cultures" (Elazar 1987). Moreover, while moves from centralized to decentralized taxation over the last century are quite rare, they seem to have gone furthest in countries with very strong regional-ethnic cleavages: Spain and Belgium. Yet such cleavages are almost certainly not a sufficient condition for tax decentralization; long traditions of bloodshed, civil war, and regional antagonism in Argentina, Mexico, and Nigeria have not preserved subnational fiscal sovereignty.

Political Parties Revisited

Some version of William Riker's classic argument about the importance of decentralized political parties in maintaining decentralized federalism provides another possible explanation. Indeed, from some of the preceding chapters emerges a relatively clear correlation between the intertwining of federal and provincial party systems, the relative centralization of taxation, and the blurring of subnational sovereignty. The federal and state party systems in Germany and Australia have grown increasingly intertwined since World War II, as have the federal and state fiscal systems. Moreover, the two path-breaking intergovernmental reform episodes discussed in the previous chapter – Australia in the 1990s and Germany in the 1960s – also involved important shifts in the arenas of intergovernmental decision making. In each case, policies and revenues that were previously in the hands of individual states were moved to intergovernmental bargaining arenas like the Council of Australian Governments or a variety of sector-specific intergovernmental bodies. At these key moments in both countries, state-level leaders realized their electoral fates were partially out of their hands, which strengthened incentives to put aside aggressive regional agendas and cede unilateral authority over revenue and policy decisions to multilateral bodies in exchange for electoral credit for popular reform. In Brazil, after the dust settled from the reforms instituted by Cardoso's coalition, the states appear to have ceded considerable autonomy over public finance to the executive, the Central Bank, and the judiciary. As the levels of government have become increasingly intertwined over time in Germany, creditors have received clearer signals that state governments should not be treated as fiscal sovereigns. By reducing their borrowing autonomy and attempting to make them beholden to the center through a dense new set of rules and requirements, the reforms of the Cardoso administration reduced even further the possibility that anyone could view the Brazilian states as fiscal sovereigns.

As the Canadian federation has unraveled somewhat, however, credit markets have received clear signals that the debts of the provinces should be treated as sovereign. Provincial governments have strong incentives to guard their jurisdictional and fiscal turf. A common observation is that federal-provincial relations resemble international diplomacy, and often Ottawa's only option is to negotiate separate bilateral deals with individual provinces (Simeon 1972). In contrast to Australia and Germany, where intergovernmental pacts and oversight bodies serve to coordinate joint involvement in the same policy field, each Canadian government often proceeds as if the other does not exist. Kenneth McRoberts (1985) refers to this as "double unilateralism." In the absence of electoral externalities, each government is concerned only with receiving credit (or avoiding blame) for its own activities. The previous chapter noted that this mode of intergovernmental relations undermines reform. Moreover, critics of Canadian federalism view it as the source of inefficiencies like a fragmented internal market, overlapping but uncoordinated involvement of federal and provincial governments in similar expenditure projects (Haddow 1995; Migué 1997), and taxation of the same base (Dahlby 1994; Dahlby and Wilson 1996).

Yet if one is attracted to the notion of competitive fiscal discipline, Canada's fragmented political parties may have a virtue if they undermine the type of multilateral reform deals that chip away at subnational sovereignty. The decline of electoral externalities in Canada may help explain why the provinces regained their prominent role in taxation. Canada seems to have come very close to sacrificing provincial fiscal sovereignty in the 1940s. Alberta and Saskatchewan were bailed out in the 1930s, and the Dominion government assumed Newfoundland's debt when it entered the federation. The Rowell-Sirois Commission of 1938 recommended that as part of a major reorganization of fiscal federalism the federal government take over a dominant role in taxation, assume the debts of all the provinces, and then back up and regulate future provincial borrowing (Perry 1955). As described in the last chapter, the outbreak of World War II was the last moment at which a supermajority of provinces was controlled by a relatively integrated national political party. This facilitated an agreement whereby the central government temporarily "rented" provincial authority over income and corporate taxation during the war.

The tax rental agreements were renegotiated during the 1950s, but intergovernmental bargaining was increasingly contentious, and Ottawa found it impossible to simultaneously satisfy the demands of the provinces – especially Québec. For most of this period, the party in control in Ottawa controlled fewer than half the provinces, and intraparty strains between federal and provincial organizations grew. The Liberal party in Québec was losing ground to the Union Nationale, which portrayed the Liberals as a party of centralization. Partially in response, the provincial Liberals broke their ties with the federal party. And throughout the 1950s, the regional Social Credit Party and the Cooperative Commonwealth Federation (CCF) made gains in the western provinces based on anti-eastern sentiment, which forced the provincial branches of the two major parties to distance themselves from Ottawa as well.

Led by Québec, several provinces started reasserting their rights to independent corporate and income taxation. Intraparty accommodation was impossible, and it was no longer clear to the central government that there were advantages to collecting taxes that would be spent by partisan enemies in the provinces. By the 1960s, the provinces had regained their autonomy over corporate and income taxes, and the central government had reduced its own taxes accordingly. Without Québec's dogged insistence on tax autonomy and the fraying links between federal and provincial parties during this crucial period, it is possible that the Canadian experience would have resembled Australia, where wartime dominance in the field of direct taxation never disappeared and the central government took over the role of organizing state borrowing.

In short, at moments when perceived crises create demands for centralizing reforms in democracies, centralizing pacts appear to emerge more easily in the presence of integrated federal and provincial political parties. Yet as with William Riker's original argument, it is difficult to show that the organization of political parties *causes* the long-term level of tax centralization. In fact, Chhibber and Kollman (2004) use several case studies to assert that the opposite causal relationship is at work: The level of fiscal centralization shapes the relative centralization of the party system. For instance, it is possible that reforms to the constitutional contract first reduce the autonomy of provinces, and voters eventually respond by turning their eyes to the central executive as the locus of credit and blame, which ultimately strengthens electoral externalities.

It is also quite possible that the strength of electoral externalities, the relative centralization of taxation, and ultimately the strength of the center's no-bailout commitment are jointly determined by some other underlying facets of society. In Canada, for instance, it is difficult to explain the fraying links between federal and provincial parties without the "quiet revolution" in Québec or the alienation of Westerners on which political entrepreneurs were able to build.

An additional possibility is explored by Diaz-Cayeros (2004), who argues that in Mexico a dominant, centralized party – the PRI – came together in the first place as a way of cementing a centralizing pact. Centralizing political entrepreneurs found it difficult to commit not to expropriate the resources and patronage that sustained rural elites. The hegemonic PRI emerged as a commitment device that promised rural elites a guaranteed flow of resources in the future. In this story, neither tax centralization nor party centralization caused the other, but both emerged as part of a pact among self-interested elites.

Inequality and Economic Geography

Another hypothesis is that decentralized taxation is difficult to maintain in the long run in the presence of pronounced interregional income inequality, especially if a large portion of the country's wealth is generated in one dominant jurisdiction. In fact, such a pattern emerges quite naturally in early stages of economic development, when agglomeration effects lead to pronounced income differences between the industrializing center and the poor, largely agricultural periphery. As a legacy of this, in most decentralized fiscal systems the median jurisdiction is much poorer than the mean.

Because a decentralized system of taxation with a weak center would only allow the wealthy regions to provide public goods like infrastructure investment and education and get further ahead while the periphery lags further behind, it is not difficult to understand why political entrepreneurs in the periphery would push for tax centralization aimed at capturing some of the wealth generated in the core. In contrast, decentralized taxation might be most sustainable in the presence of a relatively even and fluid interregional income distribution that limits the demands for centralized interregional tax transfer systems.[3]

It may also be fruitful to add intraregional inequality and class conflict to the story. Capitalists in the urban core may actually prefer a centralizing fiscal pact with rural elites if they fear that the urban poor would tax them at an even higher rate under decentralization. This logic could provide an intriguing interpretation of the centralizing fiscal pacts in Latin America: Urban capitalists form an alliance with rural elites, who are intentionally overrepresented in the legislature. A share of the urban industrial surplus – a part of which is to be used on patronage – is exchanged for rural support in maintaining a low level of redistribution from rich to poor.

Moreover, as demonstrated by the Brazilian and Argentine experiences with wealthy giants like São Paulo and Buenos Aires, and perhaps the early German experience with Prussia, the presence of one or two wealthy, dominant jurisdictions can create a too-big-to-fail dynamic characterized by subnational debt crises that ultimately play into the hands of centralizers.

Once tax centralization has been achieved and the fiscal affairs of the center and provinces have become intertwined, interregional income inequalities help explain why centralization is often so stable. Consider the resistance of countries like Germany, Italy, and the UK to demands for tax decentralization. When the Italian North and wealthy German states like Bayern demand tax decentralization, they are clearly outnumbered by jurisdictions – home to a majority of the population – that benefit from the status quo tax transfer system. However, even if the wealthy regions with preferences for decentralized taxation are outnumbered, they may be able to limit centralization if they are in a position to make credible secession threats, as in Belgium and Spain – the two European countries that have made the boldest recent moves toward increased subnational tax autonomy. As with arguments relying on political parties, it is difficult to ignore the role of

---

[3] For a closely related model based on the median voter logic, see Bolton and Roland (1997).

ethnic, religious, and linguistic cleavages that so often provide the logic of the federal bargain in the first place.

III. Conclusion

Whether authoritarian brutes, crafty democrats, or some combination of the two, centralizing political entrepreneurs often attempt to seize upon moments of perceived crisis in federations. In these moments, the political rhetoric echoes Hamilton's skepticism, and the fragmentation and competition associated with decentralized federalism – especially in the realm of taxation – can easily be portrayed as a problem to be solved through centralization.[4] Some of the most impressive bouts of fiscal centralization in this century appear to have taken place in conjunction with war, depression, and subnational debt crises, and many involved spells of authoritarianism. Yet the previous chapter also discussed a subtler intertwining of federal and provincial fiscal sovereignty in response to perceived inefficiencies in democratic federations. Once centralizing entrepreneurs succeed in assuming subnational debts and replacing subnational taxes with grants and loans, the trend is difficult to reverse.

But some countries have avoided this trend; and in hopes of spurring further research, this chapter has speculated about the reasons. Some interrelated possibilities include mutually suspicious region-based groups, decentralized parties, and the structure of geography and income inequality. Many important questions remain unresolved and amenable to research, though identification of causality will be difficult.

By carefully examining some possible explanations of cross-national differences and diachronic changes in some of the basic fiscal and political institutions emphasized in earlier chapters, hopefully this chapter and its predecessor have solidified this book's claims that these institutions are not epiphenomenal. The game of fiscal federalism can and does change, and antecedent factors like economic and ethnic geography probably help structure the conditions under which fiscal structures and patterns of party organization are stable. Yet once they take shape, we have seen that these institutions can be quite stable over long periods – sometimes frustratingly so – with predictable effects on the credibility of the central government's no-bailout commitment.

---

[4] Sometimes the perceived crisis has nothing to do with federalism. Witness the recent replacement of popularly elected Russian governors with hand-picked allies of President Vladimir Putin, allegedly as a response to terrorism in Russia.

These chapters also present a useful reality check before moving on to a discussion of policy implications in the next chapter. When confronted with institutions that promote unpleasant outcomes, the natural response is to advocate institutional reform. Yet we have seen that the institutions required for the type of competitive, market-based fiscal discipline so often idealized in the literature are probably not easy to build, and semisovereign provincial governments can emerge quite naturally, especially during transitions to democracy. These observations call for care and subtlety in the dispensation of policy advice.

11

Conclusions

This final chapter draws together the key conclusions of the book, places them in a larger context, and assesses policy implications. It starts by revisiting the basic paradox that motivates the book: two seemingly irreconcilable views of federalism. It then summarizes the arguments and evidence that have been mobilized to show that vastly different incentive structures from one country to another – and from one province to another – can help sort out some of the promise and especially the perils of fiscal federalism in recent decades. These findings allow for some fairly solid conclusions about conditions under which the perils of fiscal federalism are greatest, and these translate into some useful contemporary policy implications – especially for newly decentralizing countries. Finally, this chapter concludes with a discussion of future research that might address some questions that have been raised but not answered in this book.

I. Hamilton's Paradox Revisited

This book started with the paradox of Alexander Hamilton's writings and actions in the realm of fiscal federalism. He believed that federalism – if it implies divided sovereignty – inevitably leads to inefficiency at best and at worst "renders the empire a nerveless body" (*Federalist* 19). Yet as part of his centralization strategy, he was forced to throw some bones to his opponents from Virginia. He joined in writing some essays that, while pointing out its perils, defended the principle of divided sovereignty more eloquently than any treatise before or since.

Evidently, Hamilton was quite right when he said, shortly before his death, "[I]n everything which gives opportunity for juggling arts our adversaries will nine times out of ten excel us."[1] The legacy of the juggling arts in *The Federalist* has been fully expropriated by his adversaries. According to Vincent Ostrom, "A limited constitution cannot rely upon the expediency of vesting 'ultimate authority' or the 'last say' with any particular governmental body. The design of a limited constitution, thus, requires reference to a theory of political organization which stands in marked contrast to a theory of unlimited sovereignty" (1987: 67). According to Ostrom, such a coherent theory of the "compound republic" congealed during the revolutionary period and was articulated in *The Federalist*. The notion that federalism is a way of protecting liberty and property rights against the encroachment of Leviathan, especially when capital and labor are mobile, has informed a great deal of scholarship running from Friedrich Hayek to James Buchanan and Barry Weingast, who argue that federalism should engender smaller, more efficient government and perhaps even faster economic development. Combine this logic with Charles Tiebout's famous sorting mechanism and the notion from public economics that decentralization facilitates improved information revelation and accountability. Then consider a century of stability and economic growth with a relatively small public sector in the United States, Canada, and Switzerland, and it is easy to understand the enthusiasm for decentralization that has captured intellectuals and policymakers – especially conservatives who are skeptical about redistribution and the welfare state.

Yet at the beginning of the twenty-first century, in light of macroeconomic crises in Argentina and Brazil and serious concerns with subnational debt ranging from Nigeria to Germany, Hamilton's skepticism about what he viewed as an irrational "rage for liberty" seems more prescient than some of the disingenuous praise for the notion of divided sovereignty in *The Federalist*. This book has focused on the fiscal decisions of subnational governments and the externalities they produce for federations. It has asked why subnational governments in some countries exhibit tight fiscal discipline, while in others they overfish the common revenue pool and undermine macroeconomic stability. The answers help shed light on larger questions about the promise and peril of divided sovereignty.

II. Key Arguments and Findings

The central argument starts with a basic dynamic commitment problem facing the center in all decentralized systems of government. As with

---

[1] Attributed by Miller (1959: 567).

governments and state-owned enterprises in socialist economies, when the center dominates the power to tax and takes on heavy obligations to fund subnational governments, it cannot credibly commit to withhold bailouts in the event of a local fiscal crisis. Knowing this, subnational officials face weak incentives *ex ante* for fiscal discipline. Voters and credit markets, believing that the center ultimately will not tolerate default, will be slow to punish subnational officials for running unsustainable deficits. Chapter 4 showed that credit-rating agencies perceive implicit federal guarantees of subnational debt in the vast majority of the world's decentralized systems – even the majority of formal federations. Truly divided fiscal sovereignty is quite rare.

The case studies suggested that the details of intergovernmental financing arrangements matter a great deal. Depending on the context, bailout expectations are shaped, for example, by whether grants are general- or specific-purpose, rule-based or discretionary, population-based or income-redistributive, by the flexibility of the tax base allotted to subnational governments and the nature of federal expenditure mandates. But even though it is a relatively blunt proxy, the overall level of local dependence on intergovernmental transfers appears to capture the central government's commitment problem reasonably well.

Thus, decentralized finance poses a moral hazard problem for countries – federal and unitary alike – in which subnational governments are funded primarily through revenue sharing and grants. Knowing that creditors and voters have relatively weak incentives to discipline local governments, it is in the central government's interest to place firm limits on their borrowing. And in fact, using a large sample of countries, Chapter 4 demonstrated a negative correlation between transfer dependence and formal borrowing autonomy allowed by the center.

This is where political federalism – defined as a special type of incomplete constitutional contract between the federal government and provinces – becomes important. Hamilton was correct in pointing out that the central government in a federation is often "incapable of regulating its own members." Chapter 4 showed that central governments in federations are much more inclined than those in unitary systems to allow subnational governments access to credit markets, even when transfer dependence is high and the moral-hazard problem looms large. As the case studies illuminate, this is often because the states have such strong representation in the legislature and, more importantly, because the basic rules of the game were negotiated by the states and require their agreement for reform. Thus, once the central government takes on heavy cofinancing obligations – often as a part of a centralization drive in response to some perceived national crisis – federations are in danger of falling into a bad equilibrium in which the center's lack of commitment is painfully obvious, yet the basic contract makes it difficult to impose a hierarchical solution. In this equilibrium, neither market-based nor hierarchical discipline functions properly and debt levels can skyrocket.

The literature on soft budget constraints in socialist economies identifies a similar problem: Simply giving more autonomy to enterprise managers without cutting their reliance on the government for funding only exacerbates the soft budget constraint problem if it reduces the center's ability to monitor the quality of the projects selected by managers (Kornai et al. 2003; Wang 1991). In this literature, the surest solution to the soft budget constraint problem is to finance projects through a decentralized, competitive banking system rather than a single government (Dewatripont and Maskin 1995). In this book, the analogous solution for subnational governments is a highly decentralized system of taxation.[2]

The real fiscal danger in the twentieth century was not the divided sovereignty feared by Hamilton, but rather a murky semisovereignty that comes about when a politically constrained center dominates taxation but not spending and borrowing. In a sense, the peril of fiscal federalism is most acute when Hamiltonian centralizers achieve only partial success, asserting long-term central government preeminence in taxation but not borrowing. Canada, Switzerland, and the United States stand out among the world's federations in that creditors clearly view all of their constituent units essentially as sovereigns. Though there are important differences between them, these federations have reached a relatively stable equilibrium in which the provinces, states, and cantons – even the poorest – are primarily funded by broad-based taxes over which they have considerable autonomy. At the provincial level, they abide by Hamilton's dictum that the creation of debt should always be accompanied with the "means of extinguishment." In most other federations, a stable system has emerged where in the aggregate, the

---

[2] A related point is made in the classic literature on the firm. In highly centralized unitary organizations, incentives for innovation are reduced, but so are opportunities for the worst forms of opportunism. In the highly decentralized, multidivisional organization structure touted by Oliver Williamson (1985), divisions are autonomous, self-financing profit centers, harnessing the discipline of the market while strengthening incentives for innovation. The most troubled form of organization, supposedly exemplified by General Motors in the 1930s (Chandler 1966), was the holding company, where the center is little more than a forum for horse trading in which each division manager exchanges votes with fellow managers for favored projects, thus introducing cross-subsidization and a common resource problem.

constituent units are funded in much larger part through revenue sharing and grants, and even the taxes allocated to them are highly regulated and inflexible. In these federations, the "means of extinguishment" for some or all of the debts of the constituent units are in the hands of the central government, leading to perceptions by voters and creditors that subnational debt ultimately carries an implicit federal guarantee.

But among these cases of "semisovereign" borrowing, there is considerable diversity both within and across countries. Especially in developing federations, there are often striking differences between the fiscal incentives faced by the wealthiest and poorest jurisdictions. For instance, intergovernmental transfers make up a minuscule portion of the budgets of Buenos Aires, São Paulo, and Navarre, while comprising virtually the entire budget of the poorest units in Argentina, Brazil, and Spain. Thus, the relatively wealthy, self-sufficient states might be creditworthy without federal guarantees, and one might expect that market discipline, even if implausible for the poorest rural states, can at least rein in the fiscal behavior of the wealthy industrialized states.

Yet there is often a countervailing logic. The wealthy states might understand that they are too big to fail because of the externalities they produce for the nation's economy and credit reputation. They might use their greater credit market access to borrow even more aggressively than other states. If they perceive the center's credibility to be low, cycles of borrowing and bailout demands might be rational strategies in a larger game of distributive politics for the wealthy states, especially if the poor states can usually dominate them in the legislature and extract resources from them. Such distributive battles rooted in the asymmetry of jurisdictions' size and clout has undermined fiscal discipline in both Argentina and Brazil on and off since the 1800s.

The problem of asymmetric jurisdiction size is related to another key issue: distributive politics and legislative representation. In practice, because the legislative process in federations is driven by interregional bargaining, the distribution of federal grants and loans often follows a political logic much more closely than any of the prescriptions of welfare economics. Presidents in countries like Brazil and leaders of majority parties in parliamentary federations like Germany and India must build and maintain legislative coalitions across regions. Thus, provincial-level officials might have expectations that they can extract benefits from the center if their representatives in the legislature are in a strong bargaining position. When subnational governments believe they are well positioned for future bailouts because of some political characteristics, they will demonstrate less fiscal discipline in the current budget period. For instance, the Brazilian and German case studies suggested that small states with more legislative votes per capita not only receive larger grants and spend more than other states, but they also run larger deficits. Though the finding was less robust, it also appears that the same can be said about the states where the executive is controlled by the party or coalition of the federal executive.

A key question about troubled semisovereign federations is why some, like Brazil, develop widespread problems with fiscal discipline that extend to a broad cross-section of states, while the problems have been relatively small and limited to only a few states in countries like Germany. There are likely a plethora of context-dependent answers, but this book has paid special attention to the role of political parties. Opportunistic attempts by large, especially wealthy German states to overborrow and trigger bailouts would be damaging to the careers of state officials and to the reputation of the political party. German state officials, like those in Australia, are embedded in a highly integrated national party system that shapes their career prospects. Protecting the value of a national party label is generally not a priority for state-level officials in Brazil, providing few electoral incentives to avoid debt and bailout demands.

German party ties place limits on aggressive regional self-seeking in the legislative arena as well. Party discipline is quite strong even in the Bundesrat, and many intergovernmental disputes are resolved within the parties, whose leaders wish to avoid open public disputes. In Brazil, on the other hand, even though Cardoso was able to forge a stable legislative coalition, party discipline is relatively weak in general, and the legislative process involves a good deal of logrolling among representatives of states, especially in the Senate, which translated into bailout expectations (and actual bailouts) for a large number of states.

Using a sample of federations going back to the 1970s, Chapter 5 showed that higher levels of "partisan harmony " between the federal executive and the states are associated with lower overall public sector deficits. But the findings in Chapters 7 and 8 suggest that if this is true, at least in two cases it is apparently not because allies of the center always exhibit more fiscal restraint than those of the opposition. In fact, under some conditions co-partisans of the central executive might hope to extract extra resources from the federal government though "redistributive" bailouts. But if the electoral success of provincial politicians is driven by the value of their nationwide party label, this puts a ceiling on what they have to gain by "throwing their burdens onto their neighbors," as Hamilton put it. Thus, electoral externalities can limit incentives, especially for large states, to extract bailouts that will have collective costs for the federation. Electoral externalities might also place limits on the central government's incentives to shift its burdens onto the states through such actions as unfunded mandates and dramatic cuts in transfers.

Finally, electoral externalities have an important role to play in the renegotiation of the intergovernmental contracts that structure the rules of the game in federations. The socially inefficient equilibrium, in which provincial governments overfish the common revenue pool, can be quite resistant to reform efforts even though its costs are well known. However, provincial politicians who gain from the status quo contract are more willing to drop their opposition to reform when they can receive sufficient electoral credit by doing so. And this is most likely to be the case when electoral externalities are strong. Chapter 9 discussed the experiences with intergovernmental reform in four federations and pointed out that although it is not a sufficient condition, popular reform efforts are more likely to succeed in countries where electoral externalities are strong and at times when the crucial states are controlled by the same party as the federal government.

III. Policy Implications[3]

These arguments and findings lead directly to some policy implications for newly decentralizing countries. The most important lesson is that policymakers and institutional designers should be deeply skeptical about the prospects for the rapid development of market discipline among subnational governments in newly democratizing, formerly centralized countries in which expenditure authority is shifting to provincial and local governments. In these situations, the central government's commitment is often seriously undermined by its involvement in provincial and local government finance and the political interests of legislators. Credit-rating agencies, bondholders, local banks, and voters will easily pick up on the center's lack of commitment and, as a result, provide insufficient punishment for imprudent fiscal behavior.

A quick read of the dominant literature on fiscal federalism flowing from the optimistic legacy of *The Federalist* can lead to a mistaken notion that fiscal

---

[3] For a more detailed and technical set of policy recommendations based on a wider set of case studies (including unitary countries), see Rodden, Eskeland, and Litvack (2003). For a discussion of the European Monetary Union, see Rodden (2005).

decentralization – especially when federal contracts and strong upper legislative chambers limit the center's discretion – will lead to rapid improvements in the efficiency, accountability, and prudence of government. These notions implicitly assume American-style subnational tax autonomy and divided sovereignty. These are simply not realistic short-term options in most decentralizing countries, where local tax administration capacity was either destroyed long ago or was never built in the first place. Moreover, political federalism can make things worse by making hierarchical solutions difficult and undermining reform efforts.

The prospects for effective market discipline are diminished even further in countries marked by severe interregional inequalities. A common trait of developing federations – virtually all of which emerged from the era of colonialism – is an extremely uneven pattern of economic development leading to one or two urban, industrialized giants and a vast, impoverished, often sparsely populated hinterland. The histories of these federations, going back even before the construction of an effective central authority, are often characterized by battles – now played out in the legislature rather than on the battlefield – between these jurisdictions. It is difficult to introduce market discipline in a context where the budgets of a handful of governments are funded largely from their own taxes and the vast majority is highly transfer dependent. Even if the center could commit, the majority of transfer-dependent provinces would not sanction a pure market-based system because no rational creditors would lend to them without federal guarantees. Moreover, as we have seen, even the large, potentially creditworthy jurisdictions might try to claw back some of the resources lost through intergovernmental transfers by overborrowing and demanding federal assistance.

The most pessimistic inductive conclusion based on the cases would be that effective market discipline requires a prehistory of provincial independence, relatively even economic development, and over a century of democracy and tax autonomy. However, this book provides little basis for such a claim. After all, the U.S. federation was christened with Hamilton's debt assumption. Moreover, Canadian provincial fiscal sovereignty was very questionable as recently as the 1950s. A more reasonable conclusion is that market discipline and subnational sovereignty ossify slowly; they do not spring into existence when the central government – even after negotiating a new constitution – suddenly makes a pledge to eschew bailouts. The central government must not only allow subnational governments significant tax autonomy and disentangle its books from those of the subnational governments, but it must demonstrate through costly action that it will not assume subnational liabilities when times get tough.

Perhaps credible central disengagement from subnational finance is possible. It happened in the 1960s in Canada, as described in the previous chapter, but the center's dominance of taxation was tenuous and short-lived. The Australian central government has recently renounced its role in organizing and guaranteeing state borrowing in an explicit attempt to transition from hierarchical to market-based discipline. Australia would seem to be a good candidate for market discipline, because its states do have some tax autonomy and the constitution opens the way towards further autonomy. However, Chapter 6 demonstrated that credit markets still view the central government as implicitly guaranteeing the debt of poor states like Tasmania. Canberra's response to the next state-level fiscal crisis will be crucial to future iterations of the game. It will be an interesting case to watch in the decades ahead.

More generally, reformers and institutional designers who wish to capture some of the efficiency and accountability gains commonly associated with decentralized expenditures and borrowing should focus on finding ways to increase the ability of subnational governments to rely on taxes they raise themselves. The challenge of developing local taxation and user fees under conditions of poverty, capital mobility, and weak institutions is daunting but potentially worth the effort.

It should be stressed, however, that most decentralizing countries are moving in a very different direction. Wide-ranging tax autonomy at the state and local levels is quite rare, and, with only a few exceptions, decentralization around the world is being funded by increased intergovernmental transfers rather than new taxes. In these countries, effective market discipline is not a realistic option in the short run. What can be done? Realizing the potential for moral-hazard problems, central governments in many decentralizing unitary countries have moved to impose new regulations that restrict the borrowing autonomy of municipal and local governments.[4]

Perhaps the greatest challenges, though, are in federations where the provinces are able to stand in the way of such regulations or undermine their enforcement. In decentralizing federations with weak and uneven subnational tax capacity, it may be necessary to implement restrictions on subnational borrowing before a vicious cycle of debt and bailouts emerges – even if it offends the sensibilities of those attached to the optimistic side

[4] For example, see Wetzel and Papp (2003) on Hungary.

of Hamilton's legacy. The obvious problem, though – exemplified by the Brazilian Senate – is that if the center cannot commit not to provide bailouts, perhaps it also cannot commit to effectively regulate subnational borrowing. Thus, reformers should try to find ways of regulating intergovernmental finance that reduce the discretion of the center, especially the legislature. For instance, rather than relying on the center to regulate the links between state governments and the commercial banks that they own or control, reform efforts should focus on privatizing these institutions. This was a critical aspect of recent reforms in Brazil and Australia, but remains as a problem in Argentina, Nigeria, and even Germany. Delegation to a legitimate, independent judiciary with strong enforcement powers is also an attractive strategy. Though the no-bailout commitment of the German federal government is clearly undermined by the basic federal bargain and its rather unusual interpretation by the high court, it is helpful that the distributive burden of bailouts is to some extent determined by the courts rather than political bargains. An important question for the future in Brazil is whether the judiciary will have the legitimacy, strength, and independence to enforce its aggressive new regulations.

Next, the findings in this book may provide grist for the mill in debates about the future of the European Monetary Union and whether it is necessary for the union to impose numerical limits on the deficits of member states. At least for now, the independent tax capacity of the central government is extremely limited, and the constituent units of the European Union are considerably more reliant on direct own-source taxation than the Swiss cantons, Canadian provinces, or U.S. states over the last century. While not impossible, it seems doubtful that voters and creditors perceive any implicit guarantees from Brussels. While the center has been steadily increasing its fiscal role, it has not undertaken the kinds of obligations that would clearly undermine its commitment to ignore future fiscal crises of member states.

Given the experiences of other federations, this book encourages skepticism about the bailout problem as the central justification of the Stability and Growth Pact, which imposes monetary fines on countries that run "excessive deficits." The incentive structure in the EU is a far cry from those of the Brazilian or German federations, and it has much more in common with the cases of dual sovereignty. Over the last fifty years, in the absence of federally imposed borrowing restrictions, neither the American, Swiss, nor Canadian central banks have been forced to monetize the deficits of their federated units. While there may be other justifications – above all that debt accumulation by one EU member (especially a large one) could put pressure on interest rates for the EU as a whole – the bailout problem may be something of a red herring.[5]

On the other hand, since the 1997 adoption of the Stability and Growth Pact, which makes central governments accountable for all public sector deficits, several vulnerable central governments have passed legislation aimed at enhancing the central government's ability to control subnational borrowing. In this respect, the European Monetary Union may have had a well-timed beneficial impact, especially in countries like Belgium, Italy, and Spain, where political decentralization in the late 1990s had been moving forward along with expansions of subnational spending and borrowing powers in contexts where taxation was still highly centralized and citizens expected national standards. In fact, two of the European countries aside from Germany in the empirical analysis in Chapter 4 demonstrating high levels of transfer dependence combined with wide-ranging subnational borrowing autonomy also demonstrated some of the largest subnational deficits in Europe in the 1990s: Italy and Spain. Both of these countries have recently adopted new restrictions on subnational borrowing, as have Austria, Belgium, and others (Balassone, Franco, and Zotteri 2002).

These efforts have been quite diverse, and the temptation to make sweeping judgments based on only a few years experience should be resisted. Most of the new "national stability pacts" adopted in response to EMU rely on cooperative mechanisms rather than formal rules, and only time will tell whether they can survive stress tests without stronger enforcement mechanisms.[6] But in any case, for most European countries – especially the majority without strong traditions of federalism and relatively little local tax autonomy – the trend is toward increased central surveillance and regulation of local budgeting.

Finally, some tentative, indirect policy implications may also be drawn from the arguments made in this book about political parties. When dual sovereignty is not possible, it may be advantageous to design institutions that encourage a vertically integrated party system. As discussed in Chapter 9, vertical partisan links may help countries escape inefficient noncooperative traps, not only in the area of intergovernmental fiscal relations, but also in other areas like interprovincial trade. Partisan links may be particularly helpful when the basic constitutional contract must

---

[5] See also Eichengreen and von Hagen (1996) and Eichengreen and Wyplosz (1998).
[6] Indeed, the EMU Stability and Growth Pact itself has proven noncredible, as Germany and France have been able to avoid fines while surpassing deficit targets.

be renegotiated. This observation might be useful in debates about institutional design – especially pertaining to the nature and powers of upper legislative chambers – in contexts as diverse as Canada, India, and the European Union. A related argument has been made by Filippov et al. (2004), who argue that strong links between federal and provincial political parties can help assuage centrifugal tendencies in federations, especially those with pronounced ethnic or linguistic cleavages.

Yet it should also be noted that partisan externalities might be a double-edged sword. While potentially useful in reducing the perils of federalism when market discipline clearly fails, as in Germany, they may also do violence to the setting in which market discipline thrives. William Riker was correct to point out that vertically integrated parties might be useful weapons in the hands of Hamiltonian centralizers who wish to smash the sovereignty of the provinces. Or less dramatically, as in Germany and Australia, they may facilitate multilateral deals that blur sovereignty. If one is fond of provincial sovereignty and compelled by the notion of competitive fiscal discipline, the unraveling of Canada's party system after World War II was a good thing if it was, as hypothesized in Chapter 10, part of the reason why the provinces regained a central role in income taxation. Yet a clearer set of policy implications regarding vertically integrated parties requires a more careful historical analysis of the coevolution of partisan links and subnational sovereignty.

IV. Directions for Future Research

Fiscal discipline is only one among many problems faced by modern federations. Though this book sheds light on larger issues like collective versus private goods, cooperation, and stability, it turned a blind eye to a variety of important normative concerns and thus does not even come close to a full accounting of the promise and peril of federalism. For instance, the strict market discipline that seems to function in the American, Canadian, and Swiss federations – while attractive to fiscal conservatives who fear big government – might serve to entrench and reinforce income inequality. It may not be a coincidence that these three federations have among the smallest welfare states and highest levels of income inequality in the industrialized world. Attempts to build market discipline might have disturbing implications for poverty reduction in decentralizing countries that are already characterized by high levels of inequality. There are many open questions about the effects of the varieties of decentralization and federalism on the nexus of issues related to income inequality, redistribution, and the welfare state.

A contribution of this book was to clarify and quantify some of the distinctions among decentralized systems, especially federations. Above all, it is clear that scholars attempting to understand the effects of institutions on things like public spending, redistribution, income inequality, and economic growth are unlikely to get much purchase out of a binary distinction between federal and unitary systems or even measures of expenditure decentralization. Future work might use some of the concepts and categories developed in this book to approach the outstanding issues where empirical research has thus far failed to find clear answers. One possibility is that this book may suggest new ways to approach the persistent argument – perhaps planted in *The Federalist* and then nurtured by public choice theorists – that under the right conditions, federalism protects property rights and enhances economic growth.

Progress on these questions requires that scholars begin to view the various forms of federalism and decentralization described in this book as endogenous. Before one can conclude with certainty that institutions affect outcomes such as fiscal discipline, inequality, or economic growth, it is necessary to comprehend the geographic, social, and political factors that lie behind the choice of institutions. Specifically, students of comparative federalism must try harder to understand the conditions under which the wide variety of vertical fiscal and political structures around the world emerge and become stable. As demonstrated in Chapter 10, today's institutions often reflect the outcomes of yesterday's battles and bargains. Perhaps the next task in the study of comparative federalism is to develop theories and empirical studies that step back in time and analyze these battles and bargains in a common framework. The historical narratives in this book only scratched the surface.

Good historical studies of federalism can teach us much about the future of governance around the world. As authority continues to shift from central governments down to provincial and local governments and up to higher-level entities like the European Union, the questions addressed by Alexander Hamilton, James Madison, and John Jay are more interesting and crucial than ever.

References

Abromeit, Heidrun. 1982. "Die Funktion des Bundesrates und der Streit um seine Politisierung." *Zeitschrift für Parlamentsfragen* 13: 467–71.

Abrucio, Fernando, and Valeriano Costa. 1998. *Reforma do Estado e o Contexto Federativo Brasileiro.* São Paulo: Fundação Konrad Adenauer Stiftung.

Ades, Alberto, and Edward Glaeser. 1995. "Trade and Circuses: Explaining Urban Giants." *Quarterly Journal of Economics* 110(1): 195–227.

Aghion, Philippe, and Jean Tirole. 1997. "Formal and Real Authority in Organizations" *Journal of Political Economy* 105(1): 1–29.

Aghion, Philippe, and Patrick Bolton. 1990. "Government Domestic Debt and the Risk of Default: A Political-Economic Model of the Strategic Role of Debt." *University of Western Ontario Papers in Political Economy* 9.

Ahmad, Junaid. 2003. "Creating Incentives for Fiscal Discipline in the New South Africa." In *Fiscal Decentralization and the Challenge of Hard Budget Constraints*, ed. by Jonathan Rodden, Gunnar Eskeland, and Jennie Litvack. Cambridge, MA: MIT Press, pp. 325–52.

Alesina, Alberto, and Allan Drazen. 1991. "Why Are Stabilizations Delayed?" *American Economic Review* 81(5): 1170–88.

Alesina, Alberto, and Nouriel Roubini. 1997. *Political Cycles and the Macroeconomy.* Cambrdige, MA: MIT Press.

Afonso, José Roberto, and Luiz de Mello. 2000. "Brazil: An Evolving Federation." Paper presented at the IMF /FAD Seminar on Decentralization, November 20–21, Washington, DC.

Alt, James, and Robert Lowry. 1994. "Divided Government, Fiscal Institutions, and Budget Deficits: Evidence from the States." *American Political Science Review* 88(4): 811–28.

Alter, Alison. 2002. "Minimizing the Risks of Delegation: Multiple Referral in the German Bundesrat." *American Journal of Political Science* 46(2): 299–316.

Ames, Barry. 1987. *Political Survival: Politicians and Public Policy in Latin America.* Berkeley: University of California Press.

Ames, Barry. 1995. "Electoral Rules, Constituency Pressures, and Pork Barrel: Bases of Voting in the Brazilian Congress." *Journal of Politics* 57(2): 324–43.

Ames, Barry. 2001. *The Deadlock of Democracy in Brazil*. Ann Arbor: University of Michigan Press.

Ansolabehere, Stephen, Alan Gerber, and James Snyder. 2002. "Equal Votes, Equal Money: Court-Ordered Redistricting and the Distribution of Public Expenditures in the American States." *American Political Science Review* 96(4): 767–77.

Arellano, Manuel, and Stephen Bond. 1991. "Some Tests of Specification for Panel Data: Monte Carlo Evidence and an Application to Employment Equations." *Review of Economic Studies* 58(2): 277–97.

Aristotle. 1981. *The Politics*. Transl. by T. A. Sinclair. London: Penguin Classics.

Arretche, Marta, and Jonathan Rodden. 2004. "Legislative Bargaining and Distributive Politics in Brazil: An Empirical Approach." Unpublished paper, MIT. http:// web.mit.edu/jrodden/www/materials/rodden.arretche.aug.041.pdf.

Bakvis, Herman. 1994. "Political Parties, Party Government, and Intrastate Federalism in Canada." In *Parties and Federalism in Australia and Canada*, ed. by Campbell Sharman. Canberra: Australian National University Press, pp. 1–22.

Balassone, Fabrizio, Daniele Franco, and Stefania Zotteri. 2002. "Fiscal Rules for Sub-National Governments: What Lessons from EMU Countries?" Paper presented at the World Bank/IMF conference "Rules-Based Macroeconomic Policies in Emerging Market Economies," Oaxaca, Mexico, February 14–16, 2002.

Banco Central do Brasil. 2001. *Boletim das Finanças Estaduais e Municipais*. September.

Baron, David, and John Ferejohn. 1987. "Bargaining and Agenda Formation in Legislatures." *American Economic Review* 77(2): 303–9.

Barro, Robert. 1979. "On the Determination of the Public Debt." *Journal of Political Economy* 87(5, pt. 1): 940–71.

Bayoumi, Tamim, and Barry Eichengreen. 1994. "Restraining Yourself: Fiscal Rules and Stabilization." *IMF Research Department Working Paper* 94/82.

Bayoumi, Tamim, Morris Goldstein, and Geoffrey Woglom. 1995. "Do Credit Markets Discipline Sovereign Borrowers? Evidence from U.S. States." *Journal of Money, Credit, and Banking* 27(4): 1046–59.

Bednar, Jenna. 2001. "Shirking and Stability in Federal Systems." Unpublished paper, University of Michigan.

Beramendi, Pablo. 2004. "Decentralization and Redistribution: North American Responses to the Great Depression." Paper presented at the Annual Meeting of the American Political Science Association, September 2–5, Chicago, IL.

Besley, Timothy, and Ann Case. 1995. "Incumbent Behavior: Vote Seeking, Tax Setting, and Yardstick Competition." *American Economic Review* 85(1): 25–45.

Besley, Timothy, and Stephen Coate. 2003. "Centralized Versus Decentralized Provision of Local Public Goods: A Political Economy Approach." *Journal of Public Economics* 87(12): 2611–37.

Bevilaqua, Afonso. 2002. "State Government Bailouts in Brazil." *Inter-American Development Bank, Research Network Working Paper* R-441.

Bird, Richard. 1986. *Federal Finance in Comparative Perspective*. Toronto: Canadian Tax Foundation.

References

Bird, Richard, and Almos Tassonyi. 2003. "Constraining Subnational Fiscal Behavior in Canada: Different Approaches, Similar Results?" In *Fiscal Decentralization and the Challenge of Hard Budget Constraints*, ed. by Jonathan Rodden, Gunnar Eskeland, and Jennie Litvack. Cambridge, MA: MIT Press, pp. 85–132.

Blaas, Hans, and Petr Dostál. 1989. "The Netherlands: Changing Administrative Structures." In *Territory and Administration in Europe*, ed. by Robert Bennett. London and New York: Printer, pp. 230–42.

Black, E. R. 1979. "Federal Strains within a Canadian Party." In *Party Politics in Canada*, ed. by Hugh Thorburn. Scarborough: Prentice Hall Canada.

Boadway, Robin, and Frank Flatters. 1994. "Fiscal Federalism: Is the System in Crisis?" In *The Future of Fiscal Federalism*, ed. by Keith Banting, Douglas Brown, and Thomas Courchene. Kingston, ON, Canada: School of Policy Studies, Queen's University, pp. 25–74.

Bohn, Henning, and Robert Inman. 1996. "Balanced-Budget Rules and Public Deficits: Evidence from the U.S. States." *Carnegie-Rochester Conference Series on Public Policy* 45: 13–76.

Bolton, Patrick, and Gerard Roland. 1997. "The Breakup of Nations: A Political Economy Analysis." *Quarterly Journal of Economics* 112(4): 1057–90.

Bomfim, Antulio, and Anwar Shah. 1994. "Macroeconomic Management and the Division of Powers in Brazil: Perspectives for the 1990s." *World Development* 22(4): 535–42.

Boothe, Paul. 1995. *The Growth of Government Spending in Alberta*. Toronto: Canadian Tax Foundation.

Brennan, Geoffrey, and James Buchanan. 1980. *The Power to Tax: Analytical Foundations of a Fiscal Constitution*. New York: Cambridge University Press.

Breton, Albert. 1991. "The Existence and Stability of Interjurisdictional Competition." In *Competition among States and Local Governments: Efficiency and Equity in American Federalism*, ed. by Daphne Kenyon and John Kincaid. Washington, DC: Urban Institute Press, pp. 37–57.

Breton, Albert. 1996. *Competitive Governments: An Economic Theory of Politics and Public Finance*. Cambridge: Cambridge University Press.

Breton, Albert, and Anthony Scott. 1978. *The Economic Constitution of Federal States*. Toronto: University of Toronto Press.

Bruce, Neil, and Michael Waldman. 1991. "Transfers in Kind: Why They Can Be Efficient and Nonpaternalistic." *American Economic Review* 81(5): 1345–51.

Buchanan, James. 1975. *The Limits of Liberty: Between Anarchy and Leviathan*. Chicago: University of Chicago Press.

Buchanan, James, ed. 1990. *Europe's Constitutional Future*. London: Institute of Economic Affairs.

Buchanan, James. 1995. "Federalism as an Ideal Political Order and an Objective for Constitutional Reform." *Publius* 25(2): 19–28.

Buchanan, James, and Richard Wagner. 1977. *Democracy in Deficit: The Political Legacy of Lord Keynes*. New York: Academic Press.

Buck, A. E. 1949. *Financing Canadian Government*. Chicago: Illinois Public Administration Service.

Bulow, Jeremey, and Kenneth Rogoff. 1989. "Sovereign Debt: Is to Forgive to Forget? *American Economic Review* 79(1): 43–50.

Bury, Piotr, and Carl-Johan Skovsgaard. 1988. "Local Government Finance." In *Decentralization and Local Government: A Danish-Polish Comparative Study in Political Systems*, ed. by Jerzy Regulski, Susanne Georgi, Henrik Toft Jensen, and Barrie Needham. New Brunswick, NJ: Transaction Press, pp. 101–14.

Careaga, Maite, and Barry Weingast. 2000. "The Fiscal Pact with the Devil: A Positive Approach to Fiscal Federalism, Revenue Sharing, and Good Governance." Unpublished paper, Stanford University.

Chandler, Alfred. 1962. *Strategy and Structure*. Cambridge, MA: MIT Press.

Chandler, William. 1987. "Federalism and Political Parties." In *Federalism and the Role of the State*, ed. by Herman Bakvis and William Chandler. Toronto: University of Toronto Press, pp. 149–70.

Cheung, Stella. 1996. "Provincial Credit Rating in Canada: An Ordered Probit Analysis." *Bank of Canada Working Paper* 96–6.

Chhibber, Pradeep, and Ken Kollman. 2004. *The Formation of National Party Systems: Federalism and Party Competition in Canada, Great Britain, India, and the United States*. Princeton, NJ: Princeton University Press.

Cielecka, Anna, and John Gibson. 1995. "Local Government in Poland." In *Local Government in Eastern Europe: Establishing Democracy at the Grassroots*, ed. by Andrew Coulson. Aldershot, England: Edward Elgar, pp. 23–41.

Coate, Stephen. 1995. "Altruism, the Samaritan's Dilemma, and Government Transfer Policy." *American Economic Review* 85(1): 46–57.

Courchene, Thomas. 1984. *Equalization Payments: Past, Present, and Future*. Toronto: Ontario Economic Council.

Courchene, Thomas. 1994. *Social Canada in the Millennium: Reform Imperatives and Restructuring Principles*. Toronto: C. D. Howe Institute.

Courchene, Thomas. 1996. "Preserving and Promoting the Internal Economic Union: Australia and Canada." In *Reforming Fiscal Federalism for Global Competition: A Canada-Australia Comparison*, ed. by Paul Boothe. Edmonton: University of Alberta Press, pp. 185–221.

Craig, Jon. 1997. "Australia." In *Fiscal Federalism in Theory and Practice*, ed. by Teresa Ter-Minassian. Washington, DC: International Monetary Fund, pp. 175–200.

Crémer, Jacques, and Thomas Palfrey. 1999. "Political Confederation." *American Political Science Review* 93(1): 69–83.

Cukierman, Alex. 1992. *Central Bank Strategy, Credibility, and Independence: Theory and Evidence*. Cambridge, MA: MIT Press.

Dahlby, Bev. 1994. "The Distortionary Effect of Rising Taxes." In *Deficit Reduction: What Pain; What Gain?*, ed. by William B. P. Robson and William Scarth. Toronto: C. D. Howe Institute, pp. 44–72.

Dahlby, Bev, and Sam Wilson. 1996. "Tax Assignment and Fiscal Externalities in a Federal State." In *Reforming Fiscal Federalism for Global Competition: A Canada-Australia Comparison*, ed. by Paul Boothe. Edmonton: University of Alberta Press, pp. 87–101.

References

De Figueiredo, Rui J. P., Jr., and Barry Weingast. 2005. "Self-Enforcing Federalism." *Journal of Law, Economics, and Organization* 21(1): 103–35.

Deutsche Bundesbank. 1997. "Die Entwicklung der Staatsverschuldung seit der Deutschen Vereinigung." *Monthly Report* 3 (March). Frankfurt: Deutsche Bundesbank.

Dewatripont, Mathias, and Eric Maskin. 1995. "Credit and Efficiency in Centralized and Decentralized Economies." *Review of Economic Studies* 62(4): 541–55.

Diaz-Cayeros, Alberto. Forthcoming. *Overawing the States: Federalism, Fiscal Authority and Centralization in Latin America*. New York: Cambridge University Press.

Dillinger, William. 1997. *Brazil's State Debt Crisis: Lessons Learned*. Washington, DC: World Bank.

Dillinger, William, and Steven Webb. 1999. "Fiscal Management in Federal Democracies: Argentina and Brazil." *World Bank Policy Research Working Paper* 2121.

Dixit, Avinash. 1996. *The Making of Economic Policy: A Transaction-Cost Politics Perspective*. Cambridge, MA: MIT Press.

Dixit, Avinash, and John Londregan. 1998. "Fiscal Federalism and Redistributive Politics." *Journal of Public Economics* 68(2): 153–80.

Dougherty, Keith. 1999. "Public Goods and Private Interests: An Explanation for State Compliance with Federal Requisitions, 1775–1789." In *Public Choice Interpretations of American Economic History*, ed. by Jac Heckelman, John Moorhouse, and Robert Whaples. Dordrecht, The Netherlands: Kluwer Academic Publishing, pp. 11–32.

Dyck, Rand. 1991. "Links between Federal and Provincial Parties and Party Systems." In *Representation, Integration, and Political Parties in Canada*, ed. by Herman Bakvis. Oxford and Toronto: Dundurn, pp. 129–78.

Dye, Thomas. 1990. *American Federalism: Competition among Governments*. Lexington, MA: Lexington Books.

Eaton, Jonathan, and Mark Gersovitz. 1981. "Debt with Potential Repudiation: Theoretical and Empirical Analysis." *Review of Economic Studies* 48(2): 289–309.

Eichengreen, Barry, and Jürgen von Hagen. 1996. "Fiscal Restrictions and Monetary Union: Rationales, Repercussions, Reforms." *Empirica* 23(1): 3–23.

Eichengreen, Barry, and Charles Wyplosz. 1998. "The Stability Pact: More than a Minor Nuisance?" *Economic Policy: A European Forum* 26 (April): 65–104.

Elazar, Daniel J. 1987. *Exploring Federalism*. Tuscaloosa: University of Alabama Press.

Elazar, Daniel J. 1995. "From Statism to Federalism: A Paradigm Shift." *Publius* 25(2): 5–18.

Ellis, Joseph. 2001. "The Big Man: History vs. Alexander Hamilton." *New Yorker* October 29: 76.

Emerson, Ralph Waldo. 1835. "Historical Discourse at Concord, MA." Speech, September 18, 1835, on the occasion of the second centennial anniversary of the town of Concord. Miscellanies 1883, reprinted 1903.

Endersby, James, and Michael Towle. 1997. "Effects of Constitutional and Political Controls on State Expenditures," *Publius: The Journal of Federalism* 27(1): 83–99.

English, William. 1996. "Understanding the Costs of Sovereign Default: American State Debts in the 1840s." *American Economic Review* 86(1): 259–75.

Fabritius, Georg. 1978. *Wechselwirkungen zwischen Landtagswahlen und Bundespolitik.* Meisenheim am Glan: Verlag Anton Hain.

Feigert, Frank. 1989. *Canada Votes, 1935–1988.* Durham, NC: Duke University Press.

Feld, Lars, and John Matsusaka. 2003. "Budget Referendums and Government Spending: Evidence from Swiss Cantons." *Journal of Public Economics* 87(12): 2703–24.

Figueiredo, Argelina Cheibub, and Fernando Limongi. 2000. "Presidential Power, Legislative Organization, and Party Behavior in Brazil." *Comparative Politics* 32(2): 151–70.

Filippov, Mikhail, Peter Ordeshook, and Olga Shvetsova. 2003. *Designing Federalism: A Theory of Self-Sustainable Federal Institutions.* Cambridge: Cambridge University Press.

Fitch IBCA. 1998. "Subnational Rating Methodology." Accessed from http://www.fitchibca.com in January 2000.

Fitch IBCA. 2000. "Spanish Regions: An Analytical Review." Accessed from http://www.fitchratings.com in November 2001.

Fitch IBCA. 2001a. "International Public Finance Special Report: Examining Canadian Provinces." Accessed from http://www.fitchratings.com in November 2001.

Fitch IBCA 2001b. "Swiss Cantons: Autonomy, Solidity, Disparity." Accessed from http://www.fitchratings.com in November 2001.

Fornisari, Francesca, Steven Webb, and Heng-fu Zou. 1998. *Decentralized Spending and Central Government Deficits: International Evidence.* Washington, DC: World Bank.

Friedrich, Carl. 1968. *Constitutional Government and Democracy: Theory and Practice in Europe and America,* 4th ed. Waltham, MA: Blaisdell.

Frisch, Morton J., ed. 1985. *Selected Writings and Speeches of Alexander Hamilton.* Washington, DC: American Enterprise Institute for Public Policy Research.

Garman, Christopher, Stephan Haggard, and Eliza Willis. 2001. "Fiscal Decentralization: A Political Theory with Latin American Cases." *World Politics* 53(2): 205–36.

Gibson, Edward, Ernesto Calvo, and Tulia Falleti. 2004. "Reallocative Federalism: Territorial Overrepresentation and Public Spending in the Western Hemisphere." In *Federalism: Latin America in Comparative Perspective,* ed. by Edward Gibson. Baltimore: Johns Hopkins University Press, pp. 173–96.

Gilbert, Guy, and Alain Guengant. 1989. "France: Shifts in Local Authority Finance." In *Territory and Administration in Europe,* ed. by Robert Bennett. London and New York: Printer, pp. 242–55.

Gomez, Eduardo. 2000. "The Origins of Brazil's Macroeconomic Crisis: State Debt, Careerism and Delayed Economic Reform." Unpublished paper, University of Chicago.

Gramlich, Edward. 1991. "The 1991 State and Local Fiscal Crisis." *Brookings Papers on Economic Activity* 10(2): 249–87.

References

Grewal, Bhajan. 2000. "Australian Loan Council: Arrangements and Experience with Bailouts." *Inter-American Development Bank, Research Network Working Paper* R-397.

Grodzins, Morton. 1966. *The American System: A New View of Government in the United States*. Chicago: Rand McNally.

Haddow, Rodney. 1995. "Federalism and Training Policy in Canada: Institutional Barriers to Economic Adjustment." In *New Trends in Canadian Federalism*, ed. by François Rocher and Miriam Smith. Peterborough, ON, Canada: Broadview.

Hamilton, Alexander, John Jay, and James Madison. 1961. [1787–88]. *The Federalist: A Commentary on the Constitution of the United States*. New York: Random House.

Harloff, Eileen Martin. 1987. *The Structure of Local Government in Europe: Surveys of 29 Countries*. The Hague: International Union of Local Authorities.

Harsanyi, John. 1967–68. "Games with Incomplete Information Played by Bayesian Players, I. The Basic Model." *Management Science* 14(3): 159–82.

Hart, Oliver. 1995. *Firms, Contracts, and Financial Structure*. New York: Oxford University Press.

Hayek, Friedrich von. 1939. "The Economic Conditions of Interstate Federalism." *New Commonwealth Quarterly* 5(2): 131–49. Reprinted in Friedrich von Hayek. 1948. *Individualism and Economic Order*. Chicago: University of Chicago Press, pp. 255–72.

Hecht, Arye. 1988. "The Financing of Local Authorities." In *Local Government in Israel*, ed. by Daniel Elazar and Chaim Kalchheim. Lanham, MD: University Press of America.

Hefeker, Carsten. 2001. "The Agony of Central Power: Fiscal Federalism in the German Reich." *European Review of Economic History* 5: 119–42.

Heins, A. James. 1963. *Constitutional Restrictions Against State Debt*. Madison: University of Wisconsin Press.

Helmsing, A. H. J. 1991. "Rural Local Government Finance: Past Trends and Future Options." In *Limits to Decentralization in Zimbabwe: Essays on the Decentralization of Government and Planning in the 1980s*, ed. by A. H. J. Helmsing, N. D. Matizwa-Mangiza, D. R. Gasper, C. M. Brand, and K. H. Wekwete. The Hague: Institute of Social Studies Press, pp. 97–154.

Henderson, Vernon. 2000. "The Effects of Urban Concentration on Economic Growth." *NBER Working Paper* 7503.

Henderson, Vernon. Dataset accessed from http://econ.pstc.brown.edu/faculty/henderson in June 2000.

Hibbs, Douglas. 1987. *The Political Economy of Industrial Democracies*. Cambridge, MA: Harvard University Press.

Hines, James, and Richard Thaler. 1995. "The Flypaper Effect." *Journal of Economic Perspectives* 9(4): 217–26.

Holtz-Eakin, Douglas, and Harvey Rosen. 1993. "Municipal Construction Spending: An Empirical Examination." *Economics and Politics* 5(1): 61–84.

Holtz-Eakin, Douglas, Harvey Rosen, and Schuyler Tilly. 1994. "Intertemporal Analysis of State and Local Government Spending: Theory and Tests." *Journal of Urban Economics* 35: 159–74.

Homer, Sidney, and Richard Sylla. 1996. *A History of Interest Rates*. New Brunswick, NJ: Rutgers University Press.

Huber, John, and Ronald Inglehart. 1995. "Expert Interpretations of Party Space and Party Locations in 42 Societies." *Party Politics* 1(1): 73–111.

Iaryczower, Matías, Sabastián Saiegh, and Mariano Tommasi. 2001. "Coming Together: The Industrial Organization of Federalism." Unpublished paper, Universidad de San Andrés, Buenos Aires. http://www.isnie.org/ISNIE99/Papers/iaryczower.pdf.

Inman, Robert. 1988. "Federal Assistance and Local Services in the United States: The Evolution of a New Federalist Fiscal Order." In *Fiscal Federalism: Quantitative Studies*, ed. by Harvey Rosen. Chicago: University of Chicago Press, pp. 33–78.

Inman, Robert. 1997. *Do Balanced Budget Rules Work? The U.S. Experience and Possible Lessons for the EMU*. NBER Reprint 2173.

Inman, Robert. 2003. "Local Fiscal Discipline in U.S. Federalism." In *Decentralization and the Challenge of Hard Budget Constraints*, ed. by Jonathan Rodden, Gunnar Eskeland, and Jennie Litvack. Cambridge, MA: MIT Press, pp. 35–84.

Inman, Robert, and Daniel Rubinfeld. 1997. "The Political Economy of Federalism." In *Perspectives on Public Choice: A Handbook*, ed. by Dennis Mueller. Cambridge: Cambridge University Press, pp. 73–105.

Instituto Brasileiro de Geografia e Estatistica (IBGE). Various years. Diretoria de Pesquisas. Departamento de Contas Nacionais, Contas Regionais do Brasil, microdados.

Inter-American Development Bank. 1997. "Fiscal Decision Making in Decentralized Democracies," In *Latin America after a Decade of Reforms: Economic and Social Progress in Latin America Report*. Washington, DC: Johns Hopkins University Press, pp. 151–214.

James, Harold. 1986. *The German Slump*: Politics and Economics, 1924–1936. Oxford: Oxford University Press.

Jefferson, Thomas. 1999. *Notes on the State of Virginia*. Ed. with an introduction and notes by Frank Shuffelton. New York: Penguin.

Jones, Mark, Pablo Sanguinetti, and Mariano Tommasi. 2000. "Politics, Institutions, and Fiscal Performance in a Federal System: An Analysis of the Argentine Provinces." *Journal of Development Economics* 61(2): 305–33.

Katzenstein, Peter. 1987. *Policy and Politics in West Germany: The Growth of a Semi-Sovereign State*. Philadelphia: Temple University Press.

Khemani, Stuti. 2003. "Partisan Politics and Intergovernmental Transfers in India." *World Bank, Policy Research Working Paper* 3016.

Kiewiet, D. Roderick, and Kristin Szakaly. 1996. "Constitutional Limitations on Borrowing: An Analysis of State Bonded Indebtedness." *Journal of Law, Economics, and Organization* 12(1): 62–97.

Kilper, Heiderose, and Roland Lhotta. 1996. *Föderalismus in der Bundesrepublik Deutschland*. Opladen, Germany: Leske und Budrich.

References

King, Preston. 1982. *Federalism and Federation*. London: Croom Helm; Baltimore: Johns Hopkins University Press.

Kitchen, Harry, and Melville McMillan. 1985. "Local Government and Canadian Federalism." In *Intergovernmental Relations*, ed. by Richard Simeon. Toronto: University of Toronto Press, pp. 215–61.

Kneebone, Ronald. 1994. "Deficits and Debt in Canada: Some Lessons from Recent History." *Canadian Public Policy* 20(2): 152–64.

Kneebone, Ronald, and Kenneth McKenzie. 1999. *Past (In)Discretions: Canadian Federal and Provincial Fiscal Policy*. Toronto: University of Toronto Press.

Kopits, George, Juan Pable Jiménez, and Alvaro Manoel. 2000. "Responsabilidad Fiscal a Nivel Subnacional: Argentina y Brasil." Unpublished paper, International Monetary Fund.

Kornai, János. 1980. *Economics of Shortage*. Amsterdam: North-Holland.

Kornai, János, Eric Maskin, and Gérard Roland. 2003. "Understanding the Soft Budget Constraint." *Journal of Economic Literature* 41(4): 1095–136.

Laufer, Heinz. 1994. "The Principles and Organizational Structures of a Federative Constitution." In *The Example of Federalism in the Federal Republic of Germany: A Reader*. Sankt Augustin: Konrad-Adenauer-Stiftung, pp. 24–48.

Lee, Frances. 2000. "Senate Representation and Coalition Building in Distributive Politics." *American Political Science Review* 91(4): 59–72.

Lehmbruch, Gerhard. 1989. "Institutional Linkages and Policy Networks in the Federal System of West Germany." *Publius* 19: 221–35.

Levine, Robert. 1978. *Pernambuco in the Brazilian Federation, 1889–1937*. Stanford, CA: Stanford University Press.

Lipset, Seymour Martin, and Stein Rokkan. 1967. *Party Systems and Voter Alignments: Cross-National Perspectives*. New York: Free Press.

Lockwood, Ben. 2002. "Distributive Politics and the Benefits of Decentralization." *Review of Economic Studies* 69(2): 313–38.

Lohmann, Susanne. 1998. "Federalism and Central Bank Independence." *World Politics* 50(3): 401–46.

Lohmann, Susanne, David Brady, and Douglas Rivers. 1997. "Party Identification, Retrospective Voting, and Moderating Elections in a Federal System: West Germany, 1961–1989." *Comparative Political Studies* 30(4): 420–49.

Love, Joseph. 1980. *São Paulo in the Brazilian Federation: 1889–1937*. Stanford, CA: Stanford University Press.

Lowry, Robert, James Alt, and Karen Ferree. 1998. "Fiscal Policy Outcomes and Electoral Accountability in American States." *American Political Science Review* 92(4): 759–74.

Lucas, Robert, and Nancy Stokey. 1983. "Optimal Fiscal and Monetary Policy in an Economy Without Capital." *Journal of Monetary Economics* 12(1): 55–93.

Madison, James. 1961 [1787]. "Federalist 10." In *The Federalist: A Commentary on the Constitution of the United States*, by Alexander Hamilton, John Jay, and James Madison. New York: Random House, pp. 53–61.

Mainwaring, Scott. 1991. "Politicians, Parties and Electoral Systems: Brazil in Comparative Perspective." *Comparative Politics* 24(1): 21–43.

Mainwaring, Scott. 1992. "Brazilian Party Underdevelopment in Comparative Perspective." *Political Science Quarterly* 107(4): 677–707.

Mainwaring, Scott, and David Samuels. 2004. "Federalism, Constraints on the Central Government, and Economic Reform in Democratic Brazil." In *Federalism and Democracy in Latin America*, ed. by Edward Gibson. Baltimore: Johns Hopkins University Press, pp. 48–70.

Matsusaka, John. 1995. "Fiscal Effects of the Voter Initiative: Evidence from the Last 30 Years." *Journal of Political Economy* 103(3): 587–623.

McCarten, William. 2003. "The Challenge of Fiscal Discipline in the Indian States." In *Fiscal Decentralization and the Challenge of Hard Budget Constraints*, ed. by Jonathan Rodden, Gunnar Eskeland, and Jennie Litvack. Cambridge, MA: MIT Press, 249–86.

McGrane, Reginald. 1935. *Foreign Bondholders and American State Debts*. New York: Macmillan.

McKinnon, Ronald. 1997. "Monetary Regimes, Government Borrowing Constraints, and Market-Preserving Federalism: Implications for EMU." In *The Nation State in a Global/Information Era: Policy Challenges*, ed. by Thomas Courchene. Kingston, ON, Canada: John Deutsch Institute, pp. 101–42.

McRoberts, Kenneth. 1985. "Unilateralism, Bilateralism, and Multilateralism: Approaches to Canadian Federalism." In *Intergovernmental Relations*, ed. by Richard Simeon. Toronto: University of Toronto, pp. 86–87.

Medeiros, Antônio C. de. 1986. *Politics and Intergovernmental Relations in Brazil, 1964–1982*. New York: Garland.

Merkl, Peter. 1963. *The Origin of the West German Republic*. New York: Oxford University Press.

Migué, Jean-Luc. 1997. "Public Choice in a Federal System." *Public Choice* 90(1): 235–54.

Millar, Jonathan. 1997. "The Effects of Budget Rules on Fiscal Performance and Macroeconomic Stabilization." *Bank of Canada, Working Paper* 97–15.

Miller, John. 1959. *Alexander Hamilton: Portrait in Paradox*. New York: Harper and Row.

Ministèrio da Fazenda, Secretaria do Tesouro Nacional, Coordinação-Geral das Relações e Análise Financeira de Estados e Municipios. Various years. Unpublished data on budgets of Brazilian states.

Moesen, Wim, and Philippe Van Cauwenberge. 2000. "The Status of the Budget Constraint, Federalism and the Relative Size of Government: A Bureaucracy Approach." *Public Choice* 104(3–4): 207–24.

Montinola, Gabriella, Yingyi Qian, and Barry Weingast. 1994. "Federalism, Chinese Style: The Political Basis for Economic Success in China." *World Politics* 48(1): 50–81.

Moody's Investors Service. 2001. "Credit Ratings and Their Value for UK Local Authorities." Accessed from http://www.moodys.com in November 2001.

Mora, Monica, and Ricardo Varsano. 2000. "Fiscal Decentralization and Subnational Fiscal Autonomy in Brazil: Some Facts in the Nineties." Unpublished paper, IPES, Rio de Janeiro.

References

Morrow, James. 1994. *Game Theory for Political Scientists*. Princeton, NJ: Princeton University Press.

Musgrave, Richard. 1959. *The Theory of Public Finance: A Study in Public Economy*. New York: McGraw-Hill.

Nascimento, Edson, and Ilvo Debus. 2001. "Entendendo a Lei de Responsabilidade Fiscal." Accessed from http://federativo.bndes.gov.br in March 2003.

Newton, Michael, with Peter Donaghy. 1997. *Institutions of Modern Spain: A Political and Economic Guide*. New York: Cambridge University Press.

Nordhaus, William. 1975. "The Political Business Cycle." *Review of Economic Studies* 42(2): 169–90.

North, Douglas. 1990. *Institutions, Institutional Change, and Economic Performance*. Cambridge: Cambridge University Press.

Nurminen, Eero. 1989. "Finland: Present and Futures in Local Government." In *Territory and Administration in Europe*, ed. by Robert Bennett. London: Francis Pinter Publishers.

Oates, Wallace. 1972. *Fiscal Federalism*. New York: Harcourt Brace Jovanovich.

Oates, Wallace. 1991. "On the Nature and Measurement of Fiscal Illusion: A Survey." In *Studies in Fiscal Federalism*, ed. by Wallace Oates. Brookfield, VT: Edward Elgar, pp. 431–48.

Oates, Wallace. 1999. "An Essay on Fiscal Federalism." *Journal of Economic Literature* 37(3): 1120–49.

Oates, Wallace, and R. Schwab. 1991. "Economic Competition Among Jurisdictions: Efficiency Enhancing or Distortion Inducing?" In *Studies in Fiscal Federalism*, ed. by Wallace Oates. Brookfield, VT: Edward Elgar, pp. 325–46.

Oliveira, Joao do Carmo. 1998. "Financial Crises of Subnational Governments in Brazil." Unpublished paper, World Bank.

Ordeshook, Peter. 1996. "Russia's Party System: Is Russian Federalism Viable?" *California Institute of Technology, Social Science Working Paper* 962.

Ordeshook, Peter, and Olga Shvetsova. 1997. "Federalism and Constitutional Design." *Journal of Democracy* 8(1): 27–42.

Organisation for Economic Co-operation and Development. 1997. *OECD Economic Surveys: Australia*. Paris: OECD.

Organisation for Economic Co-operation and Development. 1998. *OECD Economic Surveys: Canada*. Paris: OECD.

Organisation for Economic Co-operation and Development. 1998. *OECD Economic Surveys: Germany*. Paris: OECD.

Organisation for Economic Co-operation and Development. 1999. *Taxing Powers of State and Local Governments. OECD Tax Policy Studies* No. 1. Paris: OECD.

Ostrom, Vincent. 1987. *The Political Theory of a Compound Republic*. Lincoln: University of Nebraska Press.

Padilla, Perfecto. 1993. "Increasing the Financial Capacity of Local Governments." In *Strengthening Local Government Administration and Accelerating Local Development*, ed. by Perfecto Padilla. Manilla: University of the Philippines, pp. 64–88.

Palda, Filip, ed. 1994. *Provincial Trade Wars: Why the Blockade Must End*. Vancouver: Fraser Institute.

Panizza, Ugo. 1999. "On the Determinants of Fiscal Centralization: Theory and Evidence." *Journal of Public Economics* 74(1): 97–139.

Parikh, Sunita, and Barry Weingast. 1997. "A Comparative Theory of Federalism: The Case of India." *Virginia Law Review* 83(7): 1593–615.

Peltzman, Sam. 1992. "Voters as Fiscal Conservatives." *Quarterly Journal of Economics* 107(2): 327–62.

Perry, David. 1997. *Financing the Canadian Federation, 1867–1995.* Toronto: Canadian Tax Foundation.

Perry, Harvey. 1955. *Taxes, Tariffs, and Subsidies: A History of Canadian Fiscal Development.* Toronto: University of Toronto Press.

Persson, Torsten, and Guido Tabellini. 1996a. "Federal Fiscal Constitutions: Risk Sharing and Redistribution." *Journal of Political Economy* 104(5): 979–1009.

Persson, Torsten, and Guido Tabellini. 1996b. "Federal Fiscal Constitutions: Risk Sharing and Moral Hazard." *Econometrica* 64(3): 623–46.

Persson, Torsten, and Guido Tabellini. 1998. "The Size and Scope of Government: Comparative Politics with Rational Politicans." NBER Working Paper 68–8.

Persson, Torsten, and Guido Tabellini. 2000. *Political Economics: Explaining Economic Policy.* Cambridge, MA: MIT Press.

Pommerehne, Werner. 1978. "Institutional Approaches to Public Expenditure: Empirical Evidence from Swiss Municipalities." *Journal of Public Economics* 9(2): 255–80.

Pommerehne, Werner. 1990. "The Empirical Relevance of Comparative Institutional Analysis." *European Economic Review* 34(2–3): 458–69.

Pommerehne, Werner, and Hannelore Weck-Hannemann. 1996. "Tax Rates, Tax Administration and Income Tax Evasion in Switzerland." *Public Choice* 88(1–2): 161–70.

Poterba, James. 1994. "State Responses to Fiscal Crises: The Effects of Budgetary Institutions and Politics." *Journal of Political Economy* 102(4): 799–821.

Poterba, James. 1996. "Budget Institutions and Fiscal Policy in the U.S. States." *American Economic Review* 86(2): 395–400.

Poterba, James, and Kim Rueben. 1999. "State Fiscal Institutions and the U.S. Municipal Bond Market." In *Fiscal Institutions and Fiscal Performance*, ed. by James Poterba and Jürgen von Hagen. Chicago: University of Chicago Press, pp. 181–207.

Przeworski, Adam, and Henry Teune. 1970. *The Logic of Comparative Social Inquiry.* New York: Wiley-Interscience.

Qian, Yingyi, and Gerald Roland. 1998. "Federalism and the Soft Budget Constraint." *American Economic Review* 88(5): 1143–62.

Qian, Yingyi, and Barry Weingast. 1997. "Federalism as a Commitment to Preserving Market Incentives." *Journal of Economic Perspectives* 11(4): 83–92.

Ratchford, Benjamin. 1941. *American State Debts.* Durham, NC: Duke University Press.

Rattsø, Jørn. 2002. "Spending Growth with Vertical Fiscal Imbalance: Decentralized Government Spending in Norway: 1880–1990." *Economics and Politics* 14(3): 351–73.

References

Rattsø, Jørn. 2004. "Fiscal Adjustment under Centralized Federalism: Empirical Evaluation of the Response to Budgetary Shocks." *FinanzArchiv* 60(2): 240–61.

Renzsch, Wolfgang. 1991. *Finanzverfassung und Finanzausgleich*. Bonn: Dietz.

Renzsch, Wolfgang. 1995. "Konfliktlösung im Parlamentarischen Bundesstaat," In *Der Kooperative Staat: Krisenbewältigung durch Verhandlung?* ed. by Rüdiger Voigt. Baden-Baden: Nomos, pp. 167ff.

Rigolon, F., and F. Giambiagi. 1998. "Renegociação das Dívidas Estaduais: Um Novo Regime Fiscal ou a Repetição de uma Antiga História? Accessed from http://federativo.bndes.gov.br in June 2003.

Riker, William. 1964. *Federalism: Origin, Operation, Significance*. Boston: Little, Brown.

Riker, William, and Ronald Schaps. 1957. "Disharmony in Federal Government." *Behavioral Science* 2: 276–90.

Rock, David. 1985. *Argentina, 1516–1982: From Spanish Colonization to the Falklands War*. Berkeley: University of California.

Rodden, Jonathan. 2003a. "Reviving Leviathan: Fiscal Federalism and the Growth of Government." *International Organization* 57(Fall): 695–729.

Rodden, Jonathan. 2003b. "Breaking the Golden Rule: Fiscal Behavior with Rational Bailout Expectations in the German States." Unpublished paper, MIT.

Rodden, Jonathan. 2004. "Comparative Federalism and Decentralization: On Meaning and Measurement." *Comparative Politics* 36(4): 481–500.

Rodden, Jonathan. Forthcoming. "The Political Economy of Federalism." In *The Oxford Handbook of Political Economy*, ed. by Barry Weingast and Donald Wittman. Oxford: Oxford University Press.

Rodden, Jonathan, and Erik Wibbels. 2002. "Beyond the Fiction of Federalism: Macroeconomic Management in Multi-tiered Systems." *World Politics* 55(4): 494–531.

Rodden, Jonathan, Gunnar Eskeland, and Jennie Litvack, eds. 2003. *Decentralization and the Challenge of Hard Budget Constraints*. Cambridge, MA: MIT Press.

Rodden, Jonathan, and Susan Rose-Ackerman. 1997. "Does Federalism Preserve Markets?" *Virginia Law Review* 83(7): 1521–72.

Rogoff, Kenneth. 1990. "Equilibrium Political Budget Cycles." *American Economic Review* 80(1): 21–36.

Rogoff, Kenneth, and Anne Sibert. 1988. "Elections and Macroeconomic Policy Cycles." *Review of Economic Studies* 55(1): 1–16.

Roubini, Nouriel, and Jeffrey Sachs. 1989. "Political and Economic Determinants of Budget Deficits in the Industrial Democracies." *European Economic Review* 33(5): 903–38.

Rousseau, Jean-Jacques. 1985. *The Government of Poland*. Transl. by Willmoore Kendall. Indianapolis: Hackett.

Rydon, Joan. 1988. "The Federal Structure of Australian Political Parties." *Publius* 18(1): 159–71.

Saiegh, Sabastián, and Mariano Tommasi. 1999. "Why Is Argentina's Fiscal Federalism So Inefficient? Entering the Labyrinth." *Journal of Applied Economics* 2(1): 169–209.

Samuels, David. 1999. "Incentives to Cultivate a Party Vote in Candidate-Centric Electoral Systems: Evidence from Brazil." *Comparative Political Studies* 32(4): 487–518.

Samuels, David. 2000. "The Gubernatorial Coattails Effect: Federalism and Congressional Elections in Brazil." *Journal of Politics* 62(1): 240–53.

Samuels, David, and Richard Snyder. 2001. "The Value of a Vote: Malapportionment in Comparative Perspective," *British Journal of Political Science* 31: 651–71.

Sbragia, Alberta. 1996. *Debt Wish Entrepreneurial Cities, U.S. Federalism, and Economic Development*. Pittsburgh: University of Pittsburgh Press.

Scharpf, Fritz. 1988. "The Joint-Decision Trap: Lessons from German Federalism and European Integration." *Public Administration* 66(3): 239–78.

Scharpf, Fritz, Bernd Reissert, and Fritz Schnabel. 1976. *Politikverflechtung: Theorie und Empirie des Kooperativen Föderalismus in der Bundesrepublik*. Kronberg: Scriptor.

Schmidt, Manfred. 1992. *Regieren in der Bundesrepublik Deutschland*. Opladen: Leske und Budrich.

Segodi, R. 1991. "Financing District Developmenmt in Botswana," In *Subnational Planning and Eastern Africa: Approaches, Finances, and Education*, ed. by in A. H. J. Helmsing and K. H. Wekwete. Aldershot, England: Gower Publishing, pp. 239–45.

Seitz, Helmut. 1998. "Subnational Government Bailouts in Germany." Unpublished paper, Center for European Integration Studies, Bonn, Germany.

Seitz, Helmut. 2000. "Fiscal Policy, Deficits and Politics of Subnational Governments: The Case of the German Laender." *Public Choice* 102(3–4): 183–218.

Shah, Anwar. 1991. "The New Fiscal Federalism in Brazil." *World Bank, PRE Working Paper* 557.

Shankar, Raja, and Anwar Shah. 2001. "Bridging the Economic Divide within Nations: A Scorecard on the Performance of Regional Development Policies in Reducing Income Disparites." *World Bank, Policy Research Working Paper* 2717.

Sharman, Campbell. 1994. "Discipline and Disharmony: Party and the Operation of the Australian Federal System." In *Parties and Federalism in Australia and Canada*, ed. by Campbell Sharman. Canberra: ANU Press, pp. 23–44.

Sharman, Campbell, and Anthony Sayers. 1998. "Swings and Roundabouts? Patterns of Voting for the Australian Labor Party at State and Commonwealth Lower House Elections, 1901–96." *Journal of Political Science* 33(3): 329–44.

Simeon, Richard. 1994. "The Political Context for Renegotiating Fiscal Federalism." In *The Future of Fiscal Federalism*, ed. by Keith Banting, Douglas Brown, and Thomas Courchene. Kingston, ON, Canada: School of Policy Studies, Queen's University, pp. 135–48.

Sokoloff, Kenneth, and Eric Zolt. 2004. "Taxation and Inequality: Some Evidence from the Americas." Unpublished paper, University of California, Los Angeles.

Souza, Celina. 1996. "Redemocratization and Decentralization in Brazil: The Strength of the Member States," *Development and Change* 27(3): 529–55.

Souza, Celina. 1997. *Constitutional Engineering in Brazil: The Politics of Federalism and Decentralization*. New York: St. Martins Press.

References

Spahn, Paul Bernd. 1997. "Switzerland." In *Fiscal Federalism in Theory and Practice*, ed. by Teresa Ter-Minassian. Washington, DC: International Monetary Fund.

Spahn, Paul Bernd, and Wolfgang Föttinger. 1997. "Germany." In *Fiscal Federalism in Theory and Practice*, ed. by Teresa Ter-Minassian. Washington, DC: International Monetary Fund.

Standard & Poor's. 2000. "Local Government Ratings Worldwide." Accessed from http://www.standardpoors.com in March 2000.

Standard & Poor's. 2002. *Local and Regional Governments 2000*. New York: McGraw-Hill.

Statistisches Bundesamt Deutschland. Land-level fiscal data accessed from http://www.statistik-bund.de in 1999.

Statistisches Bundesamt Deutschland. 2002. *Statistisches Jahrbuch für die Bundesrepublik Deutschland*. Wiesbaden: Statistisches Bundesamt Deutschland.

Stein, Ernesto. 1998. "Fiscal Decentralization and Government Size in Latin America." In *Democracy, Decentralization and Deficits in Latin America*, ed. by Kiichiro Fukasaku and Ricardo Hausmann. Washington, DC: Inter-American Development Bank and OECD.

Stepan, Alfred. 1999. "Federalism and Democracy: Beyond the U.S. Model," *Journal of Democracy* 10(4): 19–34.

Struthers, J. 1983. *No Fault of Their Own: Unemployment and the Canadian Welfare State 1914–1941*. Toronto: University of Toronto Press.

Sylla, Richard, Arthur Grinath III, and John Wallis. 2004. "Sovereign Debt and Repudiation: The Emerging-Market Debt Crisis in the U.S. States, 1839–1843." Unpublished paper, University of Maryland.

Syrett, Harold, ed. 1962. *The Papers of Alexander Hamilton*. New York: Columbia University Press.

Ter-Minassian, Teresa, ed., 1997b. *Fiscal Federalism in Theory and Practice*. Washington, DC: International Monetary Fund.

Ter-Minassian, Teresa. 1997a. "Brazil." In *Fiscal Federalism in Theory and Practice*, ed. by Teresa Ter-Minassian. Washington, DC: International Monetary Fund.

Ter-Minassian, Teresa, and Jon Craig. 1997. "Control of Subnational Borrowing." In *Fiscal Federalism in Theory and Practice*, ed. by Teresa Ter-Minassian. Washington, DC: International Monetary Fund.

Tiebout, Charles. 1956. "A Pure Theory of Local Expenditures." *Journal of Political Economy* 64(5): 416–24.

Tocqueville, Alexis de. 1966. *Democracy in America*. Transl. by George Lawrence, ed. by J. P. Mayer. New York: Harper and Row.

Tommasi, Mariano, and Sabastin Saiegh. 2000. "An Incomplete-Contracts Approach to Intergovernmental Transfer Systems in Latin America." In *Decentralization and Accountability of the Public Sector*, ed. by Javed Burki and Guillermo Perry. Washington, DC: World Bank.

Triesman, Daniel. 1999a. *After the Deluge: Regional Crises and Political Consolidation in Russia*. Ann Arbor: University of Michigan Press.

Triesman, Daniel. 1999b. "Political Decentralization and Economic Reform: A Game-Theoretic Analysis." *American Journal of Political Science* 43(4): 488–517.

Triesman, Daniel. 2000a. "Decentralization and Inflation: Commitment, Collective Action, or Continuity?" *American Political Science Review* 94(4): 837–58.

Triesman, Daniel. 2000b. "The Causes of Corruption: A Cross-National Study." *Journal of Public Economics* 76(3): 399–457.

Tsebelis, George. 1995. "Decision Making in Political Systems: Veto Players in Presidentialism, Parliamentarism, Multicameralism and Multipartism." *British Journal of Political Science* 25(3): 289–325.

Tufte, Edward. 1978. *Political Control of the Economy*. Princeton: Princeton University Press.

Tullock, Gordon. 1994. *The New Federalist*. Vancouver: Fraser Institute.

Velasco, Andres. 1999. "A Model of Endogenous Fiscal Deficits and Delayed Fiscal Reforms." In *Fiscal Institutions and Fiscal Performance*, ed. by James Poterba and Jürgen von Hagen. Chicago: University of Chicago Press.

Velasco, Andres. 2000. "Debts and Deficits with Fragmented Fiscal Policymaking." *Journal of Public Economics* 76(1): 105–25.

von Hagen, Jürgen, and Barry Eichengreen. 1996. "Federalism, Fiscal Restraints, and European Monetary Union." *American Economic Review* 86(2): 134–38.

Von Kruedener. 1987. The Franckenstein Paradox in the Intergovernmental Fiscal Relations of Imperial Germany. In *Wealth and Taxation in Central Europe: The History and Sociology of Public Finance*, ed. by P. C. Witt. Leamington Spa, England: Berg, pp. 111–24.

Wagschal, Uwe. 1996. "Der Einfluss von Parteien und Wahlen auf die Staatsverschuldung." *Swiss Political Science Review* 2(4): 305–28.

Wallis, John. 2004. "Constitutions, Corporations, and Corruption: American States and Constitutional Change, 1842–1852." Paper presented at the Eighth Annual Conference of the International Society for New Institutional Economics, Tucson, AZ, September 30–October 3, 2004.

Watts, Ronald. 1999. *Comparing Federal Systems in the 1990s*, 2nd ed. Kingston: McGill-Queen's University Press.

Weingast, Barry. 1995. "The Economic Role of Political Institutions: Market-Preserving Federalism and Economic Development." *Journal of Law, Economics, and Organization* 11(1): 1–32.

Weingast, Barry, Kenneth Shepsle, and Christopher Johnsen. 1981. "The Political Economy of Benefits and Costs: A Neoclassical Approach to Distributive Politics." *Journal of Political Economy* 89(4): 642–64.

Werlong, Sérgio Ribeiro da Costa, and Armínio Fraga Neto. 1992. "Os Bancos Estaduais eo Descontrole Fiscal: Alguns Aspectos." *Working Paper* 203, Graduate School of Economics, Getúlio Vargas Foundation.

Wetzel, Deborah, and Anita Papp. 2003. "Strengthening Hard Budget Constraints in Hungary." In *Fiscal Decentralization and the Challenge of Hard Budget Constraints*, ed. by Jonathan Rodden, Gunnar Eskeland, and Jennie Litvack. Cambridge, MA: MIT Press, pp. 393–428.

Wibbels, Erik. 2000. "Federalism and the Politics of Macroeconomic Policy and Performance." *American Journal of Political Science* 44(4): 687–702.

References

Wibbels, Erik. 2003. "Bailouts, Budget Constraints, and Leviathans: Comparative Federalism and Lessons from the Early U.S." *Comparative Political Studies* 36(5): 475–508.

Wibbels, Erik. 2005. *Federalism and the Market: Intergovernmental Conflict and Economic Reform in the Developing World*. Cambridge: Cambridge University Press.

Wildasin, David. 1997. "Externalities and Bailouts: Hard and Soft Budget Constraints in Intergovernmental Fiscal Relations." *World Bank, Policy Research Working Paper* 1843.

Williamson, Oliver. 1996. *The Mechanisms of Governance*. New York: Oxford University Press.

Williamson, Oliver. 1985. *The Economic Institutions of Capitalism*. New York: Free Press.

Winer, Stanley. 1980. "Some Evidence on the Effect of the Separation of Spending and Taxing Decisions." *Journal of Political Economy* 91(1): 126–40.

Wirth, John. 1977. *Minas Gerais in the Brazilian Federation: 1889–1937*. Stanford, CA: Stanford University Press.

World Bank. 1995. "Brazil: State Debt: Crisis and Reform." *World Bank Report* 14842-BR.

World Bank. 2002a. "Brazil: Issues in Fiscal Federalism." *World Bank Report* 22523-BR.

World Bank. 2002b. "State and Local Governance in Nigeria." *World Bank Report* 24477-UNI.

Index

Index

Bremen, 155, 157, 160, 161, 163, 165, 166, 168, 174, 176, 179, 186, 187, 223, 242, 243

Brennnan, Geoffrey, 285

Breton, Albert, 19, 22, 41, 285

Bruce, Neil, 79, 285

Buchanan, James, 19, 21, 22, 23, 24, 41, 43, 79, 270, 285

Buck, A. E., 143, 285

budget deficits, 3, 4, 14, 21, 22, 54, 76, 78, 80, 94, 96, 98, 99, 103, 106, 107, 108, 109, 110, 112, 113, 114, 115, 116, 117, 127, 128, 131, 132, 137, 138, 142, 144, 145, 147, 148, 150, 155, 156, 157, 161, 163, 165, 166, 167, 168, 171, 172, 173, 174, 175, 177, 182, 183, 184, 185, 186, 189, 196, 200, 201, 215, 220, 221, 222, 223, 227, 248, 271, 274, 278, 279

Buenos Aires, 252, 266, 273

Bulow, Jeremey, 49, 60, 286

Bund, 155, 156, 157, 158, 159, 160, 162, 165, 166, 170, 240, 241, 243, 244

Bundesrat, 36, 156, 157, 158, 159, 162, 170, 176, 177, 179, 181, 182, 185, 223, 240, 241, 242, 243, 244, 274, 283

Bundestag, 159, 241, 242

Bury, Piotr, 286

Calvo, Ernesto, 170, 288

Canada, xvi, 9, 13, 31, 36, 37, 39, 43, 82, 88, 89, 90, 91, 93, 101, 130, 132, 134, 135, 136, 137, 140, 141, 142, 143, 144, 146, 148, 149, 152, 203, 228, 229, 232, 233, 235, 236, 237, 238, 239, 245, 249, 250, 252, 261, 262, 263, 264, 265, 270, 272, 276, 277, 278, 280, 284, 285, 286, 287, 288, 289, 291, 292, 293, 294, 296, 297

Canadian Charter of Rights and Freedoms, 236

Canadian provinces, 9, 36, 82, 88, 89, 91, 93, 141, 143, 146, 236, 252, 261, 278

Canberra, 90, 134, 277, 296

capital, 8, 14, 19, 22, 56, 57, 63, 67, 68, 79, 80, 81, 90, 123, 160, 161, 171, 196, 200, 207, 220, 236, 241, 245, 247, 249, 261, 270, 277

Cardoso, Fernando Henrique, 147, 196, 199, 203, 204, 211, 212, 214, 216, 225, 229, 245, 246, 247, 248, 263, 274

Careaga, Maite, 259, 260, 286

Case, Ann, ix, 11, 22, 284, 294, 296

CDU (Christian Democratic Union), 136, 171, 173, 174, 175, 183, 184, 241, 243

CDU (Christlich Demokratische Union Deutschland), 163

central bank, xvi, 81, 102, 108, 123, 143, 196, 198, 199, 207, 208, 209, 247, 263, 286, 291

Chamber of Deputies, 190, 196, 201, 203, 214

Chandler, Alfred, 162, 233, 272, 286

Chandler, William, 286

Cheung, Stella, 93, 286

Chhibber, Pradeep, 265, 286

Cielecka, Anna, 286

class conflict, 266

Coasian bargains, 230

Coate, Stephen, 42, 79, 284, 286

coattails, 223, 232

coffee valorization program, 257, 258

collective goods, 5, 11, 13, 17, 32, 33, 42, 65, 76, 119, 120, 121, 124, 125, 127, 128, 138, 139, 151, 168, 186, 203, 204, 223, 226, 227, 229, 231, 232, 233, 245, 248, 255

Index

Index

Index

Index

Index